WITHDRAWN

C

D

SYRIAN EMPIRE
(about 720 B.C.)

Nineveh

BABYLONIAN EMPIRE
(about 570 B.C.)

Babylon

PERSIAN EMPIRE
(about 525 B.C.)

W9-AMZ-919

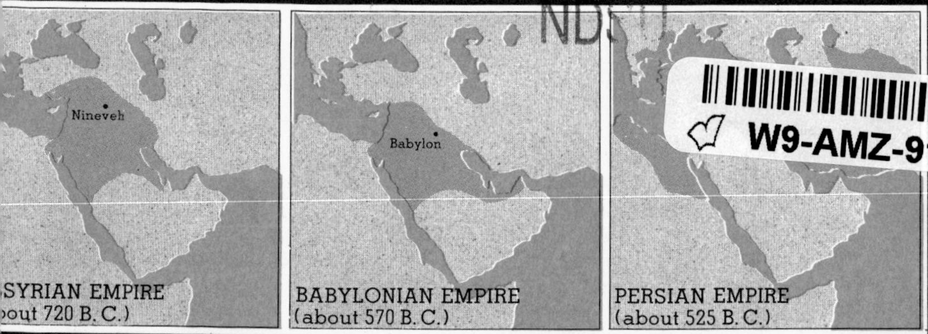

1

Kenath

Salcah

A U R A N

Edrei

moth-
lead?

G I L E A D

G A D

Succoth

Rabbah

Heshbon

River Jordan

R E U B E N

Medeba

2

GERIZIM

em

HRAIM

Shiloh

B E N J A M I N

Gilgal?

Jericho

M O

A B

Aroer

Beth-el

Ai

Gibeah

Salt

Mizpah?

Jerusalem

Kir of Moab

J U D A H

Beth-lehem

(Dead)

Sea

Gezer

J U D A H

DAN

Libnah?

Hebron

Carmel

eh

Lachish

Gath

Eglon?

Beer-sheba

dod

Ashkelon

S I M E O N

Gaza

Gerar

3

COPYRIGHT AMERICAN BIBLE SOCIETY 1954

C

D

121924

BS   Baly
630   The geography of the Bible.
B34

DATE DUE

MAR 2 3 1984			
FEB 1 2 2007			
MAR 1 2 2007			

Subject To Recall After 2 Weeks

LIBRARY
NORTH DAKOTA
STATE UNIVERSITY
FARGO, NORTH DAKOTA

DEMCO

THE GEOGRAPHY OF THE BIBLE

THE
GEOGRAPHY
OF THE
BIBLE

A STUDY IN
HISTORICAL GEOGRAPHY

DENIS BALY

HARPER & BROTHERS PUBLISHERS
NEW YORK

121924

THE GEOGRAPHY OF THE BIBLE

Copyright © 1957, by Alfred Denis Baly

Printed in the United States of America

BS
630
B34

All rights in this book are reserved.
No part of the book may be used or reproduced
in any manner whatsoever without written per-
mission except in the çase of brief quotations
embodied in critical articles and reviews. For
information address Harper & Brothers
49 East 33rd Street, New York 16, N. Y.

Library of Congress catalog card number: 56–12061

TO

RICHARD AND ROSEMARY BIRD

WITH

AFFECTION

AND

GRATITUDE

CONTENTS

LIST OF ILLUSTRATIONS

PHOTOGRAPHS

MAPS AND DIAGRAMS

INTRODUCTION

IT is now more than sixty years since George Adam Smith first wrote his classic study, *The Historical Geography of the Holy Land,* and since his day no one has attempted anything of quite the same nature in English. Even that other classic, *La Géographie de la Palestine* by Père F-M. Abel, is twenty years old, and neither of these is now easily obtainable. There have, it is true, been certain smaller studies and also more than one "atlas" of the Bible, of varying geographical value, but nothing of the scale or nature of George Adam Smith's *Historical Geography.* Even the recent and beautiful *Atlas de la Bible* by Luc Grollenberg, which at the time of writing is being translated into English, is, strictly speaking, more historical than geographical.

However, the character of the country is changing rapidly on both sides of the armistice line, and it is unreasonable to wish that this should not be so, for it is neither desirable nor possible to keep Palestine in a glass case. Nevertheless, before the changes have proceeded too far there does seem to be a need for a study of the country, which may serve to assist the Biblical scholar by giving him a picture of the stage whereon the history of our salvation had its place.

There are clearly two problems in any work of this kind. When the study is limited to the Biblical period, it is difficult not to avoid the suggestion that the history of Palestine began with Abraham and came to an end in A.D. 70, an impression which is already too firmly implanted in the minds of many Western people. However, limits of some kind are necessary, if the book is not to get completely out of hand, and it cannot be denied that the events of the Biblical period are those which most concern the ordinary American or British reader, and it seems, therefore, a useful place at which to begin, though obviously it is only a beginning.

The second problem is that expressed by a friend of mine, who read part of the manuscript, and who commented bluntly, "Theologians are not interested in geology, and geographers do not want theology in a geography book." There is much truth in what he said. Yet, on the one hand, it is impossible to understand what has been called the "personality" of a country without some knowledge of the structure and of the mechanism of the climate, and on the other hand, to attempt to study the Bible as if it were merely a work of secular history is to do violence to its nature. The moment one sets out to examine "the Land and the Book," it is necessary to take account of two facts: that the "Land," like any other land, is a complex and powerful thing, strongly influencing the lives and thinking of its people, and for this reason worthy of a thorough study in its own right; and that the "Book," from the beginning to the end of it, presupposes the existence of one God, who is both active and effective, and, who, in Karl Barth's famous phrase, is always "the subject of the sentence." Therefore, a study of the "Land" which is merely superficial and rejects the discipline of examining how the whole environment is built, and a study of the "Book" which does not take seriously the nature of the Biblical argument, are both of them studies without integrity. It is for the reader, and not for the author, to say whether this attempt to take account of both aspects of the subject has been successful. I can only say that, whatever blemishes the book may have, I have tried to write out of this conviction.

This book is the result of twenty years' work, fifteen of which were spent in the Palestine region, from 1937 to 1947 and from 1949 to 1954, when I was a member of the Jerusalem and the East Mission. During that time I visited every part of the country, and most of it very many times, by almost every means of transport known to the area, on foot, by bicycle, by horse, mule and donkey, by car, by train, by boat, and by plane (though I have to confess to my lasting regret that I never had occasion to ride on a camel). In the course of these journeys I met so many people to whom I owe a debt of gratitude that it is quite impossible to mention them all here. If this book should fall into the hands of any of them, I hope they will realize that it is only because they are so numerous that they are not thanked. However, three salutations must be given. The first is to the memory of Professor P. M. Roxby, under whom I studied at Liverpool and who first awakened in me an interest in the relations of history and geography. The second is to the members of the Civil Aviation Department in Palestine, many of whom later became members of the Meteorological Department in Israel, who put themselves and all their records at my disposal during the whole of a long summer. The third is to the Arab Legion, to both the officers and men, who never failed to be both courteous and helpful at whatever time of the day or night I arrived on their doorstep. It is impossible to praise them too highly.

It cannot be pretended that life was always placid in Palestine, and as a result of the disturbances I twice lost a large part of my maps and notes. This has made it difficult always to trace the source of my information, and though I have done my best always to give credit where it is due, I may have slipped up somewhere. If I have, it is entirely unintentional and I apologize.

The photographs are all my own, and are chosen to illustrate those features of the country which are less commonly known. For this reason I have avoided the popular views of Jerusalem and the Lake of Galilee. Some readers may think that this is a pity, but such photographs can, after all, be seen in a great many books on Palestine. For the same cause I have thought it better to have more pictures of the country east of the Jordan, which is less well known.

A word of explanation is necessary about the spelling of place names. There is, of course, an official method of transliteration from Arabic, but I find that those people who do not know any Arabic find it irritating and confusing. Moreover it is not used on most maps of the region. It has seemed better, therefore, normally to use the spelling which appears on the maps, and where a name has become familiar to the public from their newspapers, to use that spelling, e.g., Amman and Aqabah instead of 'Amman and 'Aqabah. For Hebrew words I have tried to keep to the usage of the *Revised Standard Version* of the

Bible. I know that this solution will not please the purist, but I hope that it may ease the path of the ordinary reader.

The scripture quotations in this book, except where otherwise stated, are from *The Holy Bible, Revised Standard Version,* copyrighted 1946 and 1952 by the Division of Christian Education, National Council of the Churches of Christ in the United States of America, and are used by permission.

D.B.

Kenyon College
1957

PART ONE

GENERAL

CHAPTER I

A Preliminary View

Go up to the top of Pisgah, and lift up your eyes westward and northward and southward and eastward, and behold it with your eyes.

DEUTERONOMY 3:27

IN the cathedral of Hereford, England, there hangs a map, one of the very few medieval maps we possess, and in the very center of this map is marked the city of Jerusalem. Indeed, in Jerusalem itself, in the middle of the Church of the Holy Sepulchre, tourists are shown the point which medieval geographers believed to be the exact center of the world. Visitors to either church usually smile when they are shown these things, and perhaps comment on the quaint simplicity of those former Christians who were so deluded, and even so conceited, as to hold such beliefs. Today we are coming to understand that there was more wisdom in their simplicity than we should have admitted thirty years ago. Christian historians are tending more and more to see the events of Christ's life as being in a very real sense the "center" of history, the crisis to which all previous history had looked, and without which no subsequent history can satisfactorily be explained. It was the point at which God himself entered the arena and acted directly upon history, the only point where it is possible to see visibly and concretely the eternal God at work in his temporal creation. It was no accident that the climax of this critical life took place at Passover, since the Incarnation, the Crucifixion and the Resurrection of Jesus are for the world what the Passover had been for the Jewish people—the great deliverance. "For while all things were in quiet silence, and that night was in the midst of her swift course, thine Almighty Word leaped down from heaven out of thy royal throne, as a fierce man of war into the midst of a land of destruction" (Wisdom 18:14-15).

Now, Christ's coming, though without parallel in the history of the world, was not merely an isolated incident. He came in the fullness of time. God entered history when, under his direction, history was ready for him and he came to dwell with a people whom he

3

had prepared for his reception. Equally, it is true that he came into the land which he had prepared for himself and which he had previously used for the revelation of himself during the space of well over one thousand years. Palestine was, in fact, the Chosen Land for the Chosen People; not, it should be noticed, chosen *by* them, but chosen *for* them. The Bible is very clear on this point. The Jewish historians in no sense thought of their forebears as having entered Palestine because it had appeared to them as a desirable place to live in, but because God had both prepared it for them in advance and had then summoned them to occupy it in his own good time. This is not the place to discuss whether God's action at that time gave them a claim to the land forever. That is another question with which this book is not concerned. However, it can hardly be denied by any Christian who takes his Bible seriously that it was God's intention that the Jewish people should live in Palestine during the greater part of that time when they were being prepared to receive him. It is true that God, as complete Lord and Master of his own creation, was in no sense tied to Palestine as the scene of his revelation of himself and, indeed, he took his people away, both to Egypt and to Babylon, that they might better receive the lessons which he required them to learn. Yet Palestine was as much the *normal* scene of this revelation as the Jews were *normally* the recipients of it. Hence it is surprising that theologians have paid so little attention to the country of their salvation and it is the sincere hope of the writer that this present

book may serve as an introduction to a most unfortunately neglected study.

Before we begin to study the land itself, however, there are two preliminary questions. First, it is necessary in any study of historical geography to set oneself boundaries, both in time and space. Of necessity, these will be somewhat arbitrary, if the undertaking is not to get completely out of hand, for neither in history nor in geography is it really possible to set a limit and say, "Thus far shalt thou come and no farther." In time, therefore, our limits will be the entry of the Patriarchs into Canaan and the destruction of Jerusalem in A.D. 70. We shall take only an occasional side glance at what happened before and after these dates.

The geographical limits are more difficult, since the political boundaries of the Chosen Land varied considerably and, as we have already seen, the Jews were living quite outside Palestine for two important periods in their history. However, we still know very little about their stay, either in Egypt or in Babylon. Therefore, it will probably be wise to confine our study to the Palestinian region and, for convenience, we shall take this to mean the area covered by the two modern countries of Jordan and Israel. Within these limits the great majority of the Biblical events took place.

The second question is that of names. Recent events have made this far from easy, for the words "Palestine" and "Israel" have acquired meanings which they did not have forty years ago. Therefore, we must define exactly the meaning of the names we shall use. "Israel" we shall take to mean the ancient country of Israel which lay north of Judah and "Palestine" to mean "the country of the Bible" on both sides of the Jordan, in the sense in which this word is used in many commentaries. *Neither word will be used in its modern political sense, unless this is expressly stated.* In speaking of the two regions on either side of the great Central Valley we shall follow the example of Professor Picard[1] and speak of "Cisjordan" and "Trans-jordan."

of Eurasia and Africa is so constricted that it would be possible, as it were, for a gigantic hand to get a grip on it, by inserting a thumb in the Mediterranean and the fingers in the spaces occupied by the Black Sea, the Caspian, the Red Sea and the Persian Gulf. This extraordinary narrowing of the landmass almost in the very center of it has meant that all the great continental routes must go through this area. There is no way round without taking to the sea. This

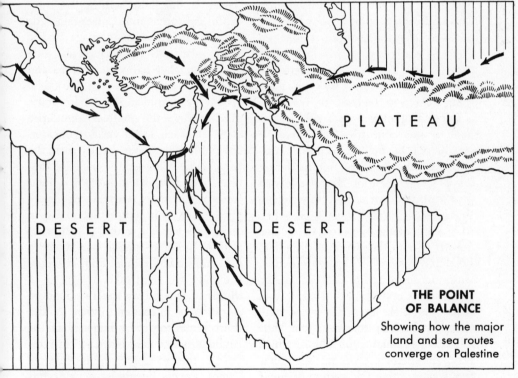

THE POINT
OF BALANCE

Showing how the major
land and sea routes
converge on Palestine

Fig. 1.

Palestine, as thus defined, lies at the "point of balance" of the Old World and forms part of an area which has aptly been described as the "Land of the Five Seas." Here the vast land mass

convergence of the major routes is even more strongly emphasized by the fact that in the Isthmus of Sinai the continental mass is cut through almost completely and Africa dangles by a mere thread. Here the routes which lead from Asia into Africa are pressed together into one narrow line across Sinai, and the place of their assembly is Palestine.

This same area of Sinai is naturally also the region where the ships, nosing their way along the Red Sea with the products of India and the East, most

from where come the lioness and the lion, the viper and the flying serpent" (Is. 30:6).

This anomaly can be explained only if we raise our eyes for a moment and cast a glance at the whole region. The Levant Coast of the "Arab Island," of which Palestine forms a part, lies

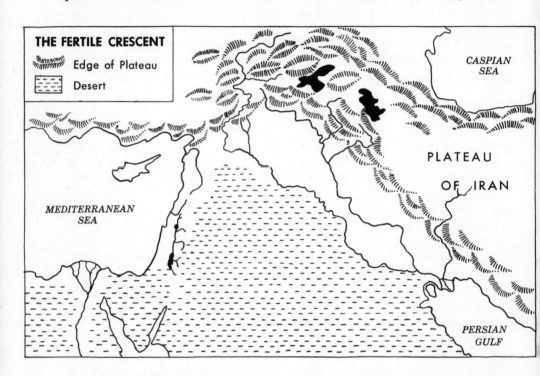

Fig. 2.

nearly touch the busy maritime commerce of the Mediterranean, for here there is less than 100 miles of land between them. Other things being equal, then, it would seem as if Sinai had been designed by God to be the mart of the world. However, history shows that not only has it never held this position, but that it has hardly been inhabited. Isaiah well describes it as "a land of trouble and anguish,

within an area known to all students of the Bible and ancient history as the "Fertile Crescent," a huge sickle of inhabited and cultivable land between the sea, the desert and the mountains. In the north lie the vast elevated tablelands of Anatolia and Iran, some 3000 feet in height. These are divided from each other by the Armenian mountain knot, where cross-movement is well-nigh impossible, and are hemmed in on almost every side by great mountain ranges, such as the Taurus, the Pontic Range, the Elburz and the mountains of Kurdistan. To the west is the sea and to the south and east the grim unwelcoming desert, where men can find no city to dwell in. The Fertile Crescent, which lies enclosed by these three great barriers to movement, is formed on the east by the broad land of Mesopotamia, watered by the Euphrates and the Tigris and by the other rivers which flow down from the Zagros. In the west is the Levant Coast. Here the main lines of relief, the mountains and valleys, run from north to south, that is parallel to the coast. Roughly speaking, there is normally a narrow coast plain and then two lines of mountains divided by a deep, longitudinal valley, and these not only help to channel movement from north to south, but also ensure moisture in a region where it would otherwise be deficient, for the air moving in from the Mediterranean is forced to rise over the two mountain ranges and thus deposit its rain, especially on the western sides, the eastern or leeward slopes being very much drier.

These two regions might have been merely loosely connected if it had not been for a fortunate combination of circumstances, which has caused them to be joined in a broad zone in the north. Here the Euphrates swings far over to the west and thus brings Mesopotamia close to the coast, and in the same region the inner line of mountains curves around to the east, in the Jebel Bishri group, so that it is no longer parallel to the coast, but runs out into the desert in a diminishing line of hills. The rainfall is more plentiful in this northern region and the summer drought is shorter and, now that there is only one barrier of mountains to check it, the rain is carried far inland and creates a broad area of fertile steppeland, joining the Mediterranean and the Euphrates. Movement across this steppeland between Mesopotamia and the coast is easily possible because, as we have seen above, the eastern barrier of mountains, which might otherwise have hindered it, has been removed by the eastward deflection of the Jebel Bishri hills.

At the southern end of the Levant Coast the rainfall peters out and the cultivated land passes into desert, but not far away to the southwest is that other fertile river valley, the Nile, with which communication is possible, though difficult, across the desert of Sinai. The Nile Valley and Mesopotamia, with their rich irrigated lands, are the homes of prosperous agricultural communities and the Levant Coast forms, as it were, a bridge between the two. All traffic from Mesopotamia to Egypt, or vice versa, had to travel the full length of this bridge. No short cut across the Arabian desert was possible, as we shall see a little later, and the history of the Levant Coast is very largely the history of the struggle between Mesopotamia and Egypt to control the bridge. Those of us who saw in the Palestinian streets during the recent World War soldiers being carried northward from Egypt for the invasion of Syria, or returning to the defense of the Nile Valley, were watching nothing new, and the small Iraqi forces which came to contend with the army of modern Israel in

1948 were but ineffective descendants of the mighty hosts of Assyria which wiped out an earlier Israel like an overflowing scourge (Is. 28:18).

Palestine lies at the southern end of this bridge and Gaza is the place where the desert begins, as we are told in Acts 8:26. Palestine, therefore, has to some extent usurped the role which might at first sight have expected to be played by Sinai. However, it is significant that the greatest trading center of them all stood on the uplifted southern plateau of Trans-jordan, where the cultivated area came closest to the Red Sea. This was Sela or Petra, at one time the pride of the Kingdom of Edom (Jer. 49:16) and later, in New Testament times, the great entrepôt city of Nabatean trade.

Within the Palestinian section of the bridge the division into the four important north-south zones of relief is maintained. First, there is the *Coast Plain*, extending from one frontier to another, though it is considerably wider in the south. Near the modern town of Haifa it is broken by the headland of Mount Carmel and to the north of that it is very narrow, for all practical purposes coming to an end at Ras en-Naqura ("the Ladder of Tyre").

Immediately to the east of this plain are the *Western Highlands*, which descend by the two great steps of Upper and Lower Galilee from the mountains of Lebanon to the low-lying Plain of Esdraelon just south of Nazareth. This plain cuts right across the highlands from northwest to southeast, joining the sea just north of Carmel to the Central Valley near Beisan. The Western Highlands reappear south of the plain in the hills of Samaria and farther south again they rise still more to the high plateau country round Jerusalem and Hebron. Here they reach over 3300 feet in places, but south of Hebron they descend again to the Negeb Uplands. It is true that these rise to 3300 feet in the Khurashe Dome almost exactly half way between Gaza and the Gulf of Aqabah, but both north and south of this dome there are wide areas of lower land, the Beersheba and Jeraya Gaps, where the land is not more than 2000 feet.

The eastern slopes of these highlands drop very steeply to the *Central Valley*. This is a vast trough extending from Syria to the Red Sea and entering Palestine from the north at about 300 feet above sea level. The Lake of Huleh is 230 feet above the level of the Mediterranean, but then it drops to 650 feet *below* sea level at the point where the Jordan enters the Sea of Galilee. The descent is continued south of the Lake, so that the surface of the Dead Sea is 1284 feet lower than the Mediterranean and the bottom is very nearly another 1300 feet below that. South of the Dead Sea the trough rises again to a point slightly more than 650 feet *above* sea level and then it descends once more until it sinks beneath the waters of the Red Sea at Aqabah. From the northern frontier to the Dead Sea this trough is followed by the River Jordan, but the southern portion, which is known as the Wadi Arabah, is waterless.

The farther side of the Central Valley is formed by the steep edge of the *Eastern Plateau,* which forms even more of a precipitous wall than that made by the highlands of the western side. This Plateau is divided by four river canyons which cut back into its edge—the Yarmuq, which is the "Brook" mentioned in the fifth chapter of I Maccabees, the Jabbok, which is the modern Zerqa and outside which lay Ammon, the Arnon or Mojjib, which was held to be the northern border of Moab, and the Zered or Hesa, which divided Moab from Edom. This plateau edge is pushed up rather higher both in the north and in the south. In the north is the swelling of Gilead and in the south the plateau reaches its greatest height in the mountains of Edom which touch 5700 feet in places. This great height of Edom is very important because it comes opposite the much lower country of the Negeb Uplands and this has meant that Edom has been able to catch the last remnants of the Mediterranean storms which coast along the edge of the Sahara and which pass, almost unhindered, across the lower-lying Negeb. It is this which explains why it was possible for there to be a settled population in the Kingdom of Edom at all, when the land nearer the sea was almost complete desert.

North of the Palestinian frontier zone, in the region now occupied by the countries of Syria and Lebanon, the general level of the land rises abruptly and the main lines of relief bend more toward the northeast. Here there is almost no coast plain and the mountains of Lebanon rise steeply from the sea to a height of 8300 feet. They form a towering and almost impassable barrier so that the present road from Beirut to Damascus has to clamber tortuously almost to the summit before it can cross them.

The Central Valley is here raised well above sea level and at Baalbek even the bottom of the valley is over 3300 feet above sea level. It is drained in the south by the Litany and in the north by the Orontes. On the eastern flank of the valley are the mountains of the Anti-Lebanon, which are divided into two by the valley of the Barada behind Damascus, Mount Hermon forming the southern section. To the east of these again is the bare plateau of the Syrian Desert.

This region is brought to an end in the north by the Homs-Tripoli Gap. Thereafter the western mountains resume their northerly direction as the Nuseiriyeh Mountains, which in their turn are broken through at their northern end by the lower Orontes. They are somewhat lower than the mountains of Lebanon and they represent the last of the series of western highlands. The Amanus Ranges which succeed them are really a southward extension of the Taurus.

The eastern mountains in northern Syria do not follow the western range in their return to a south-north direction. Instead they continue to swing round to the northeast just south of Homs, fanning out and becoming lower as they do so, and they reach the Euphrates not far north of Deir ez-Zor. These are the desert hills of Jebel Bishri and Jebel Buweidha and at their foot stands the ancient and once important oasis of Palmyra.

Within the Palestinian region the porous nature of the rock and the length of the summer drought have meant that permanent streams are few, though there are many deep wadis which were cut by the more vigorous streams of the Lower Pleistocene Pluvial Period. The Plain of Esdraelon is drained by "the onrushing torrent, the torrent Kishon" (Judg. 5:21), which for most of the year is no more than a sluggish brook, and south of Carmel a few minor streams cross the Coast Plain to the sea.

The Western Highlands form the water-parting between these Mediterranean streams and the region of inland drainage which includes the greater part of Palestine. This basin is centered on the Dead Sea and the largest stream entering it is the River Jordan, which rises on the slopes of Mount Hermon and flows almost due southward through Lake Huleh and the Lake of Galilee. It is on the last part of its course, after it has left the Lake of Galilee, that it is joined by its two largest tributaries, the Yarmuq and the Jabbok, both from the Eastern Plateau where the steep escarpment faces the rain-bearing winds. There are also some other, though smaller, scarp streams, such as the Kufrinje, the Shu'eib and the Kufrein, but from the western bank it receives only the Fari'a.

This same phenomenon is to be seen along the sides of the Dead Sea, which is entered from the east by two major valleys, the Arnon and the Zered, and by two smaller streams, the Zerqa Ma'in and the Kerak Wadi. No permanent streams, however, come down from Judaea. South of the Dead Sea the Wadi Arabah is drained by the intermittent Jeibe, which receives

most of its waters from the lofty tableland of Edom on the east. Finally, south of Jebel er-Rishe, which is the watershed of the Arabah, the wadis, all of which are short, lead southward to the Red Sea.

On the plateau most of the wadis near the western edge have been captured by the four major rivers, but beyond the present railway the wadis tend to lead eastward, following the dip slope toward the Wadi Sirhan. This is not a wadi in the ordinary sense, but a long shallow depression stretching from el-Azraq in the north to el-Jauf in the south, just outside the present Jordan frontier. The main exception to this rule is the Wadi Yatm, which collects the occasional flash floods of the extreme south and pours them into the Red Sea near Aqabah.

Within the four main north-south zones that we have described both settlement and movement have been possible only within fairly strict limits, because of the existence of what we may call "regions of difficulty." The first of these is the desert, which has some similarities with the sea, in that it cannot maintain a settled population, except where there are oases. Before the taming of the camel real desert must have been so difficult as to be almost impossible. Even after the camel was tamed certain regions in the desert provided peculiar difficulties, for the camel is limited by the fact that it has broad, soft feet which are suited to traveling on sand. It cannot, however, easily manage to walk on sharp rock or on slippery ground, such as areas which tend to remain muddy after a winter storm. The wide basalt regions of the

Trans-jordan and Syrian deserts, for example, have been almost entirely closed to them, so excessively sharp is the surface of the rock. Even to this very day men flee to the basalt for refuge from the Damascus government, for armies penetrate with difficulty into that black and forbidding region, where wood is so scarce that in the past even the doors were made from stone. This basalt forms a great barrier stretching out southeastward from near Damascus and this is the reason why it was not possible to take a short cut across the desert to Assyria.

Mountains are also a hindrance to movement and settlement and they do not need to be high in order to be difficult. It is sufficient if they are forest covered and have steep, narrow valleys, such as those in the Nuseiriyeh Mountains of northern Syria. Even quite low hills create barriers if the slopes are steep, which is why the apparently insignificant Central Carmel Range, not much more than 650 feet in height, was such an obstacle. Likewise, plateaus, though easy enough on top, are often very difficult to climb up on to and it was this fact which constituted the main defense of Judaea, Moab and Edom.

Other possible regions of difficulty are forests and marshes. Within the Palestine area forests were seldom thick enough to provide a real obstacle to movement or settlement, except on Mount Carmel, in Western Upper Galilee, in Gilead and possibly on the Plain of Sharon, but marshes could be a serious problem. This was especially true in four areas: the Huleh Basin, where they were permanent, and the

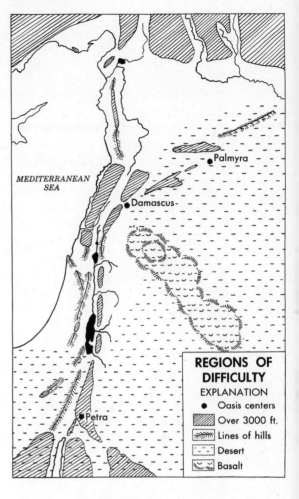

MEDITERRANEAN
SEA

●Palmyra

Damascus-

●Petra

REGIONS OF DIFFICULTY

EXPLANATION

● Oasis centers

Over 3000 ft.

Lines of hills

Desert

Basalt

Fig. 3.

plains of Sharon and Esdraelon and the coast plain north of Carmel, where they endured through the winter and largely dried up in summer. In all these regions the roads and villages clung to the edge of the surrounding hills on the slightly higher land. Far away to the north there were much larger areas of marsh all along the Orontes valley and these helped to turn the traffic of the steppes southward onto the bridge.

The final matter with which we must deal in this preliminary survey is to take a brief glance at the two countries which lay at either end of the bridge, for, apart from the fact that each owes its existence to rivers flowing in what would otherwise be desert, Egypt and Mesopotamia are strikingly dissimilar. The floods of Egypt are caused by heavy summer rain in Abyssinia and therefore provide water for cultivation during the subsequent winter. Moreover, they are controlled by a complicated natural mechanism which spreads them out over several months and causes them to rise and sink slowly so that they can be used relatively easily for agriculture, and therefore "to rise and sink again like the Nile of Egypt" became proverbial (e.g., Amos 8:8 and 9:5). The Mesopotamian floods are not controlled naturally and, unless they are controlled by man, are likely to do a tremendous amount of damage. This is particularly true of the Tigris which runs close to the mountains and receives four tributaries, the Great and Little Zab, the Diala and the Karun, rushing down unchecked from the mountain slopes. A sudden thunderstorm in any one of these may have disastrous results in the plain and the terrifying fury of the Mesopotamian rivers in spate provides the source of Isaiah's description of the King of Assyria as the "overflowing scourge." Furthermore, the floods are caused by melting snow and therefore come in early summer when the evaporation is tremendous. They may do much harm by causing the deposition of salt in the surface layers of the soil. The Mesopotamian floods have been well described by a modern geographer as "a tiger to be tamed."

Another difference is that Mesopotamia lies entirely north of 30° (i.e., the latitude of New Orleans), while Egypt lies almost entirely to the south, so that much of Mesopotamia has the advantage of a stimulating cold winter, but this is not true of Egypt. Also Mesopotamia is constantly exposed to invasion from the north and east, for from time to time the intermontane basins in Turkey and Iran overflow and pour down their inhabitants to pillage and sometimes to occupy the fertile river valleys. Egypt was not so much exposed to danger, though this meant also that she did not receive the stimulus of inoculation by new and vigorous blood.

Taken all in all, therefore, the Mesopotamian environment is the more severe and the challenge it presents correspondingly more difficult. The tendency is for it to take somewhat longer for the inhabitants of Mesopotamia to make the appropriate response, since they have more to overcome, but, when the response is made, it is likely to be more effective and to elevate the makers of it to a position of greater power. Historically, Egypt tends to be the first to be able to exercise control over the Levant Coast, but somewhat later she is likely to be replaced by Mesopotamia, whom Egypt is seldom able really to challenge. Thus, Egypt controlled the Palestinian area in the period preceding the entry of the Israelites, but in the later centuries her place was taken, first by Assyria and then by Babylon, both of whom were able, at the height of their power, to bring even Egypt under their control. We are almost certainly witnessing a similar struggle at the present time and there is some chance that the result may perhaps not be very different. It is interesting that the rise to power of modern Iraq is involving once again the taming of the Mesopotamian floods.

It is possible to extend the pattern of power even further and say that the countries of the Levant Coast attain power themselves only when both Egypt and Mesopotamia are weak, for the geographical diversity of this coast has hindered the development of a strong, unified country here. In Old Testament times this occurred during the prolonged interval between the Egyptian decline and the rise of Assyria, made even longer by the checking of her first advance at the battle of Karkar in 853 B.C., a battle in which King Ahab played an important part. This interval came to an end a hundred years later in "the year that King Uzziah died" (Is. 6:1), that climactic period which saw the deaths of both Uzziah of Judah and Jeroboam II of Israel and the accession to the throne of Assyria of the powerful Tiglath-Pileser III. During such periods of weakness the tendency is for the power to reside at Damascus, the most important single center in the area, and it is only if Damascus also is weak that the Palestinian area can rise to pre-eminence. In the Biblical period this seems to have happened only three times, during the reign of David, and then again under Omri and his son Ahab, and finally during the forty golden years of Jeroboam II and Uzziah, as well as possibly once again in the heyday of the Maccabees. It would follow that what we might call "effective independence" is exceedingly rare in the Palestine area and it is an interesting commentary upon God's methods that his revelation of himself should have been made to a people in this precarious position.

The last point that needs to be made for the moment in this pattern of power is that within the Palestine area itself the normal situation is for Trans-jordan either to be independent or to be governed from Cis-jordan. The most frequent position in the past was that southern Trans-jordan, protected by the Dead Sea and the precipitous walls of the plateau, was independent, while the north, with its easier contacts across the Jordan, was under Cis-jordanian control. In periods of great instability, however, part of Cis-jordan might be governed from a capital east of the river. This seems to have happened temporarily immediately after the death of Saul and again just after the division of the kingdom. If history, therefore, is anything to go by, the present situation in which most of the Judaean and Samarian hills are governed from Amman is highly insecure and destined to be purely temporary.

CHAPTER II

The Depths of the Earth

My frame was not hidden from thee,
When I was being made in secret,
Intricately wrought in the depths of the earth.
PSALM 139:15

By far the greater part of man's activity is pursued upon the surface of the earth. Though men "search out to the farthest bound the ore in gloom and deep darkness [and] open shafts in a valley away from where men live" (Job 28:3-4), this is not their normal life. Therefore, any study of the relation of man's life and thought to the land where he lives must concern itself almost entirely with the surface of that land. Nevertheless, the surface is not a matter of chance. The hills and valleys and the dusty, sun-bitten deserts are a stage for man's activity, brought into being both by the constant onslaught of the climate, by the fretting of the rain, the cleaving action of the frost and the hot, imperious sun, and by the slower, but no less insistent, processes of creation from within, the patient construction of the rocks, grain by grain upon the sea bottom, the titanic upheaval of the mountains and the shearing effect of fault and rift. The present surface of

any land or region cannot be understood if these two processes are not studied and it is with the second that we must begin. Those whose interest in the Holy Land is Biblical rather than geographical may perhaps be tempted to skip this chapter and the next in order to reach quickly material where the connection with the Bible is more immediately apparent. However, they are asked to be patient. The importance of what will be examined in these two chapters will become evident later in the book when we turn to a study of the country region by region. What we are doing now is establishing the basis for that study.

A difficulty certainly arises with the use of technical geological terms, which may be strange to some readers. I shall try to avoid their use, therefore, in these chapters, and, where I am forced to use them, to explain them when they occur. This in its turn may be irritating to others to whom such terms are commonplace, but it has to be done. *

Throughout geological history, at any rate as far as can be traced with any accuracy, the Palestinian region has been a coastland. On the east there has been the resistant land mass of Arabia and on the west that sea to which we give the name of *Tethys*, a sea of which the present Mediterranean is but a remnant. The shoreline has never strayed very far outside the region. For long periods it seems to have lain, very roughly, where the present Rift Valley now lies, in the region of the Jordan, but occasionally the land mass was pushed up in relation to the sea, which therefore withdrew farther to the west, leaving the whole of our region as dry land. Occasionally also the land mass was lower and the sea flowed over into Trans-jordan and even, though rarely, beyond. It would also seem to be true that the southeastern portion was almost always somewhat higher so that in any transgression of the sea it was the last part to be covered and also emerged the soonest as an island when the sea retreated. It follows, therefore, that in Cis-jordan, which was the more often covered by the sea, the rocks are mainly the result of marine deposition, limestones, chalk and the like. East of the present Jordan, however, the sea came more rarely and so the marine deposits are thinner and the desert sandstones, formed when the area was dry land, are correspondingly thicker. This is especially true of the southern

* A glossary of geological terms used in Chapters II and III will be found at the end of the book on page 267.

part of Trans-jordan, where the sandstone is often of tremendous thickness.

During the last hundred million years or so a new factor has been introduced by the creation of the great mountain ranges which curve round Arabia to the north and east. Their creation seems to have been spread out over almost the whole of this period from first to last and, indeed, cannot be said to be finished even yet. The effect of this new factor upon the Palestinian region has been limited in two ways:

(a) The main mountain-building storm occurred in the region of Anatolia and Iran and was therefore separated from Palestine by the whole expanse of Syria. This meant that Palestine was affected, not so much by the main storm, as by what Cole has well called the "ground swell" [1] and therefore the folding in the Palestinian region is relatively simple.

(b) Palestine rests upon the edge of the great solid block of Arabia. This vast crystalline mass was unable to bend and so the folding in this region was severely limited. However, the strain was so great that the crystalline block was broken, some parts being pushed upward and others thrust down. There is no part of the Palestine region where this breaking of the underlying platform has not had its effect, but the most striking result has undoubtedly been the creation of the great Rift Valley, cleaving the whole country from north to south.

This great stable block had come into existence long before the Cambrian period [*] and at the time when Cambrian began Palestine had been receiving the debris washed down from the extremely ancient mountains to the east, the Arabo-Nubid mountains. These had been worn away to their roots, largely, it would appear, by erosion while the area was above the surface of the sea.[2] During the Cambrian the sea seems to have extended well to the east, since both in the Zerqa Ma'in valley and in the Valley of the Zered (the Wadi Hesa) dark Cambrian limestone has been exposed. In the Valley of the Zered it

[*] For the benefit of those to whom such terms are unfamiliar a table of the rocks to which reference will be made is given below:

ERA or GROUP	SYSTEM	SERIES
Quaternary	Recent Alluvium, etc.	
Tertiary	Pleistocene Pliocene Miocene Eocene	
Secondary	Cretaceous	Senonian Turonian Cenomanian Albian
	Jurassic Triassic	
Primary	Permian Carboniferous Devonian Silurian Cambrian	
Archaean		

It will be seen that the oldest rocks are at the bottom of the table. The systems are all divided into series and the series themselves are subdivided. However, the major divisions of the Cretaceous only are given, since it is to this system that most of the Palestinian rocks belong.

rests directly upon the eroded ancient platform. This platform is made mainly of pink and gray granite, but is penetrated also by many dikes of porphyry and basalt, which must themselves be very ancient, since they have also been eroded and do not penetrate into the Cambrian limestone.[3]

We are still very much in the dark as to what happened in the Palestine area during the long Primary era. It is probable that the coastline fluctuated in the course of it and may have extended eastward at certain periods, though the southeastern part seems to have remained fairly consistently above the level of the sea. Here we have great thicknesses of sandstone resting on the Cambrian limestone. This sandstone is of desert origin, but it is very difficult to date, though Blake has suggested that the manganese of Wadi Dana may be Carboniferous [4] and that the lower sandstone may go back to the Triassic period in Central and South Trans-jordan.[5] We should probably not be far wrong in thinking of this sandstone, to which the name *Nubian* is given, as having been laid down on and off throughout the whole period from the mid-Cambrian to the Cretaceous and even a little later.

During the Jurassic period there certainly occurred a temporary transgression of the sea eastward and southward, for limestones of this period are found both in the Valley of the Jabbok (the Wadi Zerqa) and in the Wadi Raman and Jebel Hathira regions of southern Cis-jordan (Maktesh Raman and Maktesh Gadol on modern Israeli maps). However, this transgression did not cover the south-eastern portion, nor did it last very long, for both in Trans-jordan and in southern Cis-jordan this Jurassic limestone is succeeded by the Lower Cretaceous sandstone. Central and Northern Cis-jordan remained under the sea at this time, for limestone of the Albian period has been exposed by erosion in the center of the main arch both in Judaea and in Eastern Samaria.

With the Cenomanian we reach the beginning of the great Cretaceous transgression of the sea which produced the larger part of the rocks exposed today throughout the inhabited areas on both sides of the river. At first the sea was not very extensive and the coastline lay only just to the east of the present Jordan, but little by little the waters spread south and east until by the end of the Cenomanian they covered the whole region except only the part of Trans-jordan south of Ma'an. By the Senonian period even the, most southeasterly portion was under the sea.

This gradual extension southward and eastward of the Cenomanian sea has meant that the Cenomanian limestones are thickest in Northern and Central Cis-jordan, where they may reach 1700–2000 feet, and only 1000–1500 feet thick in the south.[6] In Trans-jordan these rocks are relatively thin in the northern part and in the south they die away altogether.

It seems likely that the first beginnings of the great mountain-building occurred during the Senonian period, producing merely gentle folding in a southwest-northeast direction. Some of the results of this folding are the

raised middle section of the Wadi Arabah between the Dead Sea and the Red Sea, where the valley bottom is humped up in Jebel Rishe to about 850 feet above sea level.

1. *Nubian sandstone.* The interior of the Temple of the Urn at Petra, showing the beautiful graining of the sandstone out of which the great monuments of Petra were carved.

After the Senonian, during the Eocene, the movements seem to have been of a somewhat different kind. Instead of folding, different parts of the coast were pushed up and down at different times, so that the sea tended to extend inland in first one region and then another.[7] It reached its greatest extent in the middle of the period when it swept right across the present Saudi border into Arabia. Nevertheless, the general tendency was for the whole region to be raised up out of the sea. At first there seems to have been an island in the form of a great dome extending from Ju-

2. *Wadi Hasma.* The underlying granite platform exposed in the extreme south of Trans-jordan, with resting unconformably upon it (a) the Cambrian limestone and (b) the Nubian sandstone.

daea into Gilead and by the end of the period all Judaea, Samaria and Eastern Galilee were probably dry land. There was already some kind of big depression dividing Cis-jordan from Trans-jordan and forming a large inland sea with its shore somewhere near Bethlehem and "the evidence appears to be in favor of the Trans-jordan plateau having been raised in Eocene times to about 2000 feet, leaving Palestine [i.e. Cis-jordan] at 1000 feet and most of the Judaean wilderness at about the level of the inland sea." [8] The short duration of the Eocene sea in the east is shown by the fact that the Eocene deposits on the Trans-jordan plateau are only about 300 feet thick [9] as compared with 650–1000 feet west of the Jordan.

During the Oligocene the coast plain of Cis-jordan remained under water and there was still an arm of the sea extending inland from the Haifa region and round to the Syrian desert, but all the rest of the area was dry land and so it has remained. This is therefore a good moment in the history at which to pause and examine the nature of the rocks which resulted

from this process of transgression and regression of the sea, before we go on to study the effect which the mountain-building had upon them.

At the bottom, of course, is the granite platform of Arabia which has been pushed up to the surface and and exposed in the extreme south of Trans-jordan where it forms the mountains round Aqabah. Upon the eroded surface of this platform was laid down the dark Cambrian limestone, which can be seen at one or two points in the deep valleys of Trans-jordan.

As the Cambrian sea retreated from Trans-jordan there ensued a very long period of desert conditions during which there were deposited great thicknesses of sandstone which form the major rock in large parts of southern Trans-jordan. It is most frequently dark red in color, but it may also be white, yellow, purple, or a brilliant flamelike orange. In the extreme south the great sandstone cliffs form the huge bastions of Edom, to which the color of the rock has surely given its name of "the Red." It is this same rock which carries the important deposits of copper, over which Edom and Judah wrestled for so long and which were thought of as one of the great assets of the Promised Land, "whose stones are iron, and out of whose hills you can dig copper" (Deut. 8:9). The formation of this Nubian sandstone was interrupted briefly in northern Trans-jordan and in the south of Cis-jordan by the influx of the Jurassic sea and the deposition of limestones, but the rocks of the lower Cretaceous period in both areas are once more sandstone.

The great Cretaceous transgression of the sea which began in the early Cenomanian period and came to an end in the later Eocene produced three major rocks, the Cenomanian-Turonian, the Senonian and the Eocene. The first and last of these are usually hard limestones which are resistant to erosion, but the rock of the Senonian period is very often a soft chalk. This distinction is of vast importance. Both the Cenomanian and the Eocene limestones form excellent building stone, of which Palestine has no lack, and they weather into a rich, deep-red soil, the typical Mediterranean terra rossa. Since they are hard, they tend to stand up as mountains and hills, and, being porous, they absorb the winter rain and pay it out regularly even during the long summer drought. It is these limestones which justify the description of the country as "a good land, a land of brooks of water, of fountains and springs, flowing forth in valleys and hills" (Deut. 8:7). The Cenomanian limestone, for instance, is responsible for the precipitous headland of Mount Carmel and the jagged palisades of upended strata in Jebel Hathira, and the Eocene for the twin mountains of Gerizim and Ebal on either side of Shechem from which, in Deuteronomy, the blessing and curses were

ordered to be proclaimed (Deut. 27:11–13). Solomon's Quarries, from which the stone for the original Temple is reputed to have come, are in the Upper Cenomanian and in Galilee the striking orange cliffs of Wadi Amad and the Valley of the Robbers are Eocene. The typical dolomite formation is less common, however, east of the Jordan.

The Cenonian chalk which lies between these two limestones is very different, being soft and easily eroded. It is so infertile that it is almost useless for agriculture and Isaiah speaks of it contemptuously as "chalkstones crushed to pieces" (Is. 27:9). Nevertheless, despite its great infertility, it has one practical virtue: it is so soft that wherever it is exposed it is immediately worn away to form a valley. Although it is inclined to be slippery in wet weather, it is very porous and dries with great rapidity and is worn by the passage of feet and vehicles into a hard, fairly smooth surface, unbroken by boulders. Therefore, it is these valleys of Senonian chalk which have provided the roads of the country, especially west of the Jordan. The passes across the limestone hills of Carmel, including the famous pass of Megiddo, follow narrow exposures of the chalk and all the towns which have served as capitals of the northern kingdom, Shechem, Tirzah and Samaria, stand at junctions of similar valleys. The narrow moat which played such a vital part in the defense of Judaea, that valley which runs from north to south past Beth-shemesh, dividing the Judaean plateau from the uplands of the Shephelah, is Senonian, the plateau to the east be-

4. *Shahba, Jebel Druze.* Volcanic cones in the Jebel Druze region. The one shown in the foreground is a basalt "plug," and the two in the rear are cinder cones.

ago the last volcanic eruption took place in Trans-jordan, though medieval writers speak of them as having taken place in North Arabia [15] and some of the cinder cones in the Jebel Druze have suffered very little erosion. There seem to be references to, or possibly remembrances of, volcanoes in more than one place in the Old Testament. Despite the rejection of the idea by certain scholars, it is exceedingly tempting to see in "the pillar of cloud by day and the pillar of fire by night" (Ex. 13:21–22) and

in Mount Sinai "wrapped in smoke" so that "the smoke of it went up like the smoke of a kiln, and the whole mountain quaked greatly" (Ex. 19: 18) vivid memories of some volcanic eruption. Similar memories seem to be enshrined in the Psalms (104:32; 144:5) and in the "waste-land that smoketh" of Wisdom 10:7.

The destruction of Sodom and Gomorrah poses a problem of its own. However, whatever additions the story may have gained in the telling, it does seem clear that there is a memory of volcanic activity of some kind. "Brimstone and fire from the Lord" and "the smoke of the land" which "went up like the smoke of a furnace" can hardly refer to anything else (Gen. 19:24, 28).

Evidences of modern volcanic activity are largely confined to the frequent hot springs, most of which are east of the Jordan, such as those

5. *Hot springs in the wilderness.* The hot waterfall at Zerqa Ma'in. Hot springs are frequent along both sides of the Rift Valley, though they are more common on the east.

found by Anah, the Edomite, in the wilderness (Gen. 36:24). During the summer of 1940, however, a small fall of rock in the Arnon valley, some distance above the present road crossing, revealed a smoking crack round which the earth was hot enough to ignite matches at the touch. Also the recent

excavations at Jericho have shown that the remarkable preservation of perishable materials, such as wood and meat, in the tombs there are the result of the exhalation of volcanic gases through cracks along the edge of the rift.[16]

The quieter activity of the Pleistocene period was the deposition of sedimentary rocks in two well-marked and separate areas, the Coast Plain and the Rift Valley.

(a) *The Coast Plain.* Three different types of rock seem to have been being formed here at roughly the same time. The first is the Kurkar of the coast, a hard, sandy limestone which is believed to be the result of ancient dune sand that became solidified by water percolating upward through capillary action.[17] There are two layers. The Lower Kurkar is a hard layer beneath the surface and seriously limiting tree growth if it is less than 3 feet deep. The Upper Kurkar was formed later, after a brief interruption due to a transgression of the sea, and is responsible for the narrow line of very low hills that borders the coast from Jaffa northward. These hills are seldom more than 70–100 feet high and are not continuous. They may possibly be what was meant by "the heights of Dor" (Josh. 11:2—left untranslated in RSV as Naphoth-dor), since these hills are well developed in the region of Dor and played an important part in the defense of the town.

The second rock is the Mousterian Red Sand of the Plain of Sharon, a bright red or orange sand which is today the citrus soil par excellence. It occurs in patches divided by allu-

6. *The gorge of the Zerqa Ma'in.* The white material in the middle of the picture is the gravel which completely filled the wadi during the pluvial period, and on the extreme right can be seen the new valley which the river was forced to cut when the base level was once again lowered, and by which it now enters the Dead Sea.

vium and appears to be material brought down by wind and water from the mountains into the basins which were formed behind the hills of the Upper Kurkar.[18]

The Loess, formed of wind-borne material from the desert, is found to the south of this in a great triangle west of Beersheba.

(b) *The Rift Valley.* At the beginning of the Pleistocene there was a series of separated basins: the Aqabah basin in the south, the Jordan-Dead Sea basin, the Tiberias-Beisan basin which lay north of the Jordan Valley "waist" near the present Jordan-Jabbok confluence, and the Huleh basin. At first these last two basins were

joined together, but the great outflow of basalt in mid-Pleistocene times built a great dam right across the valley south of the present Lake Huleh.

The next development was the changes caused by the very heavy rain of the mid-Pleistocene Pluvial period. The tremendous floods of this period brought into being a huge salt lake extending all the way from Tiberias to 'Ain Hosb and thus joining the two middle basins.[19] It was at the bottom of this lake that were laid down the whitish-gray Lisan marls of the Jordan Valley and the Dead Sea. Another result of the vastly increased rainfall was that huge masses of gravel were washed down by the rivers and choked the mouths of all the wadis leading into the Rift. In parts of the Wadi Arabah they form great alluvial fans which extend far into the Rift Valley and sometimes meet in the middle. Farther north the creation of

7. *The gorge of the Zerqa Ma'in,* showing in the upper part the outflow of basalt.

the Tiberias-'Ain Hosb Lake meant that the base level of the streams entering the Rift was raised and the material which they brought down was dropped at their entrance to the lake.

Finally the rains decreased and during the last fifty thousand years the Rift Valley has taken on its present appearance. The huge salt lake has shrunk until it is represented today only by the fresh-water Lake of Galilee and the excessively salty Dead Sea. The lowering of the base level once more has rejuvenated the rivers and led to increased erosion. Thus, the Jordan has cut through the basalt dam and, farther south, has carved out for itself a secondary valley, known as the *Zor,* several feet below the level of the Lisan marls. Likewise, the tributary valleys were forced to cut down again to the new level. Sometimes this has meant cutting their way through the vast masses of gravel which accumulated in the Pluvial period, but at least one river, the Zerqa Ma'in, was unable to do this and carved a new valley for itself in the soft sandstone.

CHAPTER III

The Earth on its Foundations

Thou didst set the earth on its foundations,
so that it should never be shaken.
Thou didst cover it with the deep as with a garment;
the waters stood above the mountains.
At thy rebuke they fled;
at the sound of thy thunder they took to flight.
The mountains rose, the valleys sank down
to the place which thou didst appoint for them.

PSALM 104:5–8

THE most obvious division of the country structurally is that made by the great Rift Valley running from north to south and dividing the whole of Palestine into that eastern area to which we have given the name of Trans-jordan and the western section which we have called Cis-jordan. However, this more obvious division cuts across another, secondary division which is less immediately apparent, but which is also in some measure marked out by faulting. This is a division of the whole area into three broad zones running from west to east right across the Rift and dying away in the desert plateau east of the present railway. The lines of demarcation between these zones are first, a line drawn through Lydda, Ramallah and Amman, the ancient Rabboth Ammon, and second, a line through Beersheba and the Valley of the Zered. Between these containing lines is the Central Section, which may be described as the *Zone of Relative Simplicity*. To the north of the Lydda-Amman line lie Galilee, Samaria and Gilead. These form the *Zone of Greater Complexity*. To the south of the Beersheba-Zered line is the southernmost section, including the Negeb, the Arabah and Edom, and this section we shall call, perhaps, the *Zone of Reversed Tendencies*.

(a) *The Zone of Greater Complexity*. East of the Jordan the level surface of the plateau has been elbowed

27

up into the high Dome of Gilead. This is the northeastern end of the ancient Judaea-Gilead island * and it has been cut across obliquely in two directions, first from north to south by the Jordan Valley and second from west to east by the valley of the Jabbok. In the Jordan Valley itself the wide rift-valley formation is less apparent here than elsewhere, because the two sides of the Rift come close together just north of the junction of the Jabbok with the Jordan, so constricting it that it looks like a single fault instead of a true rift valley. In the west, Samaria and Galilee have been built of a series of upwarps and these in their turn have been greatly complicated by faults running in three directions, from north to south, west to east and northwest to southeast. The relief here is therefore much more diversified than in other parts of the country.

(b) *The Zone of Relative Simplicity.* This is brought to an end in the north by a number of hinge faults cutting inward from the plains into the mountains. These are the Valley of Ajalon leading up to Ramallah, the great fault which curves back northwestward from Jericho and, on the eastern side of the Rift, two faults running northeastward from the corner of the Dead Sea. In the south this central zone shows some signs of being similarly limited, for there appear to be hinge faults running back to the southwest and southeast from the southern end of the Dead Sea. Within these limits the structure is somewhat less complicated than it is farther north. Thus, west of the Dead Sea

* See above, pp. 17–18.

the complexities of Samaria and Galilee give place to one broad arch, moderately varied by the gentle folding of the rocks of which it is composed. In Trans-jordan the relief is that of a broad and partly dissected plateau, dipping slightly toward the east, and the great canyons of the Arnon and the Zered reveal the strata lying one upon the other in level, uncontorted layers. Both in the east and the west of this Central Zone there is a tendency for the tremendous force of the fracturing along the major faults to have pulled the overlying strata sharply downward in plunging monoclines in the direction of the downward thrust, so that the layers of rock very nearly stand on end. The slopes on both sides of the Dead Sea are formed in this way and so is the western side of the Judaean hills, and the precipitous descents created by these cataracts of rock have played a very important part in the defense of the regions they enclose. "We have heard of the pride of Moab, how proud he was," said Isaiah (16:6) and "his arrogance, his pride, and his insolence" were in no small measure due to the fact that he felt safe behind such a defense.

(c) *The Zone of Reversed Tendencies.* In the southernmost structural band some important reversals of the general rules have to be noticed. Here the upwarps of Cis-jordan lose their height and through much of the Negeb form uplands rather than highlands as in Judaea, Eastern Samaria and Galilee. Secondly, the Rift Valley is no longer below sea level but is raised by the very early transverse folding of the Cretaceous period until it reaches over 650 feet in Jebel Rishe. Finally, east of the Rift, the plateau has been greatly disturbed by the complex faulting of southern Transjordan. Here it has been pushed up to over 5000 feet above sea level and the plateau edge is formed, not of a single plunging monocline, but of at least three huge faults which can be clearly seen from the Arabah, with the white limestone resting on the red sandstone and the hard, gray granite exposed beneath that. South of Petra the edge of the plateau turns southeastward and its place is taken along the edge of the Rift by a gigantic wedge of granite which has been pushed up between huge faults to a height of over 2000 feet. Behind this wedge is the wasteland of Wadi Hasma and Jebel Tubeiq, where huge mountains of rock rise from a sea of sand. The tremendous height of the plateau north of Petra has meant that here alone in southern Palestine, despite its distance from the sea, has settled habitation normally been possible.

TRANS-JORDAN

East of the present Hejaz Railway these three zones are no longer so apparent and instead there is the endless plateau of the desert, dipping slowly toward the east, and disturbed only by a gentle "swell" in the otherwise level rocks. In the center there is a wide, but slight, depression which has preserved the overlying Eocene limestone from erosion and in the north a somewhat sharper upfold has exposed the hard Cenomanian limestone, upon which stands the Roman castle of Hal-

labat.[1] To the east of this again the rocks dip gradually toward a very broad trough which has preserved the Eocene limestone over a very wide area. It is to be seen, however, only on the edges of the basin, since the

8. *Qasr Hallabat, Trans-jordan.* A Roman castle built to guard the desert, in which the builders made excellent use of the two major building stones, black basalt and white limestone. The oldest part of the castle may be as early as Nabatean, but the part shown here is probably third century.

lower-lying central portion received the repeated outflows of hot basalt from the Pleistocene volcanoes of Jebel Druze, which then cooled to form peaks and plateaus, rising high above the surface of the tableland and effectively concealing the rocks which lay beneath it. This broad but shallow trough, along which the basalt flowed, lies parallel to, but beyond, the present frontier of Jordan, extending from northwest to southeast, and the lowlying area just west of the stony basalt cap is the long depression known as the Wadi Sirhan. This is not a wadi in the true sense, but merely a somewhat lower portion of the plateau where water collects at the foot of the basalt cap and the traveler across the featureless, flint-strewn desert of eastern Jordan crosses the frontier and arrives at the wadi without being aware he has done so.

Between the railway and the plateau edge, with its long series of great north-south faults extending from beyond Huleh to the Red Sea, sometimes with a throw of many hundred yards, the country must be divided into the three zones we have already mentioned. In the extreme north, round the present town of Irbid and stretching across the Yarmuq far into Syria and to the foot of the towering Mount Hermon is the Plain of Bashan. Since this lies mainly outside our geographical limits, it is sufficient for the moment to say that in the part which lies south of the river the level surface of the plateau is floored mainly by chert of the Senonian period, though there is some basalt. To the north, in modern Syria, the volcanic activity has been very extensive and has had a profound effect on the character of the plain.

The upwarped mass of Gilead starts to rise out of the level plateau surface several miles south of Irbid and comes to an end in the south with the line of Senonian chalk which is marked on the geological map running almost due southwestward from just near Amman. The direction followed by this exposure of the Senonian chalk shows clearly the direction of the ancient Judaea-Gilead island of which it marks the edge. This dome of Gilead has been complicated by two events, the cutting of the Jabbok Valley at right angles to the Jordan

and thus obliquely to the dome, which is divided by this canyon into two distinct sections, and the development of hinge faults in the southern of these two sections. The northern is generally rather higher and touches over 3600 feet in many places. It is formed almost everywhere of the hard Cenomanian limestone. The Jabbok has cut down right through this limestone to the Nubian sandstone beneath and, in its lowest reaches, to the Jurassic limestone. South of the river the land rises again to the mountains round the Es-Salt and Sweileh, but these are cut by the two hinge faults which strike back from the northeastern corner of the Dead Sea. One of these has been responsible for the downfaulted basin which cuts into the plateau edge just north of the Dead Sea, known today as the Ghor Kefrein and in Old Testament times as the "Plains of Moab by the Jordan" (Num. 26:63, 31:12 and 33:48). The other lies slightly to the north of this and is followed by the modern road up from the Jordan along the Wadi Shu'eib, until the Shu'eib bridge, when the road turns off to the north toward Es-Salt. The road returns again, however, after a sharp hairpin bend above Es-Salt and crosses the fault once more near Sweileh on the edge of the great down-faulted basin of the Beqa'a, enclosed in the heart of the southern Gilead mountains.

South of the Gilead dome is the central, less disturbed section, where the strata are remarkably level, "all the tableland of Medeba as far as Dibon" (Josh. 13:9), which is perched on the edge of the tremendous canyon of the Arnon. Beyond this canyon to the south the extinct volcano of Shihan raises its head above the level surface which then continues unbroken to the town of Kerak (Kir Haroseth), from whose Crusading castle can be clearly seen the dramatic monocline by which the rocks of the plateau plunge toward the blue waters of the Dead Sea.[2] The steep valley which drops away from the castle northwestward toward the Rift is almost certainly following another hinge fault, which is continued on the eastern side of the town by the shallow, but remarkably straight, valley of Fijj el-'Aseikir and the Wadi Gheish. South of this line the ground begins to rise gently, though with little disturbance of the general plateau effect, until the last of the river canyons is reached, the Valley of the Zered.

South of this valley the land rises steadily and even rather steeply until for a distance of 45 miles the edge of the plateau is continuously over 5000 feet and reaches in places over 5600. The plateau edge is here gashed by faults running both toward the northeast and the southeast. An example of the first of these would seem to be the Wadi Dana leading down toward Feinan, the ancient Punon, and examples of the second are apparently the Zered Valley itself and the southern edge of the Edomite plateau, or Ras en-Neqb, the northern and southern limits of the Edomite plateau. The exposure of the granite in the south has already been discussed (p. 29), but another pre-Cambrian feature in this region is the long porphyry dike at the bottom of the Wadi Dana. This great dike extends for some 20 miles south of Feinan, a long spine in the valley of the Arabah. The series of parallel faults which form the eastern edge of the Rift in this region has meant the exposure over a wide area of the Nubian sandstone. The precipitous and almost unscalable cliffs which this rock develops in such a semidesert region as this is are a very important feature of the Edomite topography.

CIS-JORDAN

When we cross the Rift Valley into Cis-jordan we find ourselves at once in a region with obviously more complicated structure and the greater variety of relief that this naturally involves. However, there is in one sense rather less diversity, since throughout the greater part of the inhabited areas the dominant rocks are Cretaceous and the only variety of relief for which they are responsible is that caused by the difference between the soft chalk and harder limestones. The basalt, which is so widely exposed east of the Jordan, is here confined to a small area north and west of the Lake of Galilee, and the rocks older than the Cretaceous are exposed only in small areas and these entirely in the desert regions of the Negeb. The main exception to the Cretaceous-Eocene domination is the Coast Plain with its markedly gentle relief caused by the alternation of Mousterian Red Sand and recent alluvium, together with the triangle of loess which covers the Beersheba foreland.

We have constantly to bear in mind in Cis-jordan Picard's three tectonic forms: warping, folding and faulting. It was essentially upwarping which produced the most important topo-graphic feature—the great central line of highlands running like a spine from north to south of the country, but the shape of these highlands has been controlled by faulting. Thus, the up-warps do not run directly from north to south, but rather from NNE to SSW, that is slightly obliquely to the main north-south line of the high-lands, and placed *en echelon*. The north-south line is the result of the faults which have outlined the high-lands on either side, most noticeably on the east, but also on the west.

In the southernmost of the three transverse zones there are two fairly lowlying upwarps, each diversified by

frontier and reaches its greatest height in Jebel Khurashe (3290 feet). By far the most striking feature of this region is the great basin of Wadi Raman, about 22 miles long and 3 miles wide, shut in on all sides by high limestone cliffs, except near Qasr Mahalla, where the rare flash floods of winter break through to the Arabah.

The next upwarp, the Hathira or Kurnub Upwarp, is considerably lower, the highest point being in Jebel Hathira, which reaches only 2355 feet. The land is over 2000 feet only in rela-tively small areas and for the most part lies between 1600 and 2000. Two of the folds have broken away to form basins, similar to, but smaller than,

9. *The Ascent of the Scorpions.* Part of the plunging monocline which here forms the western side of the Wadi Arabah.

folding. The first is the upwarp which lies athwart the present Egyptian

the Wadi Raman basin. These are Wadi Hathira and el-Hadhira, the Maktesh ha-Gadol and Maktesh ha-Qatan of modern Israeli maps. The

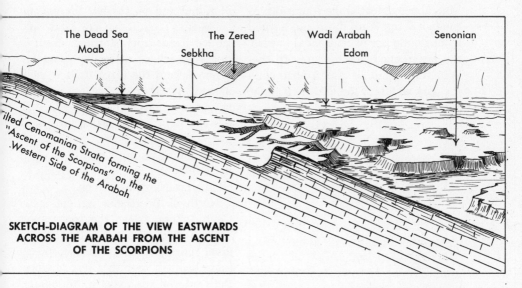

The Dead Sea
Moab
The Zered
Sebkha
Wadi Arabah
Edom
Senonian

Tilted Cenomanian Strata forming the "Ascent of the Scorpions" on the Western Side of the Arabah

SKETCH-DIAGRAM OF THE VIEW EASTWARDS ACROSS THE ARABAH FROM THE ASCENT OF THE SCORPIONS

Fig. 4.

formation of these basins is not yet completely understood, but it has been suggested that during the Pliocene period the hard limestone roof of the arch cracked and the underlying sand was washed out, thus bringing about the collapse of the arch.[3]

The present Israeli road from near Bir 'Asluj to 'Ain Hosb in the Arabah runs right across this upwarp and the traveler along it can gain a clear idea of the structure in a region where the desert climate has protected the upwarp from too much erosion. At Bir 'Asluj one is on the first of the five folds which form the covering of this upwarp and then after a little one passes the gentle rise of Jebel Rakhma, the second fold, and begins the slow ascent of the third and greatest fold, Jebel Hathira. The scenery is very featureless until suddenly one reaches the edge of the basin and the ground drops away in a series of huge steps. Here, with the collapse of the lime-

stone roof, the slightly tilted strata have been cut wide open and one looks across a vast open space to the eastern side where the downward pull of the Rift Valley has caused the rocks to turn over like a nearly breaking wave and the sharp edges of the almost vertical strata stand up on end like a gigantic *chevaux-de-frise*. The road noses its way through a gap in this colossal palisade and once more begins the slow climb of the western slope of a fold, this time Jebel el-Hadhira. This fold is broken open only in a small area north of the present road and so there is no basin to cross and the road continues to climb until with surprising suddenness the strata turn over and plunge headlong into the Arabah. This is Neqb es-Sufei which is probably the Ascent of the Scorpions, mentioned in more than one place in the Old Testament as the boundary of Judah (Num. 34:4; Josh. 15:3; Judg. 1:36) and in I Macc. 5:3 as the place where Judas

Maccabeus defeated the Idumeans. At the foot is the Wadi Fiqra and beyond it the gentle rise of Shushat el-Quseib, the last remnant of the upwarp. Beyond that again is the Arabah with the dark waters of the Dead Sea on the

THE DESERT
AND THE SOWN

Cultivated land

Fig. 5.

left and to the south of them the dazzling white marls of the Sebkha. On the far side of the Arabah is the Trans-jordan plateau, divided into two by the Valley of the Zered which has on its right the uplifted mountain

of Edom and on the left the plateau of Moab. It is a barren, stark and jagged landscape, startling even in this land where extensive views are common, and the place itself is well-named, whether by reason of the many scorpions which plague this desert country, or, as seems most likely, because of the road, which again and again must curl back upon itself, like the tail of a scorpion, to climb this Niagara of rock.

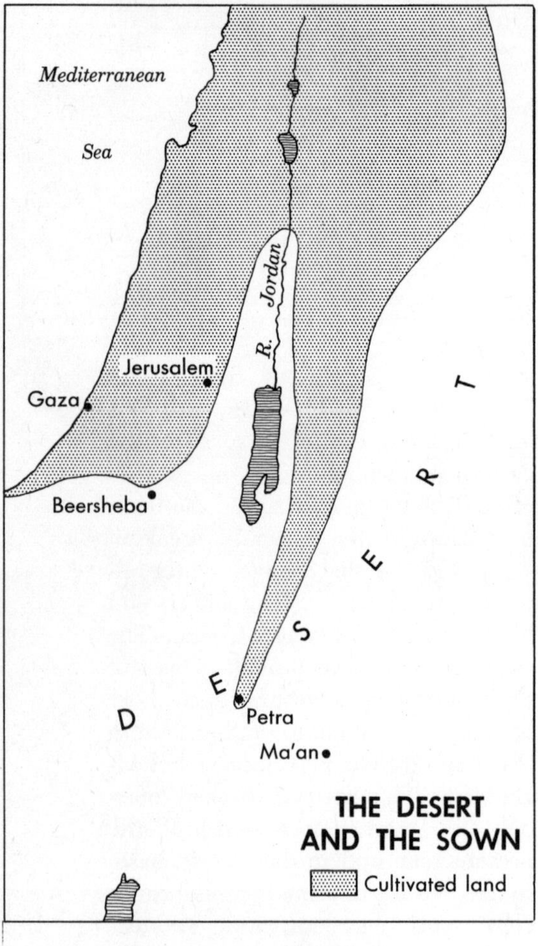

North of Beersheba we enter the Central Zone. Here the topography is dominated by one broad arch, the great Judaean Upwarp, the secondary folds being here rather less obvious. Both sides of the upwarp are marked by plunging monoclines which carry the strata steeply down to the plain. The arch rises out of the coast plain on the west, reaches its greatest height north and east of Hebron, and then bends downward toward the Dead Sea. On this side a broad trough has preserved over a very wide area the soft Senonian chalk, which is to be found also on the west in a narrow valley between the hard Cenomanian limestone which is exposed in the center of the arch and the Eocene limestone toward the coast plain. Thus, proceeding from the west we have:

(a) The broad outcrop of hard Eocene, which forms the hills of the Shephelah, that bloody debating ground between the Philistines and the inhabitants of Judaea.

(2) The thin valley of Senonian chalk which effectively divides the Shephelah from the mountains. This valley is so narrow that it is hardly apparent on the 1:250,000 map, but it

10. *The Wadi en-Nar near Jerusalem.* This is one of the wadis leading down through the Wilderness of Judaea to the Dead Sea. The picture shows the smooth and gentle slopes of the Senonian chalk in the upper part of the wadi and the narrow gorge which is formed where the wadi has cut down to the underlying Cenomanian limestone. The buildings shown here are those of the monastery of Mar Saba.

formed a vitally important moat defending Judaea on the west.

(c) The Cenomanian highlands in the center. Here erosion by the driving rain from the west has pushed the water-parting backward so that the highest land, on which the towns of Hebron, Bethlehem and Jerusalem stand, lies east of the real top of the arch.

(d) The wide exposure of Senonian chalk on the eastern flank. This exceptionally porous rock has combined with the dry climate common to the eastern flanks to produce the inhospitable Wilderness of Judaea. Where the wadis have cut down to the hard Cenomanian underneath, there have developed the narrow gorges which make such a striking contrast with the smooth slopes of the Senonian hills.

The next upwarp is the Ephraimite Arch (the Ramallah Arch of Picard), which shows some striking differences from the Judaean. Starting rather west of Jerusalem, it crosses the present Jerusalem-Nablus road near Lub-

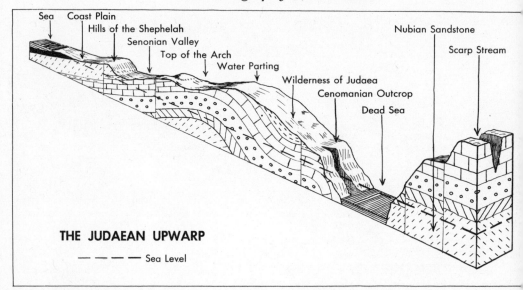

THE JUDAEAN UPWARP

— — — — Sea Level

Labels on figure: Sea; Coast Plain; Hills of the Shephelah; Senonian Valley; Top of the Arch; Water Parting; Nubian Sandstone; Scarp Stream; Wilderness of Judaea; Cenomanian Outcrop; Dead Sea

Fig. 6. *Diagrammatic Block across the Judaean Upwarp and the Dead Sea showing the main structure.* This is not an exact cut at any particular point but is a "typical" block intended to illustrate the general features.

ban and it carries over from the Central into the Northern Zone, for in the latitude of Ramallah there occur the two inward-curving hinge faults which bring the Central Zone to an end. On the west is the Valley of Ajalon, where a down-faulted valley has preserved the soft Senonian in a valley pointing up into the hills. This was the Valley of Ajalon and the easiest approach into the hills. On the other side another hinge fault north of Jericho marks the end of the wide Senonian outcrop in the Wilderness of Judaea. To the north of these hinge faults the Senonian chalk is largely absent on both sides of the arch. In this region the arch is almost entirely composed of Cenomanian with a small outcrop of Albian in the center. There is no exposure of Eocene on the west to form hills similar to those of the Shephelah.

Beyond Lubban the Ramallah Arch continues in a NNE direction into Jebel Kebir Upwarp, which forms the central portion of what was once the Judaean-Gilead Island, now cut across by the Jordan Rift. The Jebel Kebir Upwarp is itself cut by a number of cross faults at right angles to the main axis, the most important of them being the narrow rift valley of the Wadi Fari'a which cleaves the mountains and gives easy access up from the Jordan. It will be seen that here the main arch lies well to the east and the central area round Nablus and Samaria is, in fact, a basin. This fact is obscured because the hard Eocene limestone which has been preserved in the center of this basin has been pushed up until it forms the highest land in the region (3100 feet in Mount Ebal). Nevertheless, the basin character is of great importance, because the soft Senonian chalk is

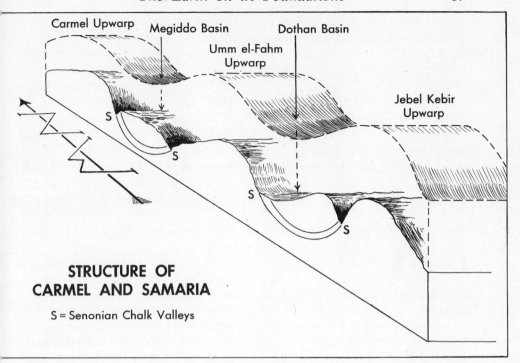

Carmel Upwarp   Megiddo Basin   Dothan Basin

Umm el-Fahm
Upwarp

Jebel Kebir
Upwarp

**STRUCTURE OF
CARMEL AND SAMARIA**

S = Senonian Chalk Valleys

Fig. 7. The dotted lines represent the original structure. The solid drawing beneath represents the present relief, showing how the basins are occupied by hills.

now enclosed within the rim of the basin instead of being on the outside of the arch as in Judaea, and has formed valleys of communication within the area rather than valleys of defense outside it.

The northwestern edge of this basin is formed by another upwarp, the Umm el-Fahm Arch, with beyond that another downwarp, the Megiddo Basin. Beyond the Megiddo downwarp is the third and final upwarp of Carmel. In the two upwarps the hard Cenomanian limestone has naturally been exposed as in all the other upwarps, and in the Megiddo region the Eocene limestone has been preserved,

though it has not been pushed up as in the Nablus Basin. This series of upwarps and downwarps has been cut across by great faults so that all that remains of it today is a huge wedge of higher land pointing toward the northwest and reaching the sea at Carmel. In this wedge the highest parts are Umm el-Fahm and Carmel, and the central portion of Megiddo is somewhat lower, though still hilly because of the hard rock of which it is composed. In between the Cenomanian of the upwarps and the Eocene of the downwarp is, of course, the Senonian chalk, and it is this which forms the vital cross valleys of Megiddo and Jokneam.

The Samaria region differs from Judaea also in that there are a large number of cross faults and down-faulted basins, floored with fertile alluvium washed down from the mountains. The Plain of Dothan is one such basin and so is Merj Sannur, north of Nablus.

To the north of the Carmel-Samaria hill country lies the great break which stretches from the Bay of Acre to Beisan and makes possible easy movement from the Mediterranean to the Rift Valley. This plain has always played an important part in the life of the country and its place in the life of the modern Jewish state is shown by the fact that it is commonly known as *Ha-Emek*, or "The Valley" par excellence. It is outlined by faults and divided into three very obvious sections.

(a) *The Jezreel Corridor* in the east. This is the narrow rift valley running down between the Hill of Moreh and the Mountains of Gilboa to Beisan, which stands upon a very obvious step where the great north-south fault of the Jordan Rift cuts across the corridor.

(b) *The Plain of Esdraelon* in the center. This is a rough triangle with a very straight base from Megiddo to Ibleam (near the modern Jenin). Near the apex in the northeast another little plain opens out, the Plain of Tabor. This would seem to be a collapsed arch, the form of which is now obscured by the outflow of basalt which created the Hill of Moreh, but the keystone of the arch still remains in the form of the rounded hill of Tabor. The isolation of this hill, which rises steeply from the plain as Carmel rises from the coast, has given it a certain majesty which seems to have impressed the Biblical writers. Thus

Jeremiah says of Nebuchadnezzar, "Like Tabor among the mountains, and like Carmel by the sea, shall one come" (Jer. 46:18) and in Psalm 89: 12 Tabor and Hermon joyously praise God's name.

(c) *The Plain of Asher.* Near Tel el-Qassis in the west the northern hills extend a spur toward the northern scarp of Carmel and the Kishon squeezes through a very narrow gap into the last of the three divisions, the Plain of Asher which is better considered, perhaps, as part of the coast plain.

The last of the mountain sections is the region of Galilee in the north. Here the structure is much more complicated and the northern part really belongs rather to the Lebanese-Syrian area. There is one vast upwarp in the south and another near the frontier, and in the east, near the town of Safad is a great basin, where the white Senonian chalk has once more been preserved and beyond that the orange-colored cliffs of the Eocene. Where the valleys near Safad have cut down through the chalk to the Cenomanian limestone we find again the sudden change from rounded slopes to steep and narrow gorges, such as Wadi Lemmun and Wadi 'Ain el-Jinn, which we noticed in the Wilderness of Judaea (page 35). The basin structure is not, however, very obvious on the ground because once again it has been obscured by the great faults which run across it.

These faults are, in fact, the most impressive feature of the Galilean landscape, and the most striking of them is the great cross fault of Esh-Shaghur almost due east of Acre.

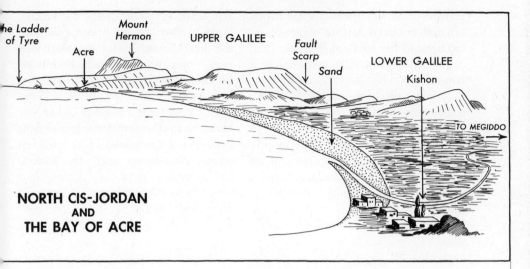

the Ladder of Tyre

Acre

Mount Hermon

UPPER GALILEE

Fault Scarp

Sand

LOWER GALILEE

Kishon

TO MEGIDDO

**NORTH CIS-JORDAN
AND
THE BAY OF ACRE**

Fig. 8.

This forms a gigantic scarp, clearly visible from far to the south, which divides Lower from Upper Galilee and is followed today by the Acre-Safad road. Lower Galilee stands at a general level of 1600–2000 feet, but is greatly complicated by many down-faulted basins, of which the most important is Sahl el-Battuf in the center, the Campus Asochis of the Romans. Upper Galilee, at the head of the huge scarp, is also broken by cross faulting, but its general level is much higher. Most of it is over 2600 feet and Jebel Jarmuq, the highest point west of the Jordan, reaches 4260. The eastern edge of Galilee is the north-south scarp of the Rift Valley. South of Lake Huleh this is much cut into by NW-SE hinge faults, which have produced, for example, the tilted valley of Ardh el-Hima and the low-lying Plain of Gennesaret. However, north of Huleh the scarp is singularly unbroken, either by faults or by erosion.

The eastern side of Galilee is further complicated by the flow of basalt which extends all over the area from Tiberias to the Hill of Moreh and includes also the basalt dam in the Rift south of Huleh. On the western side the mountains extend right to the coast at the present Israeli-Lebanese border at Ras en-Naqura. This was probably the famous Ladder of Tyre.

The Coast Plain is fairly quickly dealt with. The most important features to notice are:

(a) The line of narrow, low hills of Pleistocene Kurkar limestone which occur intermittently along the coast from Ras en-Naqura to near Jaffa.

(b) The broad areas of dune sand on the coast south of Jaffa. There is another, more limited, area farther north, near the present Hadera.

(c) The exposures of Mousterian Red Sand. These are for the most part confined to the Sharon area, that is, to a region between Caesarea and some 7 miles south of Lydda. They are farther inland than the first two features and, though there are a few isolated outcrops farther south, there are none to the north of this area.

(d) The Loess. This is found in a large triangle behind Gaza and Rafah, that is in the extreme south of the coast plain and on the edge of the southern desert.

The general outlines of the structure of the Rift Valley have been dealt with in the previous chapter. Here it is sufficient to remind the reader of the important four basins (Huleh, Lake of Galilee, Dead Sea and South-ern Arabah) and to notice the sudden limit to the low-lying rift valley in the north near Metullah. Here the very complicated Syrian system of faults cuts across the north-south Jordan faulting and produces a very complex pattern. The level of the valley is raised far above sea level (over 1000 feet at Metullah) and with Merj Ayoun one enters upon the Syrian-Lebanese section of the Rift which is structurally different, and essentially an *upland* basin.

CHAPTER IV

Has the Rain a Father?

Has the rain a father,
or who has begotten the drops of dew?
From whose womb did the ice come forth,
and who has given birth to the hoarfrost of heaven?
JOB 38:28–29

THE climate of the Palestinian region is very largely determined by two factors, the position of Palestine at the southeastern corner of the Mediterranean where the desert and the sea almost touch each other, and the well-marked division of the region into north-south lines of relief. Its position upon the globe has made it a climatic battlefield where the opposing forces of sea and desert meet head on. Normally, the influence of the sea is stronger, at any rate in the inhabited parts of the country, but there are times when the dry air from the desert sweeps right across the Judaean hills and pours down to the very edges of the sea. Since the desert lies to the south and east, it follows that these tend to be the drier areas and the greatest rainfall occurs most usually in the north and west.

This pattern is rendered more complicated by the mountains, hills and valleys running from north to south,

that is, parallel to the coast. Not only is it generally wetter and colder on the mountains, but there is a very striking difference between the western and eastern sides, for on the west the influence of the sea predominates and on the east the influence of the desert. Therefore, the western sides are markedly wetter and are more moderate in their temperature range between winter and summer, while the eastern slopes are not only drier but are exposed in winter to the bitter desert cold and in summer to its blazing heat. It is very interesting at Jerusalem to stand upon the Mount of Olives when the clouds are piling up from the west, for if you look up into the sky immediately above your head, you can watch these clouds dissolve and vanish as the air begins to slip down into the dry and overheated Jordan Valley, and then, far away to the east, you see them reform once more as the air, moving inland from the Mediterranean, has to climb again to cross the plateau of Trans-jordan.

The greatest barrier to the influence of the sea is formed by the double range of the Lebanon and the Anti-Lebanon, where the mountains are at

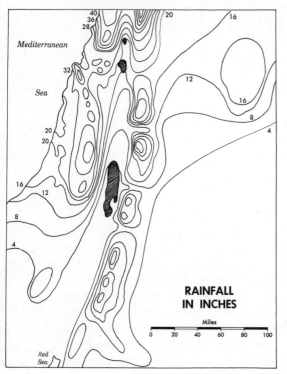

Fig. 9.

their highest. Here the desert sweeps far over to the west and reaches almost to the foot of the mountains, so that Damascus has an average annual rainfall of a mere 10 inches. This has greatly constricted the movement of traffic from north to south so that it had to pass by Damascus along the narrow passage between the desert and the Anti-Lebanon. There are, however, three places where the influence of the sea is able to extend farther inland than one would nor-

mally expect. The first is in the extreme north, where the absence of the second mountain barrier has allowed the rainfall, which in any case is greater here in the north, to sweep right inland to the Euphrates, and the second is in the extreme south where the high plateau of Edom is able to catch the last remnants of the Mediterranean storms, which have passed unhindered across the lower-lying deserts of the Negeb.* The third region is in the center, where the Mediterranan storms pass easily the low country of southern Galilee and Esdraelon and up the valley of the Yarmuq to the wide and fertile region of the Hauran. There they are even farther extended because as they pass over the plateau to the east the rising ground of the Jebel Druze causes the rainfall to increase instead of dying away. This well-watered Hauran with its rich volcanic soil was one of the great granaries of the Roman Empire and in Old Testament times it was famous for its herds and flocks.

The great Rift Valley is everywhere drier than the hill country on either side of it and south of the narrow "waist" in the middle Jordan Valley it is dry enough to merit the description of desert. Jericho has an average of 4 inches of rain in the year and the Dead Sea only 2.

The Palestinian year is divided into two major seasons, the dry summer from mid-June to mid-September and the rainy season in the cooler half of the year. The summer drought, during which no rain falls at all, is actually somewhat longer than the true "summer" and extends into the

* See above, pp. 7 and 9.

transitional seasons which divide the summer from the winter at either end. Thus, even on the coast in Cisjordan, the drought is usually complete for five continuous months, from the middle of May to the second fortnight in October. It is better to avoid using the word "winter" for the rainy season, for winter inevitably suggests to an English-speaking person a cold season, but in Palestine the cold weather is normally confined to the three months after Christmas, that is, to the second half of the rainy season. In modern Arabic the word "summer" is so emphatically suggestive of the long dry period (cf. Ps. 32:4, "My strength was dried up as by the heat of summer") that winter means more than anything else that blessed period when the rain comes. The Arabic word *shittah* is in fact used impartially for both "winter" and "rain," and there seems to be something of the same thought in Song of Solomon 2:11, "For lo, the winter is past, the rain is over and gone."

THE SUMMER PROPER

This is extraordinarily regular. It starts on about June 15 and finishes on about September 15 and during this period day after day is the same. In this season there is a low pressure centered over the Persian Gulf and a belt of high pressure in the Atlantic region over the Azores and between these two the isobars in the eastern basin of the Mediterranean run more or less from north to south. The resulting winds, tending as usual to follow the isobars, are the Etesian Winds, which are so well known to students of the classics. These winds may develop quite strongly at times and cause unpleasantly choppy seas, but they are very steady and dependable and, therefore, much less dangerous than the winds of the rainy season, and it was for this reason that summer was the period for shipping in the ancient world. The shipwreck which is so vividly described in Acts 27 occurred because the voyage had been prolonged beyond the summer well into the dangerous transitional season with its sudden changes of wind.

Throughout the summer season there is naturally a low pressure over the hot land, and this draws air in from the Mediterranean, thus deflecting the Etesian winds toward the Palestinian coast, which they reach as a westerly or northwesterly current of air. This tendency is emphasized by the presence of the island of Cyprus, over whose baking central plain a minor low develops. The air moves in an anticlockwise direction round this low pressure and so the winds over the sea to the south of the island are given a west to east direction toward the shores of Palestine. This wind does not bring rain, but it is of great importance in helping to moderate the heat of the day, particularly in the regions near the sea, and in bringing dew all along the coast and on the western slopes of the mountains, though it does not occur in the Jordan Valley south of Beisan during the summer months.[1] The value of the dew, which is largely responsible for the growth of grapes during the summer drought, was well appreciated in Biblical times and more than once is mentioned together with rain (II Sam.

11. *The morning mist.* During the summer months there may be a heavy mist in the valleys of Judaea and Gilead during the early hours of the morning, though it disappears rapidly when the sun rises. It is more than once quoted in the Bible as a symbol of impermanence. This photograph is taken at Es-Salt in Trans-jordan.

1:21; I Kings 17:1) or instead of it (e.g., "May God give you of the dew of heaven, and of the fatness of the earth, and plenty of grain and wine" [Gen. 27:28]; "Israel dwelt in safety . . . in a land of grain and wine; yea, his heavens drop down dew" [Deut. 33:28]; "Therefore the heavens above you have withheld the dew, and the earth has withheld its produce" [Hag. 1:10]. See also Job 29:19; Zech. 8:12).

In Samaria it was sufficiently heavy for Gideon to wring out "enough dew from the fleece to fill a bowl with water" (Judg. 6:38), and Isaiah spoke of God as being "like a cloud of dew in the heat of harvest" (Is. 18:4; cf. Hos. 14:5 and Mic. 5:7). In the early morning in summer the moisture in the air often hangs like a thick mist in the valleys and this was held to be characteristic of instability, because it vanishes so quickly the moment that the sun arises. Hence the force of Hosea 13:3, "Therefore they shall be like the morning mist or like the dew that goes early away, like the chaff that swirls from the threshing floor or like smoke from a window" (cf. Hos. 6:4 and Job 7:9).

At the present time researches are being undertaken to discover the value of the dew in the Negeb, where it is believed to be of great importance, especially on the western side. Ashbel has estimated that the coast south of Gaza has as many as 250 nights of dew in the year, a much higher figure than that for Athlit well to the north, which has only 100 such nights.[2] The reason for this great difference would seem to be the sudden drop in temperature at night which is characteristic of the desert regions in the south, producing more dew than in the north, where the cooling at night is less. Of course, it must not be forgotten that the days with rain are more frequent at Athlit.

In the daytime the land is naturally at its hottest and the tendency of the air to move inland is therefore greatest. Thus regularly every day the cool, damp, maritime air moves eastward across the coast and piles up on the coastal plain until it is able to pass over the mountains and pour like a flood into the Rift Valley about noon or shortly after. Its arrival east of the Jordan is somewhat longer delayed, but about three in the afternoon it overflows the plateau edge and arrives with surprising suddenness in the hot and dusty plateau villages. It reaches these villages too late to be of much use in reducing the heat of the day, which is therefore higher on the uplifted eastern plateau than it is on the low coast plain, but it is of immense value to the farmer because he uses it for winnowing his grain. One of the loveliest sights of the Pales-

tinian scene is the picture of a group of farmers on the threshing floor outside a village rhythmically tossing up the golden grain in the long rays of the evening sun, so that the chaff is blown away by the wind, but the grain falls back in a glittering cascade onto the ground. It is this picture which the Psalmist had in mind when he said that the wicked were "like chaff which the wind drives away" (Ps. 1:4; cf. also 35:5; Job 21:18; Hos. 13:3) and later John the Baptist, who said of the Messiah that "his winnowing fork is in his hand, to clear his threshing floor, and to gather the wheat into his granary" (Luke 3:17; Matt. 3:12).

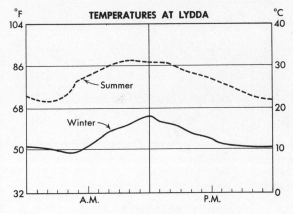

Fig. 10. *Temperatures at Lydda.* Average temperatures during the day on the coast plain in both winter and summer, showing the cooling effect of the sea breeze during the middle of the day in summer.

The course of a normal summer day in the Palestinian region is fairly easy to foretell. On the coast plain during the early hours there is almost complete calm, so that smoke rises straight into the air and hangs immediately above its source. As soon as the sun rises there is a very rapid increase in the temperature, which remains high, that is within 5° F. of the day's maximum, for as long as seven to nine hours. In part this is because the influence of the sea restrains the at any rate on the coast, but then the sea breeze starts and immediately the weather becomes bearable. This breeze increases in strength and, as we have seen, presses farther and farther inland, but soon after sunset

RELATIVE HUMIDITY

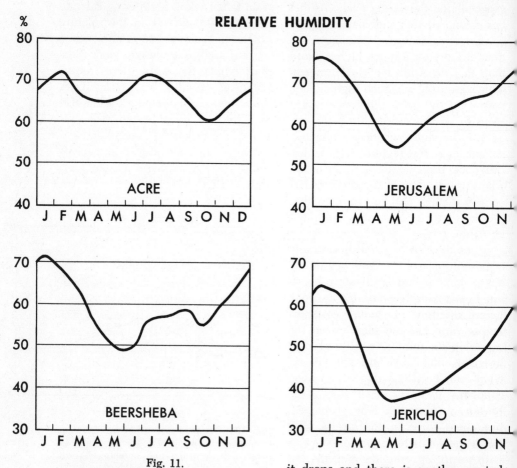

Fig. 11.

maximum from being as high as one might expect, but it is nevertheless true that the prolonged heat of a summer day is one of its most important features. This early calm and the sudden rise in temperature make the hours before nine o'clock in many ways the most unpleasant of the day, it drops and there is another period of calm until about nine or ten in the evening when the land breeze starts. Because this has to fight against the general drift of air from the sea to land in summer, and because it is slowed down by its passage over rough ground and buildings, this breeze from the land is often weak and may not be able to establish itself, with the result that the night wind is sometimes also from the sea. Despite the moderating effect of the sea upon the temperature, the summer climate of the coast is oppressive, because the nights remain warm and the dampness of the air makes the heat difficult to endure.

On the hills the nights are cool and sometimes even chilly, which makes the summer climate there much pleas-

throughout the year. During this season great high pressures prevail over the land areas of Europe and Asia in the north and Africa and Arabia in the south, leaving between them a long trough of low pressure following the line of the Mediterranean and the Persian Gulf. In good years this trough is open for the passage of cyclonic storms from the west and, if all is well, these seem to succeed each other quite steadily once a week,

MEAN AND EXTREME MAXIMA OF DAILY TEMPERATURE, LYDDA

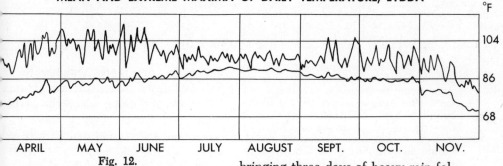

Fig. 12.

anter, even though the days may often be equally hot. In the Rift Valley temperatures are naturally very high, but in the region of Beisan and Tiberias the arrival of the sea breeze brings relief. In the south, however, round Jericho the air is so warmed by its descent and pours with such tempestuous force down the Judaean hills that its effect is most uncomfortable.

THE RAINY SEASON

In contrast to the regularity of the summer, the rainy season is very unpredictable. Not only is the weather changeable, but the total amount of rain which may fall is very variable and so is the time of its beginning and ending and its distribution

bringing three days of heavy rain followed by four of fine weather. There are thus two types of winter days, the wet days when all the world seems blotted out in a slashing tumult of water (Jerusalem, it should be noticed, has the same average annual rainfall as London, but crowded into half the year) and the dry days when the cold desert air is moving outward from the continent. On the coast these days are fresh and agreeable, but on the eastern plateau this desert wind can be as sharp as a whetted scythe and one realizes the force of Gertrude Bell's remark, "The first rule when going to a hot country is to take your thickest clothes."

The European high pressure, however, extends thin fingers along the Mediterranean peninsulas and from

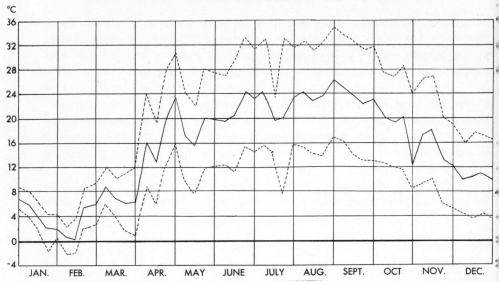

Fig. 13. *Maximum, minimum and mean temperatures at Amman during 1950.* This diagram should be compared with the preceding one for summer temperatures at Lydda. It will be seen that Amman, which is on the edge of the Trans-jordan desert, has its highest temperatures during the summer months and not during the siroccos of the transitional seasons. Nevertheless, the sudden rise of temperature caused by the siroccos of early April should be noticed together with the drop in temperature with the end of the siroccos in May. February of 1950 was unusually cold. It will be seen that the temperature range in winter is very small compared with that of summer. The drop in temperature in July caused by the inflow of cooler air from the Mediterranean should also be remarked.

time to time these may join up with the high pressure over the Sahara and thus block the passage of the cyclones, sometimes for as long as a whole month. When this happens the results in Palestine may well be disastrous. The harm may not be too great if it should happen later in the year when the crop roots are well established, but it is particularly unfortunate if the start of the rains are delayed until much after December 1, or if the

first rains come early and are then followed by a period of drought to kill the young crops which the early rains have started. During these interruptions the normal winter drift of air out of the continent asserts itself and so the winds are from the east. They bring days of sheer beauty to the coast, for the winds are warmed by their descent over the mountains, and the sea, moreover, in this region is unusually warm, the temperature for the coldest month, which is as late as March, being 61.7° F., as compared with 56.3°, which is the average for the eastern Mediterranean, and with even colder temperatures for the open ocean. On the hills the weather is fine, though often cold, and in the Rift Valley it is usually warm, though winds from the north along the narrow trough may bring sudden cold from the snows of Hermon even as far south as the Dead Sea.

The cyclones tend to arrive as already mature, though there seem to be areas in the Mediterranean where they are rejuvenated, especially in places where warm Mediterranean water is enclosed within encircling land, which in winter has rather higher pressures. Such saucers of low pressure are formed over the Gulf of Alboran and the Gulf of Sidra. When the cyclones reach the Palestinian coast they seem to pass off fairly rapidly to the northeast toward Iraq, though they may become stationary over the Gulf of Alexandretta. The rain which they bring is almost always in the form of heavy showers and practically never the prolonged drizzle of more northern countries. On the first day the rain is frequently continuous and very heavy, but on the two succeeding days it tends to occur in slashing showers interrupted by fine periods. Rain may occur with a wind from any part of the west, but it is usually strongest when the wind is southwesterly.

The rainy season begins gradually during the second half of October, though the coming of effective rain may be delayed until November or even, in bad years, until the first week in January. In 1937–38, for instance, the first effective rain at Amman was in the middle of January, though there had been a slight shower the previous November, but in the following year there were nearly 4 inches in three successive days during the first week in October. During this preliminary period the air is full of dust after the dry summer and when the westerly winds bring the first winter clouds there are often wonderful sunsets and sunrises, when men say, "It will be stormy today, for the sky is red and threatening" (Matt. 16:3). Sometimes, however, these are merely deceptive, "clouds and wind without rain" and "waterless clouds, carried along by winds" (Prov. 25:14; Jude 12), and the farmers have to wait still longer before they can begin. A very frequent effect of this early period is that the wet air from the sea moving in over the still heated land is forced to rise rapidly and produces sudden thunderstorms. These are often limited in extent, as thunderstorms commonly are, so that one village may get a good soaking which it needs before plowing can start, while another, not far away, is still dry. This explains the force of Amos 4:7, "I would send rain upon one city, and send no rain upon another city; one field would be rained upon, and the field on which it did not rain withered; so two or three cities wandered to one city to drink water, and were not satisfied; yet you did not return to me, says the Lord."

As soon as the rain comes the temperature drops, especially on the hills and plateau, and the absence of convectional currents to disturb the rain-washed atmosphere produces that glorious brilliance described by Elihu in the Book of Job, "And now men cannot look on the light when it is bright in the skies, when the wind has passed and cleared them" (Job 37:21). On such a day as this every cleft in the Trans-Jordan hills is visible from Jerusalem 40 miles away.

The beginning of this rain, those vital first showers which the Bible calls the "former rain," is earnestly longed for, and it is quite impossible to describe the sudden lifting of the spirit which the whole country feels when at last the rain begins. Even the refugees today, shivering in their sodden tents and caves, will still repeat again and again,

12. *The former rains.* The beginning of the rainy season in October or November is often marked by severe thunderstorms, which result from the rapid rise of the damp air above the still overheated land. This photograph was taken during the first storm of the 1938–39 season.

"Thank God for the rain! Thank God for the rain!" so thoroughly has it been drummed into their thinking that it is upon this that the life of the people depends. This question of dis-

tribution is almost more important than the actual amount of the rain. Generally speaking, the more rain that there is, the better will be the harvest, but it is interesting to compare the years 1937–38 and 1938–39, which have already been mentioned. In both these years the total was satisfactory with no great difference between them (Kufrinje in the Gilead district had 30.6 and 32.2 inches; Mazar in Moab 16.3 and 18.7; Zerqa 8.2 and 6.2; and H.3, far into the desert, 5.7 and 6.2 inches) but in the first year the effective rain did not start until after Christmas, while in the second it was very evenly distributed over the whole rainy season, after a very early start at the beginning of October. The result was that the first year's harvest was not more than average, but the second year produced bumper crops, vegetation grew in rank profusion right out into the desert and the Hejaz railway ran axle-deep in flowers. It is in that kind of year that "the pastures of the wilderness drip, the hills gird themselves with joy, the meadows clothe themselves with flocks, the valleys deck themselves with grain, they shout and sing together for joy" (Ps. 65:12–13).

About Christmas the cold weather begins, and frosts at night upon the hills become common. Flurries of snow may occur occasionally during the year in Jerusalem, because at this season the great pressure systems have rearranged themselves and cold air moves southward from the center of Europe. About once every five or ten years there is a heavy fall and roughly every thirty years the approaches to the city are blocked. On the eastern plateau, which is colder, snow is very much commoner and some is likely to occur every year, the Jebel Druze, in fact, being snow-capped all the winter. Job uses the snow-fed streams

13. *Snow in Jerusalem.* A little snow may fall once or twice during the rainy season, but it usually does not rest on the ground. A heavy fall of snow sufficient to block the roads occurs about once in fifteen years. Despite the utter discomfort of wet weather on the unprotected plateau, it is received with joy, because the more rain and snow that there is, the better will be the harvest.

of the desert as symbols of deceitfulness, saying, "My brethren are treacherous as a torrent-bed, as freshets that

pass away, which are dark with ice, and where the snow hides itself. In time of heat they disappear; when it is hot, they vanish from their place. The caravans turn aside from their course; they go up into the waste, and perish. The caravans of Tema look, the travelers of Sheba hope. They are disappointed because they were confident; they come thither and are confounded" (Job 6:15–20; cf. 24:19). Snow is mentioned more than once in the Bible, though always as something rather unusual, as when Benaiah "went down and slew a lion in a pit on a day when snow had fallen" (II Sam. 23:20; I Chron. 11:22), and as the great fall of snow recorded in I Maccabees 13:22.

Hail may occur quite often on the coast plain and may cause considerable damage, though it is very rare that it proves as dangerous as the freak storm described in the Book of Joshua, where it is said that "while they were going down the ascent of Beth-horon, the Lord threw down great stones from heaven upon them as far as Azekah, and they died; there were more who died because of the hailstones than the men of Israel killed with the sword" (Josh. 10:11). It was thought of in Biblical times as being one of the ever-present dangers for the farmer, and is mentioned as such many times in the prophetic writings. Thus Isaiah says to the drunkards of Ephraim that God will bring upon them "a storm of hail, a destroying tempest" (Is. 28:2).

March and April form the third division of the rainy season, when the rain is becoming less frequent and the temperature is rising. The final storm usually comes some time in April and causes a surprising drop in temperature, so that in 1949 it actually snowed in Jerusalem on April 6. This is the period of the "latter rain" of the Bible, so desperately needed to make the grain swell and ensure a good harvest. The failure of this latter rain was held to be a sign of God's displeasure and Amos says to the people in the name of God, "I also withheld the rain from you when there were yet three months to the harvest" (Amos 4:7). There may be one last shower in the first week of May, though it will be a mere sprinkling, and after that the dry weather has set in for good.

There are constant references to the "former" and "latter" rains in the Old Testament, as when Moses says, "He will give the rain for your land in its season, the early rain and the later rain, that you may gather in your grain and your wine and your oil" (Deut. 11:14; cf. Hos. 6:3, Jer. 5:24, Joel 2:23). Thus people whose knowledge of the Palestinian climate comes only from the Bible are tempted to think of the rainy season as being wet at the beginning and end, but dry in the middle. This is not so. In fact, all the figures show that the rainfall tends to get steadily greater toward the middle of the season and then to decrease again. However, the rain at the beginning of the season is that on which the farmer depends before he can start to plow and sow his grain, and the slight rains in April are those which he requires just before the harvest if the grain is to swell. If either of these two should fail, his crops will suffer.

Between the rainy season and the summer at either end are the transitional seasons, brief periods of only a few weeks each during which the sirocco may blow, a hot, dry wind from the desert, made even hotter by the fact that it is descending. The mechanism of the sirocco is not fully understood, but it is an important feature of the Palestinian climate and will be dealt with more fully later. For the moment it is necessary only to say that siroccos are confined to these two seasons; they produce the highest temperatures of the year, and those of the spring season are especially destructive of the winter vegetation, causing it to wither away almost in a night.

CHAPTER V

The Rain of the Mountains

They are wet with the rain of the mountains,
and cling to the rock for want of shelter.

JOB 24:8

ONE of the chief features of the Palestinian climate is its great variety within a very small space, not only the difference between the rain of the mountains and the drought of the deserts, which sometimes are to be found at their very feet, but also the difference within a few miles between sharp cold and almost tropical heat. These sudden variations of climate are the result partly of the rapid alternation of plain and mountain, of uplifted plateau and the deep, unnatural trough of the Jordan Rift, and partly also of the never-ending conflict between the desert and the sea. This greatly accentuates the importance of the relief so that even a slight variation of aspect may give either the maritime or the continental influence the advantage and thus bring places which are only a few miles apart under differing régimes. Jerusalem itself stands upon such a sharp divide, for though the average rainfall there exceeds 24 inches a year, yet five miles away to the east, with very little dif-

ference in altitude, is the edge of an uncultivable desert, and during a snowstorm in Jerusalem I have seen displayed for sale strawberries which had been grown in the open air only twenty miles away at Jericho.

It follows, therefore, that the climatic regions are quite sharply distinguished from each other, and, generally speaking, there are six major rules which determine the differences between these regions:

(a) Since Palestine lies at the southeastern corner of the Mediterranean, rainfall tends to *decrease* as one goes from north to south.

(b) Rainfall tends to *decrease* also from west to east, that is as one goes farther from the sea.

(c) Rainfall tends to *increase*, however, as one goes up the mountains, and this may reverse the tendency to decrease toward the south and east.

(d) Rainfall tends to *decrease* very markedly on the lee side of the mountains, that is, toward the east. This is particularly true of the eastern slopes of the hills of Cis-jordan leading down into the rift valley.

(e) Temperatures tend to *decrease* with an increase in height.

(f) The temperature *range*, however, tends to *increase* with the decrease of rainfall, that is to say, the farther one goes from the sea and to some extent also from north to south. This increase in the temperature range may be so marked that the days on the plateaus may actually be hotter than those on the coast plain 3000 feet below.

With these rules in mind, therefore, it is possible to divide the Palestinian area into the following climatic regions:

(i) The Coast Plain, including the Plain of Esdraelon as far as Affuleh.

(ii) The Cis-jordan hills, including also Carmel.

(iii) The Rift Valley, including the Valley of Jezreel.

(iv) The Trans-jordan Plateau. This region extends in the north as far east as the present Hejaz Railway, but in the south it is confined to the plateau edge and it comes to an end at Shobek.

(v) The Steppe. This is a region dividing the cultivable area from the true deserts of the Negeb in Cis-jordan and of Eastern and Southern Trans-jordan. There are two separate areas of steppe, one in Cis-jordan in the Beersheba region and one in Trans-jordan on the plateau. It does not really exist in the Rift Valley, where the change from cultivation to desert is extraordinarily rapid.

(vi) The Desert.

(i) *The Coast Plain.* This is naturally the region which is most affected by the influence of the sea at all times of the year. The summers are hot, because it is low-lying, but the sea breezes exert a strong moderating influence and the maximum temperatures during the day are not necessarily as high as those experienced at places farther inland on the Trans-jordan plateau or even on the Cis-jordan hills. However, the daily range is small and the humidity excessive, which means that one cannot get relief, either from cool nights or from the rapid evaporation of perspiration which is possible when the air is dry. For instance, when one crosses from the sunny to the shady side of the street in a coastal town, there is no immediate feeling of being cooler, such as one gets by doing the same thing in an inland region.

This excessive dampness of the atmosphere is really confined to the coast itself, and at Ramleh, which is only 10 miles from the coast, there is in the early summer as much as 10 per cent difference in the average relative humidity as compared with that of the coastal towns. Later in the summer, however, when the westerly winds from the sea become more strongly established, this difference becomes less. In the Plain of Esdraelon the decrease in humidity is even more marked and there the heat, though it is greater than at Haifa, is often easier to bear. However, the summer is never comfortable on the plain, since the nights are everywhere warm. There is, for example, very little difference between the minimum temperatures at Ramleh and at Gaza, but the maxima at Ramleh are higher.

During the rainy season the same

influence is felt. The daily range remains small and this is now pleasant, since the nights are never very cold, though the dampness of the atmosphere may cause them to seem chilly, and the days have lost the overwhelming heat of summer. Temperatures are such that it is possible to live not un-

where the range is about 18° F. There is even a tendency for the range to be somewhat less during the summer than it is in the rainy season, which is not true for any other part of the country, this being the result of the continuous influence of the sea during the summer months, uninterrupted by any

DEVELOPMENT OF THE RAINY SEASON

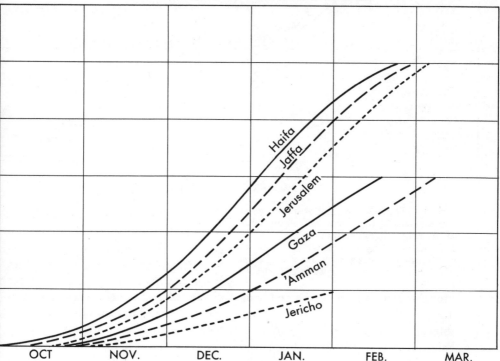

Fig. 14.

happily without heating in one's house, though in wet weather it is very pleasant to have some, for frosts are practically unknown and snow has only once been recorded, in February, 1950. One of the most striking features of the temperature graphs for places on the coast is the very even temperature range between day and night during the whole year, for example, at Gaza,

large scale movement of air outward from the desert. Thus at Haifa the average daily range from October to March is 16–18° F., but only 12–14° F. from April to September.

The rain usually starts rather earlier on the coast than it does farther inland, and it lasts slightly longer. It is also relatively heavy and fairly well assured, though the total amount which falls in a year becomes less from north to south. These two facts are well

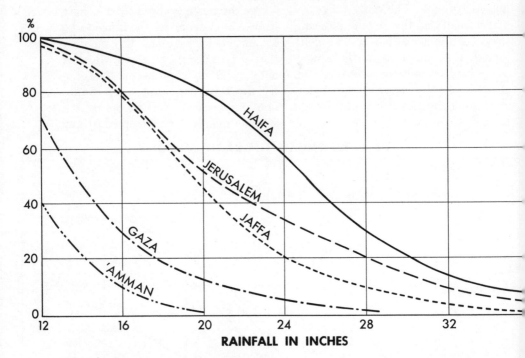

Fig. 15. This diagram indicates how great a chance one of the places marked on it has of reaching a certain total rainfall. Thus, Haifa has a 95% chance of receiving 16 inches of rain, an 80% chance of receiving 20 inches, a 57% chance of receiving 24 inches, etc.

brought out by the accompanying graphs (Figs. 14 and 15). The first, showing when various places in Palestine may expect to have received 4, 8, 12, 16 and 20 inches of rain, makes it clear that by the end of December Haifa has usually received 12 inches and Jaffa 10, but that Jerusalem has had only 8. Yet Jerusalem's final total is normally not very different from that of Haifa (Jerusalem 23.7; Haifa 24.2 inches) and greater than that of Jaffa. The second graph, that of rainfall probability, must be treated with reserve, since records have not yet been kept in every place for a sufficient number of years to make it

possible to produce a trustworthy comparison, but it may serve as a rough guide to the position. Such figures as are available, therefore, suggest that Haifa has about a 35 per cent better chance of getting 24 inches of rain in the year than Jaffa, and that the curve for Gaza drops even more steeply.

As one moves in from the coast there is a fairly rapid decrease in the total rainfall even within a few miles. Thus Ramleh has only 17.6 inches as compared with over 20 on the coast ten miles away, and Affuleh twenty miles inland from Haifa has over 8 inches less rain (15.8 inches as compared with 24.6).

(ii) *The Hills of Cis-jordan.* In this region the range of temperature, both daily and yearly, is greater than it is on the coast. Thus the difference between the hottest and the coldest months in Jerusalem is 27.9° F. and only 25.2° F. in Haifa and the mean daily range is 17.1° F. in Jerusalem and 15.3° F. in Haifa. These differences may not sound very great, but they are brought about by colder winters extending the figures for the yearly range in Jerusalem and cooler summer nights extending the daily range. The daily range during winter in Jerusalem is actually smaller than that of Haifa (January figures: 13.5° F. compared with 16.2° F. for Haifa), but the summer daily range is noticeably greater (20.8° and 13.2°). This means that the climate of the hills is much more stimulating than that of the coast, for the hot summer days are counteracted by cool, refreshing nights and the rainy season is cold enough to be distinctly bracing. The average temperature at Jerusalem in August is 75.2° F. whereas Haifa has 82.4°, but in January the Jerusalem temperature drops to an average of 47.2°, and that of Haifa only to 57.2°. During August also the daytime maxima are not far from each other in the two towns (Jerusalem 85.4° and Haifa 90.0° F., a difference of 4.6° F.), but at night the temperature at Jerusalem drops to 64.5° and at Haifa only to 76°, making a difference between the two places of 11.5°.

The rainfall tends to be greater than that of corresponding areas on the coast in the high plateau country of Judea and Upper Galilee, but rather less in the somewhat lower hills of Lower Galilee and Samaria, where the effect of distance from the sea more than counterbalances the effect of the increased height. However, even there the climate

is more stimulating than that of the coast plain, since the distance from the sea means a lower relative humidity and even at such a place as Nazareth, 1300 feet in height and 19 miles from the sea, the summer eve-

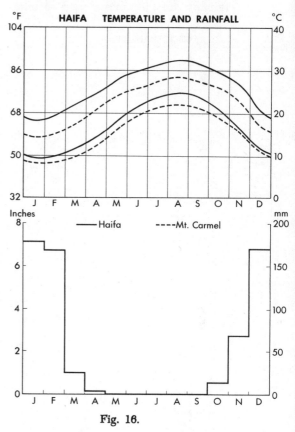

Fig. 16.

nings are cool enough to be refreshing and the nights can often be quite chilly.

The graphs for the monthly expectation of rain and for the total rainfall probability show that the hills get their rainy season rater later than the plain, but they are more likely to have years with a very heavy rainfall. Thus on the second graph the curves for Jerusalem and Jaffa lie very close together as far as the 20-inch figure, but after that they draw apart and Jerusalem has a 10 per cent greater chance of receiving as much as 28 inches in a year.

The graphs of temperature and rainfall for Jerusalem and Mount

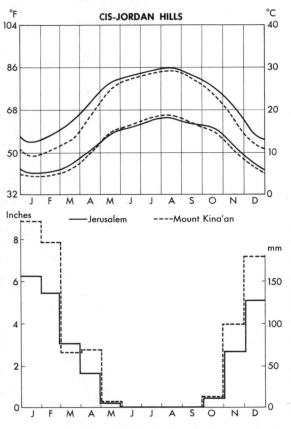

Fig. 17. Mt. Kina'an lies in the north and so the rainfall is greater. The smaller range results from the fact that Mount Kina'an is more exposed to the sea.

Kina'an show the difference between Judaea in the south and Upper Galilee in the north. Jerusalem is rather over 2600 feet and Mount Kina'an is 2950 feet above sea level, but the difference in the amount of rainfall is even

greater than this difference in height would lead us to expect, for Mount Kina'an has 9.4 inches more than Jerusalem (33.6 and 24.2 respectively). This must be explained by the tendency already noticed for the rainfall to be greater in the north than in the south. The smaller temperature range in Upper Galilee should also be noticed as an example of the fact that the range of temperature decreases with the increase in rainfall. The mean daily range in January on Mount Kina'an is very small, being only 9° F., and this is the result of the more constant cloud cover in Upper Galilee which prevents the radiation of heat at night and, in particular, reduces the temperature during the day. The climate of Upper Galilee, therefore, is much bleaker than that of Judaea, since there are fewer sunny days to provide a compensation for the winter cold.

Included within this region is the promontory of Mount Carmel, despite its nearness to the sea. It belongs to the coast plain in that it has a small daily range throughout the year (only 10° or 12° F.) and a small yearly range also (Jan. 51.8°, Aug. 75.2°), but it belongs to the mountains in that the temperatures are regularly 5°–7° F. lower than those of Haifa, and the rainfall is greater (26.1 inches as compared with 24.5). Once again, these figures may not sound very impressive, but they mean the difference between the hot and enervating climate of the plain and the more stimulating weather of the hills. In ancient times this was not of very great importance, because Carmel was thinly inhabited woodland and Haifa was a marsh, but today it makes Haifa a very much more attractive place to live in than any of the other coastal towns.

The effect of the climate upon the thinking of the Jewish people will be considered in the next chapter, but here it should be noticed that this was the climatic region in which most of them lived, and Chester McCown says of it, "So far as health is concerned, the mountain-dwelling Hebrews were much more fortunately placed than either the Egyptians or the Babylonians; they were but little behind the Greeks and Romans." [1] This is true, but we must not make the mistake of imagining that they necessarily thought so. The tempo of life was slower in those days and in the ancient Mediterranean cultures the dry summer was a period requiring little effort from the farmer beyond camping out in his vineyard to protect the vines from damage by the wild beasts. Therefore, he did not find the heat particularly exhausting, though he was always glad that it should be subdued "by the shade of a cloud" (Is. 25:5). It was only the slave who was compelled to work who longed for the shadow (Job 7:2). The winter, however, was often much more frightening, because they had so little protection against it, and the winter on the hills can be severe. It is often cold enough to make a fire a real necessity (Jer. 36:22) even as late as early April (John 18:18), and those who had no opportunity to warm themselves were forced to "lie all night naked, without clothing, and have no covering in the cold" (Job 24:7). Even the wealthy were not really comfortable in the winter months, because their form of heating was often merely a charcoal brazier (Jer. 36:22) which is a very ineffective method. Therefore ancient peoples often preferred to live in the hotter places and Josephus says of Jericho that no place can be compared with it for the excellence of its climate,[2] an opinion with which it would be difficult to find anyone to agree today.

(iii) *The Rift Valley or Ghor.* The most important feature of the Ghor is that it lies in rain shadow, quite remarkably shut off from the influence of the sea, except when the westerly sea breeze suddenly bursts into the valley during the early afternoon in summer. The effect of this rain shadow can be seen everywhere, as for instance at Beisan which has 12.1 inches, while Haifa to the west of it on the coast has 24.6. It is very marked in the Dead Sea area, where the Judaean plateau towers 4600 feet above the Ghor on the western side, interposing a tremendous barrier between the valley and the sea, and emphasizing in this region the normal decrease of rainfall from north to south (e.g., Tiberias 16 inches; Beisan 12; Jericho 4 and the Dead Sea only 2 inches).

South of the junction of the Jabbok with the Jordan the climate of the Ghor shows many features characteristic of a desert climate, such as the great daily range in summer experienced at the Dead Sea, though throughout the year temperatures are considerably higher than in the Transjordan desert, which lies on the plateau. The daily range in January is less, though surprisingly cold nights may occasionally be experienced, and those travelers who used to go during the days of the British Mandate from the north to the south end of the Dead Sea by potash barges were well advised, if they were going in December or January, to take their thickest clothes and plenty of them. With the

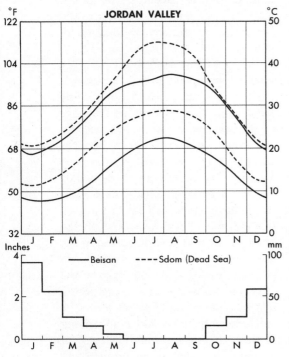

Fig. 18. Sdom is at the south end of the Dead Sea. The total rainfall is less than two inches. Notice the very large summer temperature range.

sunrise, however, the temperature climbs rapidly and even the winter days are very warm, while those of the summer are blistering.

Farther north the climate is not so grim and, indeed, it is not unattractive. Compare, for example, the temperature figures for Beisan and for Haifa. It will be seen that throughout the year the minima at Beisan are lower than those of Haifa and, in fact, the

curve agrees unexpectedly closely with that of Mount Carmel. This means that there are refreshing nights, even in summer. The daytime temperatures are naturally higher, but from December to February only slightly so, and it is not till March that the thermometer starts to climb in the Beisan region, but then the average maximum temperatures remain above 86° F. for as long as six months (May to October), whereas in Haifa they attain this figure for only three months in the year. It is this prolonged heat, with figures of over 95° F. in July and August, which has given Beisan and the Sea of Galilee their bad climatic reputation, though it is a dry heat and therefore more bearable than that of the coast. It is true that on the days when the relative humidity at Tiberias is high the effect has to be felt to be believed, for the perspiration pours down in streams even if one is merely sitting still, and there is no respite until evaporation once again becomes possible. However, such days are not common and, though the climate of Tiberias and Beisan is not entirely pleasant in summer, one may be forgiven for wondering if it deserves the complaints which the inhabitants of the northern Ghor are given to making about it. In any case, one must beware again of transferring to the people of the Biblical period the reactions that are displayed by modern man. It is worth remembering that this was a thickly populated region, especially in the New Testament time, and the one where Jesus did most of his work.

(iv) *The Plateau of Trans-jordan.* The climate of this region is very

similar to that of the hills of Cis-jordan, both in the amount and distribution of the rainfall received, and in the
temperature figures. However, the records are not nearly as complete as
those for Cis-jordan. There is, for instance, no station which has rainfall
records for a period in the very least
comparable with the one hundred
years for which they are available in
Jerusalem. Rainfall figures have been
kept at Amman for just over twenty-
five years, but for most of the stations
in Trans-jordan they are available for
no more than fifteen, and the temperature and humidity figures are even
more scanty. In view of this, a close
comparison with the weather observations for the Cis-jordan hills is obviously impossible, but certain gen-
eralizations are worth making.

The edge of the Trans-jordan plateau is almost everywhere higher than
the corresponding hill region to the
west, and therefore, the rain is often
greater (e.g., Es-Salt, which is 3000
feet above sea level, has 30.8 inches of
rain in the year, while Jerusalem, which
is just over 2600 feet, has 24.1 inches).
The winters are colder than in Cis-
jordan because of the greater height,
the greater distance from the sea and
the exposure to the icy desert winds,
and it is not uncommon for the main
road from Jerusalem to Amman to be
blocked by snow for a brief period at
least once in the year at its highest
point, which is near Sweileh, just over
3300 feet above sea level. The summer
days, however, are hotter than those
at Jerusalem and the sea breeze arrives
too late to be of much use in reducing
the temperature, which by that time
has passed its maximum. Nevertheless,

it is very refreshing and stirs the villages to activity after their midday rest.
It is very entertaining at Es-Salt to
watch the effect of this revivifying air
from the sea, which arrives with almost clockwork regularity at about
four in the afternoon, for the town is
built on two sides of a steep cleft in
the hills and from any place on one
side it is possible to see the streets
and houses of the other side rising
tier above tier as they climb the
precipitous slope. In the early part of
the afternoon the air is still and the
heat is overpowering, so that even the
noise of the market, which here is
magnified by the configuration of the
valley, is dulled to a subdued murmur,
but then, with surprising suddenness
the fresh air from the distant sea overflows the plateau rim and pours down
into the narrow valley. All the doors
in the house seem to bang at once;
clouds of dust swirl along the hillsides and in the street; children come
out to resume their endless games of
tag upon the flat housetops, and the
whole town is alive again. If you were
to climb the steep hillside then to the
flat ground above the town, you
would find the farmers hard at work
threshing and winnowing their
grain.

The nights in summer on the plateau are distinctly cool and in the early
morning, until at the latest about an
hour after sunrise, the weather is quite
fresh. It is this period of the summer
day, starting as soon as it is possible
to distinguish the rough outline of
the path beneath your feet, that is the
time for movement from one village
to another and in the gray, cool dawn
the mountain paths, which seem so

deserted at every other hour, are much used by the men and women coming down from the vineyards with their baskets of grapes for sale in the market.

This region extends a long tongue into the south because the greater

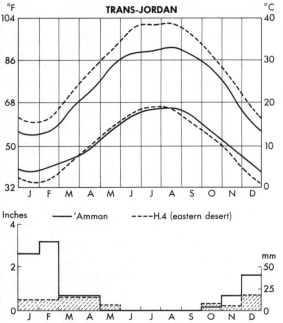

Fig. 19. H.4 is a station on I.P.C. pipeline from Iraq. The irregular winter rain and the great temperature range, especially in summer, should be noticed.

height of the plateau edge in Edom, which reaches as much as 5600 feet near Petra, counteracts to some extent the effect of the decreasing rainfall. That the rainfall does decrease from north to south is shown by the following figures—Es-Salt 30.4 inches; Mazar in Moab 16; Tafileh in Edom 11, but the region of effective rainfall is prolonged. In the south, however, the region is excessively narrow and the rain is sufficient to permit no more

than a single line of villages along the very lip of the Arabah, for it dies away with great rapidity as soon as the edge of the plateau is passed.

(v) *The Steppe.* This is a fairly narrow, and rather indeterminate, zone which may be defined as the region having between 8 and 16 inches of rainfall a year, and lying either north of the southern desert of Cisjordan or west of the deserts on the Trans-jordan plateau. It is interrupted in the Ghor because the transition to desert after the crest of the Judean hills has been passed is so abrupt that the desert there lies cheek by jowl with the cultivated land. The plateau edge in Edom, which was mentioned under the head of the previous region, ought possibly to be included here because its rainfall seldom exceeds 16 inches over very extensive areas, but it seems better to consider it as belonging to the plateau type.

The graphs for Gaza, Beersheba and Amman may be taken as typical of this type of climate. Gaza is on the coast and has the very even daily range of temperature characteristic of the Coast Plain, but already at Beersheba the winter nights become colder and the summer days much hotter. It is remarkable how the minima curve for Beersheba follows that of Gaza very closely, being 3°–4° F. lower, but the maxima curve shows a large bulge away during the summer months. This must be contrasted with the regions farther north where the greater range of temperature in the mountains as compared with the plain was the result of a greater difference in the *minimum* temperatures. Amman, which is on the Trans-jordan plateau

2600 feet above sea level, has temperatures for both the day and night in the rainy season several degrees lower than those of Gaza, but the summer days are actually hotter despite the difference in height, showing the powerful effect of the increased distance from the sea.

The rainfall regime is very similar to that of the other regions we have considered so far, though the totals are naturally less than those of any region except the drier parts of the Ghor. However, the graph for Amman shows that the eastern steppe receives its rain later and over a shorter period than the regions lying west of it.

The steppe has to be considered, therefore, as a region which is essentially marginal, for the rainfall, though on the average sufficient for agriculture, is liable to fail in dry years. It is characterized by unexpectedly hot summers with a prolonged drought which lasts later than that of the better watered regions, and during this season it displays features which are more typical of the desert than of the inhabited zone. It follows that in the steppe pastoral farming must often predominate over agriculture.

(vi) *The Desert*. East and south of the steppe, which is nowhere a very wide region, we reach the desert. How quickly this change is made is shown by the figures for Amman and for Zerqa, which lies a mere 10 miles to the northeast of it. Amman lies in the steppe zone with 13.1 inches of rain a year, but Zerqa in the desert with less than half that amount (4.9 inches). The chief characteristics of the desert climate are the great range

of temperature, shown particularly by the colder nights in winter and the very much hotter days in summer, and the smallness and variability of the rainfall. It is most important to emphasize that the desert is not a place where rain never falls, nor indeed a

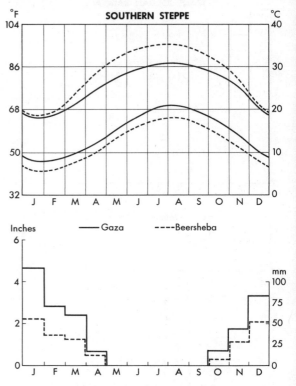

Fig. 20. Notice the very even temperature range of Gaza on the coast. Beersheba inland has minima only a few degrees lower than those of Gaza, but its maxima in summer are much higher.

place where the rainfall is never sufficient for agriculture, but *a place where the rainfall cannot be trusted*. This is especially true of the southern desert of Cis-jordan, where the figures for the number of years in which the rainfall varies from the norm are: Beersheba (in the steppe) 26 per cent;

Bir Asluj, in the desert, 43 per cent; Auja el-Hafir, on the Egyptian frontier, 65 per cent; Eth-Themed in Sinai 93 per cent. The corresponding figures for Ma'an in the eastern desert are 33 per cent, while for Jerusalem and for

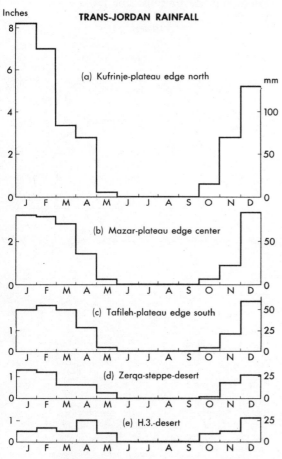

TRANS-JORDAN RAINFALL

(a) Kufrinje-plateau edge north

(b) Mazar-plateau edge center

(c) Tafileh-plateau edge south

(d) Zerqa-steppe-desert

(e) H.3.-desert

Fig. 21. Notice the decline in rainfall from north to south and the irregular rainfall of the desert.

Haifa they are 21 per cent and 17 per cent respectively.

This variability shows itself also in the fact that though the same general régime is true of the desert rainfall as of the rainfall in other parts of

Palestine, in that it is confined to the winter half of the year, yet the graphs for H.3 and H.4, which lie on the oil pipe line to Iraq, reveal that it does not show the same concentration into the middle months. In fact, there seems to be a tendency in the desert regions for the rain to fall in short, heavy storms at the beginning and end of the season. These desert storms appear to have some connection with the air masses over Abyssinia, and there is a tendency for a low pressure centered over the Abyssinian mountain region to extend an arm northward along the Red Sea and the east coast of the Mediterranean. "It is easy to recognize such a low by clouds approaching from the south-east or south, and, during the night, by electrical discharges seen in the same directions. Cases have been noted during all months between September and June. At the beginning and end of the rainy season a direct relation between these lows and the heavy Hamsins occurring at this time has been observed."[3]

The desert rain seems to be limited in extent as well as in amount. In 1938–39 Ma'an had half its total rainfall for the season in a severe hailstorm one afternoon early in April, and in March, 1940, Wadi Ram, about 40 miles away from Ma'an, had 1.6 inches in one day, though during the whole of that month Ma'an had no more than 0.24 inch. This is almost certainly the explanation of the story in II Kings 3:4–27 and I have myself, in fact, seen a very similar climatic phenomenon in the same region. In this story we are told that the two kings of Israel and Judah, being clearly unable to make a frontal attack on the tremendous western wall of Moab, enlisted the help of the King of Edom and advanced up the Zered Valley, in order to attack the Moabites from the rear. It was there that they found themselves short of water, for, although in the Ghor this stream is the second largest in Trans-jordan, most of the water is supplied by springs in the lower portion of the valley and the upper section has very much less. Elisha promised them that "you shall not see wind or rain, but that stream-bed shall be filled with water, so that you shall drink, you, your cattle, and your beasts. . . . The next morning, about the time of offering the sacrifice, behold, the water came from the direction of Edom, till the country was filled with water" (II Kings 3:17, 20). The cause of this unexpected supply was a desert thunderstorm on the plateau some distance to the east which filled the wadis and during the night poured down the Valley of the Zered toward the Arabah.

Another characteristic of the desert climate is that strong winds may develop as the result of the very rapid changes of temperature. These winds occasionally stir up dust storms which may, though fortunately rarely, be carried into the steppe zone. A bad storm will approach the observer like a wall of gigantic height; there will be a howling wind and the air will be full of whirling sand which will penetrate into the most tightly closed rooms. It is horrible while it lasts, but it will end as if cut off by a knife and the air will be suddenly clear again. Similar, though smaller, storms are sometimes met with in the Jordan Valley.

Less ferocious results of the desert winds are the spinning "dust-devils" ("the whirling dust before the storm" of Is. 17:13 and Ps. 83:13) which are to be seen chasing each other across the plateau any day during the summer. These twirling pillars of dust do no damage, but the sandstorms and the winter tempests are a real danger to the Bedouin whose tents are often ripped from their moorings by the force of the wind. It was during such a sudden storm in winter that the writer of the third chapter of Habakkuk "saw the tents of Cushan in affliction" (Hab. 3:7) and on another such day that Job suffered disaster (Job 1:16, 19).

References to whirlwinds are common in the Old Testament, though it is not always easy to see what kind of wind is meant. Elihu in the Book of Job seems to have been referring to the strong southwest wind of a winter cyclone sweeping unrestrained across the open desert plateau, because he couples it with cold, "From its chamber comes the whirlwind, and cold from the scattering winds" (Job 37:9), and the same appears to be meant by the two passages in Proverbs (1:27; 10:25) and by those in Jeremiah (23:19; 25:32; 30:23). However, Isaiah 21:1, "As whirlwinds in the Negeb sweep on, it comes from the desert, from a terrible land," seems to suggest something of the grim fury of a sandstorm. Isaiah 40:24 clearly refers rather to the parching effects of the sirocco and Isaiah 41:16 to the strong afternoon breeze by which the farmers winnow their grain. The whirlwind by which Elijah was taken up into heaven (II Kings 2:1, 11) carries the suggestion of a huge dust devil suddenly climbing up out of the dry ground and whirling across the plateau before the onslaught of a thunderstorm. The whirlwind which Ezekiel saw (1:4) and the whirlwind out of which God spoke to Job (38:1; 40:6) are surely the thunderstorm itself.*

Apart from these storms and the fury of the siroccos during the transitional seasons, the desert climate is not unattractive, for the air is dry and the very rapid changes of temperature are stimulating. Its chief defect is its monotony because it has so little rain.

* "Whirlwind" in the KJV, though not always in the RSV. The Hebrew word is either סוּפָה or some form of the root סָעַר.

CHAPTER VI

Three Special Problems

Three things are too wonderful for me;
four I do not understand.
PROVERBS 30:18

THERE remain to be discussed three special problems relating to the climate of the Palestinian area—the Sirocco, the question of whether the climate has changed at all within historical times, and the effect of the Palestinian weather in general upon man's life, with particular reference to the Bible.

THE SIROCCO

During the transitional seasons, that is any time from the beginning of April until June 15 and any time from September 15 to somewhere about the end of October, there occur periods of about three days to a week during which there develop east, southeast or even south, winds, which bring with them desert conditions to the whole of Palestine. These winds are known as "siroccos" from the Arabic word *shar-qiyyeh* meaning an east wind. Some people also speak of a "khamsin," but this name is more correctly kept for the similar wind in Egypt which does

not necessarily come from the east.

Neither the cause nor the results of the sirocco are fully understood as yet, and the most that can be said with certainty is that they are exceedingly hot, dry winds which have gained their excessive heat and dryness from the fact that they are *katabatic*, or descending, masses of air similar to the *Chinook* winds which pour down over the Rocky Mountains and melt the snows in the Prairie regions, or the *Fohn* of Switzerland. However, what causes the siroccos to descend, since there are no mountains over which they would be forced to climb, is at present quite unknown, since there is insufficient information concerning the day-to-day weather conditions in the desert. These winds of the transitional seasons are not to be confused with the east winds which develop on the dry days during the rainy season, for these are caused by masses of air moving horizontally out of the desert and are usually cold.

During the period of a sirocco the

temperature rises steeply, sometimes even climbing during the night, and it remains high, about 16–22° F. above the average, with only a slight cooling off at night, for as long as the sirocco lasts. The relative humidity drops by about 30–40 per cent and at times every scrap of moisture seems to have been extracted from the air, so that one has the curious feeling that one's skin has been drawn much tighter than usual. Sirocco days are peculiarly trying to the temper and tend to make even the mildest people irritable and fretful and to snap at one another for apparently no reason at all. Some people experience an actual rise of body temperature and may be forced to retire to bed, the chief sufferers being those with heart trouble or with nervous complaints. The fine dust in the air and the excessive dryness which parches the mucous membrane of the nose and throat often set up an irritation which is very painful for people afflicted with catarrh or sinus trouble. It is this intense dryness of the atmosphere which is so troublesome, for the other hot days, though they may be exhausting, are not so trying to the nerves. A curious feature of the sirocco is that the foreigner does not become acclimatized to it as he does to other features of the climate, and he may even find it increasingly difficult to bear. In fact, newcomers frequently seem to be quite untroubled by them during their first year, but to be fully conscious of them by the second and, indeed, if the writer's personal experience is anything to go by, may even tend to become more sensitive to dry winds in northern countries when they return to them.

It is interesting also to notice other effects: a fine, yellowish dust haze fills the air so that visibility is very greatly reduced and the sun casts only the palest of shadows; tourists therefore find them very frustrating, not only because they make traveling fatiguing, but because they drain all the color and contrast out of the landscape and make photography a mockery. Even inside the house their effect is constantly brought to one's notice, as when one discovers that one's toothbrush has become as stiff as wire, or when the soap dries on one's face even in the interval of putting down the brush and picking up the razor. If one is writing, the paper curls under the hand and it is never necessary to blot the ink before turning over the page; wood cracks, sometimes almost explosively, and pianos get out of tune; heavy curtains shrink surprisingly when they are no longer weighted down with their own moisture and return to their full length only with the change of wind to the west.

The siroccos are worse on the eastern side of the Jordan and their ferocity increases as one goes toward the desert, so that coming out of a house at Zerqa or Mafraq is like stepping straight into an oven. It is also extremely unpleasant in the Rift Valley, where the air is warmed still further by its descent over the plateau edge, but on the coast, at the very edge of the sea, there may occasionally develop a slight breeze off the sea which helps to modify the heat. In places where the mountains come close to the coast, as at Haifa and farther north, a strong sirocco will pour down the steep slopes like a river in spate and may at times reach sixty miles an hour and over. The harbors, of course, provide little protection from a descending storm of this nature and farther out to sea it can become exceedingly rough, sufficiently so to be very dangerous to the small ships of ancient times. Thus, we read in Ps. 48:7, "By the east wind thou didst shatter the ships of Tarshish," and in Ezekiel's long condemnation of Tyre, "The east wind has wrecked you in the heart of the seas" (Ezek. 27:26).

The siroccos of the spring transitional season are frequently rather stronger than those of autumn, but at both seasons they produce abnormally high temperatures, which are actually the maximum temperatures of the year. Sometimes, the autumn siroccos seem to affect only the higher parts of the country and do not descend to the Rift Valley or the Coast Plain, with the result that Jerusalem has more siroccos during the year than Jaffa.

The end of a sirocco is marked by a sudden change of the wind to the west, a rise in humidity, a drop in temperature and a wonderful feeling of relief. Owing to the radiation of heat from the parched ground, the effect of the increased humidity is often felt a little before the change in temperature, and so the first impression may be that the weather has become even more oppressive, but as the cooler air moves in ever more steadily from the sea, this impression disappears. The change of wind is very obvious, for the new west wind is usually strong and one of the first signs of the end of the sirocco is the sudden whirling about of paper and dead leaves in the street, and the tossing and swaying of the trees, what appears to be meant by the "sound of the abundance of rain" * in I Kings 18:41. Especially during the autumn, the new west wind brings heavy rain with it, for it seems to be true that siroccos are in part caused by the pulling of desert air into the low pressure of an approaching cyclone, and it is a saying among Palestinian farmers that "the east wind brings rain."

A sirocco often comes to an end after about three or four days, though Thomas Chapin records that in 1868 there was sirocco almost continuously from September 28 to October 30.[1] Usually the change takes place in the afternoon when the west wind and the sea breeze are working together, but on the coast there may be false alarms when a purely local sea breeze develops during a sirocco, and on such occasions the casual observer thinks that the sirocco is finished, but then at night the east wind re-establishes itself and the next day is equally hot.

References to the sirocco are frequent in the Bible. Elihu in the Book of Job speaks of it as being inexplicable, "Do you know . . . the wondrous works of him who is perfect in knowledge, you whose garments are hot when the earth is still because of the south wind?" (Job 37:16–17), and in Hosea it is a symbol of uselessness, "Ephraim herds the wind, and pursues the east wind all day long; they multiply falsehood and violence; they make a bargain with Assyria, and oil is carried to Egypt" (Hos. 12:1). Similarly

*קול המון הגשם which is translated "rushing of rain" in RSV, but this suggests the rain had already begun, which is incorrect. It is surely this very characteristic preliminary noise which is meant here.

also in Jeremiah, where it is contrasted with the usefulness to the farmer of the steady west wind of a summer evening, "a hot wind from the bare heights in the desert toward the daughter of my people, not to winnow or cleanse" (Jer. 4:11). Other writers refer to it as a scourge, "his fierce blast in the day of the east wind" (Is. 27:8). Thus in Jonah 4:8, "When the sun rose, God appointed a sultry east wind, and the sun beat upon the head of Jonah so that he was faint; and he asked that he might die," and in Luke 12:55, "When you see the south wind blowing, you say, 'There will be scorching heat'; and it happens." In spring the most striking fact about the sirocco is that it destroys the grass which has grown up during the winter, and it may do much damage to the crops if it comes too soon. Therefore, this picture of fruitful things suddenly laid waste by the sirocco is constantly quoted as a symbol of the impermanence of riches or of human life, "for the wind passes over it, and it is gone, and its place knows it no more" (Ps. 103:16). There is the famous passage in Isaiah 40:6–8, "All flesh is grass, and all its beauty is like the flower of the field. The grass withers, the flower fades, when the breath of the Lord blows upon it . . . but the word of our God will stand for ever." Ezekiel speaks of the rich vine of Judah dying in the ground when the hot breath of God begins to blow, "Will it not utterly wither when the east wind strikes it—wither away on the bed where it grew?" (Ezek. 17:10), and Hosea said of the Northern Kingdom, "Though he may flourish as the reed plant, the east wind, the wind of the Lord, shall come, rising from the wilderness; and his fountain shall dry up, his spring shall be parched; it shall strip his treasury of every precious thing" (Hos. 13:15). The picture appears again in the New Testament, where, for instance, St. James says of rich men, "The sun rises with its scorching heat and withers the grass; its flower falls, and its beauty perishes. So will the rich man fade away in the midst of his pursuits" (James 1:11).

CLIMATIC CHANGE

This is a question which has engendered no little heat and therefore it is necessary to define exactly what it is that will be discussed here. We are not considering the possibility of *progressive desiccation*, since that theory is now generally regarded as disproved, but of *climatic variation* within historical times. It is worth making this clear, since the opponents of climatic change have often spent their time attacking the first theory rather than the second. Nor is it suggested for one moment that at any time during the Biblical period the Palestinian climate was *greatly* different from what it is at the present day. It is therefore of very little value to argue that since the crops grown in Biblical times were the same as they are now, this proves that there has been no change at all in the climate. What is being considered is not whether there was at any time during the Biblical period a different climatic *régime* from that obtaining at present, but whether the *balance* of that regime has varied from time to time. This question is of very great importance, because the Palestinian area is crossed by the vitally important frontier between the desert and the sown, and any variation of the climate at all must in some way affect the position of this frontier. It must be remembered that it is not a sharp line, but a broad marginal zone with, in most areas, a very gentle rainfall gradient. Only a slight difference in the amount of rainfall or, which would come to the same thing, a slight difference in the amount of evaporation or in the distribution of the rainfall during the rainy season, must inevitably cause a wide advance or regression of this frontier, just as the tide sweeps far inland wherever the gradient of a beach is gentle.

It is important to recall that a desert is not necessarily a place where rain never falls, but rather a place where the rain cannot be relied upon as being sufficient for agriculture. Thus, even a slight increase in the total amount of rainfall, or a slight change in some other climatic factor bringing about an increase in the *effectiveness* of the rainfall, would give just that slightly greater reliability, which would make it worth while bringing under cultivation certain marginal areas previously considered to be just outside the cultivable region. It is not, perhaps, generally realized just how slight this change would have to be. An increase of rainfall sufficient to produce over the period of a century a rise in the rainfall averages of one inch a year would cause no change at all in the agriculture of the well-watered parts of the country, but in those areas which hover on the margin it might well help to make the difference between cultivation and nomadic pastoralism.

It must be realized from the very start that the possibility of climatic change cannot be ruled out *ex hypothesi*, as appears to be imagined by certain archaeologists. Thus, when Nelson Glueck says that during the last ten thousand years "there seems to have been no major, permanent, climatic changes in Palestine or the Near East, or probably anywhere on earth," [2] or when Dr. Albright says of Ellsworth Huntington, "Nor can a single really competent geographer be found who accepts his conclusions," [3] or when the *Westminster Historical Atlas to the Bible* states dogmatically that exploration has proved that the climate of southern Palestine has not changed,[4] they are going a great deal further than most competent geographers and climatologists would be prepared to go, since the evidence is curiously conflicting.

Part of the difficulty lies in the fact that much of the evidence for climatic change is very difficult to assess. It has been believed by many that the migrations of tribes or peoples are in some way connected with periods of drought, but it cannot be said to be agreed that there is in fact such a connection or, if there is, what it is. It is difficult, however, to believe that there is not, for certain migrations at any rate, some relation somewhere. Thus, Nelson Glueck has suggested that Trans-jordan has not enjoyed continuous settlement in its southern districts of a kind comparable to that of Cis-jordan, and he dates the periods on settled occupation in Moab and

Edom as having been between 2300–2000 B.C., 1300–600 B.C. and during the Classical Period after about 300 B.C.[5] Though it is true that much research still remains to be done on the eastern side of the Jordan before these dates can be said to be absolutely proved, the evidence so far available appears to be on his side, and there is no reason for us not to accept his thesis. Now, Moab and Edom are essentially marginal regions. Slight differences in the amount of rainfall here make considerable differences in the possibilities of effective agriculture, and so it is not unreasonable to wonder whether these alternations between cultivation and pastoralism may not have some connection with possible variations in the climate. It is far from necessary that this should be the whole explanation, but no one has yet put on paper conclusive evidence that there is no connection at all.

That climate does change is no longer a matter of doubt, though the causes of these changes have been widely disputed. It is not for us here to discuss whether the changes are the result of geographical factors, as C. E. P. Brooks would suggest,[6] or astronomical,[7] or indeed anything else at all, but rather what the nature of these changes have been. It has long been accepted, for instance, that not only has there been more than one ice age in the history of the world, but that during the last and best known there were four major advances of the ice with three main interglacial periods, and that there were several minor advances and regressions within these seven periods. Moreover, at the other end of the historical scale

it is no longer in dispute that the Northern Hemisphere has been warmer during the last hundred years than it was during the previous 250.[8] In between these limits certain other changes have taken place, which are supported by evidence both from North America and from Europe, evidence which admits of little doubt, being drawn from such widely differing fields as variations in the level of inland lakes, development of tree rings, the nature of the deposits in laminated clays, the arrangement of pollen sequences in sedimentary deposits, the advance and regression of glaciers, et cetera. As a result of the correlation of these different researches there seems fairly general agreement among climatologists that from about 5000 B.C. to 3000 B.C. the climate of both North America and Europe was warm and humid (the period of the "Climatic Optimum") and that from 3000 to 500 B.C. it was on the whole drier, becoming somewhat cooler. About 500 B.C. there was a sudden change to a colder and wetter climate, of which C. E. P. Brooks says, "This change of climate was by far the greatest and most abrupt since the end of the Ice Age and its effect on the civilization of Europe was catastrophic."[9] From about A.D. 400 to 1000 seems to have been a drier and warmer period.[10] These have not been the only changes and Hurd C. Willett goes so far as to say, "There is constantly in progress an entire spectrum of cyclical fluctuations of climate, cycles of shorter period and smaller amplitude being superposed on those of longer period and larger amplitude,"[11] and Brooks, for instance, suggests that within the "sub-boreal" period from *c.* 3000 to *c.* 500 B.C. there were at least three long droughts, as well as several shorter ones, the main droughts being *c.* 2200 to 1900, 1200 to 1000 and 700 to 500 B.C.[12] Edmund Schulman has likewise argued from the evidence provided by tree rings in North America that almost the whole of the thirteenth century A.D. was exceedingly dry, but that the fourteenth century on the whole was very stormy.

So far it has not been possible to produce such definite evidence of a similar nature for the Palestinian area, and since we are still so much in doubt about the causes of the climatic changes which have taken place in Europe, we are quite unable to say how they would have affected the climate of the Mediterranean region. However, they cannot have left the Palestinian area unaffected. One thing at least is axiomatic: any change in European climate which is marked by, or connected with, a change in the extent of the polar ice must involve either a strengthening or weakening of the westerly winds and a shifting of the zonal weather belts either toward or away from the Equator. Thus an increase in the extent of the polar ice must tend to shift the westerly winds away from the Pole toward the Mediterranean and a decrease in the ice will cause the westerly wind belt to return farther toward the north. This is true of both large-scale and small-scale changes. That such changes in the extent of the polar ice have taken place within historical times is undeniable. It would appear, for example, that from about 1000 B.C.

to the beginning of the Christian Era there was an advance of the ice,[13] which was then followed by a retreat, with another advance about A.D. 1200 [14] and an important advance between A.D. 1600 and 1900.[15] This strengthening of the polar ice would mean that a greater number of cyclones would probably be deflected south of the Alpine mountain barrier than during the periods when the ice was in retreat, and this would surely lead to a tendency for there to be somewhat greater rainfall in the Palestinian area.

That this did happen is supported, somewhat surprisingly, by a certain amount of documentary evidence for the first century A.D. in the form of a weather diary kept by Claudius Ptolemaeus, apparently at Alexandria.[16] This would suggest that the period of absolute drought was rather shorter then than it is now, and that there were more north winds in winter and more thunder and weather changes in summer than there are at the present time. Admittedly, the character of the records in this diary is not easy to determine and their value has been disputed, some people arguing that the differences are such that the diary cannot in fact have been kept at a place so far south as Alexandria.[17] However, C. E. P. Brooks suggests that the present evidence supports the possibility that the Mediterranean Belt lay slightly farther south than it does at present, and this is supported by Murray.[18] It is certainly tempting also to see a connection between the sub-boreal droughts referred to by Brooks and the periods of settlement in Moab and Edom put forward by Nelson Glueck. If the periods of drought in Europe were accompanied by a shift southward of the cyclone routes (though of course this is not yet certain), then it would seem that a somewhat increased rainfall may have been a contributory cause to the two first periods of settlement. Obviously the third period of European drought appears to be in conflict with this since it occurred at a time of pastoral nomadism in the Moab-Edom area. However, this is not necessarily so, since it is not being argued that such variations in rainfall were the sole cause, or indeed necessarily the major cause, of the alternation of agriculture and pastoralism, but a possible contributory cause. The unsettled conditions resulting from the Assyrian advance and the conflicts which developed out of it would have been sufficient to counteract any influence that possible climatic change may have had.

What is being argued here is that climate is not static, that changes in climate do take place and that significant changes have occurred between 5000 B.C. and the present day. Moreover, the climate of one area is not an isolated unit, but is related to the climate of the areas adjacent to it, and so, if important changes take place in the climate of one major area, they cannot be without some measure of effect on the climate of the near-by areas. Thirdly, while changes in climate do not automatically result in certain definite social changes, they may prove to be one of the causes contributing to social change and, indeed, even a minor variation in the weather conditions can trigger a quite important social change, if the other historic factors are favorable to change. Thus, according to Paul B. Sears, "The influence of even brief climatic fluctuations, where climate is a limiting factor, is no longer in dispute. Migration in our own Great Plains has shown that a drouth of only a few years' duration can profoundly affect segments of our own culture, despite our technological resources." [19]

The period about which there has been the greatest dispute is that from the Roman Empire to the Arab invasion, for it is certainly a fact that some areas in the southern deserts of both Cis-jordan and Trans-jordan were during the Classical Period cultivated for the only time in their history, and there has been much discussion about whether what was cultivated then could equally well be cultivated now. Unfortunately, no little of what has been said on the subject has been politically biased, since some of those whose background inclines them to view Israel with favor have often for that reason argued in favor of the modern development of the Negeb, while those who have disapproved of Jewish immigration into the area have argued in the opposite sense. Of course, not all that has been said has had this character, but there has been enough to make it necessary to view the arguments with caution.

Those who oppose the idea of climatic change have made great play of the fact that all the towns whose remains are to be seen in the Negeb were not occupied at the same time, and that the greatest care was taken to preserve water, but this cannot be taken as an argument either way. The

14. *The Negeb near S'baita.* This picture was taken just before sunset, and shows in the foreground the shadows cast by the little heaps of stones mentioned on p. 75. It is believed that these were used for the training of vines.

Negeb must always have been a marginal region, and droughts must always have been more frequent there than in other parts of Cis-jordan, but the real question is on which side of the margin it lay. It has been argued also that the excavations made at S'baita in the Negeb by the Colt Expedition show that there was no more rain there in classical times than there is now.[20] However, this is by no means certain, for the town was apparently entirely dependent on rainfall and it has been estimated that if *all* the present rainfall were collected, it would provide enough for one-third of a gallon per person per day, assuming a population of eight thousand people. This seems insufficient when one remember that there were three baths, for which much water would have been needed.[21] Furthermore, if the supposition is true that the curious heaps of stones to be seen in the fields round S'baita were used for the training of vines, then a somewhat greater rainfall seems almost essential, since it is doubtful whether the vine could be grown there in present-day conditions.[22]

The character of any possible climatic change which has taken place in the Palestine area is likely to be a matter of dispute for some time to come, but there is another matter on which we can be more definite. Whether or not there was more rain-

15. *Barren hillsides in Trans-jordan.* Over large parts of the hill country erosion has proceeded so fast that the bare rock has been exposed over very wide areas. The camels in this picture are following the Roman road to the north from Amman.

fall at certain periods in the past, it was certainly more effective over large areas than it is at present. Then there were forests and woodlands whose roots would hold back the water and prevent the drying up of the springs, but in the course of centuries these forests have been cut down and springs have disappeared. Much of the rain which falls today tends to run off immediately. Moreover, the land has been neglected for thirteen centuries, and it has been well said that it is not necessarily actively to destroy the land in Palestine—it is quite enough to do nothing.[23] Over large areas the soil has been washed from the hills, and regions, which may once have been cultivated, are now bare. So far has this process gone, in fact, that Ionides believes that large-scale erosion in Trans-jordan has now come to an end.[24]

THE EFFECT OF THE CLIMATE UPON MAN

Biblical thought is shot through and through with the conception that the climate reflects the nature of God in his dealings with man. The Palestinian farmer, as we have already seen, lived in a land of very varied climate, where an arm of the desert reached to the very gates of the capital at Jerusalem, and where he might find himself either shivering in the snow or parched by the desert wind. The prolonged heat and drought of summer were certain, at least five months without a drop of rain, but the rainy season was essentially unpredictable and from year to year might give him either famine or plenty. This means that he could never experience a sense of stability in his daily life. It is true that there was the regular rhythm of seedtime and harvest, winter and summer, but within that rhythm there was great variety, both in the daily weather and from place to place.

In accordance with the thesis that the geography of Palestine was no less part of God's plan for his people than the history, it must be understood that this unusual variety was no matter of chance. It has often been pointed out that the desert of Arabia has been the cradle of the great monotheistic religions, but it is not the only place where monotheism has been suggested, nor is monotheism inevitably the religion of the desert. Paganism persisted in parts of Arabia for centuries after the death of Muhammed, and the other deserts of the world have no great monotheistic tradition. What is probably true is that the desert, with its massive simplicity, provides an environment where monotheism is eminently reasonable, and that it was therefore necessary to the purposes of God that the Israelites should begin their education in the desert in order that they might enter Palestine with the concept of one God already implanted in them, dimly as they appear to have comprehended it.

Those who were born and grew up in a Palestinian village far from the desert knew nothing of this simplicity, but felt themselves to be at the mercy of a battery of conflicting forces, and did not know which of them to worship. Their dilemma is well described by an ancient writer, who, nevertheless, blames them for not making the final synthesis:

Surely, vain are all men by nature, who are ignorant of God
And could not out of the good things that are seen know him that is:
Neither by considering the works did they acknowledge the workmaster.
But deemed either fire, or wind, or the swift air, or the circle of the stars,
Or the violent water, or the lights of heaven,
To be the gods which govern the world.
With whose beauty if they being delighted took them to be gods;
Let them know how much better the Lord of them is:
For the first author of beauty hath created them.
But if they were astonished at their power and virtue,
Let them understand by them, how much mightier he is that made them.
For by the greatness and beauty of the creatures proportionably the maker of them is seen.
But yet for this they are less to be blamed,
For they peradventure err, seeking God, and desirous to find him.
For being conversant in his works they search him diligently, and believe their sight:
Because the things are beautiful that are seen.
Howbeit, they are not to be pardoned.
[Wisdom of Solomon 13:1–8]

One wonders whether the author of this passage was not somewhat severe and whether the final synthesis could in fact have been made by those who had not had the advantages of the Israelite training. Less to be pardoned were those who, having once been brought face to face with the Living God, should have accepted uncritically from others the idea that the works themselves were gods. That the Israelites were guilty of this is, of course, obvious from even a cursory reading of the Old Testament.

However, it appears to have been equally part of the purposes of God that the Israelites should not remain in the simplicity of the desert environment, but should be exposed to the temptations of life in an agricultural region, at the mercy of an apparently capricious nature. In the desert there is not the same dependence upon outside forces since, when times are difficult, man is sufficiently mobile to go out and try to do something about it. However, as soon as man becomes settled, there is no longer the same freedom of movement and it becomes a matter of great importance whether it rains upon one city and not upon another city (Amos 4:7). The rainfall is something which is quite outside his control, and yet upon it depends to a very large extent the difference between poverty and wealth, between life and death, for Palestine is quite unlike Egypt. There "you sowed your seed, and watered it with your foot,* like a garden of vegetables" (Deut. 11:10), kicking a hole in the soft mud embankment to admit the waters of the Nile floods, which was the action of a moment. In Pales-

* The RSV has "feet," but the word in Hebrew is singular, and the picture is of a man walking in his garden and almost casually kicking a hole in the embankment with one foot.

tine, the farmer has to wait, to wait and to pray, for he can do nothing until the rain comes.

Modern man tends to the belief that the amount of rain which a country receives from year to year is purely a matter of chance. Like Eeyore in *Winnie-the-Pooh*, they say, "Being fine to-day doesn't Mean Anything. . . . It's just a small piece of weather." The Biblical writers did not think in this fashion, for they held that God was in full control of the climate and that the kind of weather he gave them was part of his purposes for them. Thus we are told in Deuteronomy 11:13–17:

If you will obey my commandments which I command you this day, to love the Lord your God, and to serve him with all your heart and all your soul, he will give the rain for your land in its season, the early and the later rain, that you gather in your grain and your wine and your oil. And he will give grass in your fields for your cattle, and you shall eat and be full. Take heed lest your heart be deceived, and you turn aside and serve other gods and worship them, and the anger of the Lord be kindled against you, and he shut up the heavens, so that there be no rain, and the land yield no fruit, and you perish quickly off the good land which the Lord gives you.

Such teaching is found frequently in the Bible, e.g., I Kings 8:35; Haggai 1:9–11; Zechariah 10:1; Malachi 3:10 and James 5:17–18.*

* It is interesting in this connection to consider whether modern science does in fact encourage us to be so skeptical about God's control of the weather. It is usually objected, of course, that we cannot expect the course of the climate to be changed to-day, either by our prayers, or because we are being punished for our misdeeds, since the causes of today's weather go far back into history. There is surely some surprisingly

The great variation of climate, of course, took place within reasonable limits, which made possible the development of agriculture. Thus, certain kinds of weather were felt to be unseasonable and even unnatural. "Like snow in summer or rain in harvest, so honor is not fitting for a fool" (Prov. 26:1). It will be remembered also that Samuel called on God to send thunder and rain during the wheat harvest as a sign of the unseasonableness of the people's request for a king, "and the Lord sent thunder and rain that day; and all the people greatly feared the Lord and Samuel" (I Sam. 12:16–18).

Another characteristic of the climate which seems much to have impressed the Israelites was the ferocity of the weather in some of its manifestations. It was not only that drought might rob them of their food, but the rain for which they so earnestly longed could also be destructive. There is a slightly comic picture in the Book of Ezra of the people sitting "in the open square before the house of God,

---

limited thinking here about the nature of God, who sees all space as one piece and must also see all time in the same way. Thus, though we, who can see only one bit of space or time at any given moment, are left entirely free to choose whether we shall or shall not pray, yet God sees that we have already made now this free choice when he is directing that part of time which we call "the past" and acts accordingly. A good analogy is that of the chess player who acts now in accordance with a future move, which, for the purposes of his decision, his opponent "has already made." Yet his opponent is at all times entirely free. God, who is in no wise limited in the sense that the chess player is, is able to make this kind of action perfectly. It is really a question whether we have not forgotten a very important part of God's revelation.

trembling because of this matter and because of the heavy rain" and protesting to Ezra that "we cannot stand in the open" (Ezra 10:9, 13), and the dramatic story of the contest on Mount Carmel concludes triumphantly with the words "And in a little while the heavens grew black with clouds and wind, and there was a great rain" (I Kings 18:45). Jesus quoted it as a well-known occurrence that a badly built house might collapse during the rainy season (Matt. 7:27) and, indeed, it is only when one has seen a storm sweeping in from the Mediterranean across the Palestinian hills or the torrents pouring down the precipitous slopes into the Lake of Galilee that one knows quite what a concentrated fury is contained in those words, "and the rain fell, and the floods came, and the winds blew and beat against that house."

Extremes of temperature were also to be feared. The burning midday sun could be fatal to those working in the fields, as it was to the small boy who cried out to his father, "Oh, my head, my head!" and was then carried in to his mother and "sat on her lap till noon, and then he died" (II Kings 4:19–20). The snow which falls on the hills in the rainy season brought nothing but misery to those whose houses were built for the heat and had small means of warming them. "Pray that your flight may not be in winter," said Jesus to those whom he was warning of the coming destruction of Jerusalem (Matt. 24:20), and the Psalmist says of God, "He gives snow like wool; he scatters hoarfrost like ashes. He casts forth his ice like morsels; who can stand before his cold?"

(Ps. 147:16–17). In Proverbs 31:21 we are told that it is one of the marks of a perfect housewife that "she is not afraid of snow for her household." Most fearful of all was the "storm of hail, a destroying tempest" (Is. 28:2), which might beat down the grain while it was yet awaiting the sickle, smash the tender flowers of the olives, and destroy the vines (Ps. 78:47; Hag. 2:17). "Therefore thus says the Lord God: I will make a stormy wind break out in my wrath; and there shall be a deluge of rain in my anger, and great hailstones in wrath to destroy it. And I will break down the wall that you have daubed with whitewash, and bring it down to the ground" (Ezek. 13:13–14).

Thus it was that the Israelite farmer knew himself to be at the mercy of natural forces quite beyond his control. He usually explained his position by imagining that there were storehouses somewhere beyond the sky and that in these were locked up the supplies of rain and hail and snow. This is what is meant by God's question to Job, "Have you entered the storehouses of the snow, or have you seen the storehouses of the hail, which I have reserved for the time of trouble, for the day of battle and war?" (Job 38:22–23; Ps. 135:7). When one remembers that the farmer lived at subsistence level and that he probably seldom produced much more in one year than would supply himself and his family, it is not surprising that he thought that his most desperate need was to win the favor of whoever controlled these storehouses. His greatest temptation was to try to placate every power that he had ever heard of, just

in case there might be some truth in the story that this or that local deity had got the key of the storehouse. The job of his religious leaders was constantly to persuade him that in fact all these supplies were in the hand of one God, who waters the mountains "from his lofty abode" and makes "springs gush forth in the valleys" (Ps. 104:13 and 10).

The basic problem which faced the prophets in this matter was that of breaking down the persistent human desire to keep everything in separate compartments and of forcing the people to widen their horizons so that they could see everything as a whole, and it is the measure of the difference in stature between the early prophets and our own nineteenth-century religious spokesmen that the latter were incapable of making this explosive effort of the mind when they were faced with the truths revealed to them by the scientists. When the Israelites came into the country of Palestine, it was taken for granted that "Yahweh," their own particular "god," was a storm god with his home in the mountains of Edom. This conception was, so to speak, "natural." They had come to know him in that most terrifying of all natural phenomena, a volcanic eruption, and they had continued to serve him in the desert where they would see "the tents of Cushan in affliction" (Hab. 3:7) and where the storms may attain a ferocity normally unknown elsewhere.

However, even if this were "natural," this does not mean that it was any less the work of God, as if for God there were anything that is "supernatural." It seems to have been part of his purpose from the beginning that his people should conceive of him as *powerful*. Accustomed as we are to thinking of love as being the most important attribute of God, it needs an effort for us to realize that the fundamental fact which men must learn of God is that he is able—able to make his purposes succeed, "excellent in effectual working" as Isaiah has it (Is. 28:29, English R.V. margin). Other facts must be learned after this. Therefore, though insisting from the beginning that people should make no image of him, God appears to have allowed them to associate him with the most powerful manifestations of nature and, since in their stage of development they would inevitably localize him, with a place that lay outside Israel. The importance of this last has not always been sufficiently realized. It surely meant that from the very start it was established that the God of the Israelites had power outside his own territory. He had rescued them from the land of Egypt and had established them, not in his "own" country of Edom, but in the distant land of Canaan which he had chosen for them. The building of the Temple caused people to think more and more of God as belonging to Jerusalem, a fallacy which earned them the scorn of Jeremiah, but in the earlier days they had spoken of him as coming to help them from Edom, usually in some tremendous thunderstorm. Two of the earliest passages which are preserved for us in the mosaic of the Old Testament are the song of Miriam and the song of Deborah and in them we are told, "The Lord is a man of war; the Lord is his name," and "Lord, when

thou didst go forth from Seir, when thou didst march from the region of Edom, the earth trembled, and the heavens dropped, yea, the clouds dropped water. The mountains quaked before the Lord" (Exod. 15:3; Judg. 5:4–5). In one of the earliest psalms, Psalm 18 which is quoted also in II Samuel 22, the same idea is developed at length, "He bowed the heavens, and came down; thick darkness was under his feet. He rode on a cherub, and flew; he came swiftly upon the wings of the wind. He made darkness his covering round about him, his canopy thick clouds dark with water. The Lord also thundered in the heavens, and the Most High uttered his voice, hailstones and coals of fire" (Ps. 18:9–13). In Psalm 50:3 we are told that "before him is a devouring fire, round about him a mighty tempest," and the magnificent psalm which was added to the book of Habakkuk presents the same picture, "God came from Teman, and the Holy One from Mount Paran . . . . the mountains saw thee and writhed; the raging waters swept on; the deep gave forth its voice, it lifted its hands on high" (Hab. 3:3, 10). This idea persisted long after the Exile as a poetic expression, and we read in II Esdras 3:19, "Thy glory went through four gates of fire and earthquake, wind and cold."

The lesson which the people had to learn when they entered Canaan was that God, whom they thought of as associated with storms and earthquakes, was not to be regarded as confined to these wilder activities of nature, but was the master of all his creation. They were very slow to learn this, but it is perhaps not fanciful to see in the fact that the vitally important rainy season so often begins with furious thunderstorms a definite and intended connecting link. He, whom they had previously thought of as riding upon the desert storms, was also he upon whom they depended for the growth of the grain from which they lived. That so many of them did not make this connection resulted from the fact that they, like us, had been given the freedom to keep their eyes shut, if they wanted to.

Finally, the Israelites were by no means blind to the beauty of their climate and to the wonder of it, whether it was the fact that God sent "rain on a land where no man is, on a desert in which there is no man; to satisfy the waste and desolate land, and to make the ground put forth grass" (Job 38:26–27), or the fierce glory of the sun, "which comes forth like a bridegroom leaving his chamber, and like a strong man runs his course with joy" (Ps. 19:5). Almost more than aɔ̣ other ancient people, they responded to natural beauty and marveled at "the sun shining forth upon a cloudless morning" (II Sam. 23:4) and the insubstantial "mists driven by a storm" (II Pet. 2:17).

CHAPTER VII

The Earth Full of Thy Creatures

O Lord, how manifold are thy works!
In wisdom hast thou made them all;
the earth is full of thy creatures.
PSALM 104:24

THIS is a subject on which it is possible to speak only tentatively and with caution, for the natural vegetation and the animals of the Palestinian region, as we know them today, must be very different from what they were in the past. This is a plain and undoubted fact, but one which visitors to the country find very difficult to believe, for they are so accustomed to seeing "Bible pictures," the artists of which have often come out to Palestine to achieve verisimilitude, that they are quite convinced that the events of the Bible must have taken place in the kind of landscape which they see about them today.* That is not true, but we are at once in a difficulty when we start to consider just how untrue it is, since it is quite im-

possible to be at all exact. We are uncertain of the meaning of a large number of Biblical words for plants and animals and can, at best, only make a guess at them. Moreover, it is impossible to know exactly what ancient writers meant by such general words as "forest," for the Arabs of today dignify by the name of "forest" small patches of trees which we should call nothing more than a wood, and the Biblical authors may have done the same. We must observe the same caution with regard to writers of the medieval and even the modern period. Thus, George Adam Smith himself says, "Lower and Upper Galilee are almost as thickly wooded as our own land," leaving one to wonder to which part of Britain he is referring, though it is probably the sparsely wooded moorlands of the Scottish mountains that he has in mind.[1] In the same way

* Just how inaccurate such pictures can be is shown by one I saw recently in which a mosque appeared!

83

Lawrence and Woolley speak of the Wadi Arabah as being almost park-like in the Spring [2] which is very misleading to those who have in mind the vegetation of western Europe or the greater part of North America.

In view of this uncertainty, it would seem best to begin with a very short survey of the present conditions of soil and vegetation, such as the modern visitor sees them, and then attempt to suggest some ways in which the ancient conditions may have differed.

Soil is primarily the result of the climate, and, as we have seen, the climate in Palestine has a double character. In summer there is prolonged and intense heat which tends to destroy much of the living matter in the soil and to dry up the surface so that it becomes parched and powdery. In the drier regions this drying of the surface layers is so intense that the water in the soil is drawn upward by capillary action, bringing with it in solution the natural salts which are then deposited in the upper layers when the water evaporates. During the rainy season, however, the water, which has been lost by evaporation in the course of the summer, is given back by the heavy rainstorms, but these storms do much damage by washing away the powdery surface soil and leaching out the salts from the upper layers. Since most of the rock in Palestine is limestone, variations in climate are of much greater importance in determining differences in soil than variations in the parent rock, though this is not without its effect. Reifenberg has suggested that by putting together the total rainfall and the loss of water by evaporation

during the rainy season, when almost all the growth takes place, it is possible to obtain a *Rainfall Factor*, by which the effect of the climate on soil formation can be measured.[3] His formula for this is $R.F. = \dfrac{r}{t}$, where "r" is the total rainfall in millimetres and "t" is the average temperature in degrees centigrade during the rainy season. Thus, Jerusalem has an average rainfall of 614 mm, and an average temperature during the rainy season of 13° C. By dividing 614 by 13 we get a Rainfall Factor of 47.

Any area with a Rainfall Factor of less than 15 must be regarded as *desertic*. Such areas are all the southern triangle of Cis-jordan, the Rift Valley south of Beisan, and all Trans-jordan outside the cultivated zone. The typical soils here are red and yellow sandy soils and gravels, which are often rich in potash and other minerals, but inclined to be very salty. Yellow soils are to be found in southern Cis-jordan and in the east of Trans-jordan, where they are sometimes very deep,[4] while in southern Trans-jordan there are areas of red sands which have been formed from the Nubian sandstone. Two special soils of the desertic region are the Lisan Marls and the Loess. The Lisan Marl soil formed from the deposits made by the Dead Sea in the course of its prolonged shrinking is excessively salty and, unless the salt is washed out, is useless for agriculture. It is a grayish-white in color and was, for the most part, quite uncultivated in ancient times. The Loess is a windborne soil which has been brought by dust storms from the desert and deposited many feet thick in the wadis round Beersheba. It forms a very fine sand without stones and permits the passage of both air and water fairly easily. It is very fertile and well-suited to the growing of cereals, though, of course, the rainfall of the loess regions is apt to be deficient.

The greater part of the Cis-jordan lowlands, the upper Rift Valley and the Trans-jordan steppe zone, have a *moderately dry* climate with a Rain-fall Factor of between 15 and 30. In the Trans-jordan steppe there are brown soils, grading in color from the pale yellow desert soils to the deep, rich chocolate-red of the terra rossa found in regions with a Rainfall Factor of more than 30. These brown soils are found over wide areas of very level land and form excellent cereal country in the richer parts.

In Cis-jordan the southern part of the coast plain round Gaza has another excellent cereal soil, the Mediterranean Steppe Soil which is formed of loess mixed with alluvium and is rich in calcium and phosphate. Elsewhere there is much dark gray or black alluvium which is among the richest soil in the country. In ancient times, however, especially in Sharon, it must have been marshy and even today it tends to be waterlogged in a wet season. Wherever in Sharon the Mousterian Red Sand is found it breaks down into a bright red or orange clayey sand with almost perfect moisture conditions. Today these sands form the citrus soils par excellence, but in ancient times the greater part of them were isolated by marshes. Along the coast itself are the dune sands, which may extend inland to

form large, barren patches, though in the past these may have been smaller because the inward drift of the sand would have been checked by the forests of the coast plain. However, it is interesting that just inland from Cae-

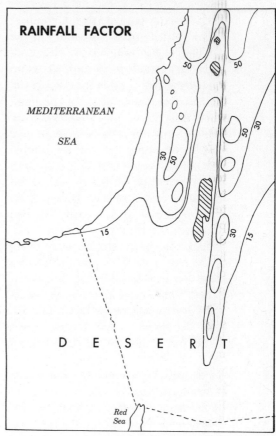

Fig. 22.

sarea the Roman Aqueduct, which was originally straight, makes a curious curve, and it is possible that a new dog-leg section had to be added because part of the old aqueduct had been blocked by drifting sand.

In the Huleh Basin the soil is of a peaty character and has been formed from the rich vegetation growing in the swamps above the shallow Huleh lake. In Biblical times the marshes in this district must have been formidable. In the area which still remained in 1935 it was still possible for a man to sink waist-deep in the mud.[5]

The greater part of the hill country, on both sides of the Jordan lies in the *moderately wet* region with a Rainfall Factor of between 30 and 50. Here the predominant soil is the terra rossa, which is so characteristic of the limestone districts of the Mediterranean. It is a deep red in color, quite unlike the bright orange-red of the Mousterian Red Sand, and is well suited to the growth of all the typical Mediterranean crops. It may, however, be poor in humus and is easily washed down from the hillsides which today have often been almost completely cleared of soil. With the terra rossa must be classed also the somewhat darker, but essentially similar, chocolate-brown soils of the basalt in Galilee. The down-faulted basins in Samaria and Galilee are usually floored with alluvium, which may become flooded in the rainy season but which produces rich crops when it dries out in the later spring.

Wherever there is an outcrop of the Senonian chalk terra rossa is not formed, but instead a whitish, infertile soil which is very easily recognizable. Cereals will grow in it, but they are very inferior to those grown in the terra rossa.

Reifenberg also distinguishes a *Wet Mediterranean Region* with a Rainfall Factor of more than 50, that is to say, Upper Galilee, parts of Carmel, central Judaea and Gilead in Trans-jordan, but the soils of these regions are very similar to those of the moderately wet region.

The kind of plants which grow by nature on these soils are curiously varied, for Palestine lies at the junction of three of the world's major vegetation regions, known technically as the *Mediterranean*, the *Saharo-Sindian* and the *Irano-Turanian*. The Mediterranean plants are predominant over most of the coast plain, the Cis-jordan hills north of Beersheba and the edge of the Trans-jordan plateau as far south as Kerak, with an interesting outlier in the Jebel Druze. It is a type of vegetation adapted to withstand the prolonged summer drought. Very many of the plants are evergreen shrubs with very small leaves and long roots which burrow deep down into the earth in search of water. The leaves are often hairy, or thick and leathery, or coated with wax, to prevent excessive evaporation in summer. There are also a great many spring flowers, including bulbs such as the tulip and iris, which come up for a brief season after the rain and disappear with the approach of summer. This period when "the winter is past, the rain is over and gone, the flowers appear on the earth" (Song 2:11) is quite extraordinarily beautiful, for the ground is often altogether hidden by the flowers, but it is short-lived and with the siroccos of April they disappear. The scorching siroccos are also probably the reason why there are relatively few different types of grasses. A characteristic feature of the Mediterranean regions is the brilliantly colored blue and purple thistles which the ancient farmers knew well and hated (Gen. 3:18 and Matt. 13:7).

The Saharo-Sindian plants are those suited to the great desert areas of the Sahara, Arabia and Sind, regions with very little rain, a very high daily temperature but sudden cold at night. The summers are scorchingly hot, but temperatures may drop below freezing in winter, and at all times there may develop powerful winds which, especially close to the ground, may be heavily charged with sharp particles of sand. In these conditions plants can exist only with difficulty and so the vegetation is normally extremely scarce and stunted, small, thorny scrub which can endure the heat, the drought and often very salty soils. These plants are very sensitive to the presence of water and the slightest increase in the supply leads to a thickening of the always sparse plant cover. This can be seen clearly wherever there is even the most gentle depression into which the water tends to drain. Where there is enough water from underground supplies the date palm is important. The area where these plants predominate is the desert, lying south and east of the Mediterranean region and extending two long tongues northward, one along the line of sand dunes on the Cis-jordanian coast and the other in the Rift Valley about as far north as the confluence of the Zerqa with the Jordan. The sand-dune region has a thoroughly Mediterranean climate, but the loose sand permits the water to run through so easily and becomes so hot in summer that it shares many of the characteristics of the desert and so here both types of plants are found growing

together, although, naturally, they are not very numerous.

Between the eastern edges of the Mediterranean regions and the desert, that is to say, on the eastern slopes of the Judaean hills and in the Transjordan steppe regions south of Kerak and round Amman and Mafraq, we find examples of the Irano-Turanian plants, which normally belong to the high plateaus of Asia, including those of Iran and Turkey. There the growth of the plants is interrupted twice in the year, once by the winter cold and once by the summer drought, with the result that the growing season is very short, though there is more rainfall than in true desert regions. In such conditions trees are absent and the vegetation is stunted, consisting mainly of steppeland grasses and small shrubs. The presence of such plants in the Palestine region reflects the increased winter cold of the steppeland regions which prevents the growth of such true Mediterranean plants as the olive.

VEGETATION REGIONS

(a) *Sand dunes of the Coast.* These have already been mentioned as having a very sparse vegetation with both Mediterranean and Saharo-Sindian plants.

(b) *The Lowlands and Plains.* Here today there is almost no natural vegetation left, and instead there are orange groves, wheatfields, oliveyards, et cetera with frequent clumps of eucalyptus. In ancient times much of Sharon and Esdraelon must have been marshy, while the Mousterian Red Sands were probably forested. The

Philistine section of the coast plain is unlikely to have had so much forest cover, but the frontier region of the Shephelah between the Philistines and

16. *Maquis.* The thick, thorny scrub bushes which cover much of the wetter Mediterranean districts. In the west of Galilee and on the northern slopes of Carmel the bushes are taller than a man and grow so thickly together that they are almost impenetrable, but in most of the Palestinian area such a thick *maquis* is unlikely.

17. *Spring at 'Iraq el-Amir.* This Maccabean fortress stands in one of the smaller scarp valleys of Trans-jordan, and there in a good spring the flowers are almost waist deep. In this picture the figure of a man can just be discerned in the extreme right, showing the height of the vegetation in which he is standing.

Judaea was famous in Old Testament times for its woodlands.

(c) *Hill Country of Judaea and Samaria.* Today the usual vegetation of this part of the country is shrubland, which is much richer on the wetter west and dies away altogether in the east. Both in the Wilderness of Judaea and in the wet Carmel region the northern slopes are more thickly covered with plants than those facing south, on account of the protection from the hot rays of the sun. On Carmel the shrubland is at its richest and on the northern slopes there is a true *maquis,* which makes movement difficult if not impossible. It consists mainly of rockrose taller than a man and gay with flowers in spring, but on the southward facing slopes the same plant is only a dwarf shrub. The carob is a common tree and there are many dwarf oaks and arbutus. In spring the carpet of flowers is altogether magnificent and of great variety, and it lasts here longer than in other parts of the country.

Elsewhere on the hills this luxuriance is not found and the vegetation is that poorer type of *maquis* known as *garigue,* where there are fewer and smaller shrubs and larger patches of bare ground. In many places the vegetation is poorer still, but almost everywhere there are plenty of wild flowers in spring. Much of Judaea round Jerusalem today has this poorest type of *garigue,* which is very barren in summer but covered with grass in the rainy season, and gay with flowers, but not carpeted with them, in spring. On the eastern slopes in the Wilderness of Judaea, there is a cover of grass only in the wettest winters.

18. *The Beqa'a in Gilead.* The Beqa'a is the down-faulted basin which is crossed by the road from Amman to Jerash. This picture of it was taken facing eastward, and shows well the greater thickness of the vegetation on the northward-facing slopes, where there is less evaporation.

(d) *The Hills of Galilee.* This is very similar to the preceding region, but the vegetation is much richer. On the western slopes of Galilee the *maquis* is even thicker than that of Carmel and in many places the hills are quite well-wooded, though the trees are nowhere large. In Upper Galilee there is an admixture of plants belonging to the Euro-Siberian types which are characteristic of regions much farther to the uorth. A very noticeable example of this is the haw-thorn whose wonderful white blossoms are common round Safad, but which is not found in other parts of Palestine.

(e) *The Western Hills of Trans-jordan.* This is the Gilead region which in Old Testament times was famous for its woodlands and which today still carries a fairly thick cover of trees in many parts, mainly Aleppo pine, oak and carob. On the present Amman-Jerash road it is interesting to notice the sudden change from the oaks of the southward-facing slopes to the pines of the colder northern ones.

(f) *The Steppeland.* This lies to the south and east of the Mediterranean regions and has many Irano-Turanian

19. *River in a desert.* The River Jabbok near Zerqa 10 miles from Amman. This picture was taken some twenty years ago, before the recent growth of the town of Zerqa, and shows the sharp contrast between the cultivated land near the river and the barren slopes on either side.

plants. It is best developed on the Trans-jordan plateau. In the rainy season it is covered relatively thickly with grass, but this soon vanishes with the advent of summer and thereafter the plant cover is very thin indeed. As far as the eye can see the ground is bare, but dotted with innumerable tiny bushes of dark green. In spring a remarkable sight is provided by the immense, deep-purple irises, known as "Moab lilies," which are not found elsewhere.

(g) *The Desert.* This is nowhere complete desert, for though the hills are often quite bare, the wadis carry a thin line of saltbush, and even the slightest hollow in the ground produces a little crop of stunted green bushes. After a good rainy season the bare earth may disappear altogether under the thin green grass, but this never lasts for long.

(h) *The Rift Valley.* Here the heat is like that of a greenhouse and where there is sufficient water, as for instance along the banks of the Jordan, the vegetation has the thickness of a jungle which is very difficult to penetrate. A great many of the plants, as well as the fish, of this region are typical of regions far to the south in the Sudan. Such a plant is the papyrus of the Huleh basin, which elsewhere is not found north of about 7° N. latitude on the river Nile. The southern part of this Rift is very desertic, but it is interesting to note that the

Sudano-Deccanian plants which grow there continue to flower in summer, which is the rainy season of the Sudan. There is much tamarisk and *spina Christi* along the edges of the Jordan.

In the past neither the soil conditions nor the vegetation were different *in kind*, though certain plants which are particularly noticeable, such as the orange, the eucalyptus and the prickly pear, have been introduced since Biblical days, but apart from these the plants and trees are essentially the same. The southern and eastern regions must always have been more or less desert, and the Philistine plain and many parts of the steppe-land may have carried only few trees. However, elsewhere the nature of the vegetation pattern must have undergone very great changes since Biblical times.

When agriculture first started the surface which was cultivated was small and the flocks maintained were limited in number. They were unable to wander at will over the countryside because of the constant danger from wild beasts, so that the trees were not attacked by the domestic animals and the "natural" conditions were allowed to continue. In these "natural" conditions there would have been very little soil erosion, for the soil, climate and vegetation together would have formed a "stable environment," that is to say, one in which the different parts were so well adjusted to one another that action and reaction were equal and no great change could take place. In this stable environment the soil was a passive member, for it did not take any great part in producing or resist-

ing change, but it was of the first importance because it was the material in which the plants grew. It was a "natural" soil producing a "natural" vegetation, both well adjusted to the climate and to each other.

20. *Hamada or stone desert.* This view is typical of much of the desert east of the railway in Trans-jordan.

This delicate adjustment, however, was destined not to continue, since man had need of wood both for fuel and for building and therefore, particularly after he had learned to make iron weapons, he started to cut down the trees and thus to expose the land to the onslaughts of the weather. The result of this interference in the environment was that the climate, which had previously been the most important factor in the production of the soil, was gradually turned into the most important factor in its destruction. The long summer drought began to dry up the valuable top surface of the soil, which was now less protected by the shade of trees from the burning heat—a preparation for destruction which went on unceasingly for five months—and then came the slashing rains of winter to beat furiously against the loosened soil, no longer held back by the clutching tentacles of the roots, and to sweep it into the wadis, staining the blue waters of the Mediterranean for days after the rain

21. *Sacred terebinth.* Such old trees as do still remain in Palestine usually owe their preservation to the fact that they were regarded as sacred. This terebinth at Yajuz in Gilead is one of a small grove in the midst of which is a Roman temple, of which part can be seen here.

had ceased. Of course, the people of the time did not know that they were doing this. The supply of wood seemed to them to be inexhaustible, and it is striking that the Law permitted the destruction of forests in time of war, though not of fruit trees. Yet even fruit trees were not always secure, for when the armies of Judah and Israel attacked the Moabites, "they felled all the good trees; till only its stones were left in Kir-hareseth," both cultivated and wild trees apparently being destroyed together (II Kings 3:25).

Thus we must imagine that, especially on the hills, the distribution of soil was markedly different from that which we see today. Thousands of

years ago the soil was thick enough for cultivation or for the growth of forest over much larger areas in the hills than at present, but the work of destruction, so long continued, has meant that the sad truth is that in many places the soil is no longer there. As the danger to flocks and herds was gradually removed, the number of domestic animals increased and they began to eat the tiny shoots faster than they could grow again. The forests were cut down for a multitude of purposes and never replanted. Under the Roman and Nabatean governments, and probably under the early Arabs, the soil was protected by terraces and dams, but then the country entered on a thousand years of neglect, for which only now are we beginning to atone. Trees continued to be cut down and the valuable oak forests of the plain, which had held back the sand dunes, were destroyed. Wars, disturbances and constant misgovernment meant the neglect of farmlands and so the terraces and retaining walls were allowed to decay. No longer was there any restraint upon the fury of the weather, and the soil was swept wholesale from the hillsides, leaving them rocky and barren as we see them today, and so complete has been this devastation that in many parts there is nothing left to be eroded. A prophecy of Isaiah has been fulfilled in a way which he did not originally intend: "In that day every place where there used to be a thousand vines, worth a thousand shekels of silver, will become briers and thorns. With bow and arrows men will come there, for all the land will be briers and thorns;

and as for all the hills which used to be hoed with a hoe, you will not come there for fear of briers and thorns; but they will become a place where cattle are let loose and where sheep tread" (Is. 7:23–25).

Just how extensive the early forests were is difficult to determine. Certainly one or two of the references to forest in the Bible must be discounted. The normal word is יַעַר, which is translated variously as "forest," "wood" or "thicket," and this has a curious double meaning. Originally, it would appear, it had the sense of richness, for it also means "honeycomb," and therefore "forest" as being the place with the most luxuriant vegetation. This appears to be the sense in Isaiah 32:15, where the desert is going to become as rich as the cultivated land and the cultivated land is to develop the overwhelming luxuriance of the forest. But a forest is also the uncultivated land and so the word can apparently mean "wasteland," similarly to the corresponding word وعر in Arabic, which is used normally for rough and rugged country, such as the basalt of Trans-jordan.* This would appear to be the meaning in Hosea 2:12, "And I will lay waste her vines and fig trees . . . I will make them a forest," and possibly also of Isaiah 21:13, "In the thickets in Arabia you will lodge, O caravans of Dedanites," though this may refer to the palm groves of the oases. In Psalm 50:10 and 104:20; Is. 56:9; Jer. 5:6; Amos 3:4; and Micah 5:8, where the reference is to wild animals, the "beasts of the forest," the exact meaning is

unimportant, since it is speaking of wild country whether wooded or not, but in other places the word seems to mean a wooded area, though it is not always clear whether it is real forest or merely scrub.

Very often there is no doubt that it is used for forests proper, such as the forests of the Lebanon (I Kings 7:2, 10:17, 21; II Chron. 9:16, 20; Is. 29: 17, 37:24, etc.), but this is not necessarily the meaning everywhere, as where Ezekiel speaks of the "forest" of the Negeb (Ezek. 20:46–47). Nevertheless, it is clear from the frequency of the references to some kind of woodland and to forest fires (Is. 10: 17–18; Jer. 21:14; Joel 1:19; Deut. 9:3, etc.) that trees were much more common in the past than they are today. Certain place names also suggest greater woodland than at present, for example, Kiriath-Jearim or "the village of the woods" (I Sam. 6:21; I Chron. 13:5 and probably also Ps. 132:6) and the modern Arabic name for the eastern part of the Carmel range which is Umm el-Fahm or "mother of charcoal."

Yet one must not imagine for a moment that the forests of Palestine were ever to be compared with those of the Lebanon. The trees can never have been very tall and, if first-class timber was needed at any time for building or for ships, it had to be brought from Phoenicia. The straight timbers of cedar and cypress were floated down to Joppa from Sidon and Tyre and then were taken up to Jerusalem ("Unto them of Zidon also and Tyre they gave carrs that they should bring cedar trees from Libanus, which should be brought by floats to the

* It is also used for the shrubland close to the seashore.

haven of Joppe, according as it was commanded them by Cyrus king of the Persians" [I Esdras 5:55]. See also I Kings 5; II Chron. 2; as well as II Sam. 5:11; I Kings 9:26–28; II Chron. 8:17–18. Judging from I Kings 9:10–

22. *The Cedars of Lebanon.* Only a few patches of these magnificent trees still survive, so great has been the deforestation of these once thickly forested mountains. This is part of the most famous group at Bsharreh, above Tripoli.

14, the price which was demanded was often heavy). Hence the name given to the great room in Solomon's palace where the armor was kept, the "House of the Forest of Lebanon," which seems to have been built with great beams of cedar and panelled as well with the same wood (I Kings 7:2, 10:17, 21; II Chron. 9:16, 20; Is. 22:8). The great height of the cedars never ceased to fascinate the Israelites, who never saw anything comparable in their own country. They marveled that Solomon had "made cedar as plentiful as the sycamore of the Shephelah" (II Chron. 1:15), and Ezekiel compared the king of Assyria to a great cedar of Lebanon which yet had been destroyed

(Ezek. 31). "The voice of the Lord is powerful," said the Psalmist, speaking of the thunderstorm, "the voice of the Lord is full of majesty. The voice of the Lord breaks the cedars, the Lord breaks the cedars of Lebanon" (Ps. 29:4–5).

Throughout the Old Testament there is constant reference to wild animals, the "beasts of the forest," which inhabited the woods and thick *maquis* which covered so much of the hills when they came into the country. They seem to have been a constant danger both to flocks and to wayfarers, so that Jacob was able to say, "It is my son's robe; a wild beast has devoured him; Joseph is without doubt torn to pieces" (Gen. 37:33). That the danger continued to be a real one is obvious from the frequency of this imagery in the prophets. "So I will be to them like a lion, like a leopard I will lurk beside the way. I will fall upon them like a bear robbed of her cubs, I will tear open their breast, and there I will devour them like a lion, as a wild beast would rend them" (Hos. 13:7–8), and again, "as if a man fled from a lion, and a bear met him; or went into the house and leaned with his hand against the wall, and a serpent bit him" (Amos 5:19). Isaiah uses similar metaphors, "As a lion or a young lion growls over his prey, and when a band of shepherds is called forth against him is not terrified by their shouting, or daunted by their noise" (Is. 31:4), and so also does Zephaniah, "Her officials within her are roaring lions; her judges are evening wolves * that

* Possibly the meaning is "desert wolves" or "wolves of the wasteland."

leave nothing till the morning" (Zeph. 3:3). There are stories of actual meetings between men and wild beasts, as when a young lion roared against Samson in the vineyards of Timnah (Judg. 14:5) and David as a youth destroyed both a lion and a bear (I Sam. 17:34). When the man of God who came from Judah disobeyed the word of God, "a lion met him on the road and killed him" (I Kings 13:24), and later the Lord sent lions among those whom the king of Assyria had settled in Samaria to replace the people who had been taken away into captivity (II Kings 17:26). The excuse of the sluggard in Proverbs 22:13, "There is a lion outside! I shall be slain in the streets!" for all that it was an excuse, was not as fantastic as it would be in our day or as it would have been in New Testament times. The lions seem particularly to have been associated with the tangled tamarisk jungle on the banks of the Jordan (Jer. 49:19, 50:17; Zech. 11:3) and they impressed the people of the time both by their ferocity and by their majesty. "The lion, which is mightiest among beasts and does not turn back before any," was one of the four things which "are stately in their stride" (Prov. 30:29–30).

The Israelites were very observant of the ways of animals and they used them frequently for similes and metaphors. They remarked "the little foxes that spoil the vineyards" (Song 2:15), the hawk soaring and spreading his wings toward the south, and the eagle mounting up and making his nest on high (Job 39:26–27). Job 40:6–24 is a description of the hippopotamus, known from Egypt, and all chapter 41

a picture of the crocodile which was to be found in the Jordan as well as in the Nile.* "Even the stork in the heavens knows her times; and the turtledove, swallow and crane keep the time of their coming; but my people know not the ordinance of the Lord," [6] said Jeremiah (8:7), speaking of the habits of migration among birds. The skill of the mountain dwellers such as the wild goats caught their attention (Ps. 18:33, 104:18) and even the smallest of the animals served to teach a lesson: "Four things on earth are small, but they are exceedingly wise: the ants are a people not strong, yet they provide their food in the summer; the badgers are a people not mighty, yet they make their homes in the rocks; the locusts have no king, yet all of them march in rank; the lizard you can take in your hands, yet it is in kings' palaces" (Prov. 30:24–28).

The animals of the desert hold a special place in the imagery of the Old Testament. On behalf of great kings like Solomon the desert might be scoured for game for the table so that they might be provided with "harts, gazelles, roebucks and fatted fowl" (I Kings 4:23), but for ordinary folk they were strange animals which shared something of the mystery of the desert itself. It was in the desert that "the Lord sent fiery serpents among the people, and they bit the people, so that many people of Israel died" (Num. 21:6); the desert was "the great and terrible wilderness, with its fiery serpents and scorpions" (Deut. 8:15) and "a land of trouble

* The last crocodile in the Jordan was killed in the middle of the nineteenth century.

and anguish, from where come the lioness and the lion, the viper and the flying serpent" (Is. 30:6). Yet, despite their fear, they admired them. They were impressed particularly by their freedom, their speed and their strength, and by the sense of desolation which overcame them when they considered the life of such animals. In the great 39th chapter of the Book of Job God silences Job by reminding him of the mysteries of desert life, of the wild goats, the wild ass, "to whom I have given the steppe for his home, and the salt land for his dwelling place" (v. 6), the strength and freedom of the wild ox (vv. 9–12), and the speed and stupidity of the ostrich (vv. 13–18). The Psalmist in his distress cried out, "I am like a vulture of the wilderness, like an owl of the waste places; I lie awake, I am like a lonely bird on the housetop" (Ps. 102:6–7). Hosea compared Ephraim to a "wild ass wandering alone" (Hos. 8:9) and in the Song of Solomon the gazelle is a constant image of speed and grace (Song 2:8–9, 17, 4:5, 7:3, 8:14).

By the time of the New Testament the picture that we have is of a more civilized and ordered countryside and references to wild animals are much less common. Our Lord refers to foxes, wolves, serpents and scorpions (Matt. 7:10, 8:20, 10:16, 23:33; Luke 9:58, 10:19, 11:11–12, 13:32) and John the Baptist speaks of vipers (Matt. 3:7; Luke 3:7). Peter likens the devil to a roaring lion (I Pet. 5:8), but other references to lions are either a picture of the arena (II Tim. 4:17) or drawn from the Old Testament (Heb. 11:33; Rev. 4:7, 5:5, 9:8, 17, 10:3, 13:2). This does not denote a lack of interest in such imagery, for domestic animals such as sheep, goats and camels are quoted frequently. It is just that they had ceased to be such a part of the daily life of the people as they had been in the past.

23. *Mosaic at Madeba.* This fifth-century mosaic, once the floor of a church, and now part of a private house, illustrates some of the typical Palestinian fauna and flora.

CHAPTER VIII

Food From the Earth

Thou dost cause the grass to grow for the cattle
and plants for man to cultivate,
that he may bring forth food from the earth.
PSALM 104:14

IT is necessary now to turn to the use made by man of the land, to the plants which he grew, the animals he kept, the towns and roads that he built, and the manner in which he lived and passed his days there. He was essentially a farmer, living in a village or a little town, for even in Roman times large towns must have accounted for only a minority of the people. It is true that the words "Canaan" and "Canaanite" seem to be associated with trading and the bridge position which Palestine holds must have made trade important, especially in the northern part of the country, but it was not by trade that the majority of the people lived. Rather it was the Phoenicans who were the traders, and it would appear that the word "Canaan" comes originally from one meaning "red purple," the famous product of the Phoenician coast.[1]

The three main products of the Mediterranean farmer have always been "wine to gladden the heart of man, oil to make his face shine, and bread to strengthen man's heart" (Ps. 104:15). When the people in other countries said of the Israelites, " 'Where is their God?' Then the Lord became jealous for his land, and had pity on his people. The Lord answered and said to his people, 'Behold I am sending you grain, wine, and oil, and you will be satisfied' " (Joel 2:17–19). The constant bracketing of these three products together in the Old Testament shows how they dominated the agriculture of the country (Gen. 27:28, 27:37; Deut. 7:13, 11:14, 12:17, 14:23, 18:4, 28:51, 33:28; II Kings 18:32; II Chron. 31:5, 32:28; Neh. 5:11, 10:39, 13:5, 12; Ps. 4:7; Is. 36:17; Lam. 2:12; Hos. 2:5, 8, 22; Joel 1:10; Hag. 1:11) and to them we should probably add the humble pulses which Daniel and his companions ate (Dan. 1:8) and by which Jacob bought his birthright (Gen. 25:29–34). In Ecclesiasticus 39:26 there is a longer list: "The principal things

97

for the whole use of a man's life are water, fire, iron, and salt, flour of wheat, honey, milk, and the blood of the grape, and oil and clothing." All these are products of the country. The salt came from the Mediterranean or the Dead Sea, and the iron together with copper from the mountains of Trans-jordan (Deut. 8:9). The milk and the honey are, of course, the two products most commonly associated with Palestine, for God had promised his people from the beginning that he would bring them into "a land flowing with milk and honey" (Exod. 3:8, 13:5, 33:3; Lev. 20:24; Num. 14:8; Deut. 6:3, 11:9, 26:9, 27:3; Josh. 5:6; Jer. 11:5, 32:22; Ezek. 20:6, 15) and when they were struggling through the desert, the people complained that far from bringing them into such a land, Moses had in fact brought them out of a land flowing with milk and honey to kill them in the wilderness (Num. 16:13–14). This was a picture of Palestine as seen from the desert, whence it appeared that the rich grass of winter would provide excellent pasture for the animals. The honey was wild honey, collected from the trees and the rocks (I Sam. 14:25–7; Ps. 81:16; Matt. 3:4; Mark. 1:6), and it was then an important source of sweetening matter and imported into the desert by the Bedouin as they now buy sugar.

It is interesting to notice that when the Israelites had finally become settled in the land where "grain shall make the young men flourish and new wine the maidens" (Zech. 9:17), and where rich olive oil replaced animal fat for fine cooking, the once longed-for milk and honey were de-spised. The expression is absent from the earlier prophets until Jeremiah, Ezekiel and the writer of the Book of Deuteronomy look back with nostalgia to the great hopes of the early days, which seemed to have been so tragically unfulfilled. Indeed, in the time of Isaiah the very things which had been a symbol of richness had come to denote poverty. When Isaiah was rebuking Ahaz for the folly of his foreign policy, he warned him that before Immanuel, the child who was to be born, would be old enough to tell the difference between good and bad, the Assyrian wars would have reduced the country to such a state that butter and honey would be the only food obtainable, "In that day a man will keep alive a young cow and two sheep; and because of the abundance [the word is sarcastic] of milk which they give, he will eat curds; for every one that is left in the land will eat curds and honey" (Is. 7:21–22).*

The cultivation of these four products, grain, wine, olives and pulses, was the basic activity of the Palestinian farmer, and the Jewish religious year revolved about this, for it is quite clear that all the major fasts and feasts in the Jewish calendar have a double significance, agricultural and religious. This had been true of the Canaanite religion which the Israelites found established in the country when they arrived, for it was concerned above all

* The Isaiah passage is sometimes taken to indicate the wealth of the food which the Messiah will eat, but the tenor of the whole chapter makes this impossible. The point is that all cultivated land will be laid waste, and men will have to take refuge with a couple of animals and gather what food they can.

things with the urgency of obtaining a good harvest. We have already seen that the Palestinian weather is capricious and though rain may fall in abundance one year, it may be withheld in the next, and ways, therefore, had to be found of persuading the gods to be kind and give the rain when it was needed. Hence there was necessity for fasting at the beginning of the year before the rain had started and there was joy and feasting when the major harvests were complete. It was these agricultural festivals which the Israelites took over and sanctified in the course of their sojourn in the country.

During the parched days of the autumn siroccos, when the weather is exhausting, and when it is still not certain how soon the rain will come, is the beginning of the New Year. At one time this month, Tishri, was the seventh month, the first being Abib or Nisan, when there seems to have been a lambing festival connected with desert life, and which was traditionally the time associated with the delivery from Egypt (Exod. 23:14–15, 34:18; Lev. 23:5–8; Num. 28:16; Deut. 16:1). However, so great was the effect of the agricultural year that the New Year later came to be placed at its beginning and to take the place of the Feast of Trumpets mentioned in Lev. 23:23–25. Ten days later comes the Day of Atonement, the most solemn of all the fasts and the only one which is binding upon every Jew (Lev. 16:1–34, 23:26–32). At this same season of the year also, when the moon is full, is the Feast of Tabernacles, which partakes of the nature of both the beginning and the end of the

year. As marking the beginning, it is the occasion of special prayers for rain, and during the time when the Temple still existed water was drawn from the Pool of Siloam and poured on the altar to symbolize the desperate need for rain. "On the last day of the feast, the great day, Jesus stood up and proclaimed, 'If anyone thirst, let him come to me and drink'" (John 7:1), and, despite the warnings of Hoskyns,[2] it is difficult not to see some connection between this and the ceremonies of the feast, concerned as they were with the pleading of the Jewish people for water.

In a good year the first rains would start on the coast shortly after this, but in the hills a little later, and then the land could be plowed and the grain planted. As the rainy season developed the grain grew, "first the blade, then the ear, then the full grain in the ear" (Mark 4:28). By the end of March and the beginning of April the weather had turned fine and hot, though there should be those vitally important storms of early April, the "latter rains," which swell the grain and ensure a good harvest. During these months the grain turns yellow and ripens in the heat of the spring sun until at last the first ears can be plucked. This is the time of the Feast of the Firstfruits, when these preliminary ears of grain were offered to God in thanksgiving at a festival which in course of time was merged with the lambing festival in the greatest of all the feasts, the Feast of the Passover, to celebrate the Exodus from Egypt (Exod. 23:14, 34:18–20; Lev. 23:4–14; hence the significance of Christ as the firstfruits of those who are to rise from the dead in I Cor. 15: 20–23).

The harvest is soon finished in the plain, but in the hills it is continued for some weeks longer. When all is gathered in there is the Feast of Weeks, the harvest festival of the grain, timed to fall seven weeks after Passover, and coming usually at the end of May or the beginning of June (Lev. 23:15–21; Num. 28:26–31).

24. *Grapes in Gilead.* An Arab farmer tending his vines near Es-Salt.

This brings us to the beginning of summer during which little could be done by the farmer because of the lack of water, but throughout the hot,

dry months God was at work on the annual miracle of the vine, whose long root, stretching far into the earth, enables it to pump up water to the grapes, which store up their energy in the form of sugar. They ripen during August and September, and during this season the farmers would go out from their homes to live in tents and little huts made of branches in the vineyards, which lay on the slopes of the hills, often at some distance from the village, in order to protect the grapes from the depradation of wild beasts (Song 2:15). When at last the whole harvest of summer fruits has been gathered in there is the Feast of Tabernacles or Booths (called in Exod. 23:16 and 34:22 the "Feast of Ingathering"), already mentioned as looking forward to the beginning of the following year. The connection of this feast with the harvest was shown by the fact that wine as well as water was poured upon the altar. This feast provides an interesting example of the new and deeper significance which was given to the ancient feasts by the Israelite religious leaders. The living in tents at this time of the year was an agricultural necessity; it is still practiced today on the hills of Transjordan and it must have been a custom among the Canaanites long before the Israelite invasion, but it was seized upon by the newcomers who said that it should serve as an annual reminder of the mercies of God to their fathers in the desert. It may be compared also with the "baptism" of the vintage festival among the Gerasenes when the region became Christian, for then the festival, which probably had previously been accompanied by much

25. *An Arab family camping out near the vineyard in summer.* This is a very common practice in the grape-growing districts, since the vineyards are often some distance outside the village and they need to be protected against the depradations of wild animals during the summer months. Rain never occurs in summer and so the tent has to do no more than provide shade from the sun.

vulgarity and drunkenness, was transformed into a ceremony in memory of the miracle at Cana of Galilee, and performed in the courtyard of the cathedral at Jerash.

After the Feast of Tabernacles the cycle begins once more with the planting of the grain, but there is another cycle which lasts two years instead of one, the cycle of the olive. This is a tree peculiarly adapted to the Mediterranean climate, and is unable to grow outside it. It can endure long periods of drought, and will grow in very shallow soils where there is even less than 8 inches of rain, but it is killed by severe frosts. It survives the drought by growing slowly, the flowers of one spring producing fruit in the autumn of the following year. The ripening process is also slow, and it does not matter very much if the olives are left on the tree for some time before they are picked, so that the farmer is able to gather his olive harvest whenever his work in the fields gives him time, either before or after plowing and sowing his grain, according to whether the first rain comes early or late. The olive has an added importance in that it stores up energy in the form of oil and not sugar and thus supplements the grape and provides a substitute for the animal fats with which Mediterranean regions are not always well provided.

26. *"A green olive tree, fair with goodly fruit."* An olive tree on the Mount of Olives, seen against a summer sky. The olive and the vine were both considered typical of richness and plenty.

The pulses were grown in the old days between the vines, the vineyards being so prepared that there were a succession of hillocks on which the peas and beans were planted, and hollows into which the water drained and which were used for the vines. Thus, these four products together formed a system which could be operated by one man, farming his little plot of land with the help of his family, and from these plants they could live throughout the year, eating meat only on special occasions. It was the ideal of the Israelites that they should sit "every man under his vine and under his fig tree" (Mic. 4:4; Zech. 3:10)

for then "you shall eat the fruit of the labor of your hands; you shall be happy, and it shall be well with you" (Ps. 128:2). The whole family were expected to work together to produce the food which they all needed: for a good wife is one who "works with willing hands" (Prov. 31:13) and "a son who gathers in summer is prudent, but a son who sleeps in harvest brings shame" (Prov. 10:5; see also Matt. 21: 28–31).

References to vines and olive trees are so frequent in the Bible that it is quite impossible to quote all of them. Both trees were symbols of richness and prosperity, Jeremiah speaking of "a green olive tree, fair with goodly fruit" and also "a choice vine, wholly of pure seed" to describe Israel in the days of her greatness (Jer. 11:16, 2:21. Cf. Ps. 128:3–4; Is. 5:1–7, 27:2; Ezek. 19:10–14; Hos. 10:1, 14:5–7; Matt. 21: 33–41; John 15:1 ff.). The grain was less a symbol of prosperity in itself, though this might be applied to an exceptionally good harvest (Ps. 65:9– 13, 72:16), but the miracle which produced such a wonderful result from such a tiny seed is mentioned more than once in the New Testament (e.g., Mark 4:2–20, 26–29; John 12:24; I Cor. 15: 36–38).

The most important cereals were, and indeed still are, wheat and barley, the first being the most esteemed and grown wherever the climate made it possible (see Ps. 147:14. Barley is never quoted in this sense and it is even possible that it has a slightly derogatory meaning in John 6:9). Today almost three times as much wheat as barley is grown in Palestine, but the ancient proportions are quite impossible to estimate, since it is likely that what is much of the best wheat land in Cis-jordan, in the lower-lying areas, was then marshy. However, the better drained Valley of Jezreel was excellent country for wheat, and so were the down-faulted basins of Samaria and Galilee (Hos. 3:22). In Trans-jordan there were very extensive wheat-producing areas on the plateau, the best being what is now the Hauran of southern Syria, the ancient Bashan, which in Roman times was one of the great granaries of the Empire.

Barley is a product of the drier south and east, "the standing grain of the Philistines" (Judg. 15:5) being very probably barley, which is mentioned as being grown together with wheat near Bethlehem (Ruth 2:23). It will grow on poorer soils than wheat and does not need such a long ripening period, but it is easily spoiled by rain during the harvest.

Olives are confined to those areas with a true Mediterranean climate, that is to say, to the Coast Plain, Galilee, Samaria, northern Judaea and the westward facing slopes of the Trans-jordan plateau. They thin out very noticeably in southern Judaea, where the influence of the desert with its cold winters begins to intermingle with the milder maritime climate, and they are not found on the eastern slopes of the Cis-jordanian mountains nor on the surface of the Trans-jordan plateau (save in the most protected parts) since these areas are exposed to the bitter winds from Arabia. In general, they are far more characteristic of Cis-jordan than of the eastern section of the country.

Vines are essentially a product of the hills, where they can be grown everywhere except in the desert stretches. It is even possible that in Roman times they were grown as far south as the Negeb,* though this is by no means certain. Today the finest grapes come from the mountains of Gilead, clusters of long, sweet, green fruit, which for table purposes are almost unparalleled, and in ancient times this was an important wine-producing region. Because of the importance of wine, it is probable that the production of grapes was much greater in the past than it is today, when the orange has become the dominant fruit of the country and the Muslim tradition, moreover, prohibits the drinking of wine.

Besides the "grain and wine and oil" there were also other minor agricultural products, such as the summer fruits. These included figs, whose early fruit was greatly appreciated (Mic. 7:1; Hos. 9:10; Jer. 24:2; Nah. 3:12), pomegranates (Deut. 8:8; I Sam. 14:2; Song 4:3, 13, 6:7, 11, 8:2; Joel 1:12; Hag. 2:19), pistachio nuts and almonds (Gen. 43:11; Eccles. 12:5). The almond tree is the first of the Palestinian fruit trees to blossom, bursting into a mass of glorious pink and white flowers when every other bough is bare, and hence it is called in Hebrew the "wakeful tree," which gives point to Jeremiah 1:11–12, where there is a play upon words on שָׁקֵד (*Shaqed,* or almond) *and* שׁוֹקֵד (*shoqed* or awake). A similar play on words occurs in Amos 8:1–2 between קַיִץ (*qaitz* or summer) and קֵץ (*qetz* or end), but here it is not merely

* See above, p. 75.

a play on words, for there were no true winter fruits, and that there was nothing to take the place of the summer fruits is well seen from Micah 7:1. Another common tree was the fig-mulberry, the "sycamore" of I Kings 10:27, Is. 9:10 and Amos 7:14. Besides these there were the garden products, the vegetables and spices, of which we have a picture in Is. 1:8, 28:27 and Matt. 23:23.

Over against the agricultural economy, and to some extent intermingling with it, is the pastoral economy, and in the early period it is almost the only economy of which mention is made. "The men are shepherds," said Joseph to Pharoah (Gen. 46:32) and he spoke the truth, though it may have been that they indulged in a little primitive agriculture, as it were on the side, much as the semi-Bedouin of the steppe do today. Throughout Genesis the keeping of flocks is the honored profession and the story of Cain and Abel reflects a pastoralist view of the agelong struggle between the desert and the sown. It was not until after the Exodus that the change took place. "Now the sons of Reuben and the sons of Gad had a very great multitude of cattle (or rather "sheep" as also in Gen. 46:34 and many other places); and they saw the land of Jazer and the land of Gilead, and behold, the place was a place for cattle. . . . And they said, 'If we have found favor in your sight, let this land be given to your servants for a possession'" (Num. 32:1-5).

With the conquest of Cis-jordan, however, there was a strong swing-over, and pastoralism ceased to hold the predominant position in the think-ing of the people. It was not until the prophets arose to challenge the careless luxury of the people of the northern kingdom that there was any return to thinking that the pastoral way of life might be in itself better than the

27. "A rod of almond." This is the first of the flowering trees to come into blossom, and for this reason was known by the Israelites by the name of the "wakeful tree" (Jer. 1:11–12).

agricultural. Amos claimed to have been a herdsman (7:14–15) and it is striking that the metaphor of the shepherd as a symbol of God's care for his people is a late one and is found only rarely before the time of Jeremiah (I Kings 22:17; Jer. 13:17, 23:1,

25:36, 31:10, 50:19; Is. 40:11; Ps. 23, 74:1, 79:13, 80:1; Ezek. 34:1–31; Hos. 13:5–8; Zech. 10:3, 13:7. It is, however, very common in the Gospels, e.g., Matt. 9:36, 10:6, 12:11, 15:24, 25:32; Mark 6:34, 14:27; Luke 12:32, 15:3–7; John 10:1–18; I Pet. 2:25).

The sheep were of the fat-tailed variety, and were kept for the triple purpose of providing milk, meat and wool (Exod. 29:22), sheepskin coats being also greatly valued by the farmers for protection against the cold at night. The Palestinian sheep are strong and can live out of doors throughout the year, but they are liable to die in large numbers if they become too heated as a result of being overdriven (Gen. 33:13), and so they limit the mobility of those Bedouin who keep them. Naturally, they are mainly to be found in the steppe regions, but they are also kept in almost every part of the hill country on both sides of the Jordan. Their milk is used for the making of *semneh* and *leben*, of which the first is a kind of liquid butter similar to the *ghi* of India, and the second is a form of yoghurt. It was this which Jael served to Sisera, "curds in a lordly bowl" (Judg. 5:25), and it was also the despised food of which Isaiah spoke to Ahaz (Is. 7:15). It remains today an important part of the Bedouin diet and the very poorest may have to make bread dipped in leben the whole of their meal.

Goats in Palestine are kept in much the same conditions as sheep, though they are able to range farther into the desert, and in most regions the two animals are kept together. They are more destructive than sheep, since they can eat even the tiniest of shoots,

and the beginning of the tragic deforestation of the country must be dated back to that period when the "flock of goats, moving down the slopes of Gilead" (Song 6:5) began to be more than the country could bear. They are kept for the same products as sheep, though they have much less fat, and their coarse, black hair is extensively used for tent-making, those tents of Kedar, which are "dark but comely" (Song 1:5).

The third of the domesticated animals is the camel, which, it is believed, was not domesticated until late in the second millennium B.C.[3] They are really a desert animal and, in fact, the only animal of the true desert, and are unable to live where desert conditions do not prevail. In winter, when the grass is fresh and green, they need water only once in three weeks or a month and quickly become ill if their food is too rich. Therefore, during the rainy season they are taken off to the east and return to the damper west only in the summer drought, so that they are bred only in Trans-jordan, Cis-jordan being essentially "camel-consuming." The Bedouin of the eastern deserts are the chief camelkeepers and they bring them into Palestine to rent to the farmers for work during the summer harvest, and this has probably been the practice ever since the time of the Old Testament. Camel milk can be drunk either fresh or sour, but it cannot be used for making butter or cheese and for that reason is less valuable than sheep or goats' milk. On the other hand the camel can stand the desert conditions much better than the sheep and therefore the camel is a fundamental source of wealth for

28. *Goats at Kerak.* The Palestinian goat can go anywhere and eat anything, with the result that it is very destructive of vegetation. The hair is used for making tents.

the true Bedouin, even the poorest of them trying to own a few camels of his own, while a rich sheikh may have as many as a thousand. Their meat is good to eat, but the killing of even one camel for a feast makes a large hole in a normal Bedouin's herd, and so the normal practice is for the Bedouin to keep both camels and sheep together.

"The restive young camel interlacing her tracks" (Jer. 2:23) can cover as much as a hundred miles in a day, and the possession of them made sudden raids from the desert upon the steppe a real and constant danger (Job 1:13–17). It was probably the fact that the camel had been only newly domesticated, and was therefore strange to the Israelites, which made it possible for the Midianites to terrorize so much of Cis-jordan when

they "would come up with their cattle and their tents, coming like locusts for multitude; both they and their camels could not be counted; so that they wasted the land as they came in" (Judg. 6:5). It is worth adding, perhaps, that the camel is by far the largest animal in the country and very ungainly, so that it is quite absurd to explain away the picture of the camel trying to go through the eye of the needle (Mark 10:25), as so many commentaries do. It is exactly the same ridiculous contrast that Jesus used again when he said that the Pharisees were "straining out a gnat and swallowing a camel" (Matt. 23:24).

Other animals were the ass, the mule, the ox and the horse. The first two were beasts of burden, while cattle were used for work and for milk, though probably very little for meat, since ordinary Palestinian beef is very tough and heartily disliked by the people of the country. They must also have been used for transport, though they were doubtless very slow (I Sam. 6:7; I Chron. 12:40). Horses were essentially animals of war and they remained fearsome animals to the Israelites, whose hilly country was little suited to chariot fighting (Hab. 1:8). Solomon seems to have imported his horses from Cilicia and Cappadocia (I Kings 10:28–29, where "Egypt" must surely be a mistake), and his chariot cities were in the plains, though he also had stables at Jerusalem (II Chron. 1:14).

These then were the plants and animals upon which the Palestinian farmer of Biblical times depended. However, it must not be thought that he obtained his food easily, for one of the most constant of the Old Testament pictures is that of the struggle which was involved for the ordinary man if he wished to maintain life at all. The picture given in Genesis 3:17–19 is an unadorned description of the daily life of the Palestinian farmer: "Cursed is the ground because of you; in toil you shall eat of it all the days of your life; thorns and thistles it shall bring forth to you; and you shall eat the plants of the field. In the sweat of your face you shall eat bread till you return to the ground, for out of it you were taken; you are dust and to dust you shall return." The same book gives another picture of the hard life of the shepherd, "By day the heat consumed me, and the cold by night, and my sleep fled from my eyes" (Gen. 31: 40). The Book of Job also describes the desperate straits to which the poor were driven both in the agricultural areas and in the steppe (Job 24:4–12;

30:1–7). On the one hand there was the ever-present threat of famine brought about either by lack of rain or by invasion of the enemy (II Kings 6:24–29; Jer. 14:2–6), destruction by hail (Ps. 78:47), or by locusts (Amos 7:1; Joel 1:2–2:10) or by blasting or mildew (Hag. 2:17). On the other there was the fear of raids from the desert or destruction by storm (Job 1:13–19), when a man might cry, "Suddenly my tents are destroyed, my curtains in a moment!" (Jer. 4:20). Against these things there was little protection and over the head of the farmer hung the everlasting fear that he might plant vineyards and not eat the fruit of them (Amos 5:11; Mic. 6:15; Hag. 1:6, 9).

29. *Cultivation in the desert.* Most of the Palestinian Bedouin do some cultivation, particularly in the wadis. This picture was taken in the Negeb of Cis-jordan near S'baita.

Palestine is not a country where crops grow easily, and nothing there can be obtained without an effort. In contrast to the relatively lazy life of the Egyptian farmer of ancient times, that of the farmer in Palestine was one of unremitting toil. The Gezer Calendar, which dates from about 925 B.C., describes how the year was divided:

His two months are [olive] harvest;
His two months are grainplanting;
His two months are late planting;
His month is hoeing up of flax;
His month is barley harvest;
His month is harvest and festivity;
His two months are vine tending;
His month is summer fruit.[4]

This shows how the work is continuous throughout the year, beginning about September 15, but it says nothing of how the farmer had to supply his garden with water, by bringing "a brook from a river and . . . a conduit into a garden" (Ecclus. 24:30–31), not of how he had to fight from very early days against soil erosion.[5] So unremitting was this toil that it must have seemed to many that they could not hope to succeed unless they were men of whom it could be said, "You shall be in league with the stones of the field, and the beasts of the field shall be at peace with you" (Job 5:23). If he were a shepherd, his troubles were no less, for he had to protect his flock against the ravages of wild beasts and find them pasture, though it might mean taking them tremendous distances to do so. The brothers of Joseph, it will be remembered, had taken their flocks all the way from Hebron to Dothan (Gen. 37:12–17).

Yet the profits from this toil could be wonderful, and an ancient writer says of Palestine, "The land is thickly planted with olives, covered with fields of grain and leguminous plants, rich in wine and honey; the other fruits and dates cannot be numbered, while cattle of all kinds are there in abundance, as well as rich pasture land for them." [6]

CHAPTER IX

Straight Ways and Cities

He led them by a straight way,
till they reached a city to dwell in.
Let them thank the Lord for his steadfast love,
for his wonderful works to the sons of men.
PSALM 107:7–8

IT is always difficult to know, when one is discussing settlements and communications, with which it is better to begin, since the two go together and react upon each other: roads develop in order to join the towns and villages, and, at the same time, towns and villages grow up where the roads meet. It is a double process which is going on all the time. There are some reasons, however, for thinking that we should do better to begin with the roads, since it has been the roads across Palestine, rather than the towns within it, which to a large extent have determined its history.

We have already seen that Palestine forms a bridge between the great empires of the Nile Valley and the fertile plains of Mesopotamia, and that within this bridge area the main lines of relief have helped to channel the trade routes from north to south. The exact line of these routes has very largely been determined by two things,

by the exposure of the soft Senonian chalk which forms narrow valleys between the mountains, and by the existence of certain regions of difficulty, such as mountains, marshes, steep slopes, woodland and desert, which men are not easily able to cross. The purpose of the present chapter is to examine a little more closely the effect of this upon man's movements.

The four major zones of movement from north to south are the Coast Plain, the Cis-jordan hill route, the Rift Valley and the surface of the Trans-jordan Plateau, and corresponding to these four zones there are, both in the north and in the south, four gates into the country. Of the northern gates, that on the Trans-jordan plateau, the Syrian Gate, was overwhelmingly the most important, because of the dominating position of Damascus. This is one of those places in the world where there must be an important town if there are any peo-

30. *The marshes of the Orontes.* These marshes, which are in the extreme north of Syria, are the only large area of marsh still left. However, in Old Testament times marshes were a very serious obstacle to movement.

ple in the region at all, for everything has combined to concentrate settlement upon one point. The two great parallel ranges of the Lebanon and Anti-Lebanon, running from north to south, form an immense double barrier both to easy cross-movement and to the passage of the rain-bearing winds, while the fact that the Lebanon mountains rise almost directly out of the sea has meant that movement by land along the coast is possible only

with difficulty. There is, it is true, the broad rift valley between the two ranges, known today as the Beqa'a and in ancient times variously as the Valley of Lebanon (Josh. 11:17, 12:7) and the Entrance of Hamath (Num. 34:8; Josh. 13:5 and in the books of the Apocrypha as Celosyria, or "Hollow Syria," always associated with Phoenicia, since then as now the two were governed as one province (I Esd. 2:17, 24, 27, 4:48, 6:29, 7:1, 8:67; II Macc. 3:5, 4:4, 8:8, 10:11). However, this was somewhat blocked at either end, in the north by the marshes of the Lake of Homs and in the south by the complicated hilly country created by the meeting there of the Syrian and the Palestinian fault systems. Therefore, though it contained within it the great pagan center of pilgrimage at Baalbek, it tended to be a place to go *to*, rather than a valley to pass *through*.

The difficulties of these two lowland zones and the utter impossibility of the mountains meant that the international routes were pushed eastward onto the plateau. Here, however, the desert sweeps right over to the west, lapping the very foot of the mountains, and forcing the caravans to keep to the mountain slopes, where occasional springs and wells made their passage somewhat easier. The lay of the land, both in the north and the south, has helped to emphasize this, because in the north the Anti-Lebanon broadens north of Damascus, throwing out lines of hills northeastward, like the fingers of an opened hand, and in the south the barrier of basalt leads off toward the southeast. Thus, anyone following the direction of these hills is conducted naturally toward the eastern slopes of the Anti-Lebanon, and especially to that point in the center where the mountains are cleft completely in two, the only place where it is possible to cross them. At that point the strong waters of the River Barada flow out onto the plateau, where they are ultimately lost in the salt marshes, but not before they have fed the huge luxuriant oasis which has made of Damascus the jewel of the Levant. The importance of this cannot be overemphasized, that everything should have conspired to bring together all the natural routes of the country to-

ward that one point where there is a nearly unlimited supply of water. Damascus is therefore the key to the Levant and the failure of the Crusaders to take it at the very beginning of their entry into the country was one of the major causes of their collapse. Its beauty and its luxury in the midst of the semibarren steppe were a never-failing source of wonder, so that Muhammed, when he saw Damascus, refused to enter it, saying that man could enter heaven only once and he did not wish to do so here on earth, and Naaman the Leper asked with reasonable astonishment, "'Are not Abana and Pharpar, the rivers of Damascus, better than all the waters of Israel? Could I not wash in them, and be clean?' So he turned, and went away in a rage" (II Kings 5:12).

From Damascus the roads to the south splay out across the plateau of Hauran, the ancient Bashan. One leads to the point where the Jordan can be crossed at the Bridge of Jacob's Daughters just south of Lake Huleh, and another follows the Yarmuq valley to the bridges south of the Lake of Galilee and so to Beth-shean (Beisan). Two others lead on to the Trans-jordan plateau via Karnaim and Edrei respectively, and a fifth follows the edge of the basalt toward the Jebel Druze.

The other northern gates, which are of less importance, are the Phoenician Gate along the coast and past the Ladder of Tyre into the territory of Asher, the Merom Gate in Upper Galilee and the Valley Gate which leads into the Palestinian rift from the Beqa'a. Of these the Merom

Gate is of largely local significance, for the land to the north of it climbs up into the impassable mountains of Lebanon, but it has to be mentioned because it was possible to come into Palestine this way from Phoenicia and

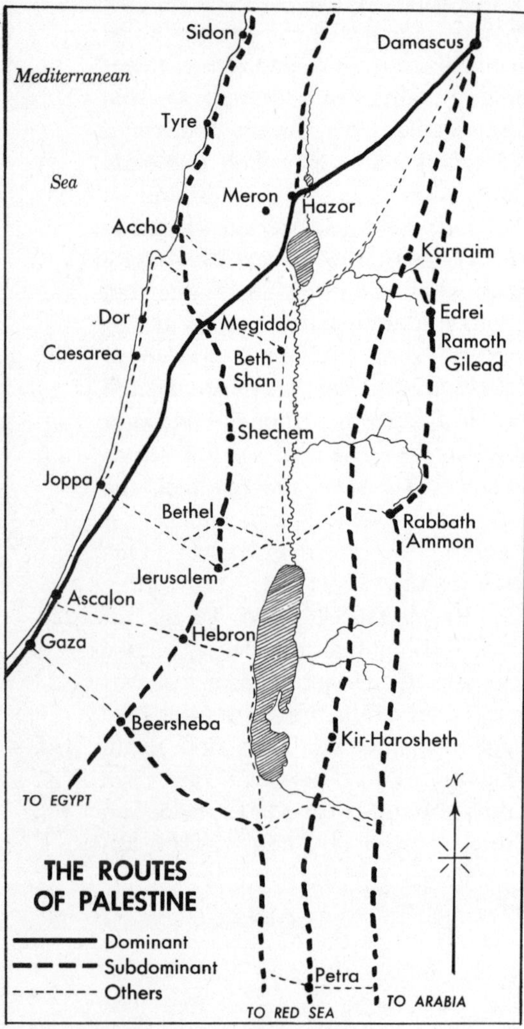

THE ROUTES
OF PALESTINE

——— Dominant
— — — Subdominant
- - - - - Others

Fig. 23.

down the Wadi Lemun to the Lake of Galilee. Merom, where Joshua is said to have defeated the kings of the northern hill country (Josh. 11:1–15),

is probably to be identified with Meirun and the Waters of Merom with Wadi Lemun, and not with the traditional site in the Huleh. The Phoenician and Valley Gates, however, were both important ways of entry into the country, though they cannot be considered the equal of the great Syrian Gate on the plateau.

The routes in from the south included the two Egyptian and the two Arabian Gates:

(1) *The Coastal Gate.* This was by far the more important road from Egypt, following the narrow strip between the desert and the sea into the Philistine territory via Gaza.

(2) *The Sinai Gate.* This is the desert road into the southern Negeb through the Kadesh Barnea region and el-Auja.

(3) *The Red Sea Gate.* This is the entry into Palestine from the Gulf of Aqabah, where was the ancient port of Eloth and Solomon's port and copper-smelting town of Ezion Geber (Num. 33:35; II Chron. 8:17). From here it was possible to go either to Cis-jordan by way of the Arabah or up on to the eastern plateau through Petra. The gate was of tremendous importance because it gave access to the sea route to Arabia, India and East Africa.

(4) *The Desert Gate.* This was the road followed by the great caravans from southern Arabia, and in post-Biblical times was to become the pilgrimage route to Mecca.

Within Palestine itself the roads run from the northern gates to the southern, but not always in a direct route. They may be classified as follows:

A. THE DOMINANT ROUTE

This is the great Trunk Road, which was followed by the armies of Egypt, Assyria and Babylon in their constant wars, and it can rightly be described as one of the primary routes of the world. It enters Palestine through the Syrian Gate, running from Damascus, across the Bridge of Jacob's Daughters and over the basalt dam to the Lake of Galilee. Thence it swings southwestward via the Pass of Megiddo to the Coast Plain and so through Lydda and Gaza to the Coastal Gate and into Egypt. This road is sometimes called "the Way of the Sea" from Is. 9:1, but it is far from certain that this is what the prophet meant and it is better to avoid the term.

B. SUBDOMINANT ROUTES

These are other north-south routes of immense antiquity and lasting importance, but they rank second to the Trunk Road, which stands in a class by itself. They are:

(1) *The Water-parting route.* This follows the hill country along the relatively flat land between the valleys and steep slopes on both the west and the east. Almost all the really important Jewish towns, especially of the Old Testament, lie along this road, the biggest of them standing where convenient valleys make possible crossroads leading up from the west and east. Beersheba is the most southerly, with desert roads coming in from both Egypt and the Red Sea. Northward from there the road mounted the plateau and struck northward through

Hebron, Bethlehem, Jerusalem, Gibeah of Saul, Ramah, Mizpah, Bethel, Shiloh and Shechem, all of which are either on, or very close to, the modern road northward through Hebron and Jerusalem. After Shechem the direction is more confused because of the greater complexity of the structure and relief, but the main road continues roughly northward through Samaria and Dothan to Ibleam, where it is interrupted by the plain of Esdraelon.

(2) *The King's Highway.* This follows the edge of the Trans-jordan plateau from the Red Sea northward through Karnaim to Damascus. In part of this was followed by the Israelites during the Exodus (Num. 21:22) and all the towns mentioned in Numbers 21:27–30 lie along it. It seems also to have been used by the four

31. *Roman camp in the Arnon Valley,* built to protect the King's Highway.

kings during the invasion which is described in Genesis 14, but it is not necessary to connect the name with that invasion, as has been done by some authorities.

(3) *The Pilgrims' Road.* This name

is considerably later than the Bible, since it refers to the Muslim pilgrimage to Mecca, but it is convenient since it emphasizes that the road leads from Damascus, round the edge of the Arabian desert, to Mecca and thence to southern Arabia. In its Trans-jor-

32.   *Roman milestones, in the Arnon Valley.*

dan section it lies in the flat steppe zone between the main river valleys and the desert, and runs through Edrei, Ramoth Gilead and Rabboth Ammon.

(4) *The Arabah.* During recent years this road, which runs from Aqabah to the Dead Sea and up into the mountains by the Ascent of the Akrabbim to Beersheba, has been of only minor importance, though it has been revived by the modern state of Israel. However, in ancient times it gave access from Judah to the vitally important copper mines of Edom and to the Red Sea.

C. MINOR NORTH-SOUTH ROUTES

(1) *The Coast Road.* This was important in its southern section where it coincided with the Trunk Road, and in the north where a road comes southward through the Phoenician Gate. However, in the central Sharon section it must have been of little significance until the Romans built the port of Caesarea, because the development of this coastal section requires the control of the Sharon marshes. Even in modern times there was no through road along the coast until 1937.

(2) *The Galilee water-parting.* This must in some measure be considered the continuation of the water-parting route in the south, which was interrupted by the Plain of Esdraelon. However, the difficulty of the terrain in Upper Galilee has meant that this road, which comes in through the Merom Gate, is of mainly local importance.

(3) *The Jordan Valley.* There is a very important road coming in through the Valley Gate from the north and following the foot of the Galilee mountains southward. Where it joins the Trunk Road stands the ancient Hyksos fortress of Hazor, which "formerly was the head of all those kingdoms" (Josh. 11:10). From there to the Lake of Galilee the Rift is followed by the Trunk Road across the basalt dam, but at Majdal, the ancient Magdala, this turned southwestward up the Valley of the Robbers, and from the Lake of Galilee to the Dead Sea the valley road must be considered to

be an internal one. There were two roads, following the foot of the mountains on either side of the river, but in the south the Dead Sea effectively brought major roads to an end.

Joining these roads to each other there were several other roads running from east to west. Of these the most important were:

(1) Gaza—Abda—Petra.

(2) Gaza—Beersheba—Ascent of the Akrabbim—Petra.

(3) Ashkelon—Gath—Hebron—Engedi. From Engedi a road led southward along the edge of the Dead Sea, so that it was possible to join the main Arabah route as 'Ain Hosb (Oboth?— Num. 33:43) or to turn across the desolate Sebkha (the valley of Salt? —II Kings 14:7) and up the valley of the Zered.

(4) Joppa—Lydda—the Valley of Ajalon ("the way of the ascent of Beth-horon" in Josh. 10:6–14)—Bethel —Jericho. Another route branched off at Lod and went up the Valley of Sorek through Jerusalem to Jericho. From Jericho the road led across the Jordan and up onto the plateau to Rabboth Ammon.

(5) Joppa—Shechem—across the Jordan at Adam (Josh. 3:16) and thence to Gilead.

(6) Accho—Harosheth of the Gentiles — Jokneam — Megiddo — Ibleam. This was the road following the foot of Carmel along the Plain of Esdraelon. From Ibleam, where it was joined by the road from the south, it curved round to Jezreel and down to Bethshean, whence it was possible to cross the Jordan into Gilead.

(7) From Accho by way of the depression of Sahl Battuf (Campus Asochis) to the Lake of Galilee. This was particularly important in Roman times.

(8) From Accho to the Lake of Galilee following the foot of the great scarp of Upper Galilee.

Within this scheme a number of towns are important as route centers, or as "ports," those places where it was necessary to change from one means of transport to another, that is, towns on the edge of the sea or the desert.

True seaports on the Palestinian coast are rare. From Carmel southward the constant deposition of silt from the Nile has produced a flat, sandy, unattractive shore with few opportunities for safe anchorage, even for those tiny barks which hugged the Mediterranean coast in ancient times. The most important harbor was Joppa, where a rocky bluff gives some protection from the southwesterly gales, and which is easily approachable from the hills, but it was not really a good port. Other points along this coast were Ashkelon, Caesarea (which was developed under the Romans and later by the building of an artificial harbor), Dor and Athlit, where the Crusaders built the great Chastel Pelerin. Gaza in the south is today three miles from the sea and, though this distance must have been less in ancient times because of the immense amount of silting which has gone on since then, it was probably never primarily a seaport.

North of the projecting headland of Carmel the picture is different. Here starts the true Phoenician coast with its fragmentary coast plain and its rocky capes and bays, rich in safe harbors, and here today is the important harbor of Haifa. In ancient times, however, this did not exist, the area then being unprofitable marsh, and the chief port was Accho, the Roman Ptolemais. This was the only harbor worthy of the name within the area allotted to the Twelve Tribes and even this did not remain long in their hands, for the tribe of Asher, within whose territory it lay, seems soon to have been absorbed by the Phoenicians who regarded the Crocodile River and the Sharon marshes as their natural frontier and the port of Accho as but one of the many important ports along their shores.

Even the other Palestinian ports were for the most part out of Jewish hands during much of Biblical history. From Joppa to Gaza inclusive was Philistine territory, of which the Jews did not get effective control until late in their history. Caesarea and Athlit hardly existed in the Old Testament period and the remaining town of Dor was a most inferior port shut in on all sides by the highlands of Carmel and the marshes of the Sharon plain. It had been strong when the Israelites entered the country and they had not been able to take it, but it was so strongly protected from the landward side that it could not develop, and though it became Jewish by the reign of Solomon (I Kings 4:11), it never played an important part in the life of the country. For this reason the sea remained an unknown medium to the Jews, who were constantly amazed at and feared the surge "of the sea that is driven and tossed by the wind" (James 1:6). "The wicked," they said,

"are like the tossing sea; for it cannot rest, and its waters toss up mire and dirt" (Is. 57:20). Psalm 107 suggests that when they did venture upon it they did not enjoy the experience.

The desert which surrounds Palestine on the east and south is not unlike the sea, in that there men find no city to dwell in. The traveler on the face of either is unable to stop. He must persevere until he finds the haven where he would be, or "a wayferers' lodging place" (Jer. 9:2) such as an island or an oasis, or he must die. There is no third possibility. For this reason the desert was as much feared by the majority of the Palestinians, clinging to the safety of their narrow bridge, as was the sea, and Psalm 107 rightly compares the two. However, the desert is not sea but land, and there is seldom a sudden junction between it and the cultivated fields, save in the Nile Basin. In the Palestinian region there is always an intermediate zone of semicultivated steppe, facilitating access from one region to the other, and there has not been that sharp line where it could be said, "Thus far shall you come, and no farther, and here shall your proud waves be stayed" (Job 38:11). The desert has thus had a very much greater influence upon the thinking of the Israelites than the sea.

Nevertheless, it has always remained a "foreign" area, which the Palestinians, if they crossed it at all, crossed with much difficulty, after considerable preparation and usually in convoy. It is essentially part of that world where one hoped devoutly that one would reach the other side, "the great and terrible wilderness" and "a land of trouble and anguish" (Deut. 8:15; Is. 30:6), and at its edge stood towns where one had to wait while the vast camel caravans were formed, and to which the Bedouin came to buy those products of the sedentary craftsman and the farmer of which they stood in need. Such towns were Gaza, Beersheba, Petra, Rabboth Ammon, Edrei and Damascus, and of these Petra and Damascus were the trading cities par excellence, the one priding herself upon her security in the clefts of the rocks (Obad. 3) and the other rejoicing in the fertile gardens of her vast oasis. Today only Damascus remains. Of Petra the words of the prophet have become true, "No man shall dwell there, no man shall sojourn in her" (Jer. 49:18).

Within Palestine there were the crossroad towns, which stand either on the spine of the hill country or in the Plain of Esdraelon, towns of the nature of Beersheba, Hebron, Jerusalem, Bethel, Shechem and Samaria and the four strongholds of Jokneam, Megiddo, Taanach and Ibleam, which guard the passes across Mount Carmel. Other important junction towns were Beth-shean and Hazor in the Rift Valley. Outside these towns lay the villages, and it was in these that the great majority of the population lived. Naturally, they are confined to the agricultural areas and grow noticeably fewer toward the desert, but it is possible within the village zone to see a definite grouping according to the nature of the land. This grouping is markedly different on the two sides of the Jordan.

East of the Jordan there are two areas of relatively level land, divided by the rugged slopes of the great westward-facing scarp—the high plateau country and the hot depths of the Jordan Valley. In the Jordan Valley there are but few villages today, but this was not true of the past, and especially of the very ancient past. Nelson Glueck speaks of seventy sites in the Jordan Valley, many having been founded over five thousand years ago, and of more than thirty-five of these as having existed in Israelite times.[1] It would seem that as man learned to exercise greater control over his environment, the climate of the plateau proved more attractive and he climbed up out of the Rift. These can never have been large settlements, and they tended to follow the springline at the foot of the eastern scarp, being, of course, considerably more numerous in the wetter north than in the south. The steep slope of the scarp interrupts the settled region, but once on the plateau the true area of settlement begins. First there are the fortresses. These stand on the edge of the plateau in a long line, where the westward-flowing torrents have cut deep and have thereby created a series of isolated hills between their headwaters, positions of amazing strength. These must have been strong points from the earliest times, and they were fortified by the successive inhabitants of the Biblical period, and thereafter by the Arabs, the Crusaders and the Turks. Petra, the "strong city" of the Edomites and Nabateans; Shobek, the "Montreal" of the Crusaders; Buseira, the ancient Bozrah of Edom; Tafileh, the Tophel of the Bible; Kerak, Kir Harosheth and the site of a huge Crusaders' castle; the Turkish capital of

Es-Salt and the Saracen castle at 'Ajlun in Gilead—these all stand upon this line. It is these fortresses which are connected by the King's Highway, though it will readily be appreciated that the travelers by this road are forced from time to time to plunge into the great canyons which cut the plateau edge, and then climb out of them again. Round these fortresses grew up towns which profited by the protection which they gave, and these were often the chief towns of the region.

Behind these castles lies the agricultural zone with its many scattered villages which get their water from springs or wells. These are much more common in the north with its greater supply of rain and, indeed, south of Kerak the agricultural region becomes so narrow that the villages tend to form but a single line with the fortresses. In Old Testament times the northern region was the rich and fertile Gilead, and in the period of the New Testament it formed part of the district known as the Decapolis, the group of ten wealthy Greek cities lying between Damascus and Amman, then called Philadelphia. Today the ruins of the ancient Gerasa at Jerash are the most spectacular evidence of the wealth of this region, but Gerasa was in its day one of the smaller cities and its buildings could not rival those of Philadelphia for example.

Farther east again is the Pilgrim Road connecting the desert ports, which we have already discussed, and then comes the desert itself. The oases in our area are few, the chief being el-Azraq on the edge of the basalt at the head of the great depression known as the Wadi Sirhan, but in the past, especially in the New Testament period in the heyday of the Nabateans, there were towns extending farther east than they do at present. Along the Wadi Sirhan was a line of wells which made it possible for the Nabateans at Petra to extend their power in a great crescent behind the Roman territory until at one time they dominated Damascus. This explains the statement in II Corinthians 11:32–33, which for so long puzzled commentators, "The governor under King Aretas guarded the city of Damascus in order to seize me, but I was let down in a basket through a window in the wall, and escaped his hands," the difficulty being that Aretas was the king at Petra and it was not then understood how he could have had so much power at Damascus.

In Cis-jordan it is not possible to draw such a schematic picture of the distribution of the settlements, since there is not the same sharp distinction into two areas of level land, one on the plateau and one in the valley. However, an examination of the map of the Arab villages of the Mandatory period, before so many of them were destroyed in 1948, which can be held to reflect in some measure the natural arrangement, reveals some interesting differences in the village distribution between region and region.

First, there are almost no villages at all east of a line drawn from Beth-shean to Beersheba, and those that do exist are small and are situated just beyond the line, which marks where the wilderness begins. If we remember that during the Old Testament period Sharon was uninhabited and that the coast plain south of Sharon was in the hands of the Philistines, it will be seen that what we may call the effective area of Israelite occupation lay within a triangle with its base along the huge fault scarp that divides Lower from Upper Galilee and its apex at Beersheba. To this we must add the Gilead region of northern Trans-jordan, but, even with this addition, that part of Palestine which the Israelites could really call their own was very small and, it is interesting to note, lies very largely outside the modern state of Israel.

Within this triangle there are five clearly marked areas:

(a) Beersheba stands by itself with practically no settlements in the immediate vicinity.

(b) In the highlands of Judaea round Hebron there are several large villages, but almost no small ones.

(c) Between Jerusalem and Shechem there are many small villages, but almost no large ones.

(d) In the hills north of Shechem both small and large villages are common.

(e) Galilee, once again, is a region of many small villages, but few large ones.

This reflects two things, the distribution of the rainfall, which is greater in the north, and differences of terrain. Thus, the lack of any village round Beersheba is to be explained by the lack of water. Villages begin to appear in the Hebron region where there are more springs, but the climate is still not to be trusted and cultivation is mixed with pastoral

farming, the tendency being for the farmers to group themselves together in large villages where there is water and to go out from the centralized settlement with their flocks. In this region was Debir, or Kiriath-Sepher, which at the original entry into the country was captured by Othniel. In reward Caleb gave him his daughter as a wife, and when he asked her what she wanted as a dowry she said, " 'Give me a present; since you have set me in the land of the Negeb, give me also springs of water.' And Caleb gave her the upper springs and the lower springs," for this is a region where water is still scarce (Josh. 15:13–19).

As one goes farther north the rainfall becomes somewhat greater and, which is even more important, more assured. Cultivation becomes more general and there is not the same need for the farmers to be concentrated in one or two favored places. The rainfall is not yet, however, sufficient to support a great population, and so the villages, while they become more frequent, remain relatively small.

It is quite natural, then, that the fourth region, which lies to the north again, should have a supply of rain which permits the scattering of the farming population over the whole area in many small villages and also the growth of several larger settlements.

What is, however, surprising at first sight is the absence of such large settlements in Galilee, the best-watered part of the whole country. The explanation of this must be sought in the nature of the landscape, which is more accidented, cultivation being per-

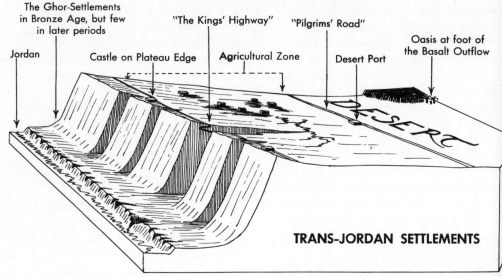

The Ghor-Settlements in Bronze Age, but few in later periods

"The Kings' Highway"

"Pilgrims' Road"

Oasis at foot of the Basalt Outflow

Jordan

Castle on Plateau Edge

Agricultural Zone

Desert Port

DESERT

TRANS-JORDAN SETTLEMENTS

Fig. 24.

force confined to the bottoms of the fertile basins. In ancient times this would have been still further emphasized by the vastly greater amount of woodland in the Galilee region. This fact must be held also to explain the absence of villages on Mount Carmel.

Naturally, the analogy between the Arab villages of the Mandatory period and the settlements of the Biblical period must not be pushed too far. Many fluctuations have taken place in the meantime, and the modern distribution can be taken only as the roughest guide. However, when the proper reservations are made it is certainly suggestive.

Of course, it must not be thought for a moment that the distribution of villages remained constant throughout the whole of Biblical history. We have already seen that the Jordan Valley was more thickly settled in the earlier

period than it was at a later date. Wars also must have caused many changes. The sudden disasters of the Middle Bronze Age surely caused many fertile lands to pass out of use, and the progressive desolation of the Assyrian advance is vividly pictured for us in the pages of the first Isaiah. During the classical period the extension of the *pax Romana* over the whole Palestinian region and the possibility (one mentions it tentatively) that there may have been then a somewhat more assured rainfall meant not only an extension of the settled peoples farther into the desert, but also an intensification of settlement within the region.

The most striking example of changes of settlement in the course of history is to be seen in the fluctuation of settlement in the southern half of Trans-jordan, where there was a gap from about 1900 to 1200 B.C. and another from about 600 to 300 B.C. During these two periods the settled population disappeared and their place was taken by the black tents of the desert nomads.

It will be seen, therefore, that what has been said about the distribution of the population on the two sides of the Jordan can be taken as true only in the general sense of the word and that at any given period there may have been important departures from it.

PART TWO

REGIONAL

CHAPTER X

The Land Before You

*Turn and take your journey, and go to the hill
country of the Amorites, and to all their neighbors
in the Arabah, in the hill country and in the lowland, and in the Negeb, and by the seacoast. . . .
Behold, I have set the land before you.*
DEUTERONOMY 1:7–8

THE geographer is concerned with the surface of the earth as it now is, and with all that passes thereon. To this end he studies such things as the geology, climate, water supply and soils, and these studies are of value to him only insofar as he can make use of them to understand the present landscape. This present landscape is a very complex thing. Underlying it all is the geological structure, which may be thought of as forming a semi-permanent stage on which the drama of history is played out. In any study of the relations between history and geography it is important to realize that this stage is not entirely perma-nent. In one sense, of course, geologi-cal changes are so very slow compared with the life of man that to all intents and purposes the stage is set and un-alterable. The mountains and valleys certainly remain permanent features throughout history, but the impor-tance of them changes. Thus, the Pass of Megiddo was in ancient times one of the major routes from north to south, but in more recent years it has carried only a secondary road, while the southern desert is again acquiring an importance it did not always have in the past. Furthermore, the climate is constantly at work, eroding the mountains, transporting the eroded material and depositing it elsewhere. Even under natural conditions this ac-tion is remarkably speedy so that no land surface has ever been uplifted so fast that it has undergone no changes from erosion before the uplift was finished. Under "unnatural" condi-tions, such as those that occur when man has stripped away the vegetation cover for his own use, changes from erosion may occur so rapidly that they constitute a serious problem within a generation or two. Consequently, we must think of our stage as comparable to the semipermanent sets which are common today in the production of

125

Shakespeare. Certain features of the scenery, such as heavy staircases and columns, are fixed and remain throughout the play, though their importance with regard to the action may vary from scene to scene, but lighter objects can be moved and the whole appearance of the stage may thus be altered. Parts of the stage may

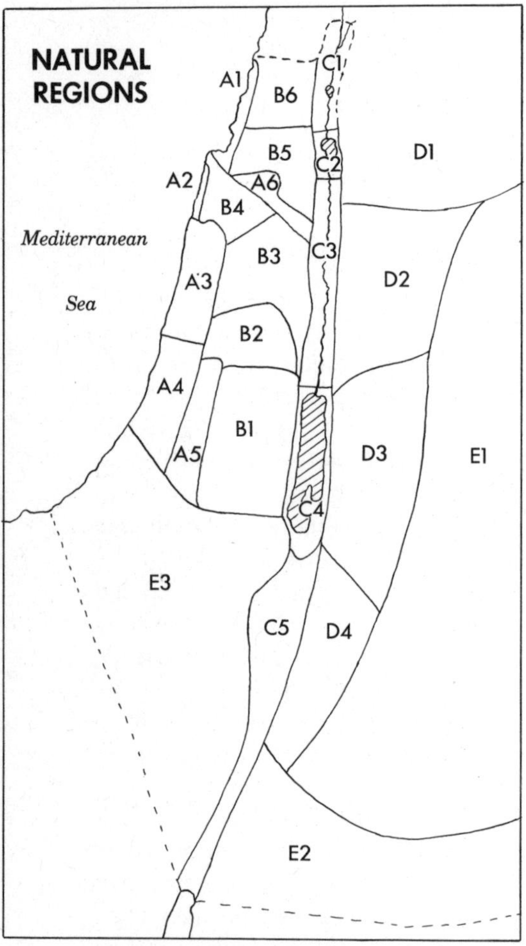

Fig. 25.

be curtained off and used only in certain scenes. This, we shall see, is comparable to the part played by the deserts on both sides of the Jordan,

for at times they were full of activity, but at other periods remained aloof and almost completely outside the drama.

We have till now been examining separately the different materials of which the stage set is made, the geology, the climate, the soils, the vegetation, et cetera. It is now our duty to see how these react upon one another to produce that complex thing which we call the environment, or what we might term the "immediate world" of the men who work and dwell within the boundaries of Palestine. It is surprisingly varied and yet surprisingly the same. There is an underlying unity given by the almost universal limestone and by the dominance of the Mediterranean climate, which makes its influence felt, though not always strongly, even to the desert frontier of the Wadi Sirhan, and this unity makes it perfectly possible to speak of the Palestine region as something recognizably distinct from the other regions which surround it. Within this Palestinian area there is, however, an obvious difference between the desert and the sown, the latter being the region of Palestine proper and the former having such strong affinities with the steppes and deserts of Arabia that, were our purpose geography alone, it would be tempting to leave it severely outside the survey. However, since this study involves the relation of the geography of the country to its history and the effect that the environment has had upon the consciousness of the people, we are bound to include it. The Book of Job alone, to say nothing of the extension of the great Nabatean empire from Petra through this region to Damascus, detaches it from the vast anonymous wilderness to the east, and makes it part of Biblical Palestine.

These two regions of cultivated and uncultivated land must themselves be subdivided into several natural regions where a local unity of structure, climate and vegetation have helped to differentiate the life of the people from that lived by their neighbors only a few miles away. These natural regions can, for the most part, be classed as what the French would call *pays*, in the sense that they have been recognized by the people of the country as each having a distinct nature of its own, and as having quite clearly defined limits.

In the chapters that follow the regions to be distinguished are:

A. THE PLAINS OF CIS–JORDAN

   1. *The Plain of Asher,* or that part of the coast lying north of Carmel.
   2. *The Coasts of Dor,* that part of the coast plain lying immediately west of Carmel.
   3. *The plain of Sharon.*
   4. *The plain of Philistia.*
   5. *The Shephelah,* or foothills of Judaea.
   6. *The central valley,* i.e., Esdraelon and Jezreel.

B. THE HILLS OF CIS–JORDAN

   1. *The hill country of Judah.*

   2. *The hill country of Ephraim.*
   3. *Central Manasseh or Samaria.*
   4. *The Carmel range.*
   5. *Lower Galilee.*
   6. *Upper Galilee.*

C. THE RIFT VALLEY

   1. *The Huleh Basin.*
   2. *Chinnereth,* or the region round the Lake of Galilee.
   3. *The Ghor,* or the valley of the Jordan south of the lake.
   4. *The Dead Sea.*
   5. *The Arabah.*

D. THE HILLS OF TRANS–JORDAN

   1. *Bashan,* the land of the farmer.
   2. *Gilead,* the land of the highlander.
   3. *Moab and Ammon,* the land of the shepherd.
   4. *Edom,* the land of the trader.

E. THE DESERTS

   1. *The eastern plateau of Transjordan.*
   2. *The Wadi Hasma,* lying south of Edom.
   3. *The wilderness of Zin,* or the Negeb of Cis-jordan.

Between E.2. and E.3. there lies the Arabah, which has been included here as part of the Rift Valley, to which structurally it belongs. However, climatically it is part of the desert, and could equally well be included in region E., thus emphasizing the essential unity of the desert crescent, which extends round the south and east of the whole Palestinian area.

CHAPTER XI

The Coastlands

Listen to me, O coastlands,
And hearken, you peoples from afar.
ISAIAH 49:1

THE headland of Carmel and the hills of Lower Galilee which approach very close to it divide the plains of Cisjordan into three groups—the plain of Asher to the north, Esdraelon and Jezreel to the east, and Sharon and Philistia to the south. Although divided by the hills, these plains are not isolated from one another, for Asher is joined to Sharon by a road which runs round the point of Mount Carmel and to Esdraelon by the Kishon gap between Carmel and Lower Galilee. From Sharon to Esdraelon there are the four passes across Mount Carmel.

THE PLAINS OF THE NORTH

A. 1. *The Plain of Asher.* This plain, which extends from Mount Carmel to the northern boundary of modern Israel, is 25 miles long and about 8 miles broad at its greatest extent. It can itself be conveniently divided into two parts by a line running inland from Accho. North of that line, as far as Ras en-Naqura, the ancient Ladder

of Tyre, where the Galilee hills crowd close upon the coast, there is a narrow alluvial plain, some 5 miles wide with a straight coast marked by an intermittent line of low hills, formed of Pleistocene limestone. The size of these hills must not be exaggerated—they are a mere thread—yet because they have hindered the free drainage from the plain into the sea, they have caused the land behind them to be marshy and this has determined very largely where in the plain men can find a place to live. At a few points along the coast the wadis from the well-watered hill country farther east gather themselves together and cut through to the sea, and at the mouth of the most important of these, the Wadi Qarn, stood the town of Achzib on the site of the modern village of Zib. This valley provides a route, albeit a somewhat difficult one, into the high hills of Upper Galilee, and so, at the point where the valley entered the mountains, the Crusaders built their castle of Montfort and in Old Testament times the town of Adnon stood near the entrance to this valley.

These two towns, Achzib and Adnon, stand on the two lines of possible settlements, the one along the coast and the other at the foot of the hills, for in between the two the land was marshy. Of coast towns there were but two, Achzib already mentioned and the vastly more important harbor of Accho, which was the only important harbor within Palestine until Herod the Great developed the artificial port of Caesarea. Accho stands at the northern end of the wide Bay of Haifa and is important because of its good communications with the interior rather than because of its harbor facilities, for it is altogether too exposed to the southwesterly gales of winter and for this reason was inferior to the great Phoenician harbors along the Lebanese coast. Immediately to its east lies the tremendous fault which divides Upper from Lower Galilee, presenting an almost unbroken face to the south. At the foot of this towering wall is the fertile basin of Esh-Shaghur leading to Ramah, which is mentioned as one of the walled towns of Naphtali (Josh. 19:36), still today one of the chief olive-growing districts of the whole country. To the south of this again is a series of down-faulted basins cutting from west to east right across Lower Galilee and making possible fairly easy passage from the sea to the lake. These include the Wadi Halazun, the Sahl Battuf or Campus Asochis of the Romans, and the Turan Valley which was followed by the road from Ptolemais (Accho) past Sepphoris to Tiberias. The concentration of these routes on Accho meant that

it was the natural outlet for Galilee and in Roman times for the rich granary of southern Syria which lay beyond.

South of Accho the plain widens somewhat and the coast curves slightly inland to form the Bay of Haifa. In this bay there has been a heavy deposition of sand as a result of the fact

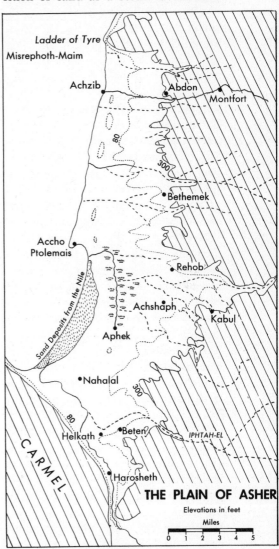

Fig. 26.

that Carmel juts out to sea across the silt-laden current from the Nile. This broad expanse of sand has completely blocked the course of the wadis so that they must seek their outlet either at the northern or the southern end. Thus, the spring which rises in the center of the plain, at what was possibly the site of Aphek (Josh. 19:30), flows northward, collecting on its way the winter floodwaters from the valleys of Lower Galilee. This part of the plain must always have been very marshy.

South of Aphek the land rises slightly, for here a westward extension of the Eocene limestone of Lower Galilee near Shefr 'Amr pushes seaward to meet an outcrop of the Pleistocene limestone. This very gentle swelling of the land divides the drainage so that the Wadi Malik is turned southward to meet the Kishon which has been flowing along the foot of Carmel to enter the sea south of the sand dunes. The Wadi Malik is the Iphtah-el which was the border between Asher and Zebulun (Josh. 19: 14, 27), and in this slightly more elevated southern region lay several towns, such as Nahalal (Tel en-Nahl ?), Beten ('Abtun ?) and Helkath (Tel Harbaj). Farther to the southwest, where the Kishon enters from Esdraelon and where the plain narrows almost to nothing, stood Harosheth of the Gentiles. This important stronghold, where Sisera, the captain of the army of Jabin, king of Canaan, had his headquarters (Judg. 4:2), cannot be identified for certain, though the name is preserved today in Jisr el-Harithiyeh where the road to Nazareth crosses the Kishon, but it is suggested it was possibly Tel 'Amr. Here the

mass of Carmel reaches its greatest height, towering 1650 feet in an almost sheer slope above the narrow valley of the Kishon. When Barak was pursuing the defeated Sisera back to Harosheth (Judg. 4:16) the normally insignificant stream was in full spate, for the battle seems to have been fought in a rainstorm (Judg. 5:20–21), and the water must have been pouring down this slope into a gorged and turbulent flood. It was no wonder that the Canaanite chariots were bogged down in the mud and at the mercy of the lighter-armed Israelites, so that "Sisera alighted from his chariot and fled away on foot" (Judg. 4:15).

This plain of Asher did not play an important part in Biblical history and, indeed, it is doubtful if it ever really belonged to the Jews. It is true that Joshua is reported to have given the whole coastland to the tribe of Asher "as far as Sidon the Great" (Josh. 19: 28), but this cannot have been more than wishful thinking, for they never got control of it. At the most the area that they can have hoped to regard as theirs must have come to an end in the north at Misrephoth-Maim and the Ladder of Tyre. As it is, the history of the tribe of Asher is rather obscure. Judging from certain references in the inscriptions of Thutmose III and Seti I, it would seem that the country was already known as that of Asher. Without going here into the vexed question of what happened during the period of the Exodus and the conquest of Canaan, it certainly seems possible that the tribes of Asher may not have been among those who went down into Egypt, and when the Israelites under Joshua entered the country, they may possibly have found them already established in this region. Here they seem to have had a very subservient position, for the account in Judges 1:31–32 suggests that they had not obtained control of any of the towns. In the Song of Deborah they are blamed because they "sat still at the coast of the sea" (Judg. 5:17), but probably they were in no position to rise against the forces of Sisera who held all the towns of the region. After his collapse, however, they were able at a later date to come to the help of Gideon (Judg. 6:35), for then they were more fortunately placed, being farthest removed from the onslaught of the Midianites, who had swept in from the east.

Nevertheless, after this they seem to have passed permanently under the authority of the Phoenicians, who took possession of Accho, and brought all the coast as far as Carmel and beyond under their control. In the list given in I Chron. 27:16–22 Asher is not mentioned, and though Solomon is reported to have appointed Baana, the son of Hushai, to be in charge of the district of Asher (I Kings 4:16), this probably means only the western slopes and not the plain. In any case he was forced to cede this same region to the Phoenicians before the end of his reign, thus giving them control of the whole of the plain and the approaches from Galilee. They were not to be ousted from this position until the Assyrian conquests in the eighth century.

A. 2. *The Coasts of Dor.* If one were to judge only from a modern physical map, it would seem as if this region ought to be counted as an extension of

Sharon and be included as part of the plains of the south, since the close approach of Carmel to the sea apparently makes a clear division of the plain. However, this division does not seem to have been so clear in the past. If we are right in understanding from the curious statement in Josh. 17:11, "In Asher Manasseh had . . . the inhabitants of Dor and its villages," that Dor was originally considered part of Asher and was later taken over by Manasseh, then it would appear that the writer thought of Dor as being part of the northern plain. Similarly, during the New Testament period this region was left outside the territory of Herod the Great, and later of Herod Agrippa and the Procurators, and was included with the northern district of Ptolemais, whose boundary ran right across Carmel. This can be accounted for only by the fact that the entry into the plain from the south was blocked by the marshes of the Crocodile River, which were then very extensive, and which completely filled the area between the mountains and the sea. Moreover, the only route from the east into this section of the plain emphasized the connection with the north, since it led to Jokneam, which lay at the extreme northwestern end of the plain of Esdraelon, just at the point where it leads northward into the plain of Asher. To this we must add that until Roman times overwhelmingly the most important sea power lay to the north, and, if the land routes of Dor be restricted, the sea is always open. Thus, the Phoenicians were always ready, whenever they were strong enough, to push southward and take control of such harbors as lay along this coast.

Physically also, this section of the coast belongs to the northern type. It is very narrow, being only 2 miles wide by 20 miles long, and along the coast the Pleistocene hills are almost continuous, though south of Dor can be seen the beginnings of the sand dunes which are such a feature of the rest

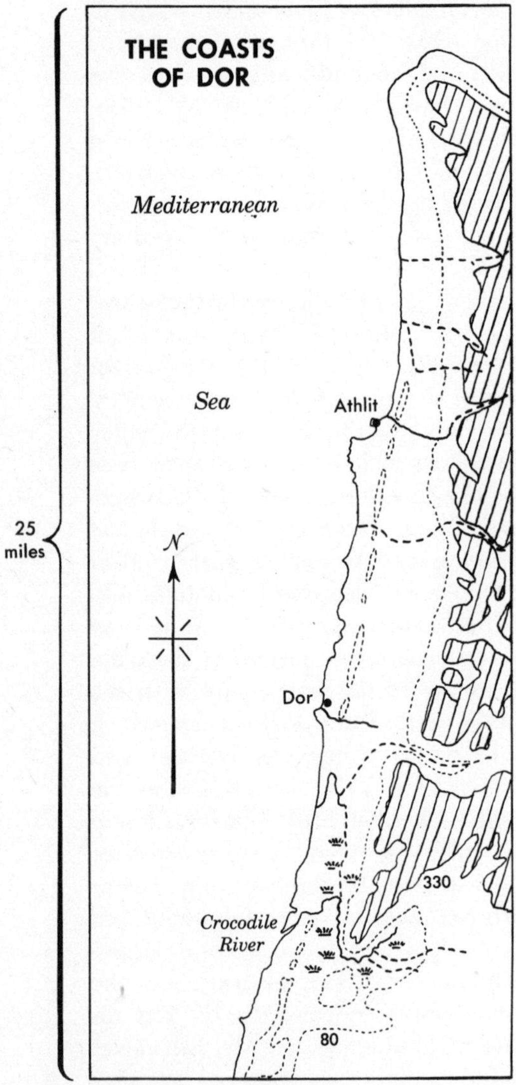

THE COASTS
OF DOR

Mediterranean

Sea   Athlit

25
miles

N

Dor

330

Crocodile
River

80

Fig. 27.

of the coast southward. The low hills and the sand have meant that the streams flowing down from Carmel are easily blocked and the land may become flooded in winter. In ancient times, therefore, the region must have been one of forest and marshland, making movement by land extremely difficult. At the time of the third Crusade it was said that the march southward from Carmel point was impeded "by the thickets and the tall, luxuriant herbage, which struck them in the face, especially the foot-soldiers." [1] Only one town in the whole of this region is mentioned in the Bible, the small harbor of Dor.

This town provides an excellent example of the truth that a position which may seem to be excellent in one period can actually become a hindrance to development in another. In the Bronze Age Dor was one of a series of small harbors in Phoenician hands, a line which stretched along most of the Palestinian and Syrian coast, and Dor must have shared in the wealth which came from the great increase in sea trade during the fourteenth century B.C. However, the upheavals of the thirteenth century and the invasions by the sea peoples in the half century after 1225 B.C. greatly reduced the power of the Sidonians and this section of the coast passed out of their control. Dor became the headquarters of a people called Thekel, who may be akin to the Sikel who gave their name to Sicily. The Israelites were not able to gain possession of Dor when they first came into the country and it is probable that they did not do so until the unification of the kingdom. By the time of Solomon it was one of the twelve districts over which he appointed officers (I Kings 4:11) and after the division of the kingdom it remained within the territory of Israel. After 722 B.C. it passed into the hands of the Assyrians, who made it the headquarters of the Province of Dor, extending southward along the coast from Carmel to Joppa, an arrangement continued later by the Babylonians and the Persians. In 219 B.C. it was besieged unsuccessfully by Antiochus III and in I Maccabees 15:10 ff. there is an account of another siege, which gives a good idea of the forces which were felt to be necessary to deal with this town. However, this was the end of its greatness, for after Herod had built the new harbor at Caesarea it declined.

Its position is the explanation both of its greatness and of its weakness. It is not in itself a good harbor, but it was admirably defended on the landward side by a triple line of defenses. First, there was the great, forested block of Carmel to the east; then there were the marshes and forests of the plain, and finally there were the Pleistocene hills, which were quarried out to form a strong wall immediately behind the town. This isolation from the often turbulent land behind it gave to the inhabitants of Dor a feeling of security from which they sucked out no small advantage. A good example of their freedom of action when no strong government mastered their landward approaches is shown by their treatment of Wen Amon, who came to them as an emissary from Pharaoh in about 1100 B.C., for not only did they maltreat him at Dor, but

pursued him also to Byblos with eleven of their ships. However, this same isolation explains the decline of the city after another harbor had been built at the northern end of Sharon, for then the lack of a real hinterland became apparent. The one clear route which led to Dor across Carmel was that from Jokneam via the Fureidis gap, below the modern wine-producing village of Zichron Yaacov, and this route gave the inhabitants of Dor access to Esdraelon, but the natural outlet for Esdraelon was always the much better port of Accho.

THE PLAINS OF THE SOUTH

A. 3. *The Plain of Sharon.* This section of the plain may be said to extend from the Crocodile River in the north to a line drawn from Joppa to the Valley of Ajalon in the south. At its northern extremity the mountains suddenly recede from the sea, leaving an area of plain some 10 miles wide, with a length of rather less than 50 miles. The Pleistocene hills continue intermittently along this coast, and there are frequent and extensive areas of dune sand, both of which serve to block the course of the rivers. The drainage from the still well-watered slopes to the east is plentiful, but there are only five exits to the sea, of which no less than three are confined to the most northerly 10 miles. The greater part of the middle of this plain is occupied by the outcrop of Mousterian Red Sand, which forms an island of somewhat higher land rising to about 180 feet. In the center this island is unbroken and stretches for over 20 miles from north to south, forcing the streams from the mountains to flow round it. In the south there is the Yarkon which rises as a strong stream at Aphek (the modern Ras el-'Ain and the Roman Antipatris) and this is joined by the Wadi Qana (the Kanah which formed the boundary between Manasseh and Ephraim —Josh. 16:8, 17:9) and by the Wadi Sa'ida from the southern side. To the south of this again is the Wadi Kebir, and it is typical of the disturbed course of the Sharon streams that this little wadi does not empty its waters into

The Red Sand hills do not reach quite to the coast and there is a narrow alluvial valley lying between them and the thin line of Pleistocene hills along the water's edge. The water which collects in this valley makes its way out to the sea by way of the tiny Wadi Faliq, the fifth of the streams which find their way through to the sea.

It will thus be seen that there are two moats, as it were, running north and south of the central higher land of Mousterian Red Sand. In these

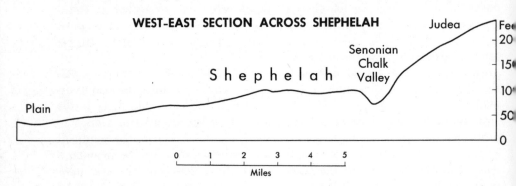

Fig. 28.

the sea at Joppa, as one might expect, but is deflected northward to join the Yarkon just north of the modern town of Tel Aviv. At the other end of the plain there is the big break through of the Iskanderuna, which has been flowing northward along the foot of the Samaritan hills and has collected the waters of several wadis along its route, and a few miles farther north is the Mifjar. This stream drains the western halves of the Wadi Ara and the Wadi Abu Nar, two of the important cross-Carmel routes, and finally there is the Crocodile River, whose marshes formed the southern boundary of the Coasts of Dor.

moats the streams move but sluggishly and tend to become choked with their own alluvium, and thus spread out into broad areas of swamp, which in places were permanent and must have provided a constant barrier to movement. The Crocodile River, the Mifjar, and the Iskanderuna are all of them perennial streams in their lower reaches and their mouths are so choked with sand that they run out to sea at an angle. Behind these clogging sand dunes the waters tend to spill over into large areas, unless they are kept under control. Even today, when so much drainage of this region has been done, the road south of Hadera is sometimes under water in a wet winter. Similarly the Faliq, although it is so tiny and drains such a minute area, tends to form a permanent marsh behind the sand dunes unless it is drained.

Farther up the wadis, where the water flows only in the rainy season, the floods would have been confined to that period and would have dried up in summer. However, it must not be thought that in Biblical times marshes needed to be permanent to discourage movement. Winter flooding was quite sufficient. The roads in those days were mere tracks, and wet weather would soon make them impassable. In regions where the water ran off quickly this was no great matter, but in regions liable to flooding, heavy rain might well render the roads unusable for a week or more, and this might mean that the road would be out of service for the whole of the rainy season, since the water would lie here and there on the road from one storm to another. It was not till the Romans came and covered the country with a network of made roads, which crossed the streams by bridges, that this problem was overcome.

This question of the marshlands of Sharon has been dealt with at some length, because they are the explanation of the extraordinary fact that though this was the only section of the coast which the Israelites effectively possessed, they never colonized it. The Old Testament mentions only two towns in Sharon north of the Yarkon, and each of these towns only once, as part of a list, and not because anything of importance took place at either of them. These towns

are Socoh and Gilgal. The first lies just north of the modern Tulkarm and was one of the district headquarters under Solomon (I Kings 4:10), and the second, whose name persists in the Arab village of Jaljulya about 3 miles north of Ras el-'Ain, was the seat of one of the petty kings who was defeated by Joshua (Josh. 12:23). Moreover, neither of these towns is really in Sharon at all, but at the foot of the hills of Samaria.

Farther south were the towns of Aphek, holding the strong source which feeds the River Yarkon, Gath-rimmon farther down the same river, and Beneberak, Jehud, Beth Dagan, Ono and Lod, which, together with Aphek, form three lines crossing the plain and converging on Joppa. In part this sudden increase of settlements is due to the existence of Joppa itself, but at the same time the problem here is less acute, for there are two valleys running fairly straight across the plain, and the towns keep to the higher land on the sides of these valleys, forming three lines across the plain: from Aphek to Ebenezer, from Ono straight across to a route leading up toward Bethel, and from Lod southeastward toward the valley of Ajalon. Moreover, here the eastern moat no longer exists.

Of these towns Aphek, with its excellent water supply, and Lod, where the Trunk Road crossed the road from Joppa to Jerusalem, were the most important. Lod and Ono are always mentioned together. In I Chronicles 8:12 it is said that they were built by the sons of Elpaal, which suggests that they were fortified towns of some importance. In Ezra 2:33 and

Nehemiah 7:37 they are mentioned as having provided with Hadid (the modern el-Haditha on the hills east of Lod) more than seven hundred of those who returned from the Exile. They were probably among the places settled by the returning exiles, and may have formed the extreme western boundary of settlement, and hence the plain of Ono formed a suitable place for the untoward purposes of Sanballat and Geshem (Neh. 6:2). The "Valley of Craftsmen," which is mentioned in connection with Lod and Ono (Neh. 11:35), was possibly the broad valley which lies between them and, though the reason for the name is obscure, it may be that we have here a memory of the days when "there was no smith to be found throughout all the land of Israel; for the Philistines said, 'Lest the Hebrews make themselves swords and spears'; but everyone of the Israelites went down to the Philistines to sharpen his ploughshare, his mattock, his axe, or his sickle" (I Sam. 13:19–20), in that far-off pre-Davidic period when the Philistines still guarded the secret of smelting iron for themselves.

The difference between the region south of the Yarkon and the region to the north of it indicates a difference between Ephraim and Manasseh, whose mutual boundary was the Kanah until its junction with the Yarkon, and thence along the Yarkon to the sea (Josh. 17:9–10). Manasseh possessed a wide area, but one which was largely useless to her, because of the marshy moat which barred her from it, while Ephraim thrust but a narrow wedge into the plain, yet a wedge where the communications were easier and which pointed to the one port, the town of Joppa. The Valley of Craftsmen was originally claimed by the tribe of Dan as their possession, but they were driven out of it by the Philistines and trekked north to the foot of Hermon (Josh. 19:40–48; Judg. 18), and their territory became a disputed region between the Philistines and the tribe of Ephraim.

There has been a curious and persistent misunderstanding among writers about Palestine concerning the attitude of the Israelites toward the Plain of Sharon. There are only six references to Sharon by name in the Bible: "They dwelt . . . in all the pasture lands of Sharon" (I Chron. 5:16); "Over the herds that pastured in Sharon was Shitrai the Sharonite" (I Chron. 27:29); "I am a rose of Sharon, a lily of the valleys" (Song 2:1); "Sharon is like a desert" (Is. 33:9); "The majesty of Carmel and Sharon" (Is. 35:2) and "Sharon shall become a pasture for flocks" (Is. 65:10). These passages by themselves, combined with our modern knowledge of the valuable citrus groves of the region, undoubtedly suggest something rich and desirable. Rich it certainly was, but too rich. The fertile Mousterian Red Sand which supports the golden orange groves today was then covered with an impenetrable oak forest, and the ancient Israelites seem to have thought of Sharon as something extraordinary, rather exotic and outside their normal experience. In Isaiah 33:9 and 35:2 Sharon is classed with Carmel and Lebanon, both typical of the extreme of luxuriance, and contrasted with the barren deserts of the Arabah. Isaiah 35:2 speaks of the "majesty" of Sharon, and the word used is הדר which has the sense of pride, of something swollen and ornate. It might almost be translated "extravagance," so that the Arabah will receive "the extravagant riches of Carmel and Sharon . . . they shall see the prodigality of our God." The result is likely to be overwhelming rather than comfortable, and there is more than a hint here of the God who is "wont to give more than we desire." *

Even the famous phrase "a rose of Sharon" from the Song of Songs indicates not so much beauty that is natural to the region as something lovely amid much that is ugly, and this is made clear in the lines which follow:

I am a rose of Sharon,
  a lily of the valleys.
As a lily among brambles,
  so is my love among maidens.
As an apple tree among the trees of the
    wood,
  so is my beloved among young men.
               [Song 2:1–3]

The picture here is of a delicate flower in the midst of a rather terrifying jungle, just as the cyclamen may be found growing in the very middle of a thornbush. Similarly in Isaiah 65:10 Sharon is paralleled with the Valley of Trouble (Achor) as two typically inhospitable places. The forests and marshes of the one are to be a place where sheep may safely graze, and the barren slopes above Jericho are to

* Collect for the Twelfth Sunday after Trinity, *Book of Common Prayer.*

carry sufficient grass for cattle. In the two passages from I Chronicles the description is not necessarily different, for the herds which Shitrai was appointed to supervise were probably not large, and it is interesting that the headquarters of Ben-hesed, who was over the plains and all the land of Hepher, was on the very edge of the region at Socoh, 330 feet above sea level (I Kings 4:10).

Historically the chief importance of this region was that at its junction with the hills of Samaria there ran the vitally important Trunk Road. After collecting the four routes from the passes across Carmel, this great highway ran southward on the eastern side of Carmel, hugging the foothills all the way. Socoh, 330 feet above the plain, guards the entrance to the Wadi Zeimar leading up to Shechem and Samaria, and Gilgal, farther south, projects rather further into the plain at a point where a bluff of land some 150 feet above sea level makes possible a settlement guarding the crossing of the Kanah and the beginning of another route up to Shechem. From there the road went to Aphek with its excellent water supply, and after that it crossed the Joppa-Judah route at Lod, before turning toward the coast in Philistia. Between Aphek and Lod the map would suggest that it turned slightly inland to follow the 150-foot contour, and thus avoid the wider sections of the wadis, which were probably difficult to cross in the rainy season.

CHAPTER XII

The Land of the Philistines

*When Pharaoh let the people go, God did not
lead them by way of the land of the Philistines,
although that was near.*

EXODUS 13:17

SOUTH of Sharon, that is south of the Joppa-Ajalon line, the character of the plain changes greatly, for instead of the eastward limit of the plain being the 330-foot contour, as in Sharon, it is now the 1500-foot contour. That it should be necessary to include as part of the coastal plain broad stretches which are well over 1000 feet above sea level may be at first sight surprising, but it is the result of two facts. First, the hill country to the east is higher, rising to 3300 feet near Hebron, and the "plain" in fact deserves its name only in relation to the mountains. Secondly, the 1500-foot contour marks a change in the nature of the landscape, for it is roughly the beginning of the outcrop of Cenomanian limestone, which makes its appearance in the Valley of Ajalon at about 1000 feet and in the district west of Hebron at about 1600. To the east of this line the land rises abruptly and the valleys are precipitous and narrow, but to the west the slopes are more gentle. At the junction of the two types of landscape there is a narrow line of Senonian chalk, extending in a somewhat irregular line from north to south, and forming a valley which can be traced from the Valley of Ajalon through the Arab towns of Deiraban and Tarqumiyeh, and thence in a south-southwest direction. The southern limit of the plain is a wide zone corresponding very roughly with the Gaza-Beersheba road.

The plain itself is divided into two by a line drawn from Lod to Libnah (Tel es-Safi) and thence southward, following the 330-foot contour at first and the 650-foot contour after Libnah. To the east of this line is the region of the Shephelah or "lowland," and to the west is the Plain of Philistia. Structurally it is Philistia which is the continuation of the coast plain, and the Shephelah is an entirely new region, the result of a broad exposure of Eocene limestone.

A. 4. *The Plain of Philistia.* Although

this is structurally the continuation of the plains to the north, yet the distribution of the rocks is somewhat different. The sand dunes are more extensive and may stretch inland for as much as 2 miles; the Pleistocene is found farther inland and is no longer the narrow thread of Sharon and the Coasts of Dor; the Mousterian Red Sand is less common and the alluvium is increasingly lightened by admixture with wind-borne material from the desert, until finally, behind Gaza, the greater part of the plain is covered with true loess. Together with these differences goes a change in topography, for instead of the low plains of the north with their wide patches only just above sea level, the land here begins gradually to rise. Everywhere it is more than 100 feet and in the south round Gaza most of the region is over 300 feet and in places reaches double that.

Despite this rise in the level of the land, the rainfall decreases, and the influence of the desert makes itself more and more felt. Thus, though the sand dunes constitute a formidable barrier along the whole of this coast, rising in places to 150 feet, yet the decreasing frequency of the winter storms and the more rapid run-off provided by the higher land behind the dunes are sufficient to prevent the formation of those marshes which were so important in the north. Instead, the landscape is one of rolling downland, with wide valleys and distant views. Even in early Biblical days the forest cannot have been so thick as it was in the north, and in the southern section trees must always have been rare, until finally they gave way al-

together to scrubland and the barren wastes of the desert. The role played by this region in history has, therefore, been very different from that of its counterpart to the north. Instead of the savage wastes, heaped with greater riches of vegetation than they could

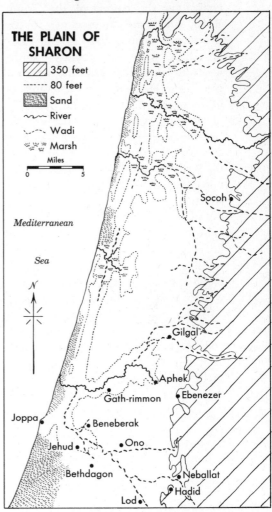

Fig. 29.

bear, a hindrance to movement and settlement alike, it is an open country, full of good grainlands and famous towns, a land where movement is seldom impossible and often easy, and which has played so big a part in history that its inhabitants gave their name to the whole land of Palestine itself.

The change in the nature of the country is immediately shown by the change in the course of the Trunk Road, which no longer clings to the dry slopes at the foot of the eastern hills, but cuts boldly southwestward until it follows the seacoast past Gaza. Henceforward its course is no more determined by the necessity of avoiding swamps, but increasingly by the necessity of finding water, a necessity that becomes more apparent the farther south that one goes. In the northern half of Philistia the villages still tend to keep to the higher part of the plain and the roads still avoid the valleys, for the possibility of winter flooding is not exhausted, but in the south, on the other hand, the villages creep down into the valleys, where water is easier to obtain, and the roads cross hill and wadi indiscriminately.

Judges 15:5 speaks of grain and olive orchards, but the former must always have been more characteristic of this region, for we are here close on the edge of the true Mediterranean climate, where alone the olive will consent to grow. Today there are good olive groves on the coast at al-Majdal, behind the ancient Ashkelon, and at Gaza, but immediately away from the coast the rolling plains, with their increasingly steppelike climate, are more suited to the growing of grain, wheat in the north and barley, together with much pastoralism, in the south. The chief problem, especially in the south, must have been the danger of drought,

and this raises a difficulty about the story in II Kings 8:1–2, where Elisha tells the Shunammite woman to go to the land of the Philistines to escape the famine. Now, Shunem is on the edge of the well-watered valley of Jezreel, whither before now people from the less-favored south have been forced to take their flocks for pasture (Gen. 37:13–17. Aref el-Aref, in *Bedouin Love, Law and Legend*, tells how the Bedouin of the Beersheba district still call 1927 "sanet Beisan," since in that year the government moved them to Beisan on account of the great drought in the south). It seems hardly possible, therefore, that the famine can have been due to a shortage of rain, and we must assume that, as in the preceding story, it was the result of war.

There are two other dangers of this region to which George Adam Smith rightly draws attention, the danger of plague and the danger of war, both of which arise from the fact that Philistia lies athwart the great route from Egypt to the north, protected by no natural barriers at either end. Gaza alone stood in the way of the Egyptians, but once they had taken it there was nothing to stop their sweeping northward to Megiddo. Hence it was there that Josiah made his futile attempt to check the advance of Pharaoh Necho, when he "went up to the king of Assyria to the river Euphrates" (II Kings 23:29). Likewise, after an army from the north had taken Megiddo, there was little to stop it from advancing into Philistia, though armies from that direction might find it necessary to protect their lines of communication by warding off the possibility of a flank attack from Samaria. So it was that the people of this plain saw the procession of Egyptian armies marching northward from the third millennium B.C. onward, and the armies of the north and of Mesopotamia trudging southward to their attacks on Egypt. All these had to pass through Philistia, which must have suffered as much from the onslaughts of war as she gained from the richness of her trade. "Rejoice not," said Isaiah, "that the rod which smote you is broken. . . . Melt in fear, O Philistia, all of you! For smoke comes out of the north, and there is no straggler in his ranks" (Is. 14:29, 31).

It is not necessary to dwell at length on the dangers of the plague. Pestilence was not unknown in the rest of Palestine, and was counted as one of the four great scourges of God (Ezek. 14:21), but the "evil diseases of Egypt" were proverbial (Deut. 7:15, 28:60; Amos 4:10), and it could not but be that the Philistines, who held the very gate into Egypt, were particularly exposed to them. It is no matter of chance that two of the best-known stories about this part of the country concern an outbreak of plague. The first is the story of the capture of the Ark and of the troubles the Philistines endured as long as it was in their territory (I Sam. 5 and 6), and the second is the story of the destruction of Sennacherib's army, which at the time was warring against Libnah (II Kings 19:8, 35–37), a story which, as is well known, is borne out by Herodotus.

The five great towns of the Philistines were Gaza, Ashkelon, Ashdod, Ekron and Gath. Gaza is one of the permanent sites in history, as necessary a place of habitation as Damascus in the north, at the meeting point on the great Trunk Road of the desert and the cultivated land. Ashkelon stands where a line of low cliffs creates a break in the sand dunes, its Philistine ruins now covered by the remains of the greater Roman and medieval cities. Ashdod (the modern 'Isdud), holds a position where the three wadis from Libnah, Moreshah and Lachish gather behind the sand dunes before cutting through them together rather farther north. There is one more coastal town on this road at Jabneel, where it crosses the Nahr Rubin, coming from the valley of Sorek. Of these four towns along the coast only the two in the north control a wadi crossing, for in the south the streams are so intermittent as no longer to provide a serious obstacle. These two northern towns were among those taken by Uzziah in his wars on the Philistines, the last time that the people of Judah were reported to have been successful against them before the exile (II Chron. 26:6).

Ekron and Gath guard the landward frontier. Gath can be placed with some certainty at 'Iraq el-Manshiyeh at the point where the Qubeiba wadi leaves the Shephelah. It stands face to face with Moreshah and Lachish, and was the scene of constant fighting, being a frontier town from which attacks on the highlands of Judah were made, and as such it passed into the Hebrew language as a proverbial symbol of the hated Philistines themselves (II Sam. 1:20; Mic. 1:10). The people of Gath seem to have been prepared to receive political refugees from Judah and to make use of them. Thus, David himself took refuge there (I Sam. 27:2) and so did the slaves of Shimei, who was forbidden to leave Jerusalem. When Shimei went in search of them Solomon seems to have been afraid that he was also disaffected and had him killed (I Kings 2:36–46). It was among the places taken fortified by Rehoboam (II Chron. 11:8), and it was taken also by Hazael who was pushing his way round by the coast in an attempt to attack Jerusalem (II Kings 12:17). Uzziah later recaptured it and destroyed it, apparently not rebuilding it as he did to Ashdod (II Chron. 26:6). Amos speaks of it as having been recently destroyed (Amos 6:2), and it is not mentioned with the other Philistine towns in the writings of the prophets (e.g., Amos 1:8; Zeph. 2:4; Zech. 9:5–6).

Ekron is mentioned several times as being one of the border towns (Josh. 15:11, 19:43; I Sam. 17:52), but it did not hold such an important position as Gath, and therefore played a less important part in history. Its exact position is uncertain, but it seems to have been somewhere near 'Aqir, southeast of the modern town of Rehovoth. Apparently it was one of the centers of soothsayers, for whom the Philistines were noted (II Kings 1:2; Is. 2:6).

A. 5. *The Shephelah.* The region to the east of the plain of Philistia, lying between it and the mountains, is one which does not occur farther north. Here there is a broad crop of Eocene limestone, divided from the Cenomanian limestone of the Judaean mountains by the long narrow valley of Senonian chalk. The region which is thus enclosed between the Philistine plain and the mountains is a rocky plateau, reaching 1500 feet in the south, but cut by frequent valleys. Its name *Shephelah* or "lowland," is derived from the root שׁפל, meaning to humble or to make low, and George Adam Smith has rightly pointed out that the word has in the Old Testament a definite geographical significance, being normally used to describe this rocky Eocene plateau, which, although elevated above the plain, is low in comparison with the much higher mountains to the east.[1] It occurs twenty times (Deut. 1:7; Josh. 9:1, 10:40, 11:2 11:16 twice, 12:8, 15:33; Judg. 1:9; I Kings 10:27; I Chron. 27:28; II Chron. 1:15, 9:27, 26:10, 28:18; Jer. 17:26, 32:44, 33:13; Obad. 19; Zech. 7:7) * and, with the possible exception of Josh. 11:2, 16, it always refers to this region between the Philistine plain and the mountains. It is therefore a pity that the Revised Standard Version does not keep to the use of the proper name, with its obvious regional significance, which it has adopted for the books of Kings and Chronicles. That it has this regional meaning is clear from II Chron. 26:10 and 28:18, for in the first passage the Shephelah is distinguished from the Plain, and in the second the Philistines, who lived in the Plain, made raids on the Shephelah.

The real problem is the meaning of the word in the 11th chapter of Joshua, where it is twice used to describe some northern region. In verse 2 it is

---

* In Josh. 12:8 the RSV omits the words "and the Shephelah" after "the hill-country," though without any explanation. That this district is intended is surely clear from the mention of Adullam, one of the Shephelah towns, in the list that follows.

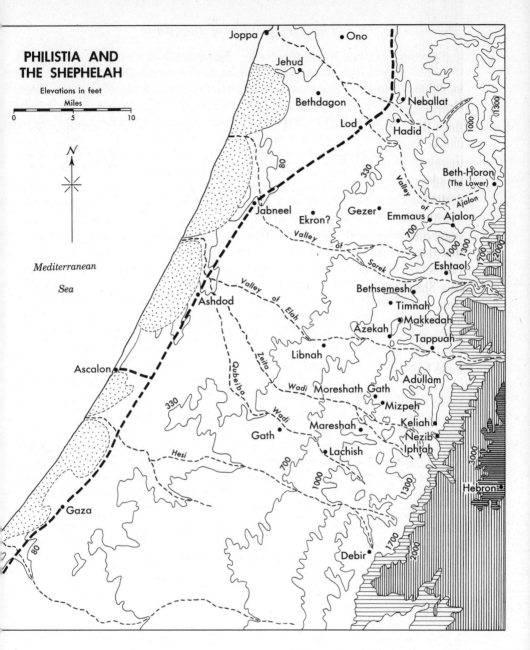

PHILISTIA AND
THE SHEPHELAH

Elevations in feet

Miles

0   5   10

N

Joppa
Ono
Jehud
Bethdagon
Neballat
Lod
Hadid
Beth-Horon
(The Lower)
Jabneel
Gezer
Ekron?
Emmaus
Ajalon
Valley
of
Ajalon
Eshtaol
Valley
of
Sorek
Ashdod
Bethsemesh
Timnah
Valley
of
Elah
Azekah
Makkedah
Tappuah
Libnah
Ascalon
Adullam
Qubeiba
Zeita
Wadi
Moreshath Gath
Mizpeh
Wadi
Mareshah
Keliah
Gath
Nezib
Iphtah
Hesi
Lachish
Hebron
Gaza
Debir

Mediterranean

Sea

Fig. 30.

grouped with the northern hill country, the Rift Valley south of the Lake of
Galilee, and the heights of Dor, which
may be either Carmel or the low
Pleistocene hills which provided the

immediate defense of the town. Then
in verse 16 mention is made of "the
Shephelah, and the Rift Valley, and
the hill-country of Israel and its Shephelah." "The Shephelah" is obviously the district between Philistia

and Judaea, but the meaning of the "Israelite Shephelah" is less clear. It is possible that it means here merely the low-lying country, which might be either Esdraelon or the coast plain. However, this is not entirely likely, since there were well-known regional names for both these districts, and therefore it would probably be best to adopt George Adam Smith's suggestion that it means the land between Carmel and Samaria.[2] This suggestion is particularly attractive in that this central section of the arm of Carmel has many similarities with the true Shephelah. It forms a rocky plateau which is above the plain but lower than either the headland of Carmel or the hills of Umm el-Fahm which form the edge of Samaria. Both of these higher areas are formed of Cenomanian limestone similar to that of Judaea, but in the central, rather lower, section the Eocene limestone has been preserved. This section is, in fact, structurally the continuation of the true Shephelah and in its general appearance is strikingly similar.

This region of the true Shephelah in the south is one of the most important historically in the whole of the country. Though bare of woods today, it seems in the past to have been famous for the number of its trees, "as plentiful as the sycamore of the Shephelah" being a proverbial simile for a vast number (I Kings 10:27; II Chron. 1:15, 9:27; also I Chron. 27:28). The most casual glance at a large scale map will furnish proof of its historical importance, for there is no other region in the whole of the country where ruins are more thickly scattered. This importance lay in its relation to the two regions on either side of it. For the people of Judah, perched on their mountains, it was the glacis which served as their first line of defense against the Philistines, but for the Philistines it was the first step to the conquest of the hills. Thus it played the part of a buffer zone, belonging neither to one country nor to the other, a debating ground whereon they waged their incessant bloody contests, so that at times the Philistines "devour Israel with open mouth" and at times Ephraim and Judah "swoop down upon the shoulder of the Philistines in the west" (Is. 9:12, 11:14).

Despite its height, it is not part of the mountains, a vital fact which the Israelites grasped when they called it the "lowland," for in between them there is the long moat of Senonian chalk. This can be traced from Ajalon, through the modern village of Deiraban to Tarqumiyeh (possibly the ancient Iphtah). Thereafter the valley is not so apparent, but the steep scarp on the east continues to Debir (Tel Beit Mirsim), after which the valley once again becomes more obvious. It was this valley which was the true defense of Judah, for it meant that whereas conquest of the Shephelah was always a necessary preliminary to the conquest of the mountains, it was only a preliminary, so that many famous armies have taken possession of the Shephelah and yet have failed to conquer Judah. The Philistines themselves, though they invaded the Shephelah again and again, never succeeded in gaining control of the mountains, and Sennacherib, though he laid waste the whole of this region, was unable to make himself master of

Jerusalem. In his turn Richard I of England, though he fortified and occupied the Shephelah, had to be content with but a distant view of the Holy City. Even today the same holds true: the modern state of Israel holds most of the Shephelah, but the mountains are denied them. Part of Jerusalem is theirs, it is true, but that is because they were already there when the fighting broke out in 1948, and it was only with the greatest difficulty that they managed to keep control of the narrow corridor which gives them access to the city.

This narrow division between Judah and the Shephelah was marked by a line of fortified towns, for it must always have been a zone of tension. In the north is Ajalon, and then in order come Asnah, Eshtaol, close to the home of Samson (Judg. 13:25), Zenoah, Tappuah, Adullam, where David gathered together "every one who was in distress, and every one who was in debt, and every one who was discontented" (I Sam. 22:1–2), Keilah, where the Philistines robbed the threshing floors and which was saved by David (I Sam. 23:1–5), Nezib and Iphtah. The interruption of the valley after Iphtah interrupts also the line of towns, so that we have only Ashnah and Saphir, standing a little back from the foot of the scarp, and finally Debir, whose frequent mention in the Book of Joshua attests its importance as guarding the back door into the mountains (Josh. 10:38, 39, 11:21, 12:13, 15:15, 49, 21:15; Judg. 1: 11; I Chron. 6:58). From Debir it was possible to go up into Judaea and approach the highlands round Hebron from the south. Joshua, it would seem,

gained control of the chief cities of the Shephelah first, then advanced on Hebron, and after that "with all Israel turned back to Debir, and assaulted it" (Josh. 10:38), since possession of Debir helped to prevent an attack on the rather lower-lying southern mountains of the country.

Running across the Shephelah from the east to west is a series of narrow valleys which form the natural routes across the region. First is the Valley of Ajalon, the most important of all the routes up into Judaea from the plain, and differing from the other valleys in being a wide down-faulted basin instead of a river valley. Through it an easy road goes up past the two towns of Beth-horon, the Upper and the Lower, and on reaching the highlands it divides, giving access either to Bethel or to Jerusalem by way of Gibeon. It was in this valley that Joshua commanded the sun and moon to stand still in the great battle in a hailstorm (Josh. 10:10–15), and it was by this route also that the Philistines fled after they had been defeated at Michmash (I Sam. 14:31) and that Judas Maccabeus overthrew the army of Seron, a prince of Syria (I Macc. 3:13–24). Beth-horon the Lower was fortified by Solomon and Ajalon by his successor Rehoboam, but in the days of the weak king Ahaz Ajalon fell to the Philistines (I Kings 9:17; Chron. 11:10, 28:18). In 1948 the Arab Legion overflowed from the mountains by this same valley to cut the Jewish life line from Tel Aviv to Jerusalem, and the present armistice line between Jordan and Israel extends from the mountains at this point to include Latrun, and thereby emphasizes the importance of this valley. Apart from Ajalon, the approach to this valley from the plain was controlled by Emmaus, Shaalbim (Josh. 19:42; Judg. 1:35; I Kings 4:9) and by Adithaim (Josh. 15:36). Farther to the west, out in the Shephelah, is Gezer, and then in a straight line Gibbethon and Ekron, all of them fortress towns (I Kings 9:15–17, 16:15–17).

The second of the transverse valleys is the Valley of Sorek (the Wadi Surar), famous for the exploits of Samson. This great wadi pierces the hill country like a trident, with all three prongs pointing at Jerusalem. On the north of it are Eshtaol and Zorah, with somewhere between them Mahaneh Dan (Judg. 13:25), and on the south is Timnah where a young lion roared against Samson and whence he took his first wife (Judg. 16). On the southern side also is Beth-shemesh, where the Philistines handed back the Ark to the Israelites, the valley of Sorek being the "highway" taken by the cattle, "lowing as they went; they turned neither to the right nor to the left." The most northerly of the three prongs of this valley leads up into the mountains at Qiriat el 'Anab, where it is crossed by the modern road, and this is probably the site of Kiriath Jearim, where the Ark was kept for some twenty years, and where it was found by the people who came with David to bring it to Jerusalem (I Sam. 7:2; II Sam. 6:2; I Chron. 13:6; Ps. 132:6). Beth-shemesh was also the place where Jehoash king of Israel and Amaziah king of Judah faced each other in battle (II Kings 14:11), for it would appear that Jehoash, who was a strong ruler,

was pressing against the Philistines in this region, as did so many of the Israelite kings, when he was challenged by the foolhardy Amaziah. The result of this battle was that Jehoash was able to make his way up the valley and plunder Jerusalem before he returned to Samaria.

The third valley is the Wadi es-Samt, the valley of Elah where Goliath was killed, between Socoh and Azekah. Socoh is probably Khirbet 'Abbad on the southern side of the valley and Azekah is the little village of Zakariyeh on the north, the contest taking place in the valley between them (I Sam. 17:1–2). At the point where this valley issues into the plain is the village of Tel es-Safi, the Libnah of the Old Testament and the Blanchegarde of the Crusaders, the white cliffs of the region having given it its name in both periods. Libnah must always have been an important stronghold, but one which lay outside the true Israelite sphere of influence, so that they held it only when the government was strong, and lost it when the central authority was weak, as in the days of Jehoram the son of Jehoshaphat (II Kings 8:22). It was against Libnah that the king of Assyria was fighting at the time of his abortive attempt to take Jerusalem (II Kings 19:8).

The fourth valley is the Wadi Zeita, the shortest route up to Hebron, and controlled on either side of the Shephelah by Iphtah and Mareshah, whose place was later taken by Eleutheropolis, on the site of the modern Beit Jibrin.

Fifth in the series comes the Wadi Qubeiba which is dominated by Lachish, the scene of many eventful happenings in Jewish history, and particulary important as being one of the frontier fortresses of of the Shephelah on the south. Joshua took it on his advance southward after he had taken Libnah (Josh. 10:31) and in the days when Judah was strong it was counted as one of the frontier posts and as such was fortified by Rehoboam (II Chron. 11:9). Amaziah fled there for refuge, though in vain (II Kings 14:19), and both the Assyrians and the Babylonians besieged and took it (II Kings 18:14; Jer. 34:7). Gath, lying rather farther to the west, owes its importance to the fact that it was able to stand guard over both the last two valleys, each of which leads up to Hebron.

This really brings us to the end of the true Shephelah, for the region to the south does not seem to have borne the name and grades off into the deserts of the Negeb. However, one might notice another valley leading across into the mountains, the wadi Suweitim, guarded at its western end by the minor fortress of Chitlish (Josh. 15:40), and at its eastern end by Debir, whose importance has already been discussed.

CHAPTER XIII

The Rich Valley

*Woe to the proud-crown of the drunkards of Ephraim,
and to the fading flower of its glorious beauty,
which is on the head of the rich valley of those
overcome with wine!*

ISAIAH 28:1

THE last of the three groups of plains on the western side of the Jordan consists of the plain of Esdraelon and the valley of Jezreel, the only two which can be said to have lain entirely within the Jewish territory, a possession for which they paid very dearly. It was the fact that this vital area lay within the boundaries of the northern kingdom which, more than any other single factor, led to its downfall a century and a quarter before the collapse of Judah, on its windswept mountains to the south. Of the two plains, that of Esdraelon is the larger, forming an isosceles triangle with its base extending along the foot of Carmel from Jokneam in the northwest to Engannim (the modern Jenin) in the southeast, a distance of some 20 miles and its apex at the modern settlement of Tel 'Adashim, 18 miles due north of Jenin. The River Kishon flows in an arc through this triangle from the southwestern corner to the north-

western, and then makes it way out through the narrow gap near Tel el-Qassis into the Plain of Asher. Though famous in history this river is often a disappointment to visitors, when they first catch sight of it on a journey from Haifa to Nazareth, for it is no more than a little brook, and in the plain of Esdraelon the bed is dry during the summer months. However, it is not fitting in any student of Palestinian geography to despise the day of small things, and the importance of this little stream was not exhausted by the part it played in the defeat of Sisera.

The whole expanse of the plain is floored with alluvium, and to the casual observer appears to be almost level, but, in fact, it descends very gradually from about 330 feet above sea level near Jenin to some 80 feet at the point where the Kishon leaves the plain in the northwest. This slow descent is interrupted in the center by a line of slightly higher land, the merest swelling, raising the level no more than 100 feet, which forms a perpendicular dropped from the apex at Tel 'Adashim to the base of the triangle at Megiddo. The slopes of this slight rise are so gradual that it is not clearly visible, even on the ground, but for the modern observer it has been made more obvious by a line of white Israeli houses built along its crest. This gentle wave in the level surface of the plain is the result of volcanic activity, and it is this which has deflected the course of the Kishon toward the north.

Structurally the plain is a fault basin, with the dominant line of faulting from northwest to southeast, which is the direction of the great fault line that forms the base of the triangle, and is repeated again in the Valley of Jezreel. Other faults cut off at an angle to this, the most striking of them being the NNE–SSW fault which forms a great scarp just south of Nazareth and towers nearly 1000 feet above the surface of the plain. Part of this scarp at Jebel Qafsa is perhaps obviously, but almost certainly wrongly, called the Mount of the Precipitation, since it is believed to be the place where the Nazarenes tried to murder Jesus (Luke 4:29), but it would hardly seem that by any stretch of the imagination it could be called "the brow of the hill on which their city was built." Another fault cuts back from this point toward Harosheth and yet another is probably responsible for the almost straight eastern edge of the plain.

From about the middle of this straight eastern edge the corridor of Jezreel leads off toward the south-east. In contrast to the almost level floor of Esdraelon, Jezreel drops steadily toward the Rift Valley, passing below sea level in about 2 miles and reaching −400 feet at Beth-shean some 11 miles farther on, where there is a sudden drop of about 350 feet over the edge of the step which forms the western boundary of the Ghor. It was on this step that stood the important fortress town of Beth-shean.

For the whole of its length the valley is but a narrow one, seldom more than 2 miles wide. It is drained by the little river Jalud, which rises at the Spring of Harod not far from Jezreel (Zir'in) toward the northwestern end. This is the place where Gideon picked out the three hundred who were to accompany him, and also "the fountain which is in Jezreel" where the Israelites encamped before the disastrous battle of Mount Gilboa (Judg. 7:1; I Sam. 29:1). The disposition of the armies at this historic battle site was very similar on both occasions, for each time the Israelites were encamped on the slopes of Mount Gilboa to the south, and their enemies on the slopes of the Hill of Moreh opposite and in the valley. However, the results of the two battles were different, for in the earlier battle Gideon's army routed the Midianites, but in the second the Israelites fled before the Philistines after one of the most shattering defeats they ever suffered at their hands.

Confined into such a narrow space between the parallel faults on either side, Jezreel cuts through between the limestone hills of Gilboa and the volcanic mass of the Hill of Moreh to provide an important strategic route from Esdraelon to the Ghor. Well supplied with water from the hills on either side, and a stranger to the cold of winter, well drained because of its slope, but not so steep that the rush of water carries away the soil, Jezreel is one of the richest sections of the country and one whose fertility is well reflected in the name ("God will sow"). Hosea makes a pregnant pun on this name when he is explaining how God uses punishment to draw his people to him again and to cause them to receive even greater treasures than they had in the past: "In that day I shall answer, says the Lord, I shall speak to the heavens, and they will speak to the earth and the earth will speak to the grain and the wine and the oil, and they will speak to Jezreel. I will sow him to me in the earth; and I will have pity upon the Unpitied, and I will say to those who were Not-My-People, 'You are my people'; and they shall say, 'Thou art our God'" (Hos. 2:21–23).* The rich harvests in the valley where Hosea had earlier prophesied disaster (Hos. 1:5) are to be the sign that God will once again have mercy on his people.

Riches and disasters—such are the grim gifts of these interior plains to their possessors. The riches came not only from the fertile alluvium, for Esdraelon indeed was always inclined to be marshy, but even more from the many routes which crossed them. Jezreel was not merely a passage to the Ghor' and Beth-shean not only the guardian of the valley, for they faced

* Author's translation. The repetition of "answer" in the RSV, though correct, is a little confusing in English, since it obscures the fact that each "answer" is a command to begin their work again.

the richly wooded mountains of Gilead whose wealth was proverbial. The fords of the Jordan here are not difficult and the ascent into the mountains fairly easy, so that Beth-shean at times seemed to belong almost more to the eastern side than to the west. Thus the Roman Scythopolis, whose name recalls the capture of Beth-shean by the Scythians in the late seventh century B.C., was the only member of the Decapolis which lay on the western side of the Jordan, and very much earlier it was from Jabesh Gilead that "all the valiant men arose, and went all night, and took the body of Saul, and the bodies of his sons from the wall of Bethshan" (I Sam. 31:12). It was from Gilead also that Jehu came to Jezreel and "slew all that remained of the house of Ahab in Jezreel, all his great men, and his familiar friends, and his priests, until he left him none remaining," a policy of savagery which prompted Hosea to use the name of Jezreel in execration (II Kings 10:11; Hos. 1:5).

Jezreel, however, is not the only route into Esdraelon. There is also the important gateway from the plain of Asher which was guarded by Harosheth of the Gentiles, so that there is a line of towns from Accho to Beth-shean marking what is unique in Palestinian geography—a lowland route from the sea to the Jordan. The land is nowhere higher than 350 feet, and the slopes are everywhere gradual, with the added advantage of relatively easy access to the eastern plateau. The importance of this corridor, therefore, is very difficult to over-emphasize.

At the apex of the triangle of Esdraelon there is another gateway from the northeast, watched over by the solitary hill of Tabor, where Barak gathered his forces before fighting against Sisera, and through this gate the Trunk Road entered the plain from the direction of the Lake of Galilee. On the southern side of the gate, on the lower slopes of the Hill of Moreh, are the twin villages of Nain and 'Indur, the Nain and Endor of the Bible. Today each is merely a huddle of cottages, nestling on the hillside above the modern road from Affuleh to Tiberias, not to be compared with the thrusting Jewish settlements which spring up almost daily on the plain below them. Yet it is difficult to pass by them unmoved, for it was to Endor that the first king of Israel made his way, demoralized and despairing, skirting the enemy camp by night in search of the magic arts which earlier he had ruthlessly condemned, and it was there that he heard his own death foretold (I Sam. 28:3–25). Not two miles away as the crow flies, at the village of Nain, the true King of Israel, whose coming the prophets had longed to see, showed his power over death itself by a word (Luke 7:11–17). Few indeed are the places, even in this country, which can seem so little, and yet which mean so much.

On the opposite side of the plain to this gateway are the four fortresses which guard the routes across Carmel, spaced some 5 miles from one another along the base of the triangle, Jokneam, Megiddo, Taanach and Ibleam. Jokneam and Megiddo stand at the exit into the plain of the two chalk valleys which mark the edge of what

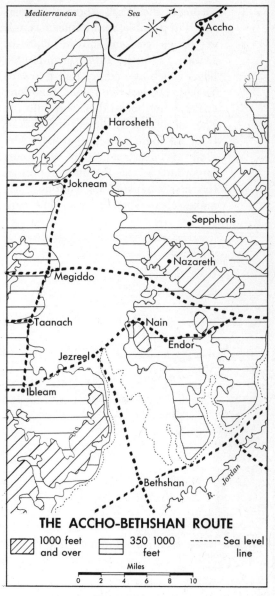

Fig. 31.

we have called the "Israelite Shephelah," the low but rocky plateau of the central section of Carmel. Near Taanach a fault line, striking southwestward across the hills toward the present village of Ya'bad, has helped to create the Wadi Abdullah, a narrow, but possible, route. Ibleam stands at the eastern end of the Plain of Dothan, a fertile little down-faulted basin which also curves round toward Ya'bad. The last two routes, therefore, coalesce and make their way into the Plain of Sharon by the Wadi Abu Nar.

Of all these routes, that past Megiddo is overwhelmingly the most important, as the Egyptian report of the first campaign of Thutmose III makes clear when it says, "The cap-

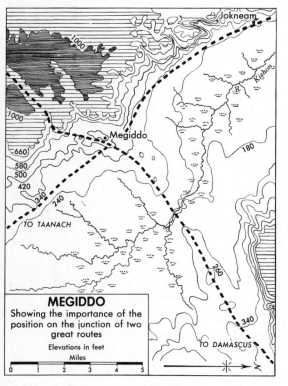

MEGIDDO

Showing the importance of the position on the junction of two great routes

Elevations in feet

Miles

Fig. 32.

turing of Megiddo is the capturing of a thousand towns." [1] This is because Megiddo controls not only the entrance to a fairly easy route across Carmel, but also the most natural

route across the plain. The hill route is the Wadi 'Ara, a narrow valley, well provided with springs, and nowhere as high as 1000 feet above sea level. The gradients are everywhere easy and, despite the narrowness of the defile, there are no serious obstacles to the passage of chariots, since the Senonian chalk wears away into a smooth, if somewhat bumpy, surface, unobstructed with boulders. This SW-NE line of the valley is continued in the plain by the basaltic causeway running across Esdraelon to Tel 'Adashim, raised slightly, but definitely, above the marshes on either side. These marshes must have been a real obstacle, for the drainage here is extraordinarily sluggish, the River Kishon being checked twice in its short course to the sea, once by the basalt causeway and then again by the restricted outlet to the Plain of Asher. In the two basins thus formed the fields are often waterlogged and even today, when modern drainage has rendered the plain fit for settlement, the floods may endure throughout a prolonged period, if the winter storms are frequent. The struggles of the early Jewish settlers in the first years of the twentieth century against the malaria and the other problems of the marshes which then existed are a famous part of the Zionist saga.

Consequently, though movement in the drought of summer would be unrestricted, the passage across the plain in winter would often be confined to the Megiddo route. The Thutmose account makes it clear that although the officers discussed the possibility of using other routes across the hills, the goal was Megiddo, and the other passages were mentioned merely as other ways round to the same point. Megiddo did not only guard the pass. It stood at a crossroads, in fact at one of the great crossroads of the ancient world. The Romans built here the fortress of Legio Maximinopolis, whose name persists in the modern village of Lejjun, and though there is no great town there today, the existence of a "Teggart Fort" in the Mandatory period, and the Jewish trenches cut in the tell of Megiddo indicate that the strategic importance of this site is not yet at an end.

The other towns held subordinate, yet strongly fortified positions. Jokneam stands at the northwestern end of the plain, and therefore away from the main line of north-south trade. However, it is the first crossing point on the seaward side and consequently the first place at which such Phoenician trade as came by land could pass over into Sharon, though most of it would naturally go by sea. It is the only pass across Carmel which has access to the port of Dor, since the western approach is a double one, and it has the further advantage of being the lowest of all the passes, the highest point being more than 300 feet lower than that of the Wadi 'Ara. It was considered as a possible alternative to the Megiddo route by the officers of Thutmose III, and, very much later in history, Napoleon chose it for his advance toward Acre.

The route by the Wadi Abdullah to Taanach is possibly the least attractive of all, for it is both narrow and steep and there is a climb up to 1250 feet. However, Taanach is near enough to Megiddo to be its rival in controlling the crossroads, and indeed the two towns tended to flourish alternately instead of at the same time, Taanach being important when Megiddo was suffering an eclipse.[2] On the other hand the Dothan route, which joins

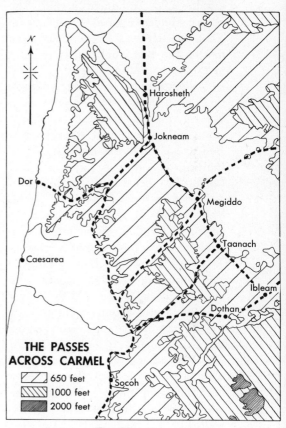

Fig. 33.

the Wadi Abdullah near Ya'bad, is both open and easy, and must often have been preferred to the Wadi 'Ara, especially if the intention were to strike toward Jezreel and Beth-shean. The entrance from the Plain of Esdraelon is a narrow defile about 2 miles long, guarded at one end by the rich, well-watered settlement of Engannim (Jenin) and at the other by the strong fortress of Ibleam (Tel Bilameh). Dothan itself is a down-faulted basin which leads not only into Sharon, but also into the heart of Samaria to the town of Shechem.

All these towns were important during the Old Testament period. The city of Megiddo which was taken by Thutmose III was by no means the first on the site. That had been built in the early Bronze Age about 3000 B.C., though there had been a village there for a thousand years previously. The Egyptians kept control of this position and of the great stronghold at Beth-shean until the second half of the twelfth century B.C. and the great battle "by the waters of Megiddo" described in Judges 5 is dated by Albright at about 1125 B.C.[3] Later the city was fortified by Solomon who made it one of his chariot cities (I Kings 9:15) and still later it saw the death of King Ahaziah, whom Jehu had slain near Ibleam, and the defeat of Josiah, who had gone north to check the advance of Pharaoh Necho against the Babylonians (II Kings 9:27, 23:29). The other towns are mentioned also in Judges 1:27 as having been too strong to be taken by the Israelites when they first came into the country, and as having finally been taken over by the tribe of Manasseh, though officially they were in the territory of Issachar.

These routes into the region are the key to its history. We have seen that the "resting place was good, and that the land was pleasant" (Gen. 49:15). Isaiah speaks of the "glorious beauty which is on the head of the rich valley" (Is. 28:1), but the wealth which came by trade must always have been greater. Of Zebulun and Issachar, who occupied these two plains, it was said that "they suck the affluence of the seas and the hidden treasures of the sand" (Deut. 33:19) and this, in large measure, was the cause of their downfall, for it was always the weakness of this region that it was too open to foreign influences. Trade brought with it not only wealth, and the insidious temptations of prosperity, but also the yet more dangerous perils of foreign worship and the strange influence of false gods. Moreover, the same roads which brought the trade brought the armies, and the soil of all this fertile corridor is soaked with blood. It is no accident that the very name of Megiddo has come to signify war in our own language, the Armageddon of Revelation 16:16, for this little triangle, the "Plain" par excellence of modern Israel, is the cockpit of Palestine. It could not but be that the great kings who sought for passage across it should sooner or later subdue the little kingdom by which is was controlled.

CHAPTER XIV

The Hill Country of Judah

The scepter shall not depart from Judah,
nor the ruler's staff from between his feet,
until he comes to whom it belongs;
and to him shall be the obedience of the peoples.
                                        GENESIS 49:10

VISITORS from the west, seeing the country round Jerusalem for the first time, are often disappointed. They have visualized the green mountains and sharp peaks of their homelands, and they find themselves face to face with an uplifted plateau, whose gentle slopes and rounded hills give them very little feeling of height, except

33. *Jeshimmon, or the Wilderness of Judaea,* the desolate and barren chalky hills between Jerusalem and the Dead Sea.

when they are standing on its edge. At any other time than the second half of winter the hillsides are brown and apparently barren, and the fields are almost unbelievably stony. For a brief period in the rainy season, it is true, the springing grain in the fields hides the multitude of stones, and the short-lived grass and vivid borage and anemones clothe the naked hillside, but, even at its best, the impression that this region gives is never one of luxury or wealth. The pilgrim to Jerusalem from the United States or Britain, or even from the north of Palestine itself, cannot but feel that the crops are being wrested from the soil, and that here, if anywhere, is the land of which it was said, "Cursed is the ground because of you; in toil you shall eat of it all the days of your life" (Gen. 3:17). It is a land where labor is unremitting, and only too ready to sink back into uselessness, should ever the ceaseless struggle of the farmer be

155

interrupted by the peremptory demands of war.

Yet one must beware of overestimating the barrenness of the region. Tre-

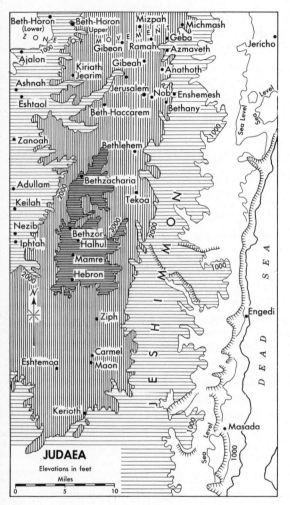

Fig. 34.

mendous deforestation has taken place since the Biblical period, for there seems to have been no lack of trees in ancient Judaea, though they can never have been very high by Western standards, or very useful for anything

except the smallest type of building. Then again, what most people see of Judaea is Jerusalem, perched just east of the water parting on the very edge of the descent to the Jordan, where the slashing storms which sweep across the hills in the rainy season are already losing their power. There are days at Jerusalem when the whole world seems blotted out by a curtain of water, but in fact the amount of rain which falls in the eastern half of the city is noticeably less than that which falls in the west, and even while it is raining a sharp edge to the clouds may be seen poised over the Mount of Olives, with the clear blue sky beyond. The hurried visitor, attempting to "do" Jerusalem and Bethlehem in a weekend, as, alas, so many do, is apt to forget that his visit has brought him to the gates of the wilderness.

The western slopes are better favored, for if the year is good, they receive a heavy soaking in the rainy season and refreshing dews throughout the summer and, by careful terracing and tending, may be coaxed into producing good supplies of grain and wine and oil. Today the Muslim dislike of drinking wine and the existence of imported cane sugar has meant that no more grapes are grown than may be consumed in the ordinary way as fruit, but in the past wine was consumed in large quantities and a rich treacle was prepared from the grapes to supply the need for sugar. Then the greater part of the village population must have encamped around the watchtowers in summer to protect the vineyards, for the parable of the man who "had a vineyard on a very fertile hill" and who "digged it and cleared it of stones, and planted it with choice vines; he built a watchtower in the midst of it, and hewed out a wine vat in it; and he looked for it to yield grapes," belonged to the life of nearly every Judaean farmer (Is. 5:1–7).

Nevertheless, when all this had been said, it still remains true that the terrain is difficult, and the rabbis used to say that it was easier to raise a legion of olive trees than one child in Judaea, and though the grape harvests may be excellent, and the dark terra rossa well suited to the growing of wheat and figs and olives, no less than half of Judah is desert and the soil of the other half, rich though it may be, is patchy.

One good thing, however, was granted to the people of Judah, and that was adequate defense. They might live high on a rocky plateau, only half of it cultivable and the other half desolate wilderness, but they were well guarded. On the east the steep ascent from the Jordan and the stern barrier of the Dead Sea coast discouraged any easy approach. There the dry climate of the eastern slopes and the unproductive chalky soil conspire together, and the sudden contrast with the orchards and vineyards west of Jerusalem is startling. The famous description of it in *Eothen* cannot be bettered, "Before me, and all around, as far as the eye could follow, blank hills piled high over hills, pale, yellow and naked, walled up in her tomb forever the dead and damned Gomorrah." It is only in the richest spring that it carries even a faint haze of grass, and such scrub as there is grows on the northern side of the hills where it can shelter from the blistering heat of the sun. In the lower parts the rounded, barren hills give way to rocky gorges of Cenomanian limestone, equally barren of vegetation, but more impressive to the view, and the edge of the Dead Sea is reached down a wall of jagged cliffs. As if this were not

34. *The Mount of Olives.* This is not a separate hill, but part of the level ridge which divides Jerusalem from the Wilderness of Judaea. It played a very large part in Jewish thinking, partly because from it one gets a truly magnificent view of the whole of Jerusalem. This view is taken from the eastern side, near the traditional site of Bethphage.

enough the Dead Sea itself stretches almost the full length of Judaea, and it is only in the northeastern corner that it is not there to give its double protection.

This region has never held cities of habitation, though the Bedouin encamp upon its slopes in the springtime and on occasions in history it has given refuge to those who shunned the towns. The monasteries of Mar Saba and Mar Jirius, clinging to the rocky walls of the narrow Cenomanian gorges, each of them occupied today by no more than a dozen monks, are the last relics of once greater com-

35. *The Monastery of the Temptation, Jericho.* The only people who have lived in the Wilderness of Judaea are religious communities who have gone there to withdraw from the world, and soldiers who have been stationed there to control the routes across it. This monastery is on the supposed site of Jesus' temptation.

munities. The number of monks who lived in the caves round Mar Saba is reported to have been some four thousand in the heyday of that movement. These were, however, exotic groups, confined to one or two areas in the lowest parts of the valleys, where water was available. The Qumran community, to whose library the Dead Sea scrolls belonged, were an earlier settlement of the same nature, but they lived in so close to the Dead Sea that they must be included rather in that region than in Judea.

David fled here to escape from Saul (Ziph is some 3 miles southeast of Hebron) and later Jesus came also to this region after his baptism. The traditional site of the Temptation is near Jericho, where the steep slopes of Jebel Quruntul rise almost sheer from the plain. However, if we are to fix on any one place, though there is no real need to do so, it must surely have been higher up in the hills, where it was indeed possible to see "all the kingdoms of the world in a moment of time" (Luke 4:5). There one may stand and look out across the Rift, and see the whole plateau of Trans-Jordan in one amazing panorama. In the far south are the lands of the Nabateans, shimmering in the haze which hovers over the Dead Sea, and in Jesus' days Petra, which was hidden in their cliffs, was rich with all the fabled wealth of the East. Immediately opposite lay Perea and the castle where Herod imprisoned John. These had been the ancient lands of Edom and Moab. Farther to the north were the cities of the Decapolis, heirs to the heritage of Alexander and of Greece, and all around Jesus was the power of Rome. "All this authority and their glory" would have been displayed before him, gathered together in one single landscape, as they would have been gathered nowhere else in the world.

On the west the defense is formed by the hills of the Shephelah and the great plunging monocline which flanks it on the Judaean side, with between them the vital moat of soft Senonian chalk. This swings round the southern end of Judaea to join the broad Senonian wilderness on the east, and at the place where it does so, about halfway between Hebron and Beersheba, there is a sudden descent of about 650 feet, just south of Adh-Dhahariyeh. This marks the real edge of the mountain region, and Beersheba beyond is an outlier, just as Dan is an outlier beyond the natural frontier in the far north of Palestine. To the south of Beersheba is steppeland, verging on desert, once the home of the Amalekites, a fierce pastoral people, whose sheep and cattle offended the ear of the prophet Samuel (I Sam. 15:14), and who were utterly destroyed by the Israelites. The hatred of the Jews for the Amalekites was traditional, and is ascribed in the Bible to the fact that the Amalekites prevented their advance into the country from the south (Exod. 17:8 ff.), but even if this were the origin, the hatred must have been fanned by the constant feeling of insecurity felt by the Jews as long as there were people on the southern frontier who could turn against them. After they had wiped them out there was no longer any danger from the south, for the desert itself was an added protection against attack from that direction. Much later in history the Maccabees were moved to exercise an equally firm control over this region, and forcibly converted the Idumeans to Judaism when they conquered them.

This ascent near Adh-Dhahariyeh is, it must be admitted, a less effective defense than those on the east and the west, and therefore the constant desire was to extend southward over the frontier zone, even as they fought to gain control over the frontier zone of the Shephelah. Thus we find the boundary of Judah being described as passing by the Ascent of the Akrabbim, the steep edge of the Ghor southeast of Beersheba, and later Judas Maccabeus in the same place "fought against the children of Esau in Idumea at Arabattine, because they besieged Israel; and he gave them a great overthrow and abated their courage and took their spoils" (I Macc. 5:3). This extension of the frontier southward not only gave the inhabitants of Judaea greater protection, but brought under their sway the approaches to the trade route which led along the Arabah to the Red Sea.

The northern frontier is less well-defined, for here there is no outcrop of soft Senonian chalk to form a protective valley against the hard Cenomanian slopes, and the plateau surface extends well northward into the territory of Ephraim. It was only here that access to the plateau from either side could be said to be easy, and here was an important zone of movement dividing the Kingdom of Israel on the north from that of Judaea to the south, the frontier region being occupied by the little tribe of Benjamin. Although there seems little on the surface to cause it to do so, the frontier between the two kingdoms remained curiously constant, Bethel marking the southern edge of Israel and Geba, not more than 5 miles away, being the northernmost town of Judah. We find, in fact, the expression "from Geba to Beersheba" being used to describe the extent of the kingdom of Judah in just the same way as "from Dan to Beersheba" had previously been used to describe the whole country (II Kings 23:8).

Between the two towns was a kind of No Man's Land which each country tried from time to time to take to itself. Not long after the revolt of Jeroboam Abijah of Judah pushed northward beyond Bethel, and even halfway to Shiloh (II Chron. 13:19), but he did not hold the territory for long, since in the next reign "Baasha king of Israel went up against Judah, and built Ramah, that he might permit no one to go out or come in to Asa king of Judah" (I Kings 15:17). Now Ramah, the birthplace of Samuel, is but 5 miles from Jerusalem as the crow flies—it is not always realized

how desperately close to the frontier the Judaean capital stood—and the present city can be clearly seen from the little hill on which Ramah stands. Asa was at his wit's end and he "took all the silver and gold that were left in the treasures of the house of the Lord and the treasures of the king's house . . . and sent them to Benhadad . . . king of Syria, who dwelt in Damascus," begging him to attack from the north. When Baasha learned of this attack he left off building Ramah. "Then King Asa made a proclamation to all Judah, none was exempt, and they carried away the stones of Ramah and its timber, with which Baasha had been building; and with them King Asa built Geba of Benjamin and Mizpah" (another frontier town, possibly Tel en-Nasbeh not far away).

This vivid little story is the key to a great deal of Old Testament thinking. It has often been pointed out that in Judah one family reigned from the beginning to the end of the kingdom, interrupted only by the brief usurpation of Athaliah in 845 B.C. In contrast to this there were constant revolts and changes of dynasty in Israel, where reigns were sometimes counted in months instead of in years, and occasionally only in days. This is held to indicate a greater stability in Judah, a greater freedom from the political turmoil, which too great contact with the outside world may sometimes bring. There is some truth in this, but it must not be thought that Judah was therefore immune from outside pressure, living out her life in an ivory tower of God's devising. Nothing could be further from the truth. Judah's strong natural defenses gave her pro-

tection from the invasion to which
less fortunate nations astride the great
Trunk Road were often exposed, and
this gave her a breathing space, but
only a breathing space. It is clear that
she lived in perpetual fear that invasions would come, and it cannot have
been only once in the history of the
House of David that "his heart and
the heart of his people shook as the
trees of the forest shake before the
wind" (Is. 7:2). Her position is best
described by saying that she was insu-
lated, but not isolated.

This nagging fear of war is such a
persistent feature of Judaean thought,
and such a contradiction of the normal
"textbook" distinction between Israel

36. *The Wadi Farah, near Anathoth.* This
is probably the "Euphrates" of Jer. 13:4.

and Judah, that it demands a little
further consideration. It is only recently that we have come to know
this threat of war as a permanent factor in our lives, so that we wonder
whether it is worth while starting this
or that job which requires time for its
fulfillment, and we are tempted to
think of this as abnormal, and to resent
it as making creative activity impossible. We forget that practically all
the training of the people of God, and
certainly the whole of the teaching of
the greater prophets, was done in just
such a situation. Given Judah's position, it could not have been otherwise.
When David first began to reign, his
capital was at Hebron, suitably and
centrally placed so long as he controlled only Judah, but when the
northern tribes joined him in the
eighth year of his reign, he sought a
town more central to the whole country, and for this purpose built a new
capital at Jerusalem. After Solomon's
death, however, the division of the
kingdom left Judah with its capital no
longer securely placed in the center
of the tribal territory at Hebron, but
almost on the frontier, a mere 5 miles
from the border towns. In Isaiah 10:
28–34, the prophet pictures the advance of the Assyrian army in staccato
phrases suggestive of speed: "He has
reached Ai; he has by-passed Migron,
dumped his equipment at Michmash
and gone over the pass. He has encamped at Geba, Ramah is terrified
and Gibeah of Saul has fled. Cry for
help, people of Gallim, listen Laishah
and answer them Anathoth! Mad-
menah are refugees; the people of
Gebim are running away. This very
day he will halt at Nob and shake his

fist at the mount of the daughter of Zion, the hill of Jerusalem." * These places cannot all be identified with certainty, but it is clear that they are not strung out many days' journey from one another, as are Calno, Carchemish, Hamath, Arpad, Damascus and Samaria, which the king of Assyria himself had quoted (Is. 10:9–10, 37: 12–13). When a man heard of those places he could comfort himself with the inaccurate, but consoling, thought that "it cannot happen here!" But the

37. *Bethlehem of Judaea.* The interior of the great Church of the Nativity, which is built over the cave in which it is believed that Jesus was born. People in the West are sometimes skeptical about this tradition, but the reasons for accepting it are very strong. Caves were very often used for stables, and are still used for this purpose in our own time. The great columns shown here belong to the church built by Justinian, but below the floor it is still possible to see the mosaics of the original church built at the direction of Queen Helena, the mother of Constantine.

places which Isaiah speaks of are close to Jerusalem, and Ai, the first of them, no more than 10 miles distant. Nob, where the dreaded conqueror is to stand this very day and shake his

* Author's translation.

fist at Jerusalem, is probably the village of et-Tur on the Mount of Olives, where Jesus stood and wept over the city (Luke 19:41).

At this present time, as one moves about the hill country of Judaea, one is very conscious of the nearness of the armistice line, for there is no road to the west which can be followed very far without reaching a road block and the information that ahead is enemy territory. Yet, save for the spearhead of the Jerusalem corridor, the armistice line of today is no nearer than the ancient frontier. In their stronger moments the people of Judah may have extended their control over the Shephelah, but then they would be pushed back onto their hills again, and on these hills it is no more than a comfortable afternoon's walk from Jerusalem to points whence one can look right across the Shephelah and the Philistine country to the sand dunes of the coast. Arab refugees today will turn round in the bus and point out the villages from which they fled, and so near are they that it is almost possible to distinguish the houses. So the ancient Israelites must have paused for a moment on their journeys and seen the smoke rising from the plundered villages of the plain and have wondered whether it would be their turn next.

George Adam Smith says of Judaea that one cannot live in it "without being daily aware of the presence of the awful deep which bounds it on the east," [1] and that may be so if one is a foreigner to whom the wasteful wilderness is a strange and rather terrifying novelty, but the inhabitant of the country is less conscious of its existence. On that side, at any rate, he is well protected, and a man who has been brought beside Jeshimmon all his life does not usually think of it as an "awful deep." On the other hand he cannot but be aware of the coast plain. For the first three hundred years of Judah's existence on these mountains, before Jerusalem had been taken from the Jebusites, the great enemy in the west were the Philistines, perpetually at war with the Hebrews, and the frontier swung backward and forward between them according to the fortunes of the fighting. After they had been defeated there was peace in that quarter for a time, but after the division of the kingdom they again became a danger, and not only they, but the kings of Syria, of Assyria and Babylon in their turn. Throughout all those troubled centuries the people of Judah watched the armies from their hilltops, and sometimes from even nearer, for twice in the eighth century B.C. an invading army reached the walls of Jerusalem itself, and the prophets strove to teach them the meaning of these things.

It is no accident that a constant term for a prophet's work is that of a watchman (Is. 21:6; Ezek. 3:17, 33:7; Hab. 2:1). Of the rulers it might be said, "They prepare the table, they spread the rugs, they eat, they drink" (Is. 21:5), thinking, as they were so often tempted to think, that by some well-managed piece of diplomacy they had contrived to stave off the dangers of war, saying, "We have made a covenant with death, and with Sheol we have an agreement; when the overwhelming scourge passes through it will not come to us" (Is. 28:15), or

that the great powers were too busy elsewhere to turn against Judah. But the prophet knew that when he saw "riders, horsemen in pairs, riders on asses, riders on camels, then he must hearken very diligently" (Is: 21:7). It was essential to God's purpose that his people should have no excuse for complacency, for complacency, as Jesus was to show, saps the will and the spiritual strength of even the best of men. Therefore, God put them in a position of constant danger and when, in the face of all the facts, they insisted on saying to the prophets, "See not . . . prophesy not to us what is right . . . let us hear no more of the Holy One of Israel" (Is. 30:10–11), and when many prophets gave them consoling answers, saying, "You shall not see the sword, nor shall you have famine, but I will give you assured peace in this place" (Jer. 14:13), then even the perilous safety of Judea had to be denied them.

The fortress which is enclosed by these walls and bulwarks is very small. The distance from Geba to Beersheba is but 50 miles in a straight line, and that from Geba to the steep descent of Adh-Dhahariyeh, the real southern edge of the plateau, is no more than 30. From Kiriath Jearim, where the Ark rested, on the western edge of the mountains, to the Dead Sea is just over 18 miles. The whole area thus enclosed is a rough oval, and this minuteness must be borne in mind in relation to the overwhelming vastness of the great empires which threatened to engulf them. It was never the purpose of God at any time that the people of Judah should "vaunt themselves against him, saying 'My own hand has delivered me'" (Judg. 7:2). Rather they must say, "We seemed to ourselves like grasshoppers, and so we seemed to them" (Num. 13:33). From before they had come into the country they had known this feeling, and they were to know it from then on. It is of the first importance to grasp this tremendous disproportionateness in size between Judah and her enemies, if we are ever to understand the fantastic assertion of Isaiah to the king of Assyria, "She despises you, she scorns you—the virgin daughter of Zion!" (Is. 37:22).

Such a small area as this would not seem likely to show much variety within it, but Judah, draped as it is over the back of the Judaean arch, and dragging its skirts in the desert of the Negeb round Beersheba, has three quite clearly defined subregions. The most obvious division is that between the eastern and the western slopes, a division coinciding fairly closely with the road from Jerusalem to Hebron. To the east of this line lies the barren wilderness, and to the west are the cultivated lands. South of Hebron there is a third subregion, though the distinction is not so sharp. This is the pastoral district of Carmel and Maon, the home of the churlish Nabal, who had three thousand sheep and a thousand goats (I Sam. 25:2), and also of Judas Iscariot. Most of this country is broad open hills with wide, open valleys, and both on the south and east it grades off into desert. Carmel and Maon are both on the plateau, just short of 3000 feet, but south of the plateau edge, which can be followed on the map by the 2000 foot contour which is a little below the lip,

the land is seldom higher than about 1300 feet. From Maon, and again from Adh-Dhahariyeh, secondary folds on the broad Judaean upwarp run off to the southwest. The Maon fold divides the steppe country from the southward extension of the wilderness of Jeshimmon, and the other, which might have formed a dangerously easy route up onto the plateau, is fortunately cleft by the Wadi Daiqa, cutting back across it to the north. In between the two folds, the broad basin which they enclose is the Wadi Khalil, which opens out toward Beersheba.

The western slopes northward from Hebron are increasingly agricultural lands, though they still have many flocks of sheep and goats, the steep hillsides here being pre-eminently suited to vines, which grow well on the natural terraces of the limestone. In the valley bottoms the rich silt supports good orchards of summer fruits, and both here and on the plateau wheat and olives are grown. The rainfall is still treacherous, however, and a bad year may well be a disaster. The striking difference in the number of villages between this western region and that to the east of the Jerusalem-Hebron road can be seen on any map.

The three chief towns of Judah all of them lie on crossroads. They are Beersheba, Hebron and Jerusalem. Beersheba, which is really an outlier, is in the steppelands beyond the essential Judaea, and on the very edge of the desert. It is, for an inland town, surprisingly low-lying, being only 1000 feet above sea level, and it owes its importance, not only to its excellent water supply in such a barren region, but also to the fact that several routes meet here. From the northwest, following the Wadi Zumeili, is the road from Gaza, and directly from the north is a road from Gath, 25 miles away. Divided from this by the spur of the Judaean hills is the road to Hebron along the Wadi Khalil, and due east runs a road to the southern end of the Dead Sea. The two routes to the south are determined by the existence of a

38. *The Wadi Qilt.* The lower part of the Wadi Farah is known as the Wadi Qilt and it may be the Valley of Achor (or Trouble) of Josh. 7:26, which reappears in Hos. 2:15.

patch of dune sand known as Rumeilat Hamad, one road running southwestward to join the Trunk Road south of Gaza, and the other running east of the sand toward the Sinai Gate into Egypt. Another road runs off from this to the Ascent of the Akrabbim and so to the Red Sea.

Hebron, David's first capital, is the highest town in Judah, standing 3300 feet above the sea. Here two roads come up from the plain, one from Mareshah and one from Lachish, and here also is one of the few routes across the wilderness to the Dead Sea, which it reaches at Engedi. This is a far from easy route, but it seems to have been much in use, the road from Engedi southward along the western shore of the Dead Sea being possible for animal transport, though water is obtainable only at rare intervals. Less than 5 miles north of Hebron, guarding the routes which lead westward to Mareshah and Libnah, is Bethsura, which was so important in the time of the Maccabees.

The third of the three cities is Jerusalem, "the city where David encamped" (Is. 29:1). In general its position is not unlike that of Hebron, for in the same way there are important valleys leading up onto the plateau from either side. The valley leading up from the west is the Wadi Surar, the Valley of Sorek, and coming up from Jericho is the valley of Adummim, or the Ascent of Blood (Josh. 15:7, 18:17), the name by which it is still known today. It is so called because of the patches of red ocher exposed along its course, which can be seen clearly near the present Inn of the Good Samaritan. The valley of Achor was said to lie north of this ascent, and so it is possibly the present Wadi Qilt. This is the road followed by the unhappy King Zedekiah when

39. *The Inn of the Good Samaritan.* At this point, which is halfway between Jericho and Jerusalem, there has always been some kind of police post to protect the road through the dangerous Wilderness of Judaea. The building shown here is Turkish and part of an old caravanserai, and higher up the hill is the ruin of a small fort of the Crusading period, from which this photograph was taken.

Jerusalem was besieged by the Babylonians and "a breach was made in the city; the king with all the men of war fled by night by the way of the gate between the two walls, by the king's garden, though the Chaldeans were around the city. And they went in the direction of the Arabah. But the army of the Chaldeans pursued the king, and overtook him in the plains of Jericho" (II Kings 25:4–5). It was also the road followed very much later by Jesus when "he went on ahead, going up to Jerusalem" (Luke 19:28). The journey up from Jericho to Jerusalem was normally done in two days, and half way along the road there was a caravanserai and police post, where travelers could rest for the night, and whence the authorities could maintain some control of the road which has often been a dangerous one. The region between Jerusalem and Jericho is so desolate that in times of civil strife, such as Palestine has so often seen, rebel bands are able to take refuge there, a fact which became very apparent in the days of the Arab rebellion from 1936 to 1939. It was a dangerous journey in the time of Jesus, and it is thought by many that the caravanserai which stood halfway along the route was the one he had in mind when he told the story of the Good Samaritan (Luke 10:29–37). This may be so, though there is actually nothing in the story to say that the inn was not in Jericho.

The city itself stands where three steep-sided little wadis gather together to form one valley. They are the Kidron Valley, the Tyropoeon Valley and the Valley of Hinnom. Between the Kidron and the Tyropoeon valleys a long narrow spur extends southward, and it was on this narrow spur that the first town was built, the town of Jebus. This was the town which was taken by David and which he made into his capital. It is very strongly defended by steep descents on all sides except the north, where it is joined to the main plateau, and when David captured it the level land on top of the spur must have been thickly covered with houses, for it is a very small area. He therefore started a process, which was to continue later, of building out northward, and it was on that side that he built his palace and bought the land on which the Temple was later to be erected. This was the threshing floor of Araunah the Jebusite (II Sam. 24:18), part of the flat land on the plateau such as is to be found outside every Palestinian village, where the farmers thresh and winnow the grain. The city remained roughly like this until the time of the Captivity, though it must have continued to spread out rather farther to the north and west, for Zephaniah speaks of "the inhabitants of the Mortar" (Zeph. 1:11), which suggests that the hollow formed by the Tyropoeon Valley had been at any rate partly included, for the word מכתש is used elsewhere for a hollow place (Judg. 15:19). This is the picture of the city given in Psalm 48:2, "His holy mountain, beautiful in elevation, is the joy of all the earth, Mount Zion in the extreme * north is the city of the great king." It is by no means the highest part of the plateau, but is surrounded with higher land, the "mountains that are round about Jerusalem" (Ps. 125:2), and there is no need, therefore, to equate Jerusalem with "a city set on a hill" (Matt. 5:14), as is often done.

By the time of the New Testament the extension to the north and west had proceeded much farther, and the whole of the western hill between the Tyropoeon Valley and the Valley of

* RSV has "far north."

40. *The Dome of the Rock, Jerusalem.* This shrine is built over the great Rock of Sacrifice, which was once part of the Jewish Temple. It is today part of a Muslim mosque, one of the most lovely buildings in the world.

Hinnom had been included. The Tyropoeon Valley was then much lower than it is at present, for it has gradually been filled up with rubble during the centuries, and two great bridges were built across it, leading

41. *Medieval fountain, Jerusalem.* Jerusalem has a very small natural water supply, and many rulers, among whom were Hezekiah and Pontius Pilate, acquired merit by bringing in water from outside.

from the western hill to the Temple. In later Roman times the city extended far to the north of the present medieval walls, which were built by Suleiman the Magnificent in the sixteenth century A.D. These surround what is

known today as the Old City, which includes the area of the ancient Temple and its southeastern corner. Until the middle of the nineteenth century no building was allowed outside the walls, but since that date the city has grown greatly, always to the north and west, leaving entirely outside it the most ancient part of all, the town of Jebus.

The problem at Jerusalem, especially as it grew in size through the centuries, has always been to supply it with water. The little spring of Siloam which rises just outside the walls of Jebus in the Kidron Valley provides a very moderate supply of water, though sufficient for the little Jebusite town, and Isaiah speaks of those who doubt the ability of Jerusalem to stand a siege as those who "have refused the waters of Shiloah that flow gently" (Is. 8:6). In chapter 22 there is a vivid picture of the necessity of conserving water in time of war: "In that day . . . you saw that the breaches of the city of David were many, and you collected the waters of the lower pool, and you counted the houses of Jerusalem, and you broke down the houses to fortify the wall. You made a reservoir between the two walls for the water of the old pool. But you did not look to him who did it, or have regard for him who planned it long ago" (Is. 22:8–11).

More than one ruler of Jerusalem improved its water supply. Hezekiah, in the time of Isaiah, had strengthened the city by extending the wall so that it included the pool of Siloam and had even contrived a long tunnel to bring the waters from the spring to this pool and therefore inside the city

(II Kings 20:20). This was the reservoir between the two walls of which

42. *The Wailing Wall, Jerusalem.* This is practically all that remains of Herod's great Temple, and there is no place which shows more vividly the great change which has come over the city during the past ten years, for now no Jew can come to it, and it is visited only by tourists and by an occasional child at play.

Isaiah speaks. Pontius Pilate has at least this to his credit that he built a long aqueduct to bring water to Jerusalem from beyond Bethlehem, from what are known today as Solomon's Pools. In modern times water is pumped up to the Arab side of the city from 'Ain Farah below Anathoth,* and to the Jewish side from Ras el-'Ain on the coast plain, but even now there is always the danger of water shortage.

This reminds us that today, alas, there are two cities, one Arab and one Jewish, and that the impassable barrier of No Man's Land divides the two more completely even than the division of the city of Berlin. It is a tragic situation, for Jerusalem is no longer "built as a city that is bound firmly together" (Ps. 122:3). "Look upon Zion, the city of our appointed feasts!" said Isaiah, "Your eyes will see Jerusalem, a quiet habitation" (Is. 33:20). Yet never in history has this been so; it is eternally a promise for the future. "Pray for the peace of Jerusalem! May they prosper who love you!" (Ps. 122:6).

* 'Ain Farah, with its steep, rocky sides, is surely the "Euphrates" where Jeremiah was told to hide his waistcloth (Jer. 13:1-7), since it is the nearest water to his village. The words are very similar in Hebrew.

CHAPTER XV

Ephraim and Manasseh

His firstling bull has majesty,
and his horns are the horns of a wild ox;
with them he shall push the peoples,
all of them, to the ends of the earth;
such are the ten thousands of Ephraim,
and such are the thousands of Manasseh.
DEUTERONOMY 33:17

THEORETICALLY the Kingdom of Israel, formed after Jeroboam's revolt, included all the territory of the ten northern tribes, those in the south remaining loyal to the house of David. Of these northern tribes two, Manasseh and Ephraim, which claimed to be descended from the two sons of Joseph, were overwhelmingly the most important, and generally speaking, the history of the northern kingdom is the history of the territory which they controlled, the other tribes being essentially marginal.

The distribution of the land among the Israelite tribes dates back to their first entry into the country in the period of the Exodus during the last part of the thirteenth century B.C. However, this movement into the country was neither so rapid nor so unified as the Biblical records would suggest, for during that troubled and uncertain

period, when difficulties at home had weakened the Egyptian control of Palestine, at least two waves of Hebrew tribes, and very possibly more, moved in to take possession of the country. The stories of the adventures which they encountered in doing so are telescoped in the Bible into the one continuous story of the Book of Joshua. These two waves were the occupation of the northern half of the country under the leadership of the Joseph tribes, that is Ephraim and Manasseh, and the occupation of the southern half of the country under Judah. It was a time of considerable upheaval and confusion. The Ammonites, Moabites and Edomites had established themselves east of the Jordan only just before the Israelites came in, and Sihon, king of the Amorites, and Og, king of Bashan, appear to have developed their territory at the expense of their neighbors at about the same time. We have really no exact knowledge of what happened, but it would seem to be true that the Israelites were able to take advantage of the confusion and weakness to move in and stake out a claim for themselves, and that this process was a movement which extended over a period of some time rather than a sudden invasion.

Within the country into which they came there are four dividing lines, three of which are obvious, while the fourth has received less attention than its importance deserves. The three obvious lines are the great Rift Valley of the Jordan and the Dead Sea, the secondary rift valley of Esdraelon and Jezreel, and, thirdly, the line which marks the junction of the coast plain and the mountains. The fourth division is that created by what may be called a zone of movement between Joppa and Jericho. Here there is no sharp cleft of the mountains as there is farther north in the plain of Esdraelon, but movement is fairly easy from Joppa southeastward by the Valley of the Craftsmen along that region which divides the marshes of Sharon from the Philistine country, and then up into the hills by the valley of Ajalon, the famous Ascent of Bethhoron, toward Bethel, or by the Valley of Sorek to Jerusalem. From both Bethel and Jerusalem valleys lead down to Jericho and, since near Jericho is one of the few fords in the lower part of the Jordan, communication with the eastern half of the country is possible.

Now, a zone of movement by itself does not normally create a division between the areas on the two sides of it, and that it should have done so here is the result of two factors, one geographical and the other historical. The geographical reason is that the two areas which this zone of movement divides are in fact somewhat different from each other, for this zone of movement corresponds fairly closely with the division between the two geological regions of "Relative Simplicity" to the south and "Greater Complexity" to the north, discussed in Chapter III. The historical reason for this division is partly that the occupation of the country did not take place all at once, and that therefore the northern and southern halves were occupied at different times, and partly that the tendency was for the stronger tribes to move *away from* the main lines of movement.

It must be remembered that the Israelites, when they came into Palestine, were not powerful, and indeed they were very conscious of this fact. "It was not because you were more in number than any other people that the Lord set his love upon you and chose you, for you were the fewest of all peoples" (Deut. 6:7), and they always considered that there was something miraculous about their entry into the country at all. At that time they were really only semi-nomadic Bedouin, apparently as yet without the use of the camel and ignorant of the secret of iron-smelting, which put them at the mercy of the Philistines and Canaanites who had already learned this secret. The tendency was, therefore, for the Israelites to turn away from the major zones of movement, which were already fairly strongly occupied with fortified towns and villages, and to establish themselves in the hill country on either side of these zones. In those days the hill country must have been only thinly inhabited, because of the forest and woodland with which it was covered, and for this reason it was attractive to the incoming Israelites, who were in no position to drive out the better armed inhabitants of the more open areas. There is a vivid little picture both of the impossibility of occupying the lowlands and of the forested character of the hills in Joshua 17:14–18, and in view of this the pattern of occupation is not surprising: the great tribes occupy the mountains and the smaller tribes are left to find what security they can round the edges of the mountains and within the zones of movement, where they were forced to eke out their existence in between the fortified towns, which they were completely unable to subdue (see Judg. 1).

The mountains and plateau south of the Ajalon-Jericho zone of movement were occupied by Judah, with Simeon on the southwestern edge. North of this zone of movement the mountains were taken over by Ephraim and half the tribe of Manasseh, the other half having their lands on the highlands east of the Jordan. The remaining eight tribes were scattered round Ephraim and Manasseh in three groups, one in the southwest, one in the southeast, and one in the north. the southwestern group consisted of Dan and Benjamin in the Ajalon-Jericho zone, though the territories of both were very small, since the better

defended land on either side was held by their stronger neighbors. The southeastern group was formed of Gad and Reuben east of the Jordan, Reuben being on the flat country round Madeba, northeast of the Dead Sea, and Gad in the area enclosed by the curve of the river Jabbok. The northern group included the four in Galilee, Asher, Zebulun, Issachar and Naphtali.

The position of these eight tribes was insecure in the extreme, and more than one of them flickered out in the course of history. Thus Dan were unable to hold their position in the Valley of Ajalon and the Valley of the Craftsmen, and were forced to take up their tents and seek a camping ground elsewhere (Judg. 18). By this time the land was fully occupied, and they finally came to rest in the extreme north, where the Jordan rises on the southern slopes of Mount Hermon. Benjamin, lying between Ephraim and Judah, was preserved from outright conquest by a foreign kingdom, but the territory was a cockpit in the wars which so often rent the country, for it was the first to be reached by any enemy invading the mountains from the coast plain. The central position of this tiny tribe became important whenever there was a question of balancing the claims to leadership of Ephraim and Judah, for the same reason for which it was decided to make Washington the capital of the United States, just because it was small and central and threatened nobody's prestige. Thus Saul, the first king, was a man of the tribe of Benjamin (I Sam. 9:1–2), and when David wished to build a capital which would be acceptable to the people both of the north and the south of the country, he chose Jebus, a hitherto independent city within the territory of Benjamin (Josh. 18: 28; Judg. 1:21; II Sam. 5:6–10, but cf. Josh. 15:63).

Of the history of the southeastern group we know little. Reuben seems to have been overwhelmed by the Moabites not long after the division of the kingdom, and it disapears from the records. Gad likewise is hardly mentioned after the end of the Book of Joshua, and it was probably overrun by the Ammonites (Jer. 49:1). The position of the northern group was equally precarious. Asher soon passed under the domination of the Phoenicians, and Naphtali on the eastern side of the Galilean hills was the first to be sacrificed when the Israelites were forced to give ground before the invasions which came upon them from the north.* Zebulun, which was more centrally placed, was slightly better protected than either Asher or Naphtali, and may have profited by Asher's disappearance, for although the boundary as outlined in Joshua 19:11 extended no farther west than Jokneam, yet in both Genesis 49:13 and Deuteronomy 33:19 the people of Zebulun seem to have contact with the sea: "Zebulun shall dwell at the shore of the sea; he shall become a haven for ships, and his border shall be at Sidon," and

again, "They suck the affluence of the seas and the hidden treasures of the sand." Nevertheless, it could not long endure if Naphtali had been conquered, and Isaiah speaks of both Zebulun and Naphtali as having been "brought into contempt" (Is. 9:1).

Issachar's territory around the Hill of Moreh and Mount Tabor was crisscrossed with routes, with the powerful stronghold of Beth-shean at the southeastern corner, and consequently Issachar early gained the reputation of being at the mercy of those who controlled these routes and strongholds. The tribe is not even mentioned in Judges 1, and in Genesis 49:14–15 the judgment is that "Issachar is a strong ass, crouching between the sheepfolds; he saw that a resting place was good, and that the land was pleasant; so he bowed his shoulder to bear, and became a slave at forced labor." The people of Issachar helped Barak against Sisera, but they do not appear in the story of Gideon, possibly because theirs was the territory overrun by the Midianites. Later, it is true, the tribe is said to have provided one of the Judges, a man called Tola, but his headquarters were not in Issachar itself but in the hill country of Ephraim (Judg. 10:1).

When at last the fortresses along the Trunk Road fell to the Israelites, it was to the great tribe of Manasseh that they fell, and not to the smaller tribes within whose territory they lay: "Also in Issachar and in Asher Manasseh had Beth-shean and its villages, and Ibleam and its villages, and the inhabitants of Dor and its villages, and the inhabitants of Endor and its vil-

---

* If the translation of Gen. 49:21 which is preserved in the margin of the RSV is correct—"Naphtali is a hind let loose, who gives beautiful words"—it may be a suggestion that the tribe had a reputation for following a line of its own and putting off the others with promises.

lages, including the three heights." The "three heights" * are probably Carmel, Tabor and the Hill of Moreh, which stand alone and for this reason seem to have impressed the Israelites more than their low elevation (between 1600 and 2000 feet) would suggest. In this account of Manasseh's expansion Zebulun is not mentioned, nor is the town of Jokneam which it controlled, though it is in the same line as Megiddo and Taanach, and this suggests that the people of Zebulun were better able to hold their own against Manasseh than their neighbors could.

This expansion of Manasseh, when they took under their control the important central plain and the three heights at its edge, cannot have happened effectively until the time of David, because at the end of Saul's reign the Philistines still controlled Beth-shean and, therefore, presumably the routes which led to it.

This leaves us with what may be called the "essential Israel" of the central hill country, as far southward as Bethel and the transverse zone of movement which was inhabited by Dan and Benjamin. This hill country was held by the two Joseph tribes, between whom there seems to have been a bitter rivalry, for we learn from Isaiah 9:20-21 that "they snatch on the right, but are still hungry, and they devour on the left, but are not satisfied; each devours his neighbor's flesh, Manasseh Ephraim, and Ephraim Manasseh, and together

* The Hebrew is שְׁלֹשֶׁת הַנָּפֶת which is obscure. The RSV translation is "the third is Naphath," but I have preferred the suggestion of the English Revised Version (Josh. 17:11).

they are against Judah." It is probable that a very great deal of the constant internal insecurity of the northern kingdom is to be explained by the tensions between tribe and tribe, and it would be very interesting to know more about the different usurpers who rose up there to overthrow one ruler after another. We do know that in the first place the division of the kingdom after Solomon's death was brought about under Ephraimite leadership, both Jeroboam and Ahijah the prophet being from Ephraim (I Kings 11:26-40), and that Jeroboam's son, Nadab, was murdered by Baasha, a man of Issachar, a tribe whose history would give its members small reason to like the overweening dominance of the two great tribes (I Kings 15:27). Jehu, who overthrew the house of Omri, may have been from the eastern half of Manasseh, since he was chosen by Elijah of Gilead and was anointed at Ramoth Gilead (I Kings 19:16; II Kings 9:1-13), and it is true that there was often friction between the two halves of the kingdom on either side of the Jordan, but it is possible that he was merely a member of the garrison, for Ramoth Gilead was a critical frontier town.

In view of this rivalry it is worth examining a little more closely the territory occupied by the two great tribes in order to see whether it throws any light upon the history of their relations with each other. By far the bigger of the two tribes was the great sprawling community of Manasseh, the "fruitful bough" whose "branches run over the wall" (Gen. 49:22), but the leadership at the first was clearly in the hands of Ephraim, which not only led the revolt against Rehoboam, but was so important in the early period that the name became attached to the whole country, and is often used by the prophets as a synonym for the complete northern kingdom. It was also in Ephraim that the Ark was kept until it was captured by the Philistines in the days of Eli, first at Bethel and later at Shiloh (Judg. 20:27; I Sam. 4:3), and the fact that Ahijah was a Shilonite was probably an added reason for his dislike of Solomon, who had made Jerusalem the center of worship and had, in his view, corrupted the true worship of God.

An explanation of this apparent anomaly that the less numerous tribe was the stronger is offered in Genesis 48, where we are told how Joseph brought his two sons, Manasseh and Ephraim, to their grandfather Jacob in order that he should bless them, presenting Manasseh, the elder, toward his right hand. However, the blind Jacob deliberately crossed his hands over, despite Joseph's protests, "and thus he put Ephraim before Manasseh" (Gen. 48:20).

B. 2. *The Hill Country of Ephraim.* Ephraim started in Palestine with several advantages, for the territory was central, exceptionally well defined and remarkably fruitful. It differs markedly from the regions to the north and south of it in that the soft Senonian chalk is hardly to be seen, the important exposures of chalk to the south having been brought to an end by inward-curving hinge faults, and instead a broad, domelike upwarping has exposed the hard Cenomanian limestone right across the whole of the arch. Much of the region is high, sur-

passing 3300 feet in the east, and the hard rock forms steep and difficult slopes. The rainfall here is greater and also more assured than it is in Judaea to the south, and the soil is everywhere a rich and fertile terra rossa. This has made Ephraim very productive, so that today this section of the country is dotted with orchards of summer fruits and here the oliveyards are very nearly continuous, and in ancient times it was blessed "with the finest produce of the ancient mountains, and the abundance of the everlasting hills" (Deut. 33:15). The valleys leading down to the west are sufficiently precipitous to cause little danger that an enemy might use them as a route up into the mountains, and the roads, in fact, tend to follow the spurs between the valleys rather than the valleys themselves. However, there is no protective moat to the west as there is in Judaea, and movement between the hills and the coast plain, though not necessarily easy, was always possible. There is, for instance, an important route leading down from Shiloh, high up in the hills, toward the plain along the southern edge of the rocky Sarida valley, and passing Zaredah, from which Jeroboam came, and Ramathaim-Zophim, the birthplace of Samuel (I Sam. 1:1) and later the home of Joseph of Arimethea. There was another possible route leading up from Aphek, where the Philistines captured the Ark.

This fact that the Ephraimites were able to communicate with the Trunk Road, but could, if they wished, remain aloof in their mountains, was of great assistance in raising them to their early leadership, and it was down these communicating valleys to the west, as well as down the valley of Ajalon on their border, that they overflowed when they took over the towns of the plain, which had at first been assigned to Dan. It is surely significant of the strength of Ephraim's position that chapter 1 of Judges, which speaks of the many towns which the Israelites were unable to subdue at their first entry into the country, mentions only one city which is said to have withstood the Ephraimites, and that was Gezer, which was not really in their territory at all, but lay in the region which the people of Dan had been forced to vacate (Judg. 1:29). The northern frontier of Ephraim against her vigorous rival, Manasseh, was also a strong one, for it followed the rocky plain of the Kanah up from the coast plain just north of Aphek as far as Tappuah, and then seems to have curved northward, leaving the low-lying Sahl Mukhnah outside its borders, before descending to the Jordan along a convenient hinge fault, which provided a strong northward-facing scarp. The Book of Joshua twice refers to "the towns which were set apart for the Ephraimites within the inheritance of the Manassites" (Josh. 16:9, 17:9), which suggests that the boundary had originally been disputed between the two tribes, but that Ephraim had been able to strengthen itself at Manasseh's expense, so that almost all along the frontier there was a steep and difficult slope facing northward to deter the people of Manasseh from attacking their stronger brethren to the south.

B. 3. *Central Manasseh or Samaria.* Ephraim was not destined to remain forever in the lead. Though in the period of the Judges and up to the division of the kingdom the towns of Ephraim receive frequent mention in the Bible, and though the Ephraimites provided the leaders in the revolt which brought about that division, yet, with the one exception of the sanctuary of Bethel on the southern frontier, no town of Ephraim occurs in the history of the northern kingdom. From the formation of the kingdom of Israel onward the dominant region was the territory of Manasseh.

The geography of Manasseh is very different from that of Ephraim. First, it is no longer true that the highlands of the country are formed by the great upwarps. These upwarps have in general a tendency to run NNE and, therefore, when the Ephraimite dome is left behind, it is discovered that the main arch now lies well to the east, though it steadily decreases in height. Just how far to the east it is can be seen if one draws a line with a ruler from Beth-shean due SSW to Artuf. This line marks the western edge of the central upfolded region and coincides with the outcrop of the soft chalk. This chalk outcrop is interrupted by a fault scarp at Beth-horon the Lower on the southern boundary of Ephraim, but reappears at Tappuah on the northern boundary, and after this it is unbroken until it is hidden beneath the alluvium of the Jezreel Valley.

The tendency for the eastern upwarped region to decrease in height toward the northeast is shown by the following figures: the highest point of the scarp forming the Ephraimite frontier near Taanath-Shiloh is 2880 feet;

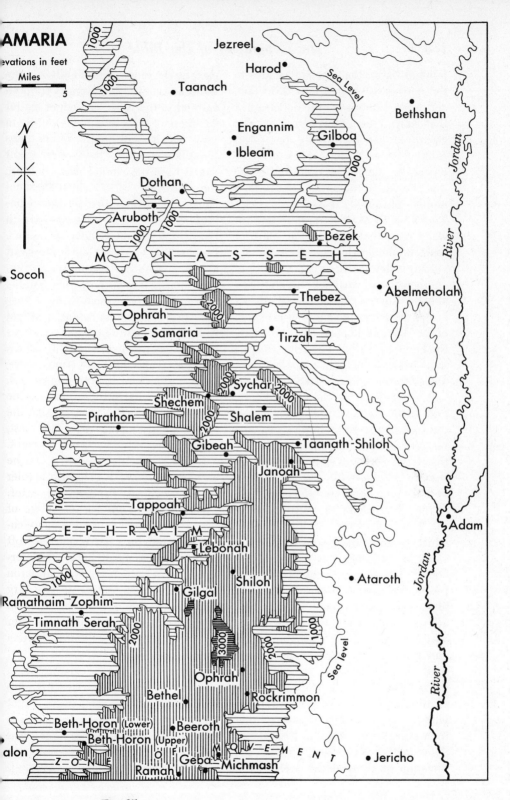

Fig. 35.

Jebel el-Kabir, the next line of hills to the northeast, reaches only 2575 feet; and Jebel Tammun to the northeast of that only 1780. This region is also greatly broken by faulting, one series running from NNE to SSW and the other very nearly at right angles, so that the whole region is carved into a number of roughly rectangular blocks. The NNE-SSW faults outline the upwarp on either side, a long line of them following the course of the Senonian valley on the western side and another line of weakness running parallel to this farther to the southeast and in part forming the lower section of the Wadi Malih near Abel-Meholah, the home of Elisha. The largest of the fault basins which cut across at right angles to the upwarp is the small rift valley occupied by the Wadi Fari'a, and to the south of it is the basin at the foot of the Ephraimite scarp, the basin of Salim. On the other side of the Wadi Fari'a is the basin of al-Buqei'a, drained by the Abu Sidra and leading down from Tubas, and beyond that again the depression at the head of which is Tayasir and which contains the headwaters of the Wadi Malih. Since this section of the country is in general rather lower than the central part of Samaria to the west of it, the rainfall is not so abundant and the villages are very few. Oliveyards and orchards, in fact, come to an end east of a line drawn north and south through Tubas.

The central area of Manasseh, west of this main arch, is a broad basin whose edge is formed on every side by upwarps, by the broad Ephraimite dome in the south, by the main continuation of the Judaean arch in the east, by the mountains of Gilboa in the north and by the beginnings of Mount Carmel in the west. The edges of this basin on all sides except the south are very much broken by faults. The basinlike structure, however, is not easy to see on a relief map, because the youngest rock, which has, of course, been preserved in the center, is the hard Eocene limestone, which tends to stand up in hills not merely because it is hard and therefore resistant to erosion, but also because it has been pushed up between parallel faults. This would seem to be the explanation of the great height of Mount Ebal and Mount Gerizim on either side of the town of Shechem, which reach 3100 and 2910 feet respectively. Thus, the picture that one must have in mind, so to speak, is of a wide saucer containing a lump of pudding which stands higher than the edges of the saucer itself.

Nevertheless, the fact that it is a basin is important, because the central hills, though usually higher than the edges of the basin, are not in themselves very high, reaching more than 2000 feet only in a few places, and are on the whole much lower than the mountains of Ephraim. Also, because it is a basin, the valleys of Senonian chalk are contained *within* the region, and indeed run right round inside the rim, instead of forming a moat outside it. As this rim is broken in a great many places by faults, it has always been possible to cross it with very little difficulty and, once inside the rim, movement along these valleys is very easy. It has been made even easier by the fact that the central highlands of Eocene limestone are themselves broken in many places by down-faulted basins similar to those which occur in the upwarped region to the southeast.

This Eocene limestone is not especially fertile and the soil which is formed from it is less attractive than the rich terra rossa of Ephraim. Moreover, west of Shechem the rock is mainly Senonian with its broad gentle slopes and white, infertile soil. Consequently, the oliveyards and orchards are very much fewer in number than they are in Ephraim and are usually found either on the westward or north-ward-facing slopes, those to the south and east being too hot and dry. In fact, the only part where they are really plentiful is the district round Tulkarm, overlooking the coast plain.

The chief wealth of Manasseh came from three facts: there are a large number of down-faulted basins, floored with alluvium and excellent for the production of grain; the tribal boundaries were extended in course of time to include the immensely fertile plain of Esdraelon and the valley of Jezreel; and communication was always easy, both from one part of the region to another, and with the outside world. However, there was a difficulty in that the district of Manasseh is singularly indeterminate; it has no clear frontiers and could easily be invaded. Thus the early history of Manasseh is the story of their attempts to establish themselves by securing the approaches, which could be done only by overflowing onto the plain. In the north they pushed outward until they controlled Esdraelon and the three heights which enclosed it, and on the west they extended onto the coast plain

until they had the protection of the Sharon marshes. This meant that they brought within their borders not only Jezreel and Esdraelon, but also a large section of the great Trunk Road and the vital crossroads at Megiddo. Once this had been done, their ultimate leadership of the northern tribes was assured, but, naturally, they could not do it alone, and, in fact, it was not done until the kingdom was united, but thereafter they became the most important northern tribe. Consequently, though Ephraim led the revolt which brought the northern kingdom into being, the capital of that kingdom was always inside Manasseh.

It is another sign of the indeterminateness of the district of Manasseh that it provided no obvious site for a capital. Three places were tried, first Shechem, then Tirzah, and finally Samaria. The truth is that the tendency of the routes to follow the Senonian chalk round the inside of the rim of the basin meant that there was no natural focal point in the center of the basin, and such focal points as there were stood at the junctions of low-lying valleys, which were useless for defense. As a result, it was not until Omri decided to build an entirely new town on top of a hill that a satisfactory stronghold was created.

It is interesting that all the towns that are mentioned in the Bible in this part of the country lie in the Senonian valleys with their easy communications, and none at all in the somewhat unattractive Eocene highlands, which must have been fairly thinly populated then as now. Four of these towns, including the two first capitals, are connected with the long Senonian valley which strikes into the heart of Samaria from the direction of Beth-shean. The chief of these is Shechem, the modern Nablus, the one possible "focus" that Manasseh possessed. Here, between the towering shoulders of Ebal and Gerizim, the road from the coast plain near the present Tulkarm, and also from the north by way of Dothan, cut through into that section of the valley known today as Sahl 'Askar, and then descended to the Jordan beneath the foot of the Ephraimite scarp. Such a crossroads, with a good water supply, could not be overlooked, and Shechem was important from the very earliest times. Here was Jacob's well; here stood the Roman town of Neapolis; here Jesus paused to speak to the Samaritan woman (John 4:1–42). Sychar in John 4:5 is probably the modern 'Askar and, since Jesus was coming from Judaea, it is probable that he had come along the Sahl Mukhnah and, if he was going to Nazareth, was intending to turn toward Sebastia (Samaria), or possibly to continue in the same direction through Tirzah and Beth-shean, if he was heading for Capernaum.

Tirzah, the capital from the end of Jeroboam's reign until Omri built Samaria (I Kings 14:17, 15:33, 16:8–23), stands in the same valley farther to the northeast, commanding the point where the valley is crossed by the route which leads from the northwest through Merj Sannur and down to the Jordan by the broad Wadi Fari'a. The people of Tirzah seem to have resented the moving of the capital, for a later usurper was from there (II Kings 15:14). The next town was Thebez, the present Tubas, where Abimelech was killed (Judg. 9:50–57). The crossroads here is that made by a route from the plain of Dothan through the modern Qabatiya and down to the Jordan by the valley of al-Buqei'a.

43. *Israelite Wall, Samaria.* Samaria was first built by King Omri (I Kings 16:24), and this wall belongs to his period. The type of construction shown here, with two "headers" and one "stretcher," is characteristic of Phoenician work, and he probably used Phoenician workmen.

The last of the four towns mentioned in this valley is Bezek, where Saul gathered the tribes together before going to the help of Jabesh Gilead just across the Jordan to the east (I Sam. 11:8). The other places mentioned are Samaria itself, able to control the roads from Tulkarm, from Shechem and from Esdraelon, and, in the north, Dothan and Ibleam.

B. 4. *The Carmel Range.* This final section of the central group of highlands is divided into three clear parts, the Umm el-Fahm arch, the central basin, and the main headland of Car-

44. *The Wadi Fari'a.* This was one of the valleys leading down to the Jordan which made the region of Manasseh so easily accessible from outside.

mel in the northwest. Both Umm el-Fahm and the Carmel headland are Cenomanian limestone with its fertile terra rossa, both rocky and neither of them very high—never as much as 2000 feet—but because of their exposure to the sea winds they are well watered. They were therefore both forested in Biblical times, and even today they carry a good covering of scrub woodland and *maquis*. They were thus only thinly peopled and constituted a real obstacle in the passage from north to south, so that the passes across Carmel were given an added importance. The main headland

in the north was exceptionally difficult to penetrate, for it was very thickly forested, isolated by marshes and outlined by extremely precipitous fault scarps. The result of this isolation was that it came to be regarded with superstitious awe, and traces of this mystery have lingered even to the present day.* There are several ancient sanctuaries on its heights, and it was the scene of the dramatic contest between Elijah and the prophets of Baal (I Kings 18:17–46). It was a fitting site for such an argument, for Carmel itself was disputed territory, both Israel and

* On top of Carmel, overlooking the modern cement factory at Nesher, is the grove known as the Forty Oaks and, at any rate till 1948, some villagers held it in such respect that an oath taken in its name was thought to be especially binding.

45. *Roman Basilica at Samaria*

Phoenicia claiming it as their own, and so here the claims of the Phoenician goddess were suitably matched against the demands of a God who brooked no rival.

The middle section is a little curious. It is formed of the Lower Eocene, rather than the Upper Eocene of central Samaria and the true Shephelah, and it is not attractive to settlement. Despite sufficient rainfall and singularly abundant springs, this "Israelite Shephelah" is by its infertility in marked contrast to the two Cenomanian regions. Today there is no scrub, save where a very thin covering appears on the westward slopes, and olives are nowhere to be seen; the villages are but the tiniest groups of little houses. Even in early days, this "Shephelah" can never have compared with the luxuriant covering of Carmel and Umm el-Fahm, and since it is not very high, reaching 1000 feet only near Megiddo, it is perhaps surprising that it should have been such an obstacle. However, the slopes facing the plain on both sides are steep despite their low elevation, and the Esdraelon scarp especially so, and the woodland which it carried, though probably far from dense, may well have been enough to hinder easy travel. It is a good example of how even a slight obstacle can channel all movement round itself.

In New Testament times Manasseh had become the country of the Samaritans, though it is possible that the name referred only to the central section. There was a fine city at Sebastia, and there must have been much commerce on the many roads within the region. However, the ancient enmity between the Joseph tribes and Judah had been still further embittered by the exchange of populations which the Assyrians had imposed on Samaria (II Kings 17:24–41), and by the differing histories of the two parts of the country in the succeeding years. Many Jews thought it unsafe to travel through Samaria, though Jesus certainly did so (John 4:4; Luke 9:51–56), and later many Christians fled to Samaria as a place where they would be free from Jewish attack, so that Samaria became an important Christian center (Acts 8:1–25, 15:3). More recently the people of this district, and especially of Nablus and Tulkarm, have shown themselves notably resistant to the government either of the mandatory power at Jerusalem or of the country of Jordan at Amman. The different geography has caused this to be a region apart even to the present day.

The same factors, of course, which brought wealth and leadership to Manasseh were the cause of the downfall of the northern kingdom. Enervating luxury and pagan worship came in from the outside along the great trade routes and finally the fact that Israel controlled these routes convinced the Assyrians that she must be eliminated, for they wanted to control the routes for themselves. "When a strong man, fully armed, guards his own palace, his goods are in peace; but when one stronger than he assails him and overcomes him, he takes away his armor in which he trusted, and divides his spoil" (Luke 11:21–22).

CHAPTER XVI

Galilee of the Gentiles

And he went about all Galilee, teaching in their synagogues and preaching the gospel of the kingdom and healing every disease and every infirmity among the people.

MATTHEW 4:23

B. 5. *Lower Galilee.* Immediately to the north of the plain of Esdraelon and the Valley of Jezreel begins that region which for Christians must forever be associated with the Gospels, the region of Galilee. It is very sharply divided into two sections, Upper and Lower Galilee, by the tremendous fault of Esh-Shaghur, cutting right across the country from the direction of Acre to somewhat south of Safad, and towering above the basin of Esh-Shaghur to a height sometimes of 2000 feet. North of this is the high plateau of Upper Galilee, where the elevated sections are well over 3000 feet and Jebel Jarmuq reaches as much as 3900; to the south are the shattered hills of Lower Galilee, which nowhere surpass 2000 feet.

Structurally the pattern is complicated. The upwarp which in Samaria lay on the eastern side, has here passed across the Jordan into the dome of Gilead. The central basin of Samaria continues toward Lake Tiberias, but is hidden for the most part under great outflows of basalt. The Umm el-Fahm upfold is continued northward through the central section of Lower Galilee, though considerably disturbed by faults and cross folding, and the Eocene hills which occupy the Israelite Shephelah in the central basin of Carmel are to be found again in the low hills west of Nazareth. The Carmel headland is cut off very sharply by the fault scarp overlooking the Haifa plain, but it may perhaps be traced once more in the extreme west of Upper Galilee. This pattern has been rendered more complex by folding and faulting. There are folds running more or less from west to east, one of which has produced the Nazareth trough in Lower Galilee, lying athwart the region and joining the southwestern basin with the Tiberias basin. However, once again this basin structure is obscured by the hard Eocene limestone which it contains and which forms the hills immediately

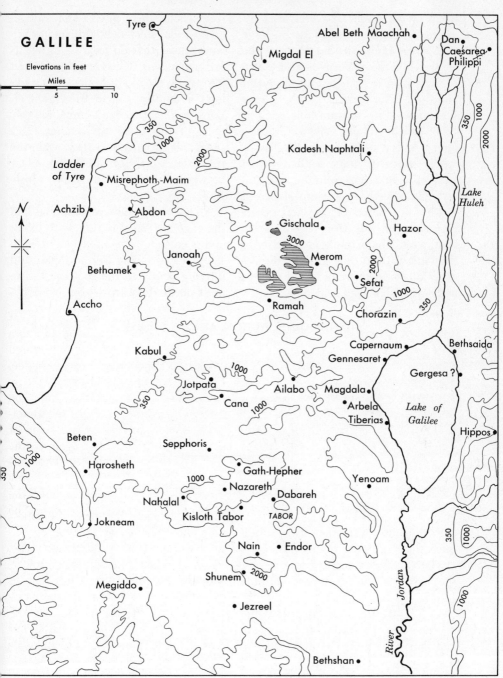

Fig. 36.

north of Nazareth. The west-east direction is followed also by a large number of faults so that parts of the central hills have been pushed down to form basins, such as Sahl el-Battuf and the Tur'an basin, and others have been pushed up to form hills, such as Jebel Tur'an. Faults, however, run in almost every direction in Galilee. A whole series of hinge faults, cutting back in wide curves from the Rift Valley, has carved the eastern slopes of Galilee into tilted blocks, and others run more or less from northeast to southwest. The extreme complexity of the fault pattern thus justifies the description given above of Lower Galilee as being a shattered region.

from Nazareth to Shefr 'Amr and remains today very nearly devoid of villages, those that do exist being on its extreme edges. Cleaving this district into two is the Wadi Malik, which follows a dog-leg course from Sahl el-Battuf along two fault lines, roughly at right angles to each other. This steep-sided, narrow valley was the Iphtah-el, which formed the boundary between Zebulun and Asher (Josh. 19:14, 27).

All the region between Tiberias and the edge of Jezreel is filled with basalt and is cut into four tilted blocks, with steep scarps facing the northeast and dipping gently to the southwest. The most northerly scarp is that overlook-

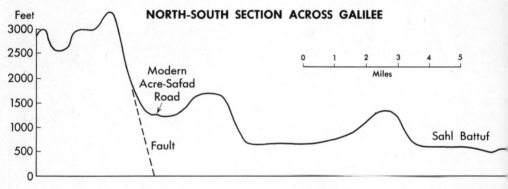

Fig. 37.

Within Lower Galilee two subregions show signs of proving rather less attractive to settlement than the rest, the basalt in the southeast and the Lower Eocene district in the southwest. This southwestern district is the continuation of the Israelite Shephelah and shares the same characteristics, so that it would not be improper to call it the "Galilean Shephelah." It lies roughly southwest of the present road

ing Magdala and the plain of Gennesaret and followed at its foot by the modern road from Majdal to Maghar. From Magdala (the name, i.e., tower, suggests that there was a fort here to guard the road junction) a rocky valley leads up to the plateau at the Horns of Hattin, where Saladin defeated the Crusaders, and in this valley also the caves in the precipitous Eocene cliffs beneath the basalt were a refuge for the Jewish rebels under

46. *The Valley of the Robbers.* This was one of the routes leading down from Lower Galilee to the Lake. In the foreground is the plain of Gennesaret and near here was Magdala, which controlled the entrance to this valley.

Bar Kochba. This valley lies very nearly at the northwestern edge of the continuous basalt.

The second scarp is that which curves round from the southwestern end of the Lake to the Horns of Hattin themselves, and on its southwestern side the block slopes down to the basin of Ardh el-Hima which is drained by the Fajjas. The third scarp may be called the Yavneel scarp from the name of the *kibbutz* which lies at its foot, and it swings back into the plateau from near the confluence of the

Yarmuq with the Jordan. The stream which drains the basin to the south-west of this is the Bira, flowing from near the foot of Tabor southeastward to the Jordan, but this valley, which appears on a small-scale map to be such an easy and convenient route, is narrow, rocky and difficult. The fourth scarp, to which we may give the name of Belvoir, from the great Crusading castle which crowned the highest point overlooking the Jordan Valley, is not so high as the preceding one and Belvoir is not much above 600 feet above sea level, though it is about 1400 feet above the Rift Valley. Belvoir stood on the site of the present village of Kaukab el-Hawa and in Roman times the fort of Agrappina stood at the same place. This part of the basalt is more easily negotiable and tracks cross it today in every direction.

This basalt region has never been thickly populated and the map of Roman Palestine reveals it to have been an empty corner also in New Testament times, though a road followed the Ardh el-Hima to the Jordan. This emptiness must be ascribed to the extreme rockiness of the land, which is, therefore, far from easy to cultivate.

Connecting these two less attractive regions is the Nazareth basin, much dissected by faults and rising on the southern side to the steep scarp of Jebel Qafsa, which overlooks the plain of Esdraelon. This scarp formed part of the southern boundary of Zebulun, though they seem to have overflowed into the plain at the expense of the weaker tribe of Issachar, for Chesulloth (or Chisloth-Tabor) in Esdraelon is named in Joshua 19:18 as being part of Issachar, but in Joshua 19:12–13 it forms the boundary of Zebulun, together with Daberath, which also is in the plain (Chesulloth = Iksal; Daberath = Daburiyeh). Nazareth itself lies in a basin of Senonian chalk behind this scarp and at the foot of another fault which marks the southern edge of the harder Eocene hills. These hills are here but a narrow line, and at their foot there is a spring, known today as the Well of the Virgin, round which the little village of Nazareth grew. Throughout Biblical times, of course, it was no more than a village, though today it is the largest town in the district.

When Jesus lived at Nazareth the chief town of the region lay a few miles farther to the northwest on another fault line at the edge of an outcrop of Cenomanian. This was Sepphoris, the modern village of Saffuriyeh, just south of the main Roman road from Ptolemais to Tiberias. This road ran almost in a straight line from Ptolemais to just north of Sepphoris, through Asochis at the western end of Sahl el-Battuf, whose marshes it avoided. It swung round to join what is now the Tiberias-Nazareth road near Tur'an and then divided, one branch following very much the line of the present road to Tiberias, and the other continuing down the Ardh el-Hima depression. This road was of great importance for carrying the grain from the Hauran east of the Lake to the port at Ptolemais, and was surely much trodden by Jesus himself in his journeys about Galilee.

North of the Nazareth trough, in which there are quite a number of villages, there is a series of fault basins aligned from west to east. The first of these is the Tur'an basin, with the steep slope of Jebel Tur'an (1780 feet) rising immediately to the north of it, and beyond that again is the much bigger basin of Sahl el-Battuf which is enclosed on the north by a wedge-shaped block of hills rising to 1710 feet and outlined by two faults which converge in the east near the modern village of 'Eilabun. North of this wedge of hills is the Halazun basin drained toward the west by the Halazun and closed by a great semicircular fault at the eastern end. Jebel Kammana, which rises to the north of this is 1950 feet high and so it is clear that the general level of the plateau is steadily rising, despite its dissection by so many faults. Beyond Jebel Kammana is the long narrow basin of Esh-Shaghur occupied by the Acre-Safad road, and then comes the tremendous wall of Upper Galilee.

These basins naturally provide a number of easy passages across Lower Galilee from the coast plain to the Lake area, where there is a tendency for all the routes to converge on the little plain of Gennesaret on the northwest, even the main Tiberias road being connected with this by the narrow valley which debouches on Magdala. However, the passages are not necessarily quite as easy as they appear on the map, for the exits at either end are very often closed and the drainage finds its way to the sea by devious routes. Thus the Tur'an basin drains northward into the Sahl el-Battuf by a narrow cleft in the Cenomanian hills, and the Sahl el-Battuf in its turn is drained by the narrow and zigzag valley of the Iphtah-el, which makes its way, somewhat indirectly, to the Kishon across the Galilean Shephelah. Similarly, the Basin of Esh-Shaghur is drained southward to the Halazun, the only one of the basins which appears to have a direct outlet westward to the sea. However, in its exit from the basin to the plain of Acre the Halazun valley is narrow and rocky and unsuited to easy communications. In fact, anyone who has done much cross-country walking in Galilee soon discovers that it is unwise to follow a wadi, however direct it may appear to be on a map, for as they leave the plateau, even in the passage from the low-lying basins to the plain, these valleys become steep and precipitous, and occasionally quite impassable. The roads and tracks, therefore,

in Galilee very often follow the spurs rather than the valleys in climbing onto the plateau, and then skirt round the edge of the basins, avoiding the areas which may become flooded in the rainy season.

This curiously indirect drainage has meant that some of the basins are waterlogged in winter, though, as a result, they are floored with very fertile alluvium. The villages consequently keep to the edges of the basins, or climb halfway up the slopes of the confining hills. It is here that the olives are to be found, covering the gentler slopes and the alluvial fans, vines also being produced on the hillsides, while the rich alluvial soil of the lowest lying areas forms the fields in which the wheat is grown. Of these villages of Galilee, so many of which must have been visited either by Jesus or by his disciples, for we get the impression from the Gospels that they attempted to cover the whole region, only three are mentioned in the New Testament, Nazareth where he passed his boyhood, Nain and Cana. Nain is in the extreme south on the slopes of the Hill of Moreh, and Cana is traditionally associated with Kafr Kanna on the road from Nazareth to Tiberias. However, it is more probably to be identified with Kana, a ruin on the northern edge of Sahl el-Battuf, which even today is called by the Arabs "Cana of Galilee." The other towns mentioned are round the Lake and must be considered therefore as belonging to the Rift Valley region.

This section of Lower Galilee comes to an end on the east at the road which runs today almost due north from Kefar Tavor to Kafr Inan, and which also marks the eastern edge of the most thickly populated section, for the land to the east is either the less attractive basalt country or the dry, eastward-facing slopes which drop down to the Lake and the plain of Gennesaret. Thus, it is clear that of all the northern tribes Zebulun was in the strongest position. Naphtali, it is true, was "full of the blessing of the Lord" and had been told to "possess the lake and the south" (Deut. 33:23) as well as the less tempting basalt, but, like Asher, she turned her back on the rest of Israel and was too easily exposed to attack, while Issachar in the rich valley of Jezreel was soon enslaved. Zebulun, however, was not only more central, but included the most thickly settled part of Lower Galilee, the interior zone of down-faulted basins and intervening blocks of hills, only some 19 miles long by 12 wide, but very pleasing to the sight. Here there is no lack of rain, the desert is nowhere to be seen, and in spring every hillside is ablaze with flowers and every basin rich with grain. Outside the main stream of Israelite life in Old Testament times, Galilee came into its own in the New Testament, for then the stern Roman control had freed these hills from the fear of enemy attack. By that time it had become a region with a consciousness of its own and a tendency to independent thought which was encouraged by its easy contacts with the outside world. It was for this reason that the strict Jews of the south despised the people of Galilee, feeling certain that no prophet could arise from such a free-thinking group (John 1:46, 7:41, 52). However, it was in Galilee that Jesus

chose to teach, rather than in the true center of Judaism, to which he seems to have paid but occasional visits, and it was from Galilee that he chose his closest friends. In the end it was not a Galilean who betrayed him.

When we are told that Jesus went about all Galilee, it is Lower Galilee and the shores of Lake Tiberias that is meant, and it is therefore against this background that we must picture him. As he went from village to village among the wooded hills, he would have skirted the fertile basins, rich with grain, taking perhaps a little over an hour to walk the full length of the largest of them, and have climbed up through the olives and vineyards which clothed the slopes. Even in the long summer, when the brilliant thistles took the place of flowers among the rocks and the stubble had gone from the fields, it would not have been a barren landscape, for the trees and shrubs must still have been many. As he trudged the dusty footpaths that cut across the hills, he would have met the farmers with their laden donkeys, taking grapes and vegetables to sell in Sepphoris or the lakeside towns, using the cool hours of the gray and very early dawn to make their journey. Sometimes he would have used the great trade routes which led from the lake shores to Ptolemais or the south and would have passed the long trains of pack animals which carried the grain of the Hauran or the rich fruits of Damascus, and sometimes he would have turned aside along a narrow track to a little village, such, indeed, as Nazareth then was.

But even away from the main highroads he would never have been far from the busy commerce and the restless coming and going of the Roman world, since Galilee is so very small, and whenever he was down beside the Lake he would have been in the thick of it. The "merchant in search of fine pearls" (Matt. 13:45), "a man going on a journey" (Matt. 25:14), the younger son who "gathered all that he had and took his journey into a far country" (Luke 15:13), as well as the farmers and the fishermen, would have been among the people he met upon his normal visits to the towns and villages round about.

B. 6. *Upper Galilee*. This last of the highland regions stands apart, aloof and windswept on its lofty heights. Here, well to the north, the rain is heavy and assured, and the westward-facing slopes especially are so thickly clothed with scrub that even at the present time they are not easily passable, and in the better wooded past all these mountains must have been truly forested, and therefore, in a sense, the beginning of Lebanon. It is not a region which enters much into Biblical history, and even in Roman times the villages here were very small and few. The most important section is the trough which lies east of the Jebel Jarmuq range, running more or less due north and south. Immediately east of Jarmuq is the more easily eroded Senonian chalk and then comes once again the harder Eocene, which forms the hills upon which Safad stands, Jebel Kinaan just behind the town rising to somewhat over 3000 feet. This section between Safad and Jarmuq, though still uplifted, is nevertheless lower and more open than the rest, for the fact that it is in a rain shadow

from the Jarmuq range combined with the less fertile soil to produce a lessening of the forest cover. This is the Gate of Merom and slightly to the north was the Roman fortified townlet of Gischala, the present village of Jish.

47. *Upper Galilee*. The windswept moorland near the frontier of Lebanon. In Biblical times it would have carried a considerable forest cover.

It was the least important of the roads into the country, but its existence meant that this lofty plateau was not entirely closed to movement.

Upper Galilee gave to the north what every other important section of Palestine possessed, a region of escape. This has been a very important feature of Palestinian geography and has contributed in no small measure to its turbulent history, for the existence of these regions helps to explain why such a tiny country has always been so very difficult to control. In the first place, Palestine is divided, as should surely be evident by now, into a number of little regions, each very small, but sharply different from one another and possessing a very definite local consciousness. Thus the people of Judaea, of Samaria and Galilee, lived their lives apart; the interests of each group were different, and, though it is clear that men traveled about from one region to another, they tended to be loyal to their own community and to resent the claims of others. When a strong government tried to impose a unified control, it was difficult, if not impossible, to reconcile the wishes of the different communities. This might have been overcome in time, if the dissidents in every area had not had somewhere to which to escape, where they might take refuge from the punitive efforts of the military and might have time to recoup their forces. Thus, the people of Judah fled either to the Shephelah or to Jeshimmon, leaving the soldiers to search for them, "like one who hunts a partridge in the mountains" (I Sam. 26:20), and those who lived in Samaria took refuge either in Carmel or across the fords of the Jordan in the forested heights of Gilead. Likewise the Galileans, who were not behind the rest of their countrymen in resistance to domination, were able to slip away into their own upper plateau and lose themselves in the forests of Lebanon.

Even though today the forests are fewer and communications easier, the importance of these regions of escape still holds true, as witness the difficulty the British had in subduing the Arab rebellion of 1936–39. In fact, the efforts of the modern world to solve the "Palestine problem" to some extent parallel the efforts of the Romans to do exactly the same thing, though, naturally, new factors are involved today which render the problem greatly more complex.

CHAPTER XVII

The Entrance of the Hamath and the Arabah

Jeroboam restored the border of Israel from the entrance of Hamath as far as the Sea of the Arabah, according to the word of the Lord, the God of Israel, which he spoke by his servant Jonah, the son of Amittai, the prophet, who was from Gath-hepher.

II KINGS 14:25

C. 1. *The Huleh Basin.* Slicing across the whole Palestinian region, very nearly directly from north to south, until the valley bottom disappears beneath the tepid waters of the Red Sea, is the great Rift Valley. On a relief map it looks as if it were the continuation of the similar valley of Celosyria, which divides the Lebanon from the Anti-Lebanon, but structurally this is not so. The Palestinian rift is a prolonged depressed area between two parallel series of faults, but the Syrian rift has only one great fault scarp, that on the west, for the slopes of the Anti-Lebanon on the east are formed instead of very sharply tilted strata. Moreover, the direction of the faulting is different, for the Syrian valley is aligned more toward the northeast, while the valley of the Jordan lies due north and south, and its continuation in the north must be traced in the

headland of Beirut, rather than in the great central valley. Finally, there is a marked difference in elevation, the Syrian rift being everywhere an upland valley with its highest section well over 3000 feet, while the Palestinian rift is for the most part far below sea level, and rises to 650 feet above the sea only in the southern part of the Arabah.

The point of junction of the two rift systems is Metullah, the modern frontier village between Israel and Syria, not far from Tel Abil, which was the site of Abel Beth Maacah, the frontier settlement between the ancient Syria and Israel. Here the valley descends in a steep and sudden step from Merj Ayoun in the north, lying somewhat above 1600 feet above the sea, to the Huleh basin in the south, which is everywhere below 300 feet. From Merj Ayoun come the two smaller of the four streams which feed the Jordan, the Bareighit and the Hasbani, the former leaping over the threshold in a remarkable little waterfall near Metullah and postponing its junction with the Jordan until just before reaching the Huleh marshes, and the latter joining the two major streams nearer the head of the basin. Towering above Merj Ayoun on the east stands Hermon, that tremendous shoulder of the Anti-Lebanon, which from every aspect dominates this landscape, climbing up from the plain to 9100 feet, the highest point in the whole of the long stretch of the Levant coast. This great mountain, which is heavy with snow in winter and retains a few patches even during the long, hot summer months, is variously named in the Bible, being called by the Phoenicians Sirion and by the Amorites Senir (Deut. 3:9, 4:48; Song 4:8), and it is normal to identify it also with the "many-peaked mountain, mountain of Bashan" in Psalm 68:15. However, it may be that this mountain, which is said to look with envy upon the glory that God has bestowed on the much smaller hill at Jerusalem, is really the volcanic Jebel Druze, which is more truly many-peaked than Hermon.* The cold snows of Hermon cause the Jordan to flood when they melt in the late spring, and they were credited with supplying the dew which refreshes the dry Palestinian hills in the long summer drought (Ps. 133:3).

At the foot of Hermon rise the two major streams of the Jordan, the Liddani and Banyasi, springing not far from each other at Tel el-Qadi and Banias. Tel el-Qadi is probably the an-

* See below, pp. 220 and 222.

cient Dan, and Banias was Caesarea Philippi, the first of them in the basin itself, and the second a little farther to the east and rather higher up the mountain slope. Both are quite incredibly lovely, for at each the cold water flows from the rock as an already notable stream, and around them there is lush green everywhere even in the height of summer.

Here is a curious corner in Palestinian history, for though it is far from the great centers of Israelite life, it keeps recurring in the records. It is first an important frontier, for here met the pretensions of three countries, Israel, Syria and Phoenicia, even as today Syria, Lebanon and Israel meet at the same place. The first mention is of Abraham pursuing the kings who had captured his nephew as far as Dan and beyond before he overtook them (Gen. 14:14), but that was long before the tribe of Dan lived there. In the early days the place was called Laish and the people "dwelt in security, after the manner of the Sidonians, quiet and unsuspecting, lacking nothing that is in the earth, and possessing wealth . . . they were far from the Sidonians and had no dealings with any one" (Judg. 18:7). Upon this unsuspecting people, too far from Sidon to get Phoenician help, came the people of Dan, themselves driven out and in search of somewhere to settle, and the Danites "smote them with the edge of the sword, and burned the city with fire" (Judg. 18:27). From that time on the name of the town was changed to Dan, and it was held to be the most northerly town in the country. Lurking in their rich woodlands, the people of Dan were "a lion's whelp, that leaps forth from Bashan" (Deut. 33:22), and harried the travelers on the roads from the north, "as a viper by the path, that bites the horse's heels so that his rider falls backward" (Gen. 49:17), but when war came upon the country from the north the villages of Dan were the first to suffer, for no invader dared leave this nest of vipers to threaten his lines of communication (I Kings 15:20; II Kings 15:29). Such a distant tribe could normally pursue a role somewhat independent of the authority of Jerusalem, and it was in Abel Beth Maacah that the rebel Sheba sought refuge (II Sam. 20:14), but in those days the authority at Jerusalem was strong and widespread, and so his flight was vain.

The second cause of Dan's importance was religious, for in primitive times it was impossible that the rocks which gave forth these two broad streams should not have been accounted the abode of gods. "They were wont to say in old time, 'Let them but ask counsel at Abel'" (II Sam. 20:18), and today one may see at Banias the niches which recall the ancient worship. When the Danites first settled at Laish, they were said to have set up a graven image (Judg. 18:30) and later it was one of the towns where Jeroboam put a golden calf (I Kings 12:29; II Kings 10:29). Amos speaks of the people saying, "As thy god lives, O Dan!" (Amos 8:14), and Josephus mentions the temple of the golden calf at Daphne, as it was then called.[1] In Roman times Banias was the center of the worship of Pan, from whom it was called Paneas, the name which persists today in its Arabicized form. Herod built a temple here to Augustus

and later, when it became part of the tetrarchy of Philip, the name of the town was changed to Caesarea, called Caesarea Philippi to distinguish it from the important seaport on the coast.

It was at Caesarea Philippi, in this haunt of pagan worship where stood shrines both of Caesar and of Pan, representing the adoration of the state and of the useless gods of the heathen, that Jesus chose to ask his disciples the critical question, "Who do you say that I am?" (Mark 8:29), and amid the ancient idols Peter answered him, "You are the Christ," the person we have all been waiting for. With this answer he pronounced the death sentence upon all the gods which stood about him, not one of whom could save mankind, and in a sense the death sentence also of Christ himself, for we are told that immediately "he began to teach them that the Son of man must suffer many things, and be rejected by the elders and the chief priests and the scribes, and be killed, and"—herein lay the difference—"after three days rise again" (Mark 8:31). It is difficult, therefore, now to stand amid the ruins of these discredited shrines unmoved by the climactic importance of this little frontier village.

"And after six days Jesus took with him Peter and James and John, and led them up into a high mountain apart by themselves; and he was transfigured before them" (Mark 9:2). Traditionally this high mountain was Tabor, but more probably it was Hermon, whose slopes rise steeply from the Jordan's source at Caesarea Philippi. It is true that there would have been no great difficulty for those who were used to traveling about the country-side on foot in getting to Tabor within a week, but there is no necessity to think that they did when the highest mountain of all stood just above them. It is, however, a little surprising that the name of the Mount of Transfiguration is nowhere mentioned, if it is to be identified with either Tabor or Hermon, for the names of both were as much part of common speech as the name of the Mount of Olives, and it is therefore possible that it was neither of them. The presence of the scribes in the crowd which Jesus found assembled when he came down from the mountain makes one wonder whether it was near Hermon, for it is unlikely that they would have been in the pagan Caesarea Philippi, and it seems clear also that the father of the epileptic boy was a Jew, for Jesus expected him to believe and was shocked when he did not (Mark 9:14–29). Of course, it may be that we have here two stories of events which took place separately and which St. Mark placed side by side for effect, but the account as we have it certainly suggests that it was at the foot of the mountain that the healing took place.

The Huleh basin which lies to the south of this is very small, only some 9 miles long by 3 wide. At the southern end is the shallow lake of the same name, which is now certainly smaller than it was in the past, for it has been slowly filling with sediment behind the basalt dam which blocks the course of the Jordan beyond it, creating the almost impenetrable papyrus marshes, which together with the lake fill fully half the basin. Above the marshes the three headwaters first join about 2 miles south of Dan, and then almost immediately divide again to enter the lake in two main streams, the Jordan and Tur'an. On either side rise the steep scarps of Upper Galilee and the plateau of Bashan. The Galilee scarp is unbroken almost to the southern end of the basin, but the volcanic slopes on the east are seamed by many short scarp streams, which are too steep and rocky, however, to form easy lines of access to the plateau. Hemmed in between the marshes and the mountains, the main road from the north clings to the foot of Galilee until it reaches the uplands of the basalt dam. In the north a road curved round the foot of Hermon through Caesarea Philippi and Abel Beth Maacah, and thence made its way across the mountains to Tyre, but south of this there is no road from the east until the great Trunk Road comes in beyond Hazor.

This crosses the Jordan just below Lake Huleh, by the Bridge of Jacob's Daughters, the only possible bridge point, since to the south of it the river enters the confines of the rocky basalt gorge, where the hills stand more than 1200 feet above the stream. The dam itself is a small, generally level, but rocky, area, whose surface is about 1200 feet above sea level, and which, in contrast to the larger basalt region to the south, carries many ruins of earlier habitation. The two places on this little plateau which are mentioned in the Bible are Hazor, which in the days of Joshua commanded the junction of the route from the north with the Trunk Road, and Chorazin, on the edge of the basalt overlooking the lake, one of the places where many of Jesus' mighty works were done (Josh, 11:10; Matt. 11:21).

C. 2. *Chinnereth.* To the south of this dam the river Jordan, now a little more than 600 feet below sea level, breaks free from the restricting valley walls and enters the blue waters of Lake Tiberias or the Sea of Galilee. This little, heart-shaped lake, only 12 miles long by five broad at its widest point, is closely shut in by hills on nearly every side. The broadest plain is the tiny triangle of the plain of Gennesaret in the northwest, and on the northeast also the hills withdraw a little from the shore in the region of Buteiha, but elsewhere they crowd closely in upon it. Nowhere, however, are they impassable, for roads can descend to the water at many points and everywhere there is sufficient space for a track to pass right round the lake. The warm winters and very long, hot summers mean a rich production of almost every kind of Palestinian crop, for there is plentiful water from the surrounding hills, and in spring the gaily colored slopes glow with a brilliance which is nowhere surpassed, even in the Palestinian scene.

Today this little region has a placid beauty which is wonderfully satisfying to those who seek a quiet retreat where they can meditate upon the Gospel story. It is not easily possible to imagine the loveliness of the Sea of Galilee, where distant Hermon presides over the green, enfolding hills and the deep blue waters of the lake, and so it is not surprising that those who come here from the West do not want it changed, and protest at every modern house, which seems to them to mar the hallowed shores. Yet this was not the Galilee which Jesus knew. It was not then a scene of rustic beauty, with only an occasional fishing boat upon the surface of the lake. In his day the shores were bustling with life, the fishing boats were more plentiful and in the right season also there must have been much transporting of the grain across the water from Bashan, for this would have been much easier than taking it round by road. Moreover, the Trunk Road in part skirted the western shores, and from the little plain of Gennesaret several routes ran up across the Galilean hills toward Ptolemais on the coast. It was, therefore, not among simple village folk that most of his mighty works were done, but among the practical businessmen of Chorazin, Bethsaida and Capernaum, and it was they who were condemned because they did not repent (Matt. 11:20–24).

It is not easy to identify all the places mentioned. An important town of the period was Tiberias, for there the steep hillside close upon the lake makes possible the building of a fortified city, but there is no record of Jesus' ever having gone there, since in his day it was a Gentile city into which no Jew would enter. Not far to the south of Tiberias are the hot springs to which, then as now, people came for relief from their diseases, and beyond the southern end of the lake, a little way up the valley of the Yarmuq, there are the other hot springs of el-Hamme, which, possibly for no better reason than that they are more difficult to reach, are often more highly esteemed. These medicinal springs and the mild winter climate combine to make the shores of the lake an invalid resort, and this may have some bearing on the amazingly large number of miracles of healing which are recorded as having taken place beside the lake (Mark 1:32–34, 3:10, 6:53–56).

Magdala is Majdal at the foot of the Valley of the Robbers, and Capernaum and Chorazin are also certain, the one being Tel Hum on the northwestern shores of the lake, and the other Khirbet Kerazeh on the basalt hills above it. However, beyond that we can only guess. Bethsaida was somewhere on the northeastern shore, and Chinnereth may have been Tel el-'Oreimah in the plain of Gennesaret.

48. *The River Jordan.* This picture was taken near Adam, the modern ed-Damiyeh, where landslides have caused the damming of the river on more than one occasion in history.

Dalmanutha is quite impossible to identify and there is some possibility that it was the same as Magdala.

The eastern side of the lake was largely Gentile, and was part of the region of the Decapolis, from which many people came to hear Jesus, but to which he seems to have gone only

when he wished to get away for a quiet conversation with his disciples. Somewhere on this shore took place the incident of the Gadarene swine, but since the name is rendered variously as Gerasene, Gergasene and Gadarene, and since in any case the description is of a district and not of an exact place, there is no knowing for certain where it happened. Gerasa was Jerash, far away from the lake in the hills of Gilead, and Gadara was Umm Qeis on the southern edge of the Yarmuq valley, but Gergasa is unknown, unless it was, as some suggest, Koursi on the eastern shore of the lake, but this is very dubious.

C. 3. *The Ghor.* Beyond the lake the Rift continues agreeable until it narrows some 25 miles to the south. There is still sufficient rain for cultivation, even without irrigation, and also frequent streams, especially on the eastern side, from which water may be drawn. The Jordan is not yet sunk too far beneath the general level of the plain to be easily fordable, and there are many bridge points along its course. On the eastern side it is joined not far below the lake by the Yarmuq, which brings as much water into the common stream as the Jordan itself, and then in order come the 'Arab, the Taibeh, the Ziqlab and the Yabes, as well as certain smaller streams. Near the entrance of the Yabes into the plain was Jabesh Gilead, which sent men secretly across the river to Beth-shean to rescue the body of Saul in remembrance of the time when he had rescued them from the Ammonite attack (I Sam. 11:1–11, 31:8–13), and, slightly to the north of this, was Pella at Khirbet Fahl, one of the cities of the

Decapolis. Across the river to the west is the broad opening of the valley of Jezreel before it narrows west of Beth-shean.

In the latitude of Samaria the Rift is crossed by the line of the Judaean-Gilead dome, and here the mountains close in upon the river, constricting the valley into a narrow "waist," to the south of which the character of the landscape changes from easily cultivable land to desert. As the Ghor opens out again it is joined by the Jabbok valley on the east and the rift valley of the Fari'a on the west, the last of the fords until Jericho being just south of the Jabbok confluence. Here is Adam (Josh. 3:16), where more than once in history a landslide has dammed the Jordan floods. Not only is the climate drier here, but the valley is wider, 12 miles in places, large areas of the plain are more than 1000 feet below sea level, and the river has cut deeper into the valley bottom, all of which helps to differentiate this section from that to the north of the "waist."

It is in this section that is most fully developed the triple division of the Rift which had already begun to make its appearance in the north. First, sloping steadily from the foot of the hills on either side to the river in the center is the main valley floor, the true "Ghor," and here, when water is available, are the cultivated fields and pasture lands. But then, as the river is approached, the ground breaks away suddenly into the desolate badlands of the *qattara*, which exhibit in miniature all the features of a dis-

Fig. 38.

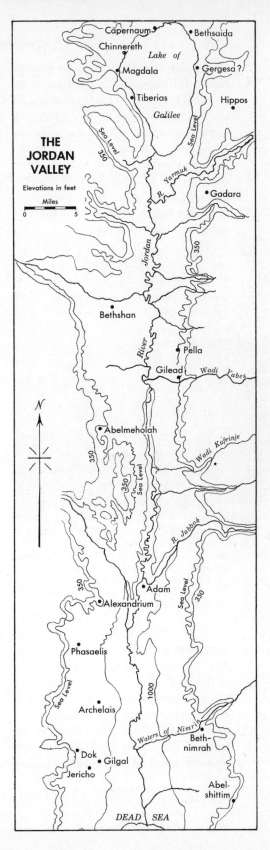

THE JORDAN VALLEY

Elevations in feet

Miles

0   5

N

sected desert landscape. It is a fascinating little region for the student of physical geography, for it contains, all in manageable size, the plateaus, buttes and mesas which normally are to be seen only on a much grander scale. It is exhausting to explore, however, for the ash-gray marl is horribly slippery after rain, and, when dry, crumbles under the foot. It is uncultivated and uncultivable.

49. *The jungle of the Jordan.* The thick and almost impenetrable *zor,* through which the river flows and which in ancient times was a terrifying haunt of wild beasts. Boar are still hunted there today.

Within the confining walls of the *qattara* is the real valley of the Jordan, the narrow, impenetrable jungle of the *zor,* where the river twists and turns in innumerable meanders amid a tangled confusion of tamarisk and other shrubs. Some 150 feet below the level of the Ghor and attaining in places a width of over a mile, the *zor*

is the part which is flooded by the melting snows of Hermon when "the Jordan overflows all its banks throughout the time of harvest" (Josh. 3:15) and its dense thickets of tropical woodland are still today the home of wild beasts, though the lion, the most famous of them, has long since disappeared. The Hebrew word for this impenetrable shrubbery is גָּאוֹן, which elsewhere has the meaning of "pride" or "excellency" (Jer. 12:5, 49:19, 50:44; Zech. 11:3; cf. Ps. 47:4, 59:12; Prov. 16:18), and the use of this metaphor to describe this kind of vegetation should be compared with the use of הֲדַר to describe the luxuriant Sharon.

It is the *qattara* and the *zor* which together have made the Jordan such a strong division between the peoples on either side, rather than the river alone, which, it must be confessed, is narrow, muddy and almost despicable, and nowhere especially difficult to cross, though the swift current may sweep an unwary traveler away. Naaman not unreasonably thought it less impressive than the clear streams which feed the rich gardens of Damascus (II Kings 5:12). However, so difficult to penetrate are the two regions which enclose it that the peoples it divides tend to be suspicious of each other even to the present day.* North of the "waist" where fords are more frequent communication was easier and the tribe of Manasseh sprawled across the hills on either side, and yet even there the people were

* There are, of course, new causes for the tension between eastern and western parts of the Hashemite kingdom, but these new causes are themselves not unrelated to the geography.

but uneasy companions, as the stories of suspicion, rivalry and bitterness between them record (Josh. 22; Judg. 8:4–17, 12:1–6, 21:8–12). It was the measure of the greatness of Saul that he was able to rouse all the western tribes to go to the help of Jabesh Gilead, a town which earlier had refused to come to the common meeting (Judg. 21:8–12), and the fact that he had done this was the ground of their gratitude to him. South of the "waist" the comings and goings across the stream were always fewer, and the plateau to the east of the Jordan was often under the domination of the Ammonites or Moabites.

It must not be imagined, however, that the fact that the Lower Ghor was desert meant that it was uncultivated. Far back in the time of Abraham there had been many little settlements along the edges of the hills, and under the Roman genius the Ghor was made to flourish, for the waters from the hills were brought in aqueducts (a lengthy one descends the Wadi Qilt near Jericho) and spread out among the palm groves of the plain. Pliny speaks of more than forty-nine kinds of dates grown here, and of a special very sweet type of wine, and there was also a milkwort used in Roman medicines which was peculiar to this region.[2] Phasaelis (Kh. Fasayil), Archelais (Auja et-Tahta), and all the district of Jericho were thus cultivated and were very valuable. Phasaelis stood where the road at the foot of the Ephraimite scarp came down from Neapolis, and above it, guarding both this road and the Wadi Fariʻa, was the fortress of Alexandrium. Similarly, above Jericho and guarding the var-

ious routes up into the central zone of movement was Docus, on a sugar-loaf hill above Duyuk. These Herodian forts, perched on pinnacles above the Ghor, reflect the inability of this lower section to provide any sites for strongholds, owing in part to the nature of the land and in part to the exhausting tropical heat, which saps the strength of even the sternest warrior. Jericho seems to have been content to belong to whoever was strongest, for though theoretically it was in Benjamin, apparently both Manasseh and Ephraim laid some claim to it, since the common boundary between them came southward along the edge of the hills to this point. The stories in I Kings 16:34 and II Kings 2:4–6 suggest that the town was then part of Israel rather than of Judah. The Romans built defenses for Jericho, it is true, but George Adam Smith has neatly summed up the position when he says, "She has been called 'the key' and 'the guardhouse' of Judaea; she was only the pantry. She never stood a siege, and her inhabitants were always running away."[3]

On the other side of the Jordan from Jericho are the "plains of Moab" (Num. 22:1), where the Israelites encamped in the last tense days before crossing to the attack, a fertile little enclave of the Ghor well watered by the plateau streams. The waters of Nimrin (Is. 15:6) are the Wadi Shuʻeib, which the present road follows up to Es-Salt, and the little village of Shunat Nimrin at the edge of the plain still carries the ancient name. Shittim, whence the spies were sent out to Jericho (Josh. 2:1), is a little farther to the south at Kufrein, and here the wadi Nusariyeh makes cultivation possible. Gilgal, where they first encamped after crossing the river, and where they set up the stones they had taken from it, cannot be identified for certain, though it was very probably in the region of Khirbet Mefjir just north of modern Jericho.* Traditionally, the site of the baptism of Jesus is near here also, and yet this is equally uncertain, for there is no indication in the Gospels as to exactly where it took place. We can only guess at the site of "Bethany beyond Jordan" of which the Fourth Gospel speaks (John 1:28).

50.　*The Dead Sea from the hills of Moab.*

C. 4. *The Dead Sea.* South of Jericho the width of the valley shrinks from 12 to 6 miles, the steep scarps approach each other, and the whole of the valley floor sinks beneath the surface of the Dead Sea. This remarkable body of water, 43 miles long by 9 miles wide, lies 1274 feet below the level of the Mediterranean and, in the

northern part, is more than 1300 feet deep. Shut in between steep and barren hills on either side, it is not only the lowest point on the earth's surface, but also the most salty body of water in the world, for it contains some 25 per cent of solid matter, including common salt, bromide, magnesium chloride and calcium chloride. Today its chief commercial importance is for the production of potash, which is extracted from the extreme southern end, but in the Biblical period it was valued rather for its salt and for the bitumen which at times was found floating on its surface. This excessive density is the result entirely of evaporation, for the streams which empty their waters into the Dead Sea contain no more solid matter than is normal. However, the heat is so tremendous that the loss of water more than keeps pace with the intake, and there is more or less constantly a heavy bluish haze above the surface of the lake. The water is poisonous to fish, and is singularly unpleasant to the taste, being like a concentrated dose of Epsom salts. Bathing in it is amusing, for one bobs about in the water like a cork, but swimming is difficult, because one's arms and legs tend merely to rest upon the surface. The greatest care has to be taken in bathing, since the water is not only unpleasant to taste, but also excessively painful if it gets into the eyes or any cut or sore. Moreover, people have been known to be drowned by getting their heads under the water and then being unable to right themselves.

The surface of the Dead Sea is usually calm and, because of the great density, is not easily ruffled by a light

* James Muilenburg, "The Site of Ancient Gilgal," in B.A.S.O.R. No. 140 (Dec. 1955) pp. 11–27. I am indebted to Dr. Millar Burrows for calling to my notice this article, which previously had escaped me.

breeze. However, the strong winds
which pour down the western slopes
in late afternoon can stir up very
choppy water and during the rainy
season quite dangerous storms may
develop. Rain is rare, the average for
the year being only 2 inches, but when
it does fall, it is likely to come as a
very heavy thunderstorm.

The two sides of the Dead Sea are
not the same. The mountains on the
west are less high than those on the
east, and the rock exposed there is
either Senonian chalk or Cenomanian
limestone, the former creating bare,
rounded hills and the latter narrow
gorges and steep cliffs. Because this
side of the valley is in a rain shadow,
it is exceedingly dry, and no rivers flow
from it into the sea, though there are
one or two important springs close to
the water's edge, and these form little
oases of green in an otherwise brown
and barren landscape. The first of
them in the north is 'Ain Feshkha, not
far from the Qumran monastery, to
whose library the Dead Sea scrolls belonged. Five to ten miles farther south
are 'Ain el-Ghuweir and 'Ain et-Tu-
raba, and then, about thirteen miles
south of that, is the strong spring of
Engedi, almost opposite Hebron on
the high Judaean plateau. Since the
slopes on this side, though often extremely steep and rocky, everywhere
leave sufficient room for a track to
pass along the water's edge, these
oases were very important for supplying water along this route, which
was fairly considerably used, especially south of Engedi.

The eastern shores tend to be much
more precipitous, and there can be
no continuous track, for as soon as the

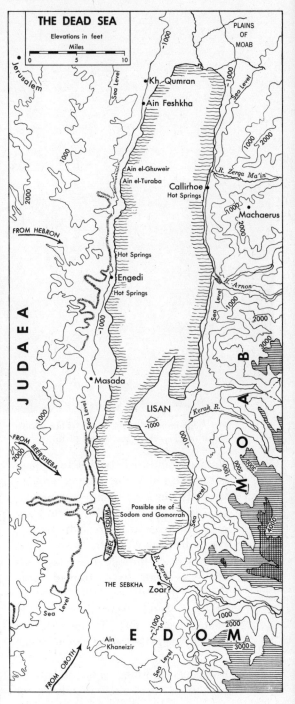

Fig. 39.

51. *The mountains of Moab.* This photograph is taken from the fertile plain.

Nubian standstone begins to appear out of the water, the tall, perpendicular cliffs block every attempt at passage round their foot. This forbidding coast is broken at intervals by narrow gorges through which the rivers of the plateau reach the sea, and where this happens there have formed little deltas of tangled vegetation and piles of dead wood swept down by the winter floods. Of all these eastern gorges the greatest is the Arnon, which is but a narrow passage between towering sandstone cliffs; it can be penetrated for some hundreds of yards, but then the way is blocked by waterfalls and further passage is impossible.

Some two-thirds of the way along this eastern shore the cliffs recede from the sea and leave quite a broad plain for the last 15 or 20 miles of the coast. From the northern part of this section the Lisan, a broad peninsula of marl, extends to within 2 miles of the other shore, and in Roman times it was possible to ford across the narrow strait. This crossing, which is said to have been possible also in 1846,[4] was guarded by the imposing fortress of Masada in the rocky western foothills. This was a Maccabean fortress, which Herod the Great had strengthened as part of the chain of forts which he

52. *The Dead Sea*. The Nubian sandstone cliffs beginning to climb out of the sea on the eastern side.

maintained along the edges of the Rift, and after the destruction of Jerusalem in A.D. 70 it was the scene of the last desperate resistance of the Jews, who all committed suicide rather than fall into Roman hands.

The Lisan itself is of the same unattractive material as the *qattara* on either side of the Jordan, but the plain which lies at the foot of the plateau is entirely delightful, for it has a plentiful supply of water from the westward-facing slopes and is still green even in the summer. It is a prolonged oasis, and wheat, barley, dates, indigo, cotton and vines can all be grown here, and sheep, goats, cattle and camels kept. However, it has not become important because of the distance from any important market, and because of the fierce and enervating heat which reduces the inhabitants to passivity. In the lawless days of the Turks they were forever oppressed by the great sheikhs of the more vigorous plateau tribes, and the only time they appear in the Bible story they are defeated in a battle (Gen. 14:1–12).

The part of the Dead Sea south of

the Lisan peninsula is really a large and shallow bay, never more than 3 feet deep, and it has been suggested that it is of fairly recent formation, having been created by an earthquake which lowered the level of this section of the Rift by several feet, and thus caused the waters of the Dead Sea to flood over into what is now the southern basin. It is held that if this did happen, it would explain the destruction of the five cities of the plain (Gen. 19:15–28), which were in reality no more than small settlements in an extended oasis, such as would have existed if the Zered had been able to spread its waters farther into the plain than it does at present. This is certainly possible, but it must be admitted that no very definite geological evidence has so far been adduced in its favor, and aerial reconnaissance has failed to reveal any traces of such settlements beneath the water.

Opposite the rich oasis of the Zered delta is Jebel Usdum, a strange salt mountain nearly 6 miles long and 650 feet in height, fretted and dissolved into fantastic shapes by the occasional

53. *The Dead Sea*. This picture shows (a) the vegetation on the southeastern plain, and (b) the dazzling white peninsula of the Lisan in the distance and (c) the plateau of Judea beyond.

winter storms, and the origin without a doubt of the story of Lot's wife (Gen. 19:26). At its foot the Dead Sea shelves gently to its end, passing almost imperceptibly into the barren waste of the Sebkha, the glistening salt marsh in which the wadis from both sides lose themselves in unprofitable meanders, a flat plain of soft, impassable mud which is brought to an end by cliffs of 'Ain Khaneizir, some 8 miles to the south.

Western travelers, confronted by this "awful deep," are frequently overwhelmed by a sense of desolation and destruction. It seems such a fit setting for the grim end of the defense of Masada, for the wanton murder of John the Baptist at Herod's other palace on the eastern rim, and for the dire punishment of Sodom and Gomorrah, forever the symbol of the wrath of God upon the children of disobedience. As they view the stark landscape, so vividly portrayed in Holman Hunt's picture of "The Scapegoat," they are apt to think that if there was any purpose in the creation of such an unnatural trough, whose waters give not life but death, it must have been to drive home the lesson of God of vengeance and austerity. So Kinglake says, inaccurately, that "no fly hummed in that forbidden air," [*] and George Adam Smith begins his chapter on the Dead Sea with the words, "Perhaps there is no region of our earth where Nature and History have more cruelly conspired, where so tragic a drama has obtained so awful a theatre." [5] Yet, for the Biblical writers the lesson was

not one of simple destruction. Sodom and Gomorrah, and the other cities of the plain, were, it is true, proverbial for the disaster which must ultimately come upon the wicked, and as such are often quoted both in the Old Testament and in the New,[**] and the barren and desolate Sebkha, "a land possessed by nettles and salt pits, and a waste for ever" (Zeph. 2:9), was a constant warning to those who would not hear the Word of God. But what struck these writers with almost equal force was the fact of life triumphant even in the midst of this very evident desolation, and so the Dead Sea became for them a reminder of the *goodness* of God, of whom it could be said, "Thou sparest when we deserve punishment, and in thy wrath thinkest upon mercy." [6]

It was for them incredible that God had of set purpose created a place so inimical to life, and so we are told that "before the Lord destroyed Sodom and Gomorrah" it was "well watered everywhere like the garden of the Lord" (Gen. 13:11), and they dreamed of its restoration to utility and fruitfulness. Ezekiel, who knew that the Spirit of God could make dead bones live (Ezek. 37:1–14), has a wonderful vision of a swelling river pouring out of the Temple at Jerusalem, with many trees growing beside it in the dusty wilderness of Jeshimmon. The effect of this river was to sweeten the waters of the Dead Sea, so that "wherever the river goes, every

---

[*] It is almost unbelievable that he actually took off his clothes to swim, and still thought that there were no flies!

[**] Deut. 29:23, 32:32; Is. 1:9, 3:9, 13:19; Jer. 23:14, 49:18, 50:40; Lam. 4:6; Ezek. 16:46–56; Hos. 11:8; Amos 4:11; Zeph. 2:9; Matt. 10:15, 11:23; Luke 10:12, 17:29; Rom. 9:29; II Pet. 2:6; Jude 7; Rev. 11:8.

living creature which swarms shall live, and there will be very many fish; for this water goes there, that the waters of the sea may become fresh; so everything will live where the water goes" (Ezek. 47:9). Only the marshes at the side were to remain salt, for salt was essential to the preserving of food and the purification of the sacrifice. This is in the same vein as the story of Elisha's purifying of the water at Jericho (II Kings 1:19–22), for it is not in the nature of the God of the Old Testament to destroy unless there shall be an even more glorious renewal.

Ezekiel's vision, which included fruit trees whose leaves did not wither and which bore fruit every month, fruit for food and leaves for healing, was not of an exotic reversal of nature, but of an intensification of the present reality. Once given that the water should be fresh and not salt, the rest followed, for life is abundant wherever there is fresh water in this singular oven; leaves do not wither and food can be grown at all times in the year, and not food only but also balsam and other plants from which medicines were made. Such was the effect of the sweet-scented gardens of these luxuriant oases that it was to "a cluster of henna blossoms in the vineyards of Engedi" that the amorous shepherd likened his beloved (Song 1:14).

An aspect of the Dead Sea's usefulness which is not mentioned in the Bible is its value for transport. Perhaps this is not surprising, since the Jews thought of ships as treacherous vehicles, and things which their enemies possessed, and indeed preferred

a place "where no galley with oars can go, nor stately ship can pass" (Is. 33:21), but it is impossible that it was not so used. The early fruit and vegetables of the southeastern plain could have been transported so much more easily by boat than by patient donkeys on the rocky hills. It is true that during much of the Old Testament period the people on each side of the Dead Sea were bitter enemies, and they could make attacks on each other by sea, more usefully from the east than from the west, whose inhabitants would be checked by the stern Moabite cliffs. Such attacks would be small raids rather than invasions, and, though much doubt has been cast on the authenticity of II Chronicles 20:1–30, when we read that "some men came and told Jehoshaphat, 'A great multitude is coming against you from

54. *Callirhoe.* The ruins of the fort which guarded the hot springs beside the Dead Sea, where Herod used to go for treatment.

Edom, from beyond the sea; and behold they are in Hazazon-tamar' (that is Engedi)," we have there the remembrance of the kind of thing which actually happened from time to time. Cer-

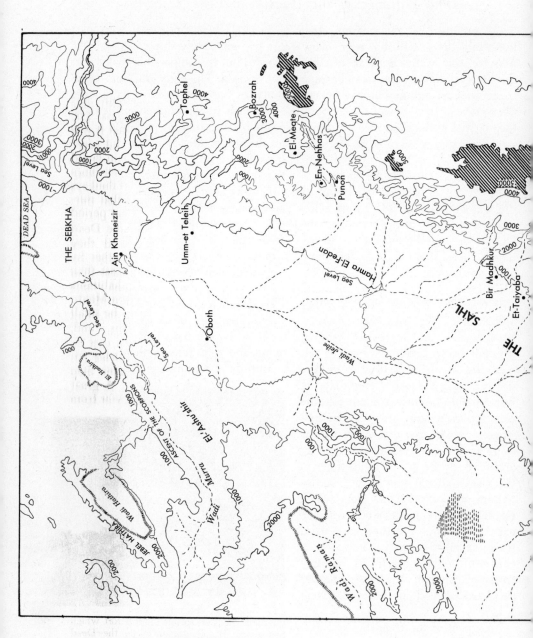

Fig. 40.

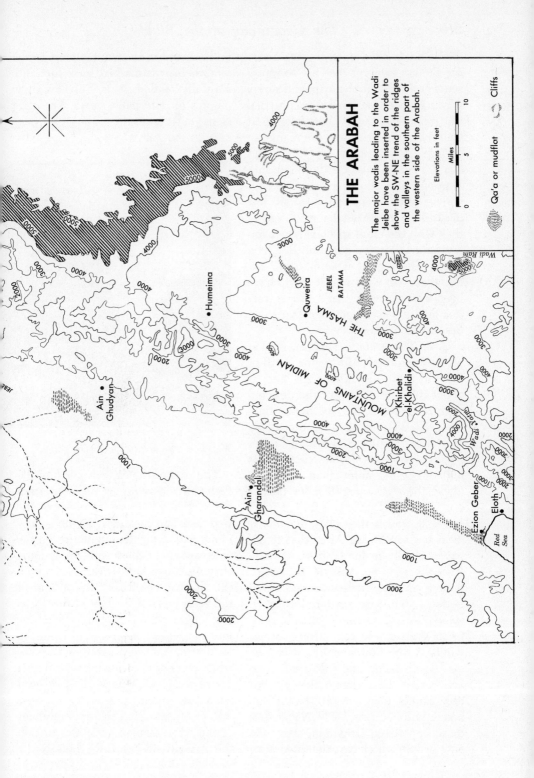

THE ARABAH

The major wadis leading to the Wadi Jeibe have been inserted in order to show the SW-NE trend of the ridges and valleys in the southern part of the western side of the Arabah.

Elevations in feet

Miles

0   5   10

░░░ Qa'a or mudflat

﹏﹏ Cliffs

• Humeima

• Quweira

JEBEL RATAMA

THE HASMA

MOUNTAINS OF MIDIAN

Khirbet el-Khalidi •

Wadi Ram

Ain • Ghudyan

Ain • Gharandal

Ezion Geber •

Eloth •

Red Sea

4000

5000

3000

2000

1000

tainly, boats plied upon the sea under the Roman rule, for they are so represented on the Madeba map, and surely it was by boat that Herod was carried for treatment to the hot springs at Callirhoe. Though there are many hot springs around the shores of the Dead Sea, Callirhoe must be identified with Zara on the northeastern shore, where still stand the ruins of the square fort marked on the Madeba map, rather than with the more spectacular steaming waterfall in the gorge of the Zerqa Ma'in. Although it is common to say that there was Callirhoe, it would have been a cruel journey for a desperately sick man to have negotiated that steep descent in a litter.

C. 5. *The Arabah.* This last section of the Palestinian Rift begins south of the cliffs of 'Ain Khaneizir, and is about 100 miles in length and directed slightly more to the southwest than the Ghor. The bottom of the valley now rises steadily, and after 30 miles passes above sea level, reaching its highest point, more than 650 feet above the sea, some 18 miles farther on, where the Cretaceous fold of Jebel er-Rishe crosses the valley diagonally from the southwest. After that it descends slowly to the Gulf of Aqabah. Everywhere the Arabah is desert, though in the better-watered wadi bottoms there are scattered trees of *spina Christi*, characteristically umbrella-shaped by the strong desert winds. A rare thunderstorm, it is true, may cover the ground with fresh grass and revive the dormant flowers, but they cannot long endure, for the sun here is without mercy. The Nabateans, those experts in irrigation, were the only people who have attempted agri-

culture, and in their day almost every waterhole was marked by a fort and carefully tended fields, but now only clumps of date palms mark the occasional oasis and relieve the dusty passage to the gulf.

55. *The entrance to the Arnon gorge.*

The part of the Arabah north of the Rishe divide is rather different from the section which slopes down to the Red Sea. This northern portion is very much wider, for the mountains on the west swing back sharply in a long, curving, hinge fault which has carved the naked precipices of the Ascent of the Scorpions. At the foot of this scarp the lengthy Wadi Murra extends far into the Negeb and receives from the Mediterranean coast a route which nowhere touches as much as 1500 feet above sea level. This wadi is divided from the Arabah proper by the low hills of el-'Ashu'shir, the final remnant of the Wadi Raman anticline, and on the Arabah side of these hills is the

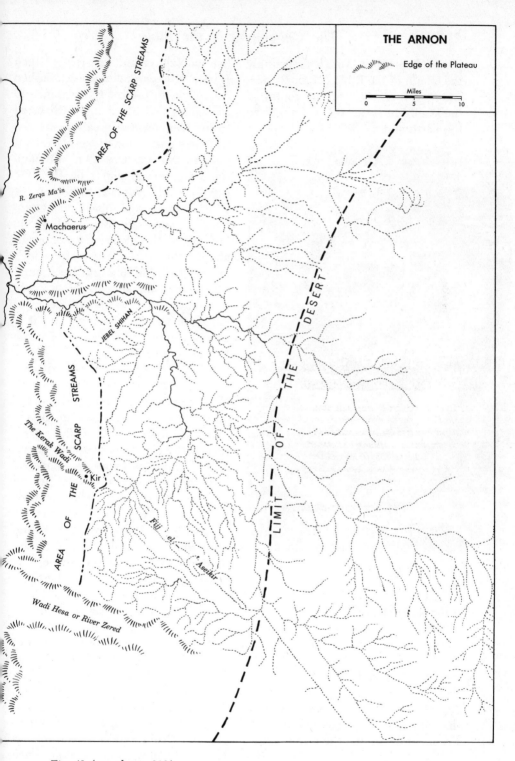

Fig. 41 (see also p. 219).

plentiful spring of 'Ain Hosb, possibly the Oboth of the Bible (Num. 33:43), where gather together the routes of the Wadi Murra, as well as those from the north and south.

56.   *Inside the Arnon gorge.*

To the northeast, on the other side, is the Nabatean settlement of Umm et-Teleih, and somewhat farther to the south is the Punon embayment, where faulting has caused a slight retreating of the gigantic scarp, here 6200 feet above the bottom of the Arabah. Across the mouth of this embayment is the hard porphyry dike of Hamra el-Fedan, and within it the copper mines of Punon (the modern Feinan), Khir-

bet en-Nehhas and el-Meqte. Upon Hamra el-Fedan Solomon established a garrison to protect the entrance to the mines,[7] which, though exhausted today, were once of great importance and were part of the reason for Edomite and Nabatean wealth. Although there are several points on the long exposure of Nubian sandstone at which copper was mined, the group round Punon were of especial value, because of the plentiful water available at the foot of the scarp, which made it possible to work these mines even during the summer. Punon was the only place where copper was mined in the Bronze Age [8] and it is almost certainly the place where the brazen serpent was set up by Moses in the wilderness (Num. 21:4-10, 33: 42-43). In the Iron Age it was rivaled, if not surpassed, in importance by the mines in Wadi Meneiaieh, in the extreme southwest, for there the extraction of the copper is unusually easy.[9] The work in the mines was done by prisoners and slaves and in Roman times such prisoners, who included many Christians in times of persecution, were brutally crippled before being set to work, in order to hinder their chances of revolt or escape. The misery of their existence is best left to the imagination.

Although all the places mentioned cannot be identified with certainty, it is not difficult to determine the general route of the Exodus after leaving Punon. The Israelites were moving northward along the Arabah, thus skirting the main Edomite stronghold on the plateau, because of the Edomite enmity (Num. 20:21), pausing at Punon probably for some time, since the Kenites, who were coppersmiths, were their friends. Then they found their way blocked by the Dead Sea and turned eastward up the Zered (Num. 21:12), moving between Edom and Moab, who were probably equally hostile. Passing round to the east of Moab, they attempted to move westward again down the Arnon valley, which was then the northern boundary of Moab, but were checked once more by the narrow Arnon gorge. When the Amorites on the northern side of the Arnon in their turn refused to give them passage, there was no alternative left but to fight, and so ensued the battle which gave the Israelites possession of the northern Trans-jordan (Num. 21:24–26).

The whole of the eastern wall is intensely dramatic, since the Transjordan tableland is here at its greatest height, and rises by a series of huge fault scarps, in a multichrome succession of rock, limestone upon sandstone, white upon red. It is well-nigh impassable, for the winter storms have carved the desert sandstone into deep, unfinished gorges, and only rarely does one of the valleys which seam the scarp provide a possible route up onto the plateau, the most important being the Wadi Musa, which permitted the caravans from the Arabah to come up into Petra, but even that is notoriously difficult. Here in the Arabah are Bir Madhkur and 'Ain et-Taiyaba, 7 miles apart, and at both these places the Nabateans established forts to guard the entrances to Petra.

In contrast to this jagged, unscalable wall, the western side of the Rift is less impressive, being for the most part only a third of the height, and made up of tumbled chalk and limestone hills, between which many narrow wadis lead up into the distant higher parts of the southern Negeb.

Throughout all this section of the Arabah the wadis drain toward the center, into the Wadi Jeibe, an intermittent stream which has carved a secondary valley, not unlike that of the Jordan, 30 to 150 feet below the general valley bottom. This wadi, which is nowhere very difficult to cross, has been pushed well over to the west by the more powerful flash floods from the eastern wall, and the great alluvial fans which these have created have built up at the foot of the scarp a broad piedmont zone known as the *sahl*, a wide stretch of rolling gravel and sand.

After Jebel er-Rishe the character of the Arabah changes. Quite suddenly it narrows, and from there to the Red Sea the two sides are sometimes no more than 6 miles apart. There are, moreover, steep cliffs now on both sides, for upon the west the Nubian sandstone appears, typically sheer and difficult, and in the extreme south the granite platform is exposed. On the east the hills are granite for almost the whole length of this section, since the underlying platform has here been forced up between two great faults in a huge wedge, sometimes called the Mountains of Midian, though where these mountains are joined to the high sandstone cliffs there is a small shattered zone where the scarp is lower and where frequent faults create narrow passages into the broad interior basin of the Hasma. This eastern wall still remains the higher, because the average height of the Mountains of

Midian is 4000 feet, while the western scarp passes 2000 feet only in the south, and nowhere reaches as much as 3300.

Another new feature of this southern section are the broad, flat areas of dried mud, called *qa'a*, formed where sediment from the two scarps has been washed down into the valley basins, and since such areas of *qa'a* are very slippery after rain, the tracks tend to cling to the foot of the scarp on either side. In this section of the Arabah the alluvial fans on the east are no longer much greater than those on the west, for though the higher eastern scarp continues to have more rain, this is compensated by the greater resistance to erosion of the granite.

The important springs are three, 'Ain Gharandel at the northern end, 'Ain Ghudyan in the center, and Aqabah at the south. 'Ain Gharandel, where water is very plentiful, gains added importance from the fact that it lies at the foot of the shattered section of the scarp, and therefore controls the entrance of the narrow passages into the Hasma. Aqabah in the far south, with its rich water supply and green, luxuriant palm groves, lies where the blue waters of the Red Sea form a broad bay between the granite mountains, now to be seen on both sides, and where also a convenient wadi, the Yatm, cuts through the mountains of Midian and makes possible a route into the Hasma. Here was Eloth, one of the places visited by the Israelites during the Exodus (Num. 33:35) and a bone of contention between the people of Judah and the Edomites.

The temptation which made the kings of Judah covet the control of the long passage of the Arabah was first its rich supplies of copper, and second the trade to which it was the gate. The copper was itself an important article in this trade, and Solomon built a highly developed copper foundry at Ezion Geber, not at Aqabah, but at Tel el-Kheleifeh, halfway round the bay.[10] It is not a pleasant site, for it is waterless and exposed, but the foundry was built here to make the best use of those howling winds, which everywhere develop in a desert, but which

57. *The Gulf of Aqabah.* Here was Eloth, which the Israelites visited during the Exodus, and at the head of the bay, at the back of this picture, was Solomon's copper foundry.

58. *Travelers from Arabia.* Aqabah is the gateway to Arabia, from which these men are coming. The mountains in the background are granite.

are here intensified by the confining walls of the narrow corridor and the differing air pressures over the land and sea. Once smelted, the copper was exported, along with wine and other products of the country, on the "ships of Tarshish" which returned the following year, "bringing gold, silver, ivory, apes and peacocks" (I Kings 10:22). The peacocks were possibly baboons, and there would have been also incense, spices, ebony (perhaps the "almug" of I Kings 10:11) and precious stones. It was the gateway to incredible wealth, and one for which the Judaeàn kings were prepared to strain their military resources to the uttermost. When for the first time

Jewish merchants penetrated to the farther end of the Red Sea in Solomon's ships, the Queen of the South, alarmed by this threat to her monopoly, came herself "with a very great retinue" to see who had sent these men, not from idle curiosity, but because she feared for her own wealth and livelihood.

It can never have been easy for Judah to maintain control of this route to Aqabah. For some 150 miles the difficult desert road stretched out from Beersheba, a journey of several days for the convoys of camels and donkeys, slowly winding down the long Ascent of the Scorpions into the Arabah. Once there, they had to run the gauntlet of the proud Edomites, who dwelt, restless for plunder, high on their exalted plateau, and there were many points at which an ambush might be attempted, especially in the final corridor, where the road was squeezed between the high cliffs and the frequent *qa'as*. Nor were the dangers only from their fellow men, for there was often the menace of sudden flash floods from the highlands of the Khurashe Dome, pouring down the Jerafi and Heiyani wadis, with a quick fury that could overwhelm a slow-moving caravan. Even at Ezion Geber there had to be constant vigilance, since the Edomites would not have been unready to pour down upon the town, either by the Arabah or the Wadi Yatm, and burn the ships which the Jews had prepared to fetch the gold of Ophir. Fortunately from the Judaean point of view, Ezion Geber was an outpost even for the Edomites, and so it was possible for a king at Jerusalem, if his strength were very great, to stretch out his arm and grasp this precious harbor.

Nevertheless, it was in no sense a permanent possession, and was held, in fact, only at peak periods of Jewish strength, being mentioned in the Old Testament only during such periods. Thus, David conquered Edom and made the king his vassal, and it was his son, Solomon, who first built a Jewish town at Ezion Geber (I Kings 9:26). The Edomites recovered it at the division of the kingdom, but later became the vassals of Judah again, for in the time of Ahab and Jehoshaphat "there was no king in Edom; a deputy was king" (I Kings 22:47). Jehoshaphat, therefore, fitted out a fleet at Ezion Geber, but it was destroyed before it could put to sea, probably because the Edomites revolted (I Kings 22:48). The third and final time that Judah gained control of the port was in her last period of greatness. Then Amaziah killed "ten thousand Edomites in the Valley of Salt [i.e., probably near the Sebkha] and took Sela by storm" (II Kings 14:7), and it was his son, Uzziah, who "built Elath and restored it to Judah" (II Kings 14:22), but in the reign of the ineffective Ahaz Elath passed out of the hands of Judah for good (II Kings 16:6).

CHAPTER XVIII

Beyond the Jordan Eastward

Gad and Reuben and half the tribe of Manasseh have received their inheritance beyond ·the Jordan eastward, which Moses the· servant of the Lord gave them.

JOSHUA 18:7

ANYONE who stands upon the Mount of Olives, or on any other point along the eastern edge of the Cis-jordan hills, sees the ground drop away in front of him in a succession of tumbled, yellow slopes, and the clouds dissolve into nothing above his head, as the air starts its tumultuous descent into the Rift. Far away in the distance, some 25 miles as the crow flies, is an unbroken wall of rock, dwarfed by the distance but still tremendous, and poised above it are the clouds, forming again where the air has cooled in its steep ascent from the Jordan. This wall is the edge of the great Arabian tableland, and it stretches, very nearly in a straight line, the extreme length of the country, from the foot of Hermon to the Red Sea.

If you go there, snaking down between the barren hills of Jeshimmon and across the muddy Jordan, you go to another country. This is immediately apparent when you leave the hot and dusty lowlands of the Ghor, and begin to climb up beside the waters of Nimrin. The frowning honey-colored cliffs, the stream which is so rare west of the Jordan, the glorious pink oleanders which line the waterside, all proclaim a landscape unknown among the western hills. In Cisjordan the oleanders are found only in one short valley in Carmel, but here they line the westward-flowing streams in rich profusion, a wonderful splash of color in the summer drought, and surely the Brook of the Willows derives its name from them (Is. 15:7).

The road continues to follow the valley until it reaches the spring at Es-Salt, once the Turkish administrative

217

center, and one of the long line of fortress towns which follow the edge of the scarp. Soon one is speeding across the broad, open tableland to the Ammonite capital at Rabboth Ammon (or Amman), the vast windswept expanse of the plateau ever more apparent, though it is not until one is beyond Amman that the limitless steppes are really to be seen. The olive has been left behind for, though it will grow in the westward-facing valleys, it cannot stand the icy desert winds which scour this plateau in winter, and the vineyards have also gone. Of the classic trinity of Mediterranean products, the bread, the wine and the oil, only the bread is left, for the level tableland continues to produce excellent wheat and barley, until at last the decreasing rainfall makes all cultivation impossible and the animals alone survive, the sheep and goats and camels and the magnificent Trans-jordanian horses.

It is necessary to insist upon the "otherness" of the country east of the Jordan, because it goes a long way to explain the constant tendency of the Trans-jordanians to feel that they are a separate people. Of course, the Jordan itself is a barrier, especially in the south where the *qattara* and *zor* are well developed, but this alone would not have been enough to explain this separateness, for one of the unexpected features of the historical geography of Palestine is that quite formidable barriers have tended not to serve as frontiers, if the land on either side of them is similar. Thus the great headland of Carmel, which would seem to be such a natural division of the coast plain, was no obstacle to the Phoenicians, who pushed as far south as the Crocodile river, for it is there that the essential character of the coast plain changes. Similarly, we shall find that the huge gashes in the plateau surface made by the Trans-jordanian rivers were seldom permanent frontiers, because they did not divide people of a different way of life. Therefore, it is of no small importance that the impressive triple barrier of *qattara, zor* and river divided, not like from like, but regions where the way of life was essentially different, so that there developed a regional consciousness and a feeling of separateness, one from the other. In brief, the difference is between the Mediterranean life of the hills and valleys west of the Jordan, where the classic trinity of grain and vines and olives grew together, and the economy of the steppes, which either were predominantly pastoral, or else forced the farmer to concentrate mainly upon one crop.

On the plateau the problem is the same, since there are really two different sets of divisions of the country. The first, and most immediately obvious, is that created by the pattern of the plateau drainage, which has developed as a result of the fact that heavy rain falls only on the steep, uplifted, western edge. This rain naturally tends to run off in two opposite directions, either straight down the steep scarp into the Rift, or else along the more gentle dip slope eastward to the desert. Of these two sets of streams, those flowing down the scarp are stronger and erode more rapidly, partly because they flow very much faster, and partly also because it is the scarp which receives the full force of the rain-bearing winds from the west. The eastward-flowing streams, moreover, are not only less swift, but move toward a region of little rainfall, since the increasing drought is very marked as soon as the plateau edge is passed. Occasionally the scarp streams, already the stronger, have been assisted still further by lines of structural weakness, and where these occur erosion has been particularly rapid, so that such streams have been able to cut back far into the plateau, and have captured the waters of the dip-slope streams. Therefore, we have today a system of small wadis in the narrow zone just west of the present railway, flowing eastward and then gathering themselves together to form the main wadi, which carries a permanent stream. At first, this may flow almost parallel to the plateau edge, but then it turns westward, and cuts its way down through a magnificent canyon to the Jordan or the Dead Sea. Such are the canyons of the Yarmuq, the Jabbok, the Arnon with its tributary the Wala, and the Zered in the south.

These great clefts in the plateau surface form very evident possible frontiers, and are now the boundaries of the administrative districts. There seems to be some evidence in the early parts of the Old Testament that then also they were so regarded, for at several points it is argued that Edom lies south of the Zered, Moab between the Zered and the Arnon, and Ammon outside the curve formed by the Jabbok. The territory between the Arnon and the Jabbok had been held by the Amorites under King Sihon, but they had

been defeated by the Israelites and their land had passed to the tribes of Reuben and Gad. In Numbers 21:24 the Jabbok is spoken of as being the frontier of the Ammonites; in Deuteronomy 3:16 Reuben and Gad are said to have been given the land between the Jabbok and the Arnon, and in Judges 11:12–28 Jephthah argues that the Ammonites can have no complaint against the Israelites, because Israel has not extended beyond the boundaries formed by these rivers.

Nevertheless, it is clear from the Jephthah story that the Ammonites did not agree that the Jabbok formed their frontier, and Moab also, fairly early in the history of the kingdoms, drove northward across the Arnon and took back the territory of Reuben, which they regarded as part of their own land. Certainly, it had once belonged to them, as we are told in Numbers 21:26–30, but the Amorites had driven them out of it. It would seem, therefore, that victorious newcomers, such as the Amorites who had driven a wedge between Ammon and Moab, and the Israelites who drove out the Amorites, tend to regard as natural frontiers those obvious strategic lines of defense created by the great river valleys, but that in course of time an older pattern re-establishes itself, the pattern of the four different ways of life. These four ways of life are the way of the Farmer of Bashan, the Highlander of Gilead, the Shepherd of Moab, and the Trader of Edom, and lying to the east of all of these is a fifth region, the desert, where the way of life is that of the nomad.

E. 1. *Bashan, the Land of the Farmer.* This is essentially tableland, wide open plains between 1600 and 2300 feet in height, and magnificently fertile. Bounded on the west by the edge of the plateau, Bashan extends in the north to the foot of Hermon, in the south across the Yarmuq to the mountains of Gilead some 6 miles beyond the present Irbid-Mafraq road, and on the east to the black, volcanic mass of Jebel Druze. On account of the lowness of the southern hills of the Galilee to the west, this is one of the three regions where the rains sweep farther inland, and over large areas the soil is a rich volcanic alluvium. Here the primary crop is wheat, and the life is an endless cycle of plowing and sowing, threshing, winnowing and gathering into barns, for, flat, well-watered and fertile, the plateau is dotted everywhere with villages and produces harvests which are the envy of the surrounding people. In the New Testament, when it included the districts of Gaulanitis and Batanea, it was one of the great granaries of the Empire, exporting its grain across Galilee to the port of Ptolemais at Acre, and in the Old Testament it seems to have been proverbial as well for the richness of its pasture. "Strong bulls of Bashan surround me," said the Psalmist (Ps. 22:12); "Cows of Bashan . . . in the mountains of Samaria" was Amos' description of the gross and lazy noblewomen of Israel (Amos 4:1); and much later Ezekiel spoke "of rams, of lambs, and of goats, of bulls, all of them fatlings of Bashan" (Ezek. 39:18). Nor does this insistence upon cattle invalidate the importance of Bashan as a granary, for cows are the animals of the agricultural land, for they need the richer

pasture and are used to do the labor of the farm.

In the writings of the prophets the trees of Bashan are also frequently mentioned. Thus, Isaiah speaks of the Lord as being "against all the cedars of Lebanon, lofty and lifted up; and against all the oaks of Bashan" (Is. 2:13), and Ezekiel says of the ships of Tyre, "They made all your planks of fir trees from Senir; they took a cedar from Lebanon to make a mast for you. Of oaks of Bashan they made your oars; they made your deck of pines from the coasts of Cyprus, inlaid with ivory" (Ezek. 27:5–6). This bracketing of Bashan with Lebanon and Carmel is very common, as in Isaiah 33:9. "Lebanon is confounded and withers away; Sharon is like a desert; and Bashan and Carmel shake off their leaves," and in Jeremiah 22:20, where the prophet pictures the people flying for refuge to Lebanon, Bashan and Abarim.* In Jeremiah 50:19 the promise is given that Israel shall "feed on Carmel and in Bashan," and a similar promise that they shall feed in Bashan and Gilead appears in Micah 7:14. In both Nahum and Zechariah the destruction of a proud empire is pictured as the withering of Bashan and Lebanon (Nah. 1:4; Zech. 11:1–2).

Such coupling of Bashan with thickly forested areas is somewhat surprising, since this fertile tableland must surely have been among the earliest regions to be cleared of trees, and those that were left would have been in clumps of woodland rather

---

* Abarim (see also Num. 27:12; Deut. 32:49) was apparently the hilly country west of Heshbon, the last trace in Trans-jordan of the Judaean-Gilead Dome.

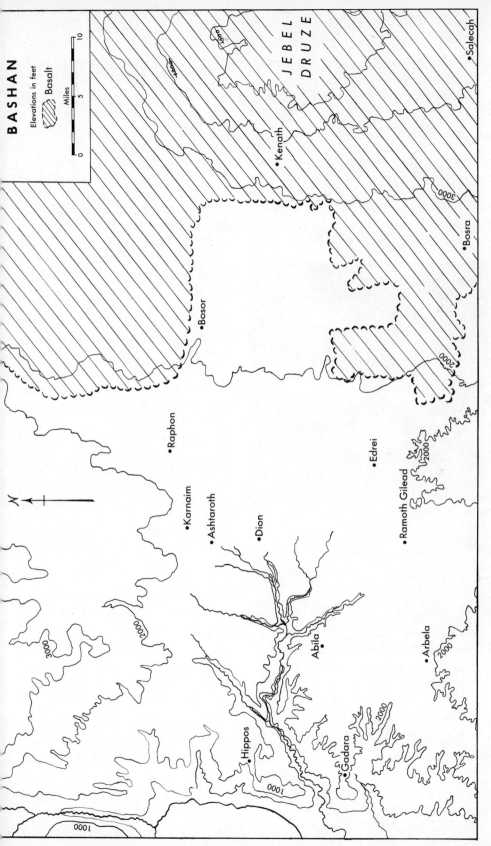

BASHAN

Elevations in feet

Basalt

Miles

0 5 10

J E B E L
D R U Z E

•Salecah

•Kenath

•Bosra

3000

•Bosor

2000

•Raphon

N

•Karnaim
•Ashtaroth

•Dion

•Edrei

2000

•Ramoth Gilead

3000

2000

•Abila

•Arbela
2000

•Hippos

•Gadara
2000

1000

1000

Fig. 42.

than continuous forest. Moreover, Lebanon, Carmel and Gilead are all mountains and regions of refuge, where the villages were hidden among the still extensive forest cover. Consequently, one must ask whether in the mind of the prophets Bashan was not thought of as extending eastward to include the Jebel Druze, which would admirably fulfill the conditions of providing a parallel with Lebanon, Carmel and Gilead, and this seems to be supported

59. *Canatha, or Kenath,* the modern Qanawat. This Jebel Druze town was claimed by Manasseh (Num. 32:42), though it is doubtful whether they were allowed to hold it for long. In New Testament times the Jebel Druze was part of the tetrarchy of Philip. The temple shown here dates from the Roman period.

by the fact that Salecah (the modern Salkhad) was in Bashan (Deut. 3:10; Josh. 12:5, 13:11; I Chron. 5:11), and that Kenath, the modern Qanawat, was held to be part of Manasseh (Num. 32:42), for both these towns are undoubtedly within the limits of the Jebel Druze. This would agree with the possibility that the "many-peaked mountain, mountain of Bashan" is really Jebel Druze, especially as later in the same Psalm Bashan is mentioned as a place to which people have fled for refuge (Ps. 68:15, 22). It may be objected the Hermon is more truly a "mighty mountain" than the Jebel Druze, but it is difficult to know how much weight to attach to this, since before the days of exact map-making people were curiously incapable of judging relative heights. It is still true today in the Hauran that when men speak of "el-Jebel" or "the mountain" without giving it a name, they mean Jebel Druze rather than the higher, but more aloof, mountain of Hermon. Moreover, there are parts of the eastern Palestine area, from which Hermon is invisible, but where in winter the snowcapped Jebel Druze is clearly to be seen, and it may have been such a view that the Psalmist had in mind.

The Jebel Druze is an entirely fascinating region, but one which lies so much on the margin of the Bible that it is not possible to examine it here in detail. It was the chief center of the great volcanic outflows and the last part to become extinct; some of the soft cinder cones, in fact, have been very little eroded, though it is not possible to determine with any exactness when the last eruption was. The hard basalt of which it is composed has made agriculture tedious and difficult, and has filled every tiny field with an incredible mass of stones, though vines can be grown and sheep and goats are kept, and its great height has made it bitterly cold in winter when the snow lies long upon the

60.   *Stone door at Qanawat.*

ground. Nevertheless, the summers are cool and refreshing. Movement about this region is difficult even today, and for this cause the people have always been fiercely independent and resistant to the authority of the Damascus government, the northwest of the country, though lower than the Jebel, being so difficult that it has earned the

name of el-Leja, or The Refuge par excellence. In the time of Jesus this part was called Trachonitis and was part of the territory of Philip (Luke 3:1), and it is argued by some that it was also the Argob of the Old Testament (Deut. 3:4, 13, 14; I Kings 4:13), but the fact that Argob contained sixty cities "fortified with high walls, gates and bars, besides very many unwalled villages" suggests that it was rather the fertile plain to the west.

Although the western slopes of the Jebel Druze are well watered and thickly covered with bushes, the forests, even in the past, must always have been stunted, for the hard rock gives no room for the roots of trees to develop, though doubtless it was very dense and impenetrable. This scarcity of wood good enough for building purposes is reflected in the ancient houses, where stone is used even for roofs, doors and windows, which are everywhere constructed out of the gloomy basalt. Ezekiel, it is true, suggests that the wood was in demand by the shipbuilders of Tyre, but a certain poetic license may have to be allowed to prophets.

The cities of the plain certainly needed their high walls, gates and bars, for they were without any other protection and, in times of war, at the mercy of any invader who might come upon them. A strong government might maintain the peace, as Philip seems to have done during the days of Jesus' ministry,[1] but whenever the hand of the government was weakened the robber bands of the Jebel Druze would descend upon them. In the Old Testament almost every appearance of this region in history is an account

61. *The Yarmuq Valley* from near Gadara. The dark line in the center of the valley is the steep cliffs which enclose the river, and beyond is the plateau of Bashan.

of some invader sweeping unopposed across it. So in the distant Bronze Age "Chedorlaomer and the kings who were with him came and subdued the Rephaim in Ashteroth-Karnaim," and marched through into Gilead (Gen. 14:5), and when Og attempted to oppose the Israelite advance they swept triumphantly across his whole kingdom ("there was not a city which we did not take from them" [Deut. 3:4]) in a victorious wave which lived forever after in their memories (Num. 21:35; Josh. 9:10; Ps. 135:11, 136:20). Even during the reign of the powerful King Ahab, who had forced the Syrians to pay tribute to him (I Kings 20:34), we find the Israelites fighting in defense of Ramoth Gilead, on the very southern edge of Bashan, and later Hazael pressed even farther south (I Kings 22:3; II Kings 10:33). Bashan was in fact a vast battlefield where Israel and Syria were constantly at war with each other, the great valley of the Yarmuq apparently making very little difference to their movements, for in the time of Jeroboam II the people prided themselves on having been able to take Karnaim from the Syrians (Amos 6:13), and in I Maccabees 5:24–52 there is an account of an expedition made by Judas

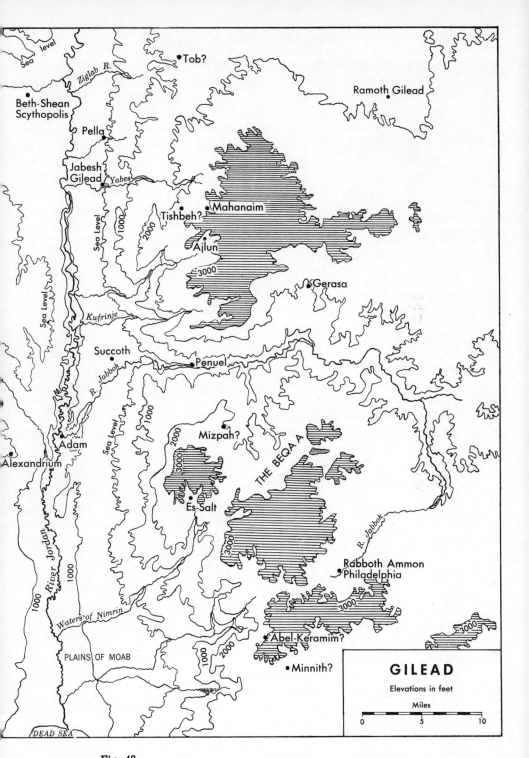

Fig. 43.

62. *Salecah, or Salkhad.* This was one of the towns captured from Og, king of Bashan. Built on the "plug" of an old volcano, it holds a very commanding position in the south of the Jebel Druze.

Rabboth Ammon, seems to have been known as Gilead, and both Gad and half the tribe of Manasseh are said to have held lands there (Num. 32:40; Deut. 4:43). Probably the boundary between them was intended to be the river Jabbok, so that Manasseh had the mountains round Ajlun, and Gad the mountains of Es-Salt, for this was the boundary between the territory of Og who controlled "half Gilead," and that of the Amorites (Josh. 12:2, 5). So we are told that "half Gilead" was given to Manasseh, and "half the hill country of Gilead with its cities" to Gad (Josh. 13:31; Deut. 3:12). How-

Maccabeus to rescue the Jews of Bashan, and of how town after town fell rapidly before him.

The chief towns of the region were Karnaim (Sheikh Sa'ad), Ashteroth (Tel 'Ashterah) and Bosra or Bosora (Busra eski-Sham), all of which lay on the Bashan plain, while Kenath (Qanawat) and Salecah (Salkhad) were more to the east in the true Jebel Druze.

D. 2. *Gilead, the Land of the Highlander.* Eighteen miles south of the Yarmuq the plains of Bashan come to an end, and the land starts to rise rapidly until it reaches a height of well over 3300 feet in the Gilead Dome. Here the plateau has been arched up in a huge upwarp, formed mainly of hard Cenomanian limestone, and carved into two clearly defined sections by the valley of the Jabbok, which has cleft the dome into two, and has cut down through the limestone to the Nubian standstone beneath. The whole of this mountainous region, as far south as the latitude of

63. *Mukheibeh,* on the river Yarmuq, which brings as much water to its confluence with the Jordan as the Jordan does itself.

ever, this division does not seem to have been effective, for Ramoth Gilead, although it lay to the north, is mentioned more than once as part of Gad (Deut. 4:43; Josh. 20:8, 21:38; I Chron. 6:80), and in Josh. 13:27 the territory of Gad is said to be "all the cities of Gilead, and half the land of the Ammonites, to Aroer . . . having the Jordan as a boundary, to the lower end of the Sea of Chinnereth, eastward beyond the Jordan," which would have given them everything between the Yarmuq and Heshbon, an area which is clearly excessive. It is possible that in the first place the tribe of Manasseh had no territory east of the Jordan, for it is not mentioned in Numbers 32:1 and appears only at the end of the story in verse 33, but that the original settlers were only Reuben and Gad. However, Manasseh spread outward from west of the Jordan, as described in Joshua 17:14–16, at the expense of the people of Gad.

In any case, the difficulty in drawing the tribal boundaries is due to the uncertainty as to where the true division of the country is to be made. On paper, so to speak, it would seem sensible to draw the boundaries along the river valleys in the tidy manner in which the writer of Deuteronomy describes the frontier of Reuben as being "as far as the valley of the Arnon, with the middle of the valley as a boundary" (Deut. 3:16), but the strong consciousness of the east Jordanian people that there were four separate regions whose limits did not coincide with the major wadis prevented this ever really happening. Furthermore, the tendency of the surrounding peoples to press inward upon the Israelites until they

were confined to the mountainous region of Gilead probably served to confuse the tribal boundaries, since Gilead had to shelter all three tribes. "Blessed be he who enlarges Gad!" is the saying preserved in Deuteronomy 33:20, and the parallel blessing in Genesis 49:19, "Raiders shall raid Gad, but he shall raid at their heels," is more than a play upon words in Hebrew (גד גדוד יגודנו והוא יגד עקב); it is a commentary on the insecurity of the land in which they lived.

The region of Gilead forms a rough oval some 35 miles long from north to south and 25 from east to west. Raised high above the surrounding plateau, it receives an excellent rainfall during the winter months and heavy dew in summer, and there are many strong permanent springs, and consequently many villages tucked away among the limestone hills. Even today, when deforestation has been going on for centuries, the highest parts are still clothed with a thick cover of scrub oak, carob and pine, and in early times the rich forests of Gilead were almost as famous as those of Lebanon, the two often being mentioned together (Jer. 22:6; Zech. 10:10). The people of Gilead lived from the forest. The balm, of course, was proverbial (Jer. 8:22, 46:11), and was exported to the Phoenicians at Tyre (Ezek. 27:17) and also to the Egyptians, for Joseph was sold to a traveling company of Ishmaelites who were "coming down from Gilead, with their camels bearing gum, balm, and myrrh, on their way to carry it down to Egypt" (Gen. 37:25).

The very hilly nature of the coun-

* *Gad gedud yegudenu wahu yagud aqev.*

try and the thick forest cover meant that wheat could no longer be grown extensively, but trees and shrubs are at home here, and so the labor of the farmer was spent on their cultivated equivalent, and especially on the vines, which are quite superb, no other part of Palestine producing grapes to compare with those of Gilead. In summer half the population encamps in the vineyards to protect the precious fruit and while away the night in conversation under the stars, and in the morning every village is freshly supplied with grapes. Olives also can be grown in some measure in the sheltered valleys, and this is almost the only region east of Jordan where they can be persuaded to flourish.

Such a valuable district was, not unnaturally, a temptation to the neighbors, and both Ammon and Syria invaded it from time to time, for, though it is not an easy country to fight in, it is a frontier district and tended, therefore, to share the fate of Galilee whenever a determined attack was made on Israel. In the period of the Judges the Ammonite menace was very serious and occasioned the victory of Jephthah and the first victory of Saul (Judg. 11:29–33; I Sam. 11:1–11). The cause of Saul's intervention was an Ammonite attack on Jabesh Gilead in the depths of the Jordan Valley, so far had they been able to penetrate, but unfortunately it is not possible to identify with certainty the places mentioned in the story of Jephthah. Tob where Jephthah took refuge (Judg. 11:3) is possibly et-Taiyibeh, near the edge of the scarp in the north, and Na'ur and Kh. Hamzeh 3 miles northeast of Heshbon have been suggested for

Abel-keramim and Minnith (Judg. 11:33) [2] but with no real certainty. Mizpah, where Jephthah lived and where Jacob met Laban (Gen. 31:49), is also unknown, though the village of Jala'ad south of the Jabbok has been suggested.[3]

Conversely, when it has not been a question of outside attack from the north or east, but of internal trouble in Cis-jordan itself, the historic role of Gilead, as of other mountain regions, has been that of providing a refuge. So the family of Saul retreated here after his disastrous defeat on the mountains of Gilboa (II Sam. 2:8),

64. 'Ajlun. This is a Saracen castle, one of the line of fortresses along the edge of the scarp. The scrub oak is typical of western Gilead.

and David likewise fled to Gilead during the revolt of Absalom (II Sam. 17: 21–22). Mahanaim, which occurs in both stories, and which was also the scene of a vision of angels by Jacob (Gen. 32:2), and a city of refuge in Gad (Josh. 21:38), is also unknown and widely different places both north and south of the Jabbok have been suggested. Later, after the division of the kingdom, Jeroboam I seems, temporarily at least, to have established his capital at Penuel, where Jacob had wrestled with the angel (Gen. 32:30), and whose inhabitants had been punished by Gideon for refusing to come to his help (Judg. 8:8–9, 17; I Kings 12:25). We may be fairly certain that this was Tulul edh-Dhahab in the Jabbok valley, not far above Succoth, which lay where the Jabbok entered the Ghor. Again, in the tragic years at the end of the first century A.D. after the destruction of Jerusalem, large numbers of Palestinian refugees fled over the Jordan to the Decapolis, which then included part of Gilead, and in 1948 the same sad trek occurred again.

The uncertainty of the sites in Gilead makes it difficult to discuss with any exactness the role of the different parts of Gilead. The Jabbok valley, though steep-sided, is somewhat less precipitous than the other three, because of the exposure of the Nubian sandstone. This friable rock, which in the south stands up in tremendous cliffs, is here easily eroded by the heavy rainfall, and movement up and down the valley from the Jordan is, therefore, not especially difficult. It was for this reason that such an important town as Penuel was in the valley bottom, an

exceptional position for a Trans-jordanian town. Nevertheless, the Jabbok cannot have made no division at all in the life of the country, and Gilead must have resembled the two regions to the south of it in that it was divided into two halves, each of which had a different center. Today these two centers are 'Ajlun in the north and Es-Salt in the south, but we have insufficient evidence to know for certain what the

65. *Gerasa*. This was one of the smaller of the Decapolis towns. The gate shown here is the triumphal gate on the southern side.

two Old Testament centers were. Mahanaim was probably one of them, but we do not know which. The southern section is different from the northern in one important feature: it contains within it the large, down-faulted basin of the Beqa'a, where grapes give place to wheat in the economy.

The Decapolis, among whose inhabitants, as St. Mark tells us (Mark 5:20), the fame of Jesus spread, was a league of Greek cities of which the number has been given variously as ten, fourteen and eighteen. The original ten as listed by Pliny, are Damascus in the north, Philadelphia in the

66. *Gerasa.* The dark line of "trees planted by the waterside" which line the river, and the Circassian village beyond, are clearly shown. In the foreground is the "Viaduct Church," which was built by enclosing a piece of a street that at one time had led to a bridge across the river. The columns on each side of the street were then used as the columns of the nave. This is a good example of how churches were built "on the cheap," for the importance of Gerasa, one of the Decapolis, was already declining when the Empire became Christian.

south, Canatha in the east, and Scythopolis in the west (i.e., Damascus, Amman, Qanawat and Beisan), the last being the only one on the western side of the Jordan. Within the area enclosed by these four cities were Pella in the Ghor, Hippos and Gadara on the edge of the plateau, Dion and Raphana in Bashan, and Gerasa in the center of Gilead.* These cities did not form a political division with a clear frontier, but were a loose confederation of independent townships founded to protect the trade routes of this fertile region from the onslaughts of the Bedouin and the fierce inhabitants of the Jebel Druze (hence the outposts at Philadelphia and Canatha), and to

* Pella is Tabaqat Fahl; Hippos is Fiq; Gadara is Umm Qeis; Raphana is er-Rafeh and Abila, which in a second-century list replaces it, is probably Quweilba just south of the Yarmuq. Gerasa is Jerash. Dion has been variously placed at Tel el-Ash'ari north of the Yarmuq, and el-Husn south of it.

provide a strong block of Hellenistic culture in the midst of the Semitic world. What St. Mark describes as "the region of the Decapolis" through which Jesus went on his way from Sidon to the Sea of Galilee (Mark 7:31) is probably the country immediately east of the lake, including Hippos and Gadara, and extending southeastward through Gerasa to Philadelphia. This would mean that he crossed over from Sidon with his disciples to Caesarea Philippi, and then turned southward in the direction of the lake, but on the eastern side of the Rift, presumably because he wished to have time for teaching the disciples away from the crowds which always encompassed him in the Jewish regions.

67. *Gerasa.* In the foreground are the pillars of the great forum and on the hill to the right is the dark mass of the Temple of Zeus. Silhouetted against the hills in the background can just be discerned the arch of the triumphal gate.

CHAPTER XIX

Ammon, Moab and Edom

Thus says the Lord:
"For three transgressions of Edom,
*   and for four, I will not revoke the punishment;*
because he pursued his brother with the sword,
*   and cast off all pity. . . .*
For three transgressions of the Ammonites,
*   and for four, I will not revoke the punshment;*
because they have ripped up women with child
*   in Gilead,*
*   that they might enlarge their border. . . .*
For three transgressions of Moab,
*   and for four, I will not revoke the punishment;*
because he burned to lime
*   the bones of the king of Edom."*

Amos 1:11–2:1

D. 3. *The Land of the Shepherd (i) Ammon.* A little to the south of the present road from Es-Salt to Amman the last vestiges of the great dome of Gilead die away beneath the surface of the plateau, and the vast, rolling tableland stretches away into the almost limitless distance. Not only have the mountains disappeared, but the rainfall is also becoming less toward the south, and so there are fewer streams and increasingly less dissection of the plateau surface. Indeed, if it were not that the plateau continually rises southward, and thus presents an ever and ever higher obstacle to the Mediterranean storms, the rain would have died away altogether, and the desert would have poured over the edge of the scarp to join its fellow in the Ghor.

Theoretically, this was the territory of Reuben, which had its northern boundary on or near the Wadi Hesban, while the Ammonites were cramped between the desert and the river Jabbok, which rises at Amman in a strong spring that gave to the town its name of "the city of waters" (II Sam. 12:27). However, Amman was the ancient Rabboth Ammon, the chief city of the Ammonites, and it is incomprehensible that they should have planted their capital on the border. We must remember again, therefore, that these theoretical boundaries were an attempt to "freeze" a strategic situation which existed at the time of the Exodus, when the Amorites from the west had driven in a temporary wedge between the newly established Transjordanian kingdoms. Before the thrust of this attack Ammon and Moab had withdrawn behind the strong defensive lines of the Jabbok and Arnon valleys, for "fire went forth from Heshbon, flame from the city of Sihon. It devoured Ar of Moab, the lords of the heights of the Arnon" (Num. 21:28). When the Israelites in their turn arrived to dwell "in the land of the Amorites, and Moses sent to spy out Jazer, and they took its villages, and dispossessed the Amorites that were there" (Num. 21:31), they regarded themselves as heirs to all that the Amorites had conquered, and argued that "Israel did not take away the land of Moab or the land of the Ammonites," and that it was therefore the duty of the Ammonites to be content with what Chemosh their god gave them to possess (Judg. 11:15, 24).

Naturally, neither the Ammonites nor the Moabites could be expected to look at it in the same light, for to them all the land of Jazer was *terra irredenta*, from which they had been driven out, and to which they had every right to return, and inevitably the Ammonite view of the Exodus was that "Israel on coming from Egypt took away my land, from the Arnon to the Jabbok and to the Jordan" (Judg. 11:13). The justice of this claim that the land had once belonged to Ammon is supported by the statement in Joshua 13:25 that the inheritance of the tribe of Gad included "half the land of the Ammonites," but the Israel-ites felt that their own claim to the country was secure because it had been the God of Israel who had driven out the usurping Amorites, while Chemosh sat helpless on the great citadel of Rabboth Ammon (Judg. 11:23).

The territory within which the Ammonites had been confined is a strangely indeterminate area of steppe, part of that narrow belt which is constantly disputed between the desert and the sown, and at first sight it seems difficult to understand how the Ammonites escaped complete annihilation at the hands of their more powerful neighbors. However, they were defended by the tremendous strength of their citadel and the presence of the desert, into which a remnant of them

68. *Ammonite fortress.* The Trans-jordanian kingdoms were protected by a line of square fortresses along their frontiers, many of which can still be seen today.

could always escape, and there remain to raid and trouble their conquerors. Yet this same desert was also their enemy, for while they remained in possession of the fertile valley of the upper Jabbok there were always other desert

69. *Philadelphia.* The seats of the great theater, the largest in Palestine, at Amman, which was the southernmost of the cities of the Decapolis. In Old Testament times it had been Rabboth Ammon, the capital of the Ammonites.

tribes ready to raid and trouble them. "I am handing you over to the people of the east for a possession," said God, "and they shall set their encampments among you and make their dwellings in your midst; they shall eat your fruit, and they shall drink your milk. I will

70. *"Mesha king of Moab was a sheep breeder."* The flocks of sheep which are reared on the eastern plateau have long been famed for their excellence, and they form the mainstay of the economy of Moab.

make Rabbah a pasture for camels and the cities of the Ammonites a fold for flocks" (Ezek. 25:4–5).

Such was the history of Ammon. Shortly before the Jews first entered the country from Egypt this little kingdom had been carved out of the enfolding desert and established around the headwaters of the Jabbok, where the converging valleys had isolated an immense, flat-topped, dog-leg hill. They had been driven back onto this citadel by the Amorites, but their constant and inevitable purpose thereafter was to enlarge their border, allying themselves with whoever would assist them in this purpose, sometimes with the king of Moab (Judg. 3:13), and sometimes with the Syrians (II Sam. 10:6). Often they preyed on Israel in her time of weakness, penetrating even to the Jordan (Judg. 10:9; I Sam. 11:1), but never able to maintain their hold upon their gains. In the time of David they were subdued, their great city being taken at last in the infamous siege which cost Uriah his life (II Sam. 11:17), and the people for a time were reduced to slavery (II Sam. 12:31). After this they reappear but occasionally in the history of Israel and Judah. Some time previously to the period of Amos they had clearly re-established a certain amount of independence, for they tried to extend their territory into Gilead (Amos 1:13), but Jotham forced them to pay tribute again to Judah (II Chron. 27:5). After the Assyrian conquests Judah was no longer able to hold this outpost, and in the last days before the Exile the Ammonites make their final appearance, raiding the borders of Jehoiakim's weakened kingdom, and plotting to overthrow

71. *The plateau of Medeba*. This area was disputed between Israel, Ammon and Moab. It is a wide, open plateau of considerable fertility, and, though it is bare in this picture, which was taken in summer, in spring it is green with rich fields of wheat.

the miserable Gedaliah, ruling over the remnant of Judah at Mizpah (II Kings 24:2; Jer. 40:14). They were ever the weakest of the three Transjordanian kingdoms, oppressed by both the Moabites and the Jews, and constantly brooding on revenge. When Jerusalem was overthrown they naturally rejoiced, and Ezekiel says of them, "You have clapped your hands, and stamped your feet and rejoiced with all the malice within you" (Ezek.

25:6), but their joy was short-lived, for they passed even more completely out of history in the same convulsion, and when Rabboth Ammon was restored to glory, it was as Philadelphia, one of the Decapolis.

The Land of the Shepherd (ii) Moab. "Now Mesha king of Moab was a sheep breeder; and he had to deliver annually to the king of Israel a hundred thousand lambs, and the wool of a hundred thousand rams. But when Ahab died, the king of Moab rebelled against the king of Israel" (II Kings 3:4–5). These two verses sum up admirably the character of Moab, for they reflect not only the pastoral na-

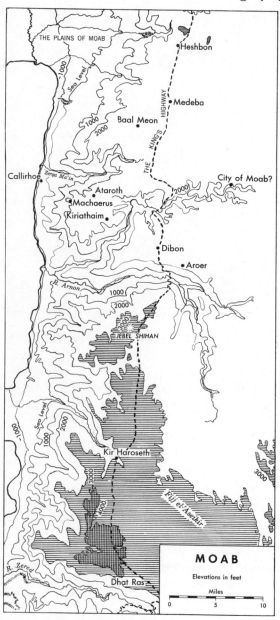

Fig. 44.

Moab to pay tribute to them, but whenever Israel showed signs of weakening, Moab threw off her overlordship and pursued a proud, independent role behind the protection of her towering Dead Sea cliffs.

The disputed territory between them was the plateau round Medeba, stretching as far south as the Arnon, where Reuben had originally settled, and which was claimed also by the Ammonites (Judg. 11:13). Reuben, however, soon vanished from the scene, swallowed up by the vengeful Moab, and after the time of Joshua the tribe is mentioned only three times. Far back in the early period of the Judges Deborah asked the clans of Reuben, "Why did you tarry among the sheepfolds, to hear the piping for the flocks?" (Judg. 5:16), but not again is this region called "the land of the Reubenites" until Hazael swept southward from Damascus to include it in his conquests (II Kings 10:33). The final mention is by Ezekiel, who prophesied their restoration, though apparently to a place *west* of the Jordan, between Ephraim and Judah, for the eastern border of the country was to be "along the Jordan between Gilead and the land of Israel" (Ezek. 47:18, 48:6). In the prophetic books Heshbon and the surrounding towns are always Moabite.

Within this region the geological strata, now that the Gilead Dome has been left behind, are remarkably level, and the traveler along the King's Highway crosses only gently rolling country, until he reaches Dibon and Aroer on the edge of the Arnon, and sees the road plunge in a sudden descent to the river nearly 2300 feet below. Three

ture of the country, but also the dingdong history, wherein the Israelites, when they were strong, pushed southward over the plateau, and forced miles away to the south is the other lip of the canyon, where Jebel Shihan raises its black head slightly above the general level, and then again is the undisturbed tableland beyond. It is the dark basalt from Shihan which has preserved the hard edges of the canyon and prevented their erosion by the tributary wadis, and this view from Aroer is that which the prophet had in mind when he said, "Come down from your glory, and sit on the parched ground, O inhabitant of Dibon . . . stand by the way and watch, O inhabitant of Aroer! Ask him who flees and her who escapes; say, 'What has happened?' Moab is put to shame, for it is broken; wail and cry! Tell it by the Arnon, that Moab is laid waste" (Jer. 48:18–20).

It is surprising that this tremendous cleavage in the plateau, carving it open like the first cut in a saddle of mutton, was not a more effective frontier. Its steep cliffs and precipices would seem to be almost a textbook case of an impregnable bastion, and yet it did not defend Sihon from the onslaught of the Israelites, nor the tribe of Reuben from the fury of Moab, determined to recover the land she once had owned. We have here, in fact, yet another illustration of the truth of the Palestinian frontiers, that they are no frontiers at all if they divide like from like. In the west the frontier between Judah and Ephraim stayed remarkably constant, though there was little on the ground to suggest an effective strategic division since the territory on either side was essentially dissimilar, but here in Moab a staggering obstacle to movement proved ineffective as a barrier, since

the land on each side of it was essentially the same.

Neither vines nor olives are greatly to be seen in Moab, and the villages become less frequent. Though in spring the tableland, which is but interrupted by the Arnon, may be green with wheat and barley, the area where these crops can grow is narrow, and especially narrow in the south. Everywhere, however, there are sheep, great flocks and converging lines of them, like the spokes of a limitless wheel, moving in clouds of golden dust to be

72. *"Stand by the way and watch, O inhabitant of Aroer!"* This is the view across the Arnon which Jeremiah had in mind. It is taken from near Aroer, and in the distance on the right is the volcanic hill of Shihan.

given their water at the well. Though the Bible speaks of the "flocks of goats, moving down the slopes of Gilead" (Song 6:5), the vast Moabite flocks could never have been kept there, where the beasts of the forest were an ever-present menace, and the trees gave them no room to move, but here on the boundless tableland sheep were the mainstay of the country. The black tents of the Bedouin cover the plateau, dwellings of people in all stages of the endless procession of settlement which has gone on throughout the centuries.

73. *The sheep market at Amman.* Rabboth Ammon, or Amman, has always been a desert port, where the Bedouin came in from the eastern desert to sell their products and to buy those necessities which they could not produce for themselves.

Some are fully settled, save that they have not yet built houses of stone to replace the tents of hair, as they will probably do in the next generation, while others own fields to which they return for the seedtime and the harvest, moving away in the meanwhile to find pasture for their flocks. There is great coming and going in Moab, for when the desert is safe even the true villager will take his sheep far out to the east during the rich season of spring and return to the west only in the drought of summer.

The chief town of Moab was Kir Haroseth, the present town of Kerak, an impressive stronghold at the head of a valley, and one of the greatest of the line of fortresses along the King's Highway. From its walls, successors to those on which the king of Moab in desperation sacrificed his son to placate the gods (II Kings 3:27), the ground drops away in a rush to the steep-sided wadi and the road which follows it to the Dead Sea, and thus Kir Haroseth dominated, not only the countryside around, but also the only possible road up from the west.

The parallel fortress in the northern section (for like Gilead, Moab was divided into two) was Heshbon, which was too near the frontier, however, to be a real center, though its strong position made it a permanent castle of defense (Num. 21:25, 32:37; Is. 15:4, 16:8, 9). The real center for this part of Moab was Medeba (Num. 21:30; Josh. 13:9, 16; Is. 15:2), which stands upon a slight eminence in the middle of the plain. It is not, however, a really strong point, for the slopes by which it is approached are too gentle, and for this reason it was not a wise choice for the Ammonite and Syrian stand against Joab (I Chron. 19:6–15).*

"Loftiness, pride, arrogance and haughtiness of heart" were the sins of which the Israelites accused the people of Moab (Jer. 48:29) and there was, indeed, a temptation to them to imagine that behind their bastions they were safe from conquest and foreign domination. The prophets might thunder denunciations, saying, "The hand of the Lord will rest on this mountain, and Moab shall be trodden down in his place . . . the Lord will lay low his pride together with the skill of his hands" (Is. 25:10–11), and promise that because of their taunts and boasts "Moab shall become like Sodom" (Zeph. 2:9), but the Moabites do not seem to have been deterred. In fact, when one considers the insults which both nations hurled at each other across the blue waters of the Dead Sea, there seems very little to choose between them, for Psalm 60 shows that

* Some commentators seem to imagine that because Medeba is not mentioned in the parallel passage in II Sam. 10:1–19 "the city" in the story must have been Rabboth Ammon. However, the Chronicler is probably right, for Ammon would surely have enlarged her border in the confusion at the end of Saul's reign, and Joab could not have attacked Rabboth Ammon immediately, without first ensuring his lines of communication.

the people of Judah were no less capable of pride and haughtiness of heart. Yet the pride of both was humbled, and each was forced to beg for succour from the other: when Jerusalem was taken, the Jews fled to Moab and Edom (Jer. 40:11), and when Moab was attacked, the people came to Jerusalem "like fluttering birds, like scattered nestlings," saying to the daughter of Zion, "Hide the outcasts, betray not the fugitive; let the outcasts of Moab sojourn among you" (Is. 16:2–4). It is true that a certain note of gloating is not absent from the prophecies of Moab's destruction, for the two peoples hated each other very bitterly, and yet the prophets seem to have thought of the punishment of Moab as being but parallel to that of Israel and Judah. They dreamed of Moab's restoration also (Jer. 48:47) and promised to the refugees the coming of "one who judges and seeks justice and is swift to do righteousness" (Is. 16:5).

D. 4. *Edom, the Land of the Trader.* Still farther south along the King's Highway the plateau is once again cleft by a mighty valley, striking back from the southern end of the Dead Sea. This is the valley of the Zered, the "Brook of the Willows" (Is. 15:7), and for once a valley really was the frontier, dividing this time Edom from Moab (Deut. 2:13). We do not know very much about the relations between these two kingdoms, though since we are told that the Moabites "burned to lime the bones of the king of Edom" (Amos 2:1), it is clear that between them also raged that incessant internecine warfare which devoured the lives of all these Levantine kingdoms.

74. *Kir Haroseth,* the modern town of Kerak. This stands in a very strong position on an isolated hill, and was the chief city of the Moabites. The castle shown here on the left is Crusading and the walls of the town are mainly Mamluke.

Yet, there is little suggestion that either side claimed as part of their own territory the land across the river, and the towns here which are quoted in the Old Testament remain quite steadily either Moabite or Edomite. It is true that in one place Bozrah, the modern Buseireh, is spoken of as a city of Moab (Jer. 48:24), but in the next chapter it appears as belonging to Edom and, since this agrees with every other reference, the first ascription must be an error (Jer. 49:13, 22; Gen. 36:33; Is. 34:6, 63:1; Amos 1:12). The reason why the Zered proved such a permanent frontier, unlike the other rivers, is that the land on the two sides of the river is not the same, for to the north is the plateau of Moab and to the south the highlands of Edom; the rising plateau has been pushed up

even further in the south, the dark red sandstone cliffs mounting ever higher, and even older strata being revealed. For long distances in Edom the plateau edge is over 5000 feet and at its greatest surpasses 5600, and so the thick sandstone beds are widely exposed. Moreover, it must be remembered that the scarp itself is here different, for instead of the plunging monocline of Moab, where the strata turn over headlong into the Rift, there are instead three tremendous steps, in which the whole nature of the landscape changes, the wide areas of sandstone creating a bizarre world of dark, gigantic cliffs, and deep, terrifying gorges. The road, it must be understood, keeps to the plateau, but from time to time the traveler on his journey approaches the plateau rim and peers dizzily into these tremendous depths.

The faulting and tilting of the region has raised the plateau edge so steeply that the dip slope to the east is here more sharply inclined than it is farther north, and the desert wadis run off eastward very nearly parallel to each other. It is this tilted western edge which catches the last fragments of the Mediterranean storms, though because of the steeper tilt of the dip

75. *Bozrah*. The village which can be seen in the middle of this picture is Buseirah, probably the ancient Bozrah, which was the chief stronghold of the northern half of Edom. It was strongly defended because it stood on a bluff of rock outlined by very steep valleys.

slope the decrease in the rainfall eastward is more than usually rapid. On the limestone which crowns the western scarp there is even today a surprising amount of scrub, and as late as World War I there was sufficient woodland here to make it worth the Turks' while to build a branch of the Hejaz Railway out to Shobek to tap the supply. Even when it was more extensive in the distant past, it can never have been more than a very thick scrub forest, but for all that the wood was very valuable, since it provided charcoal to smelt the copper at Punon, and fuel for the plateau, where the winters can be very bleak.

The Edomite territory, confined to this uplifted western edge, was thus curiously long and narrow. On all sides except the desert slopes it was well defended, but the eastern frontier demanded more frequent forts. There they are built within sight of each other, sometimes no more than 4 or 5 miles distant, and between 12 and 18 miles from the edge of the scarp, enclosing an area some 70 miles long from north to south, and only 15 miles wide. The true village zone, of course, is even narrower and is no more than 9 miles across. The southern frontier was the *Neqb*, the long limestone scarp at the southern edge of the plateau, which runs inland southeastward from 'Ain Gharandel in the Arabah. Beyond this there was nothing in the days of the Old Testament but rocky, uninhabitable desert, through which the merchants must have journeyed to Ezion Geber in armed convoy.

The territory thus enclosed is, in characteristic Trans-jordanian fashion, divided into two unequal parts, this time by the Punon embayment, which pushes the scarp back some 9 miles and thus interrupts the tenuous village zone. This division is reflected by the frequent mention of two centers of life in Edom, one in the north and the other in the south. The northern section is the smaller, and is highest in the south near Rashadiyeh, where it reaches 5300 feet. The scarp here is cut by three important fault valleys, the Wadi Dana in the south, running southwestward from the highest part of the plateau to Punon in the Arabah, the Wadi Hamayideh and Wadi Salim, both of which run northwestward toward the Sebkha. At the head of the

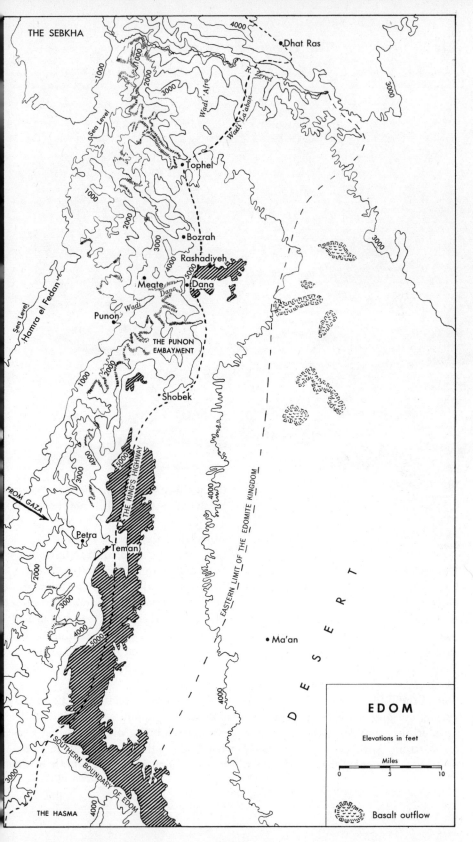

Fig. 45.

76. *Dana.* Here the edge of the Edomite plateau is more than 5000 feet above sea level and 5500 above the bottom of the Rift Valley. From here a very precipitous valley leads down to Feinan, the Punon of the Bible.

Hamayideh valley is the rocky isolated spur or which Bozrah stood, the chief stronghold of the northern section, which it was admirably able to control, being both central and very strongly defended. At the head of the Wadi Salim, which is narrow and precipitous, is Tafileh, probably the Tophel of the Bible (Deut. 1:1), the richest agricultural settlement in Edom, wonderfully supplied with water from eight strong springs and sufficiently protected, because it lies a little down the western scarp, for there to be extensive olive groves. It is not, however, easy to defend and is too easily accessible from the Zered by way of the long Wadi La'aban for it to have challenged Bozrah as the strategic center. The desert side of this northern portion, just beyond the Edomite frontier posts, is marked by a series of basalt outflows, and it is just possible that it was near here that Anah, the Edomite, found the hot springs in the wilderness (Gen. 36:24).

The southern section of the kingdom is longer and rather higher, the scarp edge being over 5300 feet very nearly throughout, and touching 5687 feet in Rujm Tal'at el-Juma'ah in the

77. *Tophel.* Tafileh, somewhat to the south of the Hesa, was probably the Tophel of the Bible. It is unusual in Edom in having extensive olive groves.

north. More or less centrally placed for this southern section is Petra and close beside it was Teman, quoted more than once as the southern parallel of Bozrah (Gen. 36:33–34; Jer. 49:20, 22; Amos 1:12). Petra did not reach its full magnificence until the Nabatean period, and the Edomite stronghold of Sela was smaller, being perched on the almost impregnable mountain of Umm el-Biyara in the middle of the city. This was what the Psalmist meant when he asked, "Who will bring me into the fortified city? Who will lead me into Edom?" (Ps. 108:10), and it was the taking of Sela by storm which made Amaziah so conceited that he foolishly challenged Jehoash of Israel to battle (II Kings 14:7–10).

A certain aura of mystery seems to have surrounded the country of Edom. Remote from all the other centers of life, dwelling in clefts of the rocks (Obad. 3), the Edomites were not like other people. They could not hope to get their wealth by farming, nor maintain the huge Moabite herds of fat-tailed sheep, but, like the Phoenicians, they were taught by the stern land in which they lived to find their fortune in trade. Their wealth came from copper, and from the lumbering camel caravans of the south, laden with the luxury products of southern Arabia and Africa, toiling wearily from the Hasma into Edom, where the cultivated land stretched out a long arm into the desert to greet them. This trade brought them in contact with that almost legendary world of the east, which the other people knew only by hearsay, and so they acquired among the Israelites a reputation for wisdom and strange knowledge. When the Edomite kingdom at last was overthrown, Jeremiah lamented the decay of wisdom among the Temanites (Jer.

78. *"Caravans of Dedanites."* These are the vanguard of a much larger group of Arabs moving northward from Edom, across the valley of the Hesa, in which this picture was taken, into Moab.

49:7), and much earlier it had been from Teman that Eliphaz had come to comfort Job (Job 2:11).

With the collapse of the agricultural communities in southern Trans-jordan in the sixth century B.C. the Edomite kingdom came to an end, but sometime in the third century the Nabateans began to move in from the desert and settle in this region. By 100 B.C. they had ceased entirely to be a pastoral society, and for the next two centuries they controlled a wide trading empire with its headquarters in the fabulous city of Petra. Although this was not the only city approached by a *siq*, or narrow corridor through the rocks, for this kind of site is characteristic of the region, it was at Petra that it attained its greatest eminence. In large measure it was a troglodyte city, though with a luxury that other cave dwellers have never known; the huge classical façades carved out of the red sandstone are, of course, world famous, and the cliffs around are honeycombed with caves which served as homes and as storehouses for the merchants. In the center a great semicircular area of open ground was filled with buildings, all but one of which have now disappeared, and the ruins of them show that in their day they were ornate and splendid.

From Petra the Nabatean power stretched forth across the deserts of Cis-jordan to the Mediterranean, and round behind Perea and the Decapolis even as far as Damascus. Perea, which in Jesus' time was part of the territory of Herod Antipas, was a narrow strip of land east of the Jordan and extending from Pella in the north to Machaerus, a typical Herodian fortress, where it is probable that John the Baptist was beheaded (Mark 6:14–29), situated north of the Arnon and not far from Ataroth (Num. 32:3, 34). Perea did not extend very far eastward, for Medeba was a few miles outside it, and it seems to have included merely the scarp towns protecting the routes down into the Jordan valley. Apparently it did not continue as far as the Arnon, which was no more of a boundary then than earlier, for the northern rim was in Nabatean hands, and they thus controlled not only Edom, but also very nearly the whole of Moab. Their connection with Damascus was by way of the Wadi Sirhan, for they extended their settlements farther into the desert than any other nation had done, and, though they refurbished the Edomite frontier fortresses, they did not allow themselves to be confined to the same narrow strip.

The immense wealth which accrued to the Nabateans from their trade enabled them to cultivate economically areas which have never been cultivated before or since, such as the Arabah and the sandy wastes south of the Edomite *neqb,* much as the wealth obtained from oil today makes it eco-

79. *Dhat Ras.* On the edge of the valley of the Hesa stood Dhat Ras, a fortress protecting the route leading down into the valley. Here there was a Moabite frontier post and, later, a Nabatean stronghold. The best preserved of the ruins still standing today is this small Roman temple.

nomically possible to develop desert regions which otherwise would have remained barren. Naturally, even though the rainfall may have been a little more assured then than now, agriculture in such areas was possible only by the most skillful methods of irrigation and water conservation, and the Nabateans were far advanced in this, but it is doubtful whether the produce of these Nabatean fields would have justified the trouble which was taken over them, if they had not assisted in maintaining the complicated network of Nabatean trade routes.

The extraordinary magnificence of Petra enters hardly at all into the New Testament records, though the merchants of whom Jesus speaks must have had to take account of it, for fine pearls from the Indian Ocean would certainly have been part of Nabatean trade (Matt. 13:45). Only twice does it stretch out a finger to touch the narrative directly, once in the Gospels and

80. *The site of Petra.* This picture was
taken from above Elji, near what was possibly the Teman of the Bible, and shows the
precipitous mountains within which Petra
lies hidden. In the foreground is the white
limestone and beyond the red sandstone.

81. *The entrance to Petra.* This was by
means of the narrow passage through the
rocks known as the *Siq.* The figures in the
foreground give a good idea of the scale.

82. *Umm el-Biyara*, or Sela, the towering rock fortress of the Edomites, round which the Nabatean city of Petra grew.

83. *The High Place at Petra.*

84. *Petra, the triumphal gate.* Today almost all that remains of Petra is the vast number of monuments cut out of the rock. However, at one time there were also many masonry buildings, round which there was a wall. This picture shows the ruins of a triple gate by which one entered the city from the west.

85. *Petra, the Khazne Fara'un.* The extreme narrowness of the *Siq* has meant that those monuments which are carved in its walls have escaped the fury of the driven sand which has done so much damage elsewhere, and the details of the carving are almost as sharp as the day that they were made.

86. *Petra, the Deir.* This is the largest of the monuments at Petra, but the details are much coarser than those of the Khazne. However, it is probably unfinished since it is doubtful whether the capitals were intended to be left so plain.

88. *Machaerus*. The characteristic sugar-loaf hill on which stood Herod's castle, overlooking the Dead Sea. It is probable that it was here that John the Baptist was beheaded.

87. *Petra, the Palace Tomb*. The damage done by wind erosion, especially at the foot of the cliffs, can be very clearly seen here.

once in the early history of the Church. The first time was when "wise men from the East" came to offer the infant Jesus gifts, "gold and frankincense and myrrh" (Matt. 2:1–12), and the second time was when "the governor under King Aretas guarded the city of Damascus" in order to seize Paul (II Cor. 11:32), for the king of whom he speaks was the same Aretas of Petra who was related in marriage to Herod the Great.

CHAPTER XX

The Wilderness and the Dry Land

The wilderness and the dry land shall be glad,
the desert shall rejoice and blossom;
like the crocus it shall blossom abundantly,
and rejoice with joy and singing.

ISAIAH 35:1–2

THE deserts which surround Palestine on the east and south may be divided easily into three regions of unequal size, but clearly different one from the other: the eastern plateau of Trans-jordan, the Wadi Hasma south of the Edomite *neqb*, and the Wilderness of Zin in the southern triangle of Cis-jordan. The last two are divided by the Arabah, but it must not be forgotten that this is also desert, and the division, therefore, is physical and not climatic.

Everywhere it is "tame" desert, and receives a certain amount of rain, sometimes only a shower or two, sometimes in a real cloudburst, coming very often either at the beginning or the end of the rainy season. If the year is a dry one, however, the rain may be very limited both in amount and in extent, and in the south it may fail altogether.

E. 1. *The Eastern Plateau of Trans-jordan.* Extending very nearly all the way from the Jebel Druze southeastward to the oasis of Jauf is the basalt, a long line of mountains and plateaus, volcanic peaks and great outflows of lava, rising at the highest points to just over 3300 feet. This lava belt is well over 60 miles wide and on an average stands 1600 feet above the level of the Sirhan depression, which lies along its southwestern edge. The height of this lava plateau, the hardness and roughness of the rock, and the great complexity of the terrain, have combined to make this a region of quite singular difficulty, and the important caravan routes made long detours to avoid it.

The southeastern end of this long tongue of basalt is almost touched by a great shoulder of sand desert, the most northerly extension of the deso-

252

89. *The eastern desert*. Much of this is flat, flint-strewn country, such as is shown here. The bus, which serves to give some idea of the scale of this picture, is coming from Baghdad.

late Nefud of Arabia. As soft sand is almost as great an obstacle as hard basalt, it is clear that the caravan routes across this section of Arabia are severely limited. The sand and basalt do not quite touch each other, however, and between them is the corridor of el-Jauf and Sakaka, through which the major routes tended to be funneled.

West of el-Jauf these routes fanned out again, one running northwestward at the foot of the basalt along the Wadi Sirhan to el-Azraq, and so through to Damascus, and another leading almost due westward through Kilwa and el-Jafr to Petra, making its way between the eastern end of Jebel Tubeiq and Qasimt el-Arnab, an area of very rocky ground near the southern end of the Wadi Sirhan. Others swung southwestward on the farther side of Jebel Tubeiq to meet the routes coming northward on the western side of Arabia. Within the triangle formed by the first two routes is the Eastern Plateau of Trans-jordan.

It is a wide tableland limited on the west by the present Hejaz Railway and on the east by the basalt, about 50 miles broad in the north and some 150 in the south. A line of Eocene hills runs roughly from northwest to southeast, and in the center of the triangle, lying in a shallow basin at the foot of these hills, is the important water supply of Bayir. Another line of higher land extends westward from Bayir in the general direction of the Punon embayment, and so there are, in general, three systems of drainage: east of the hills the wadis run in roughly parallel lines toward Wadi Sirhan; to the southwest they collect in the depression of el-Jafr; and in the northwest they run off toward the scarp streams which flow into the Jordan and the Dead Sea.

It must not be thought that because the whole of this area is relatively flat movement about it is consequently easy, for until the invention of the motorcar travel in the desert was everywhere limited by two things: where water is to be obtained and where camels can go. In this part of the desert water is available the full length of the Wadi Sirhan, fairly frequently in the northernmost part of the triangle, and also at Bayir and el-Jafr, and so routes tended naturally to converge on these places. The most difficult areas for camels were those that were either too rough or else in danger of becoming too slippery, for a camel skids uncontrollably in the mud. The particularly bad rough surfaces were the *harrah* or basalt, and the *Ardh es-Suwan,* or flint desert, east of Bayir, where the ground is covered for miles and miles with innumerable sharp nodules of flint, every particle of sand having been blown or washed away. It is incredibly barren, for not a speck of green is to be seen, and everywhere the unwinking flint throws back the light of the blazing sun.

Areas of mud flat or *qa'a* were perfectly possible in the summer, but quite impossible after rain, even the slightest shower making the surface slippery, and heavy rain rendering them impassable for long periods, since the water pours down into them through every surrounding wadi. Even slight hills might be sufficient to deflect the caravans round them, because under desert conditions slopes are often interrupted by steep cliffs, the result of the undercutting effect of blown sand, and even if these cliffs were very low, they would still deter the traveler.

The routes in this section of the desert were therefore directed either along the Wadi Sirhan or else toward Bayir. The Sirhan depression itself is a long trough of lower land, more than 150 miles long and roughly 1300 to 1600 feet above sea level. The basalt highlands, rising steeply 1600 above it, are high enough to receive a moderate supply of rain and the trough is consequently marked by a line of wells and oases, which in the classical period were the site of a series of settlements along the Jauf-Azraq trade route. It was not, however, closely colonized by the Nabateans, for there is an absence of clear-cut Nabatean pottery, at any rate in the northern part,[1] though Bayir, rather farther west, has revealed considerable evidences of Nabatean occupation, and must have been an important center for controlling the desert, then as now.

Between Bayir and the Wadi Sirhan the difficult *Ardh es-Suwan* effectively blocked any large scale movement, and this increased the importance of el-Azraq and el-Jauf at either end of the Sirhan trough, because the cara-

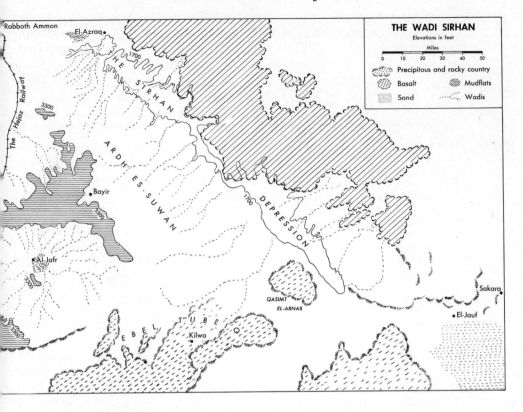

Fig. 46.

vans were deflected toward these two oases round the flint area, which extends all along the central section of the depression. It also explains why Bayir was evidently an important Nabatean center, but why the Wadi Sirhan was apparently not extensively colonized by them, for the difficulty of the flint country would have been sufficient to hinder expansion across it from the west into the Wadi Sirhan, which was, in any case, on the margin of the Nabatean empire. However, the possession of Bayir, which gave them access to el-Azraq and el-Jauf, would have enabled them to control the Wadi

Sirhan, in much the same way as traffic in the Red Sea is controlled by whoever can keep a watch on its entrances.

The northern section of the triangle, being fairly small in area and better watered, because it is farther north, is not difficult to cross, and though the routes are channeled to some extent by the fact that the higher land tends to run from northwest to southeast, the tracks lead more or less in all directions. There are here no great obstacles to movement. The Jafr basin in the south is roughly circular in shape and the rim is somewhat rocky. The wadi lines here all lead toward the center,

90. *El-Azraq.* This is an important oasis at the head of the Wadi Sirhan. The castle which can be seen here among the palm trees is a very badly built medieval Arab fortress, but it stands on the site of a Roman fort. el-Azraq also certainly played its part in the Nabatean network of trade.

15:34, 18:14–15, 29:4), keeping camels and sheep (1:3), and acquainted with the perils of the desert (1:13–19) and the caravans from Tema and Sheba (6:19), but they know also the cultivation of oliveyards and vineyards (24:6, 11) and the streets and squares of settled towns (29:7). In the great prophecies of Second Isaiah the picture is that of a tableland, for the valleys which are below the general level are to be filled, and the mountains to be made low, while the *harrah* is to be a plain (Is. 40:4), and the wealth which is to be poured upon the return-

to the wells and broad mud-flats of el-Jafr.

This eastern desert does not enter very directly into Biblical history, save as a threat to Israelite security. The Midianites, or Bedouin, had been a severe menace in the early period and the two great battles in which they had been defeated, first by Moses and then by Gideon, remained long in the Jewish memory as a picture of triumphant victory against overwhelming odds (Num. 31:1–12; Judg. 6:1–6, 7:1–25; Is. 9:4, 10:26). The picture is repeated in Psalm 83:9–12, but in a context which suggests that in the final weakness of Judah the people of the East had again become a danger (Ps. 83:6). Under the strong control of David and Solomon the Bedouin were apparently ready to accept employment under the government (I Chron. 27:30).

This part of the desert is also at the back of the thinking of both the Book of Job and Second Isaiah. In Job the people are clearly tent dwellers (4:21,

91. *El-Azraq.* The entrance to the castle, showing, once again, the use of stone for doors in regions where wood is scarce.

ing refugees is that of the flocks and
caravans of the wilderness (Is. 60:6–
7).

E. 2. *The Wadi Hasma.* Twenty
miles or so south of the present oasis
town of Ma'an the plateau comes to a
sudden end, and the whole nature of
the landscape changes. Instead of the
wide-open tableland with views that
stretch for miles there are narrow valleys and steep, gigantic cliff faces; instead of the pale browns and russets
there are dark reds and drifts of shining yellow sands; instead of freedom
of movement there is imprisonment.
The change comes where the plateau
breaks away on the southern frontier
of Edom along a NW-SE fault line,
which reaches as far as the disused
railway track and then swings round
to a more northeasterly direction.

On the west the region is enclosed
by the high granite wedge of the
Mountains of Midian, which reach
just over 5000 feet at several points in
the south, and to the east of this is a
broad, sandy plain, enclosed on every
side by high, precipitous scarps, and
floored with drifting sand, qa'a and
wide alluvial fans. Out of this plain,
like islands from the sea, rise hills and
mountains, sometimes as much as 5600
feet in height and towering 2500 feet
above the surface of the plain. At the
bottom of these island peaks is the
granite platform, and then resting
upon that a narrow band of Cambrian
limestone, crowned in its turn by enor-
mous sandstone cliffs. Though the
plain itself has a reasonable cover of
desert scrub, these hills are barren and
easily eroded, the restless sand forever
driven by the wind against the foot

92. *El-Azraq.* The salt marshes formed
where the water pours in from the surrounding wadis. Water buffalo can be kept here
and wild duck are very numerous.

of the cliffs, causing them to collapse
in huge screes and drifts at their junction with the plain. East of the old
railway, where the plateau edge swings
round more to the northeast, this same
landscape is developed and expanded
in the region of Jebel Tubeiq.

This barren archipelago of red, forbidding sandstone is the very edge of
the Biblical story, though the caravans
to Edom from the south must have
wound their way beneath these preci-

93. *A desert oasis.* A general view of Ma'an,
which today has taken the place of Petra as
the chief center of the south of Trans-jordan.

94. *View over the Hasma from the southern edge of Edom.* The Edomite kingdom did not extend south of the plateau edge, except to send armed caravans to Ezion Geber. The Nabateans, however, had a large number of posts in this region.

pices, and the Queen of Sheba passed this way. It was outside the kingdom of Edom which had "its nest among the stars" (Obad. 4) and descended from the plateau only to maintain an uncertain hold on Ezion Geber. The Nabateans, however, indefatigable in their efforts to strengthen and preserve the delicate net of commerce from which they drew their life, coaxed even these desiccated valleys to yield a little nourishment, though, when their careful schemes of irrigation fell into decay, the desert resumed its undisputed rule.

The Midian Mountains to the west are not entirely impassable, though they are difficult to cross, and the east-west route through the Hasma may be continued straight over into the Arabah by the line of the Wadi Muhtadi, though the track climbs as high as 3600 feet. Just to the north of it is Jebel el-Hafji, 4700 feet high, where first the Edomites and then the Naba-

teans had a lookout post, whence they could keep a general watch both on the Hasma and the Arabah. The Nabateans also erected forts at intervals of 10–15 miles along the road from Petra through the Hasma to Ezion Geber. This road climbed down from the plateau at its extreme southwestern corner, where the fragmentation of the Arabah scarp made it possible to reach either the Arabah or the Hasma, and thereafter it clung to the eastern foot of the Midian Mountains and passed into the Wadi Yatm. The Nabatean posts along this route were Humeima and Kalkha, controlling both the descent to the Hasma and the passages from the Hasma to the Arabah, Harabat el-Abyad in the northwestern corner of the Hasma, and Quweira some 6 miles farther south. Then came Quseir Mudeifi and Khirbet el-Khalidi, at the entrance of the Wadi Yatm, and within the narrow confines of the wadi was Khirbet el-Kithara, where the Yatm is joined by another fault valley from the southeast, the Yatm el-'Umran. Some 6 miles east of Quweira is Jebel Ratama, one of the isolated peaks in the valley, and here stood an-

95. *The route to Ezion Geber.* This is the entrance to the narrow Wadi Yatm by which a road led through the mountains of Midian to the Red Sea.

other important fort, centrally placed to watch all the western Hasma.

Although the plain is fairly level, there are few wells, and routes are confined to the passes between the sandstone blocks, passes which in the south become exceedingly narrow. Here on the southern side the islands come so close together that the archipelago becomes instead a greatly dissected plateau, cut by many north-south fault valleys, all of which were protected by Nabatean settlements. Of these fault valleys the Wadi Ram is both the most striking and the most useful. Here the two sides of the valley, Jebel 'Ishrin and Jebel Ram, both

surpass 5600 feet, and the latter, a huge mass of sandstone rising very nearly sheer for something like 2600 feet above the valley, is actually the highest point in the whole of the Palestinian region, outreaching the greatest summit of Edom by 60 feet. Because of their immense height, these two islands trigger more of the rare desert storms than the other surrounding peaks, and so there are several wells along the wadi, which carried an important tributary route into the Hasma.

E. 3. *The Wilderness of Zin.* It will be convenient to take this as including all the area south of the modern Gaza-Beersheba road and of a line running due eastward from Beersheba to the Dead Sea through Ras ez-Zuweira, though not all of this area is

96. *Wadi Ram*. This is one of the most dramatic of the Hasma valleys, since the cliffs on each side rise to tremendous heights. It is reasonably well supplied with water and, for this reason, is important as a route to Arabia. The fort in the picture belongs to the Desert Patrol of the Arab Legion.

really desert. It is divided into two parts by a zone of higher land which runs from between Ras ez-Zuweira and Jebel Usdum toward the present Egyptian frontier. This central zone is composed of two upwarps, the Khurashe and the Kurnub, and is diversified by three great basins, the Wadi Raman, the Wadi Hathira and el-Hadhira. The Khurashe upwarp is the higher and just touches 3300 feet in one or two places near the Egyptian border, but the Kurnub upwarp has only two ridges which surpass 2000 feet, and even these are broken. They are the Jebel Hathira, which is the northwestern rim of Wadi Hathira, and farther to the northwest again the Jebel Heleiqim—Wadi Juraba ridge. Cutting right across this zone of higher land, more or less between the two upwarps, is the Wadi Murra, which is the result of a huge hinge fault swinging back from the southwestern corner of the Dead Sea, and cleaving the hills so effectively that a wide scimitar of lowland divides Jebel Hathira from the higher hills to the southwest.

This broad zone of higher land divides two markedly different sections of the Wilderness. In the northwest is the moderate para-steppeland of the

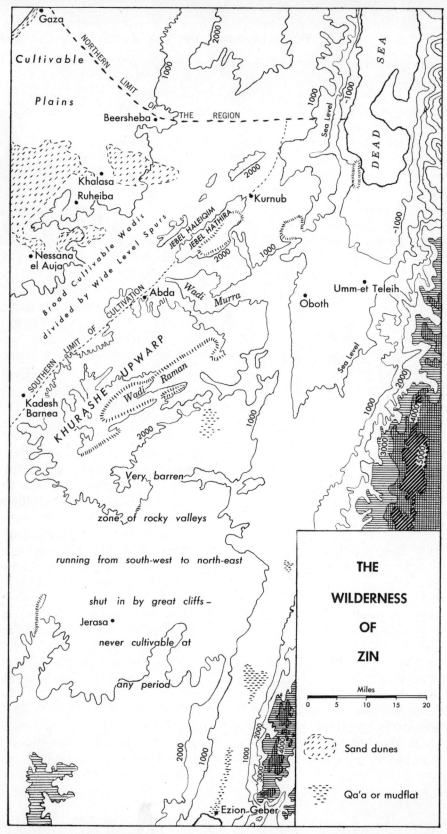

Fig. 47.

western slopes, moistened with heavy dew from the sea and the occasional storms of the rainy season, but in the southeast is one of the most desolate parts of the whole Palestinian area, a rain-shadow region in the desert.

The northwestern section could be divided again by a line from Beersheba through Khalasa to el-Auja, this being the line which divides the plain on the west from the hills, though the passage from one to the other is very gradual. The southern part of the plain is largely covered with sand dunes, those round Khalasa being of great antiquity but others being more recent, but the northern part is loess country and steppeland. This northern triangle, which lies roughly north of a line drawn due westward from a point about 6 miles south of Beersheba, is dotted with fairly frequent wells and seems always to have been cultivated. It might indeed be better to include it with the Philistine coast plain to the north than with the barren southern wilderness.*

South of the Beersheba–Khalasa–el-Auja line the land rises gently to the uplands in a landscape of broad wadis and wide, level spurs. The wadis narrow toward the east, where they become shut in by cliffs, and were cultivated somewhat ineffectively, but regularly, by the Bedouin, and in earlier days more efficiently by the Nabateans and their successors. The Bedouin of this district, in fact, tended to be cultivators rather than shepherds, and for that reason were not true Bedouin at all. This section of the Negeb forms a strip about 22 miles wide and comes to an end along a line drawn through Kurnub and Abda.

The area to the southeast of the uplands, which is by far the largest of the three divisions of the Negeb, is incredibly barren, and sharply different from the gentler region to the west. Here the storms of the Pluvial period, cutting down to the low base level of the Rift, have carved great gorges in the hills, narrow corridors between tremendous cliffs that rise almost perpendicularly sometimes more than 650 feet above the valley floor. Lawrence and Woolley say of this region, "The way down is very splendid. In the hill-sides all sorts of rocks are mingled in confusion; grey-green limestone cliffs run down sheer for hundreds of feet, in tremendous ravines whose faces are a medley of colours wherever crags of black porphyry and diorite jut out, or wherever soft sandstone, washed down, has left long pink and red smudges on the lighter colours." [2] The wadis carry some desert scrub and were used by the Bedouin for grazing in the winter, but they do not seem ever to have been cultivated, except only just around Kurnub. In many parts the surface is as fragile as meringue and breaks away under the foot of the traveler, and elsewhere there are wide stretches of flint desert, from which every speck of sand has been swept away by the wind.

The chief importance of this south-

---

* It is worth noting that modern newspaper articles, etc. which describe the cultivation of the Negeb today refer, with very few exceptions, only to this corner of it, though it is doubtful whether it ought to be counted as part of the Negeb at all.

eastern region of the Wilderness of Zin was that it had to be crossed in any passage from the coasts of Cisjordan to Arabia or the Red Sea. Naturally, the routes tended to avoid the highest land, but it was not actually this which was the greatest obstacle, for tracks run in almost every direction across the Khurashe dome. The most serious barrier to movement was precipice and cliff, of which there are two groups, the sheer confining walls of the narrow wadis which seam these eastern slopes, and the *nuqūb* (singular: *neqb*). This always refers to a steep scarp, sometimes indeed so steep as to be almost precipitous, which divides a high plateau from the lower-lying plain at its foot. Such precipices and *nuqūb* were a serious difficulty, since the grain of the country is from northeast to southwest, but the direction of movement was normally at right angles to it, from southeast to northwest. This was especially true in the southern part where the wadis all follow the downfolds, that is rising in the southwest and running in a northeasterly direction. This problem added to the unattractiveness of this southeastern section of the country, for the possible roads tended to take people where they did not want to go, though a route into Sinai led up the Wadi el-'Ajaram via the crossroad settlement of Jerasa. However, this was of less importance than the other routes which all ran north of the Khurashe dome.

These routes were gathered together at three points where it was possible to cross the hills without too much difficulty: the Wadi Murra, the Kurnub gap and the Zuweira pass. The Wadi Murra is the most obvious, for the journey from the sea to the Arabah nowhere involves climbing more than 1500 feet above sea level, and a track leads down the wadi both to the Dead Sea in the northeast and by what is known as Darb es-Sultan to Petra in the southeast. In Turkish times this Darb es-Sultan was the most important caravan route, and the journey from Gaza to Ma'an took about five days, but this route, easy as it would appear to be on the map, was only a secondary one in Nabatean and Roman times. In those days the main route to Petra lay somewhat to the south and passed through Abda and down into the Wadi Raman by Neqb el-Hemle at its northeastern end. It left the Raman basin by the gap at Qasr Mahalla, and then followed the Wadi Siq past Qasr Um-Quseir and Khirbet Moyet 'Awad into the Arabah. The crossing of the SW-NE wadis was difficult because of the steep cliffs, and it was on these cliffs that the little forts were set, to prevent any danger of a sudden raid on the caravan from above, while it was struggling up the slope. Many of these police posts were deserted after the second century A.D.

Kurnub was the collecting point for a route from Oboth to the southeast, though this meant a terrible climb up the Ascent of the Scorpions, and another from Qasr el-Juheiniyeh to the east. The final route ran along the northern border of the region, through Tel el-Milh to Beersheba in the west.

After crossing the zone of higher land the roads splayed out again, but here on the western side movement in any direction is not difficult, because the wadis are shallow and so much of the land is fairly level. This was the zone of Nabatean and Roman towns, lying between the sand dunes and the higher land. Of these Kurnub and Abda were the most easterly and guarded the passage across the hills. On the west there is a line where a good supply of water is available by digging deep wells, and on this line stood Beersheba, Khalasa, Ruheiba and el-Auja (Nessana). In between these two extremes was S'baita (Subeita), the one which has been most thoroughly excavated.

Round all these towns there were smaller, agricultural settlements, and the land between the wadis, as well as the wadi bottoms, seems at that time

97. *S'baita*. The South Church. S'baita was a town of eight to ten thousand people which flourished in the early years of the Christian era. Water, however, was always very scarce and had to be used with the greatest care.

to have been cultivated. It is doubtful whether the towns developed in the first place as farming communities, for, even if there were a slightly more assured rainfall then, this region would still have been on the margin of the cultivable area. They surely started as posts intended to control the trade routes of a difficult and troubled re-

gion, and it was the huge value of the trade which passed through them which made the agriculture economically possible. With this stimulus, however, the farms did well and persisted for several centuries. The towns were dignified and comfortable, though they must have been expensive to build, for marble was imported in large quantities and wood, which must have been imported also, was extensively used.

The relations of the Negeb were as much with Egypt as they were with Palestine, and it was the existence of this large triangle of wilderness, over which the Israelite rulers found it so difficult to maintain an effective control, which made possible the confederacy of Egypt, Edom and Philistia that from time to time menaced the well-being of the Palestinian kingdoms, for Israel could drive no wedge between them. In the wilderness those who live in the cultivated land can exercise the government only when they are unusually strong, since those who belong to the desert can evade their patrols, and two men do not meet together unless they have agreed (Amos 3:3). So, when "the Lord raised up an adversary against Solomon, Hadad the Edomite," it was to the protection and help of Egypt that the Edomites turned.

The route of the Exodus in the Wilderness of Zin and Sinai cannot be identified with any certainty, but Kadesh, where the Israelites remained for a long time (Num. 13:26, 20:14, 22), has often been identified with 'Ain Qudeis, which lies on a prolongation of the Kurnub-Abda line about 20 miles south of el-Auja, and just across the present Egyptian border. It is not certain whether this identification is correct, though somewhere in this section of the Negeb seems required by the story of the sending of spies into southern Judaea and the Shephelah (Num. 13:22–23). However, it is doubtful whether the sparse water supply of 'Ain Qudeis could have supported a multitude over a long period [3] and consequently we probably have to understand that they lived a semi-nomadic existence in the general neighborhood.

This is a fitting point at which to conclude our study of the Holy Land, for it was at Kadesh that the Israelites were given their first indication that God's promises were to be fulfilled, and that the land into which they were to go was "an exceedingly good land . . . which flows with milk and honey" (Num. 14:7–8). It is indeed a good land, but men have not used it well. Manasseh was not the first, nor was he the last, to "shed very much innocent blood, till he had filled Jerusalem from one end to another" (II K. 21:16), and the bitter strife which mars it at the present time is, alas, no new thing. In this alone may we rejoice, that here God made himself known to his people, and here, in the fulness of time, Our Lord Jesus Christ came to dwell among men.

"Would that even today we knew the things that make for peace!" (Luke 19:42).

GLOSSARY OF GEOLOGICAL TERMS

[Words followed by a dagger (†) are also explained in the Glossary.]

Alluvium. Material brought down by a river. It is usually fertile. On the geological map the symbol for alluvium has been used to include also the loess † and the deposits of the Dead Sea when it was much larger than it is now. These last are salty and infertile.

Basalt. A black, volcanic rock. It is hard and therefore not easily eroded. In the region round the Lake of Galilee and in parts of Bashan and northeastern Trans-jordan it forms the main building stone, but it is not easy to work. Basaltic soil is often very fertile, but the main basalt areas are usually fairly thinly inhabited, because the rock is very rough and hard and soil forms slowly.

Basin. Structurally this term may be used either for an area which has been depressed by faulting † or folding.† An area may have a basin-shaped structure, but the land in the middle may actually be higher than the surrounding land if the rock of which the edges of the basin are composed is more easily eroded.

Cenomanian. The rock deposited after the Nubian sandstone and before the Senonian chalk. It is usually a hard limestone and sometimes forms steep cliffs and gorges.

Chert. A hard, flinty rock which was formed in Trans-jordan during Senonian times † and covers very wide areas of the plateau.

Cretaceous. The period during which most of the Palestinian rocks were formed. It occurred just before the mountain-building storm † began.

Crystalline. Very old rocks have usually been changed in character ("metamorphosed") as a result of having been subjected to immense heat and pressure. Such rocks are very hard and resistant to erosion. The ancient platform of Arabia is composed of crystalline rocks.

Dolomite. A hard limestone which tends to form massive cliffs (adj. "dolomitic").

Dykes. Long lines of volcanic rock which has been thrust up through cracks in the surrounding rock.

Eocene. Literally, "the dawn of the recent" period. It is a term applied to the beginning of the Quaternary. The Eocene rocks were laid down after the Senonian. In Palestine they are usually hard limestones.

Erosion. The cutting away of the rocks by the action of running water, wind-borne particles, etc. The eroded material is carried away by rivers and wind and ocean currents. A river tends to erode down to its *base level* which is the level at which it enters a lake or the sea. Thus the upper Jordan is eroding down to the level of Lake Huleh, the middle section to the level of the Lake of Galilee, and the final section to the level of the Dead Sea. If the level of the lake rises, erosion is stopped and deposition begins; if the level of the lake is lowered, the river will begin to erode more vigorously.

Fault, faulting. A crack in the layers of rock so that one side slips down and the other side is pushed up. Faults can have a "throw" of only a few inches or sometimes, as often in Palestine, of hundreds of feet. A great many of the steep scarps in Palestine are the result of faulting. This faulting has been caused by the great pressure which broke the Arabian platform during the mountain-building storm † (see also *rift valley*).

Folding. During periods of mountain-building † the great pressure causes the less resistant rocks to become contorted. In Palestine this folding is relatively gentle,

267

but in areas of high mountains it is often very severe.

Granite. A hard, crystalline rock, which is the most important kind of rock in the great Arabian platform which underlies the Palestinian area. It is exposed only in the extreme south of the Wadi Arabah.

"Ground swell." A name sometimes given to the gentle folding of the rocks in areas distant from the main mountain building.† In the Middle East the center of the mountain-building storm was in Turkey and Iran and so the rocks in Palestine have been only gently folded.

Loess. A fertile, rather powdery soil which has been formed of material brought by winds from the desert. In Palestine it is found in the Gaza district.

Marl. Normally a soil consisting of clay and carbonate of lime, which is a valuable fertilizer. However, in Palestine the *Lisan Marls* are the salt-laden deposits of the Dead Sea, which are not fertile.

Monocline. A "single fold." Normally a fold, whether an upfold or downfold, has two sides. However, when a fault † occurs the layers of rock may be pulled downward in a single fold of this type. The sides of the Jordan Valley are often marked by tremendous monoclines where the layers of rock have been pulled downward toward the valley.

Mousterian. The mousterian deposits are part of the fairly recent rocks which make up the Coast Plain of Cis-jordan. They are bright red or orange sands which today form excellent orange groves, but which in the past were forested.

Nubian. A name given to the thick layers of sandstone found extensively in Trans-jordan and in one or two parts of southern Cis-jordan. They were laid down under desert conditions over a very long period.

Outcrop. An exposure of a layer of rock at the surface.

Pleistocene. The "most recent" period in geological reckoning. An important feature of the Pleistocene in Palestine is the thin thread of very low hills which line the coast and hinder the drainage.

Porphyry. A very hard, dark-red rock found

in the southern Arabah. It forms a line of hills at the foot of the Punon embayment.

Rift Valley. A valley formed by the collapse of part of the earth's surface between two parallel series of faults.† The Jordan Valley and Wadi Arabah are part of an immense system of rift valleys extending through the Red Sea to Lake Nyasa in East Africa. The faulting on each side of the great rift valley in Palestine is very complicated. There are also smaller rift valleys, e.g., the Valley of Jezreel.

Senonian. The period between the Cenomanian † which comes before it and the Eocene † after it. In Cis-jordan the Senonian deposits are usually a soft, infertile, easily eroded chalk, but over much of the Trans-jordan plateau they form a rather harder chert.†

Storm, mountain-building. The periods of mountain-building in geological history are divided by long periods of relative quiet during which new rocks are formed. Then there comes a period of slow, but tremendous, convulsion called an "orogeny" or "mountain-building storm." In the Middle East the main mountain-building occurred after the Cretaceous † and produced the high mountains of Turkey and Iran.

Stratum (pl. *strata*). A layer of rock. Rocks are laid down in level layers which may later be disturbed by *folding* or *faulting*.†

Tethys. A name given by geologists to the ancient sea which once lay in the Mediterranean-Turkey-Iran region.

Transgression. An extension of the sea over the land. This occurs when the level of the land has been lowered. Transgressions of the sea may be very extensive and endure for very prolonged periods. During a transgression marine deposits, such as limestone and chalk, are laid down.

Warping. A word used to describe the humping up of the rocks over a relatively wide area. It is really an immensely broad fold † but should not be confused with folding which is more intense, though it also may cover wide areas.

NOTES

Chapter I.
A Preliminary View

[1] Leo Picard, *Structure and Evolution of Palestine* (Jerusalem: Geological Department of the Hebrew University, 1943).

Chapter II.
The Depths of the Earth

[1] Grenville A. J. Cole. *The Geological Growth of Europe* (London: Home University Library, 1914), p. 68.

[2] Picard, *op. cit.*, p. 29.

[3] G. S. Blake, "Geology, Soils and Minerals," in M. G. Ionides, *Report on the Water Resources of Transjordan and Their Development* (London: H.M.S.O., 1939), p. 57.

[4] *Ibid.*, p. 65.

[5] *Ibid.*, p. 73

[6] Survey of Palestine, Geological Map of *Southern Palestine* 1:250,000 (Jerusalem, 1947).

[7] Picard, *op. cit.*, p. 36.

[8] Blake, *op cit.*, p. 52.

[9] *Ibid.*, *op. cit.*, p. 93.

[10] Picard, *op. cit.*, p. 22.

[11] *Ibid.*, pp. 67–68.

[12] *Ibid.*, p. 76.

[13] Blake, *op. cit.*, p. 95.

[14] Survey of Palestine, Geological Map of *Southern Palestine.*

[15] Félix-Marie Abel, *Géographie de la Palestine* (Paris: Librairie Lecoffre, 1933–38), Vol. I, p. 49.

[16] Kathleen M. Kenyon, "Excavations at Jericho 1954," in *Palestine Exploration Quarterly*, May–Oct., 1954, p. 63.

[17] Picard, *op cit.*, p. 99.

[18] *Ibid.*, pp. 99–100.

[19] *Ibid.*, pp. 116–18.

Chapter III.
The Earth on Its Foundations

[1] Blake, *op. cit.*, p. 100.

[2] *Ibid.*, pp. 54–55.

[3] G. S. Blake and M. J. Goldschmidt, *Geology and Water Resources of Palestine* (Jerusalem, 1947), p. 310.

Chapter IV.
Has the Rain a Father?

[1] D. Ashbel, *Bio-climatic Atlas of Israel* (Jerusalem, 1950), p. 51.

[2] *Ibid.*, pp. 54–55.

Chapter V.
The Rain of the Mountains

[1] Chester C. McCown, "Climate and Religion in Palestine," in *Journal of Religion*, Oct., 1927, p. 529.

[2] "It will not be easy to light on any climate in the habitable earth that can well be compared with it." *The Jewish War* IV.viii.3, quoted by Nelson Glueck, *The River Jordan*, pp. 109–10.

[3] Ashbel, *op. cit.*, pp. 1–2.

Chapter VI.
Three Special Problems

[1] Thomas Chapin, "Observations on the Climate of Jerusalem," in *Palestine Exploration Quarterly*, 1883, p. 17.

[2] Nelson Glueck, *The River Jordan* (Philadelphia: Westminster Press, 1946), p. 12.

[3] W. F. Albright, *From the Stone Age to Christianity* (Baltimore, 1940), p. 74.

[4] G. E. Wright and F. V. Filson, *The Westminster Historical Atlas to the Bible* (Philadelphia: Westminster Press, 1946), p. 64.

[5] Nelson Glueck, *The Other Side of the Jordan* (New Haven, Conn.: American Schools of Oriental Research, 1940), p. 149.

[6] C. E. P. Brooks, *Climate through the Ages* (New York: McGraw-Hill, 2nd ed., 1949).

[7] G. C. Simpson, "Possible Causes of Climatic Change and Their Limitations," in *Proc. Linnaean Soc. 152*, 1950; "Radiation Balance of the Earth as a Factor in Climatic Change," in Harlow Shapley, ed., *Climatic Change* (Cambridge: Harvard University Press, 1953), pp. 73–105.

[8] Cf. the figures given for Berlin, Paris and New Haven, Conn. in the following:

Victor Conrad, "Climatic Changes or Cycles," in *Climatic Change*, pp. 231–33.

Emile Roger, "Répartition des années chaudes et froides depuis 1757 pour le climat de Paris," in *La Météorologie, Nos. 89–91* (Paris, 1932).

J. B. Kincer, "Is Our Climate Changing? A Study of Longtime Temperature Trends," in *United States Weather Bureau Monthly Review*, Vol. 61 (Washington, 1933), pp. 251–59.

[9] C. E. P. Brooks, "Geological and Historical Aspects of Climatic Change," in Thomas F. Malone, ed., *Compendium of Meteorology* (Boston, Mass.: American Meteorological Soc., 1951), p. 1008.

[10] These dates are approximate and different authorities give slightly different limits for the beginning and end of some of the periods. However, there is general agreement among climatologists as to the nature of the changes.

[11] Hurd C. Willett, "Atmospheric and Oceanic Circulation as Factors in Glacial-Interglacial Changes of Climate," in *Climatic Change*, pp. 55–56.

[12] Brooks, *op. cit.*, pp. 1007–8.

[13] Richard Foster Flint, "Evidence from Glacial Geology as to Climatic Variations," in *Climatic Change*, p. 174.

[14] Brooks, *op. cit.*, p. 1010.

[15] Willett, *op. cit.*, pp. 55–56.

[16] Brooks, *Climate through the Ages*, p. 333.

[17] *Ibid.*, p. 335.

[18] O. W. Murray, "Desiccation in Egypt," in *Bulletin de la Société Royale de Géographie d'Egypte*, Nov., 1949 .

[19] Paul B. Sears, "Climate and Civilisation," in *Climatic Change*, p. 46.

[20] W. F. Albright, *The Archaeology of Palestine* (London: Penguin Books, 2nd ed. 1954), p. 251.

[21] T. J. C. Baly, "S'baita," in *Palestine Exploration Quarterly*, 1955.

[22] Michael Evenari and Dov Keller, "Ancient Masters of the Desert," in *Scientific American*, Vol. 194, no. 4, April, 1956, pp. 44–45. Both H. Dunscombe Colt, who directed the excavations at S'baita, and my brother, T. J. C. Baly, have told me that they believe this to be the correct explanation of these curious mounds.

[23] G. E. Kirk, "Archaeological Exploration of the Southern Desert," in *Palestine Exploration Quarterly*, Oct. 1938, pp. 211–35.

[24] M. G. Ionides, *Report on the Water Resources of Transjordan and Their Development.*

Chapter VII.
The Earth Full of Thy Creatures

[1] George Adam Smith, *The Historical Geography of the Holy Land* (London: Hodder and Stoughton, 20th ed.), p. 419.

[2] C. Leonard Woolley and T. E. Lawrence, *The Wilderness of Zin* (New York: Charles Scribner's Sons, 1936), p. 32. First published by Palestine Exploration Fund in 1914.

[3] A. Reifenberg, *The Soils of Palestine*, C. L. Whittles, trans. (London: Thomas Murby and Co., 1938), pp. 8–13. I am indebted to this book for much of the section on soils, but have ventured to make certain modifications as a result of the fuller information which there now is concerning the climate, and to extend his system to Transjordan.

[4] G. S. Blake, "Geology, Soils and Minerals," in Ionides, *op. cit.*

[5] Roger Washburn, "The Percy Sladen Expedition to Lake Huleh, 1935," in *Palestine Exploration Quarterly*, 1936, pp. 204–10.

[6] G. R. Driver suggests that these birds are the common turtledove, the swift and the wryneck. (G. R. Driver, "Birds in the Old Testament—II Birds in Life," *Palestine Exploration Quarterly*, May–Oct. 1935)

Chapter VIII.
Food from the Earth

[1] B. Maisler, "Canaan and the Canaanites," in *Bulletin of the American School of Oriental Research*, April, 1946.

[2] Sir Edwyn Hoskyns and Noel Davey, *The Fourth Gospel* (London, 2nd ed., 1950), pp. 320–21. But see also Strachan, *The Fourth Gospel* (London: S.C.M., 3rd ed.), pp. 200–201. For details of the feast see Mishnah, *Sukkah* (*The Mishnah*, trans. from the Hebrew by Herbert Darby, Oxford, the Clarendon Press, 1933), pp. 172ff.

[3] W. F. Albright, *From the Stone Age to Christianity* (Baltimore, The Johns Hopkins Press, 1940), pp. 120–21.

[4] Albright, "The Gezer Calendar," in B.A.S.O.R., 1943.

[5] Nelson Glueck speaks of terracing in some places near Jerash as going back to the early Bronze Age (see "Further Explorations in Eastern Palestine," in B.A.S.O.R., 1942).

[6] Letter of Aristeas, quoted by Frants

Buhl in his article on "New Testament Times," in Hastings' *Dictionary of the Bible*.

Chapter IX.
Straight Ways and Cities

[1] Glueck, *The River Jordan*, pp. 73, 129.

Chapter XI.
The Coastlands

[1] H. G. Bohn, *Itinerary of Richard I*, Bk. IV, para. 12–14, quoted by G. Dahl in *The Materials for the History of Dor* (New Haven, 1915), p. 116.

Chapter XII. The Land of the Philistines

[1] George Adam Smith, *op. cit.*, pp. 201–3.
[2] *Ibid.*, p. 203.

Chapter XIII.
The Rich Valley

[1] James B. Pritchard, ed., *Ancient Near Eastern Texts Relating to the Old Testament* (Princeton: Princeton University Press, 1950), p. 237.
[2] W. F. Albright, *The Archaeology of Palestine*, p. 117.
[3] *Ibid.*, pp. 117–18.
G. E. Wright, "The Discoveries at Megiddo," in the *Biblical Archaeologist*, May, 1950.
Albright argues that the phrasing in Judg. 5:19 suggests that Taanach was the capital and that Megiddo did not then exist, but it is not essential to take this poetic phrase in such a sense, though it would fit in conveniently with the archaeological evidence for the site.

Chapter XIV.
The Hill Country of Judah

[1] George Adam Smith, *op. cit.*, p. 261.

Chapter XVII.
The Entrance of the Hamath and the Arabah

[1] Josephus *Wars* iv. i. I. See also George Adam Smith, *op. cit.*, pp. 473–81.
[2] Lucetta Mowry, "Settlements in the Jericho Valley during the Roman Period," in *Biblical Archaeologist*, Vol. XV, 1952.
[3] George Adam Smith, *op. cit.*, p. 268.
[4] T. J. Salmon and G. T. McCaw, "The Level and Cartography of the Dead Sea," in *Palestine Exploration Quarterly*, April, 1936, pp. 103–11.
[5] George Adam Smith, *op. cit.*, p. 499.
[6] *Book of Common Prayer*.
[7] Glueck, "Explorations in Eastern Palestine," in *Annual of the American School of Oriental Research*, 1934–35, Vols. XIV, XV.
[8] Glueck, *The Other Side of the Jordan*, p. 69.
[9] *Ibid.*, p. 77.
[10] *Ibid.*, pp. 91–92.

Chapter XVIII.
Beyond the Jordan Eastward

[1] George Adam Smith, *op. cit.*, pp. 618–19.
[2] Luc H. Grollenberg, O.P., Atlas de la Bible, traduit et adapté du néerlandais par René Beaupère, O.P. (Paris-Brussels: Elsevier, 1955), pp. 141, 151.
[3] *Ibid.*, p. 151.

Chapter XX.
The Wilderness and the Dry Land

[1] Glueck, "Wadi Sirhan in Northern Arabia," in *Bulletin of American School of Oriental Research*, 1944.
[2] C. Leonard Woolley and T. E. Lawrence, *The Wilderness of Zin* (New York: Charles Scribner's Sons, 1936), p. 31.
[3] *Ibid.*, pp. 70–88.

BIBLIOGRAPHY

The abbreviations used in the bibliography refer to the following periodicals:

Annual of the American Schools of Oriental Research (AASOR)

Bulletin of the American Schools of Oriental Research (BASOR)

Israel Exploration Journal (IEJ)

Journal of the American Oriental Society (JAOS)

Journal of Near Eastern Studies (JNES)

Journal of the Palestine Oriental Society (JPOS)

Journal of the Royal Central Asian Society (JRCAS)

Palestine Exploration Quarterly (PEQ)

Revue Biblique (RB)

Abel, F. M. *Géographie de la Palestine.* Paris, J. Gabalda et cie, 1933–38.

——. "Le récent tremblement de terre en Palestine." RB, 1927, pp. 571–79.

——. "Le circuit de Transjordanie." RB, 1928, pp. 420–34.

——. "Notes complémentaires sur la mer morte." RB, 1929, pp. 237–61.

——. "La géologie de la Palestine d'après des travaux récents." RB. 1929, pp. 513–42.

——. "Exploration du sud-est de la vallée du Jourdain." RB, 1931, pp. 214–26, 375–400; 1932, pp. 77–88; 1933, pp. 237–57.

——. "Topographie des campagnes machabéenes," RB, 1923, pp. 495–521.

——. "Les confins de la Palestine et de l'Egypt sous les Ptolemées." RB, 1939, pp. 207–336, 530–48; 1940, pp. 55–75.

——. *Histoire de la Palestine depuis la conquête d'Alexandre jusqu'à l'invasion arabe. Tome I. De la conquête d'Alexandre jusqu'à la guerre juive.* Paris, J. Gabalda, 1952.

Abrahams, Israel. *Campaigns in Palestine from Alexander the Great.* London, Oxford University Press, 1927.

Admiralty, Great Britain. *Notes on Climate and Other Subjects in the Eastern Mediterranean and Adjacent Countries.* His Majesty's Stationery Office, London, 1916.

Aharoni, Y. "The Roman Road to Aila (Elath)." IEJ, Vol. 4, pp. 9–16.

Albright, W. F. *Archaeology and the Religion of Israel.* Baltimore, Johns Hopkins, 1942.

——. *From the Stone Age to Christianity.* Baltimore, Johns Hopkins, 1946.

——. *The Archaeology of Palestine.* Harmondsworth, Middlesex, Penguin Books.

——. "Canaanites in the History of Civilization." *Studies in the History of Culture.* Menasha, Wis., published for the Conference of Secretaries of the American Council of Learned Societies by the George Beran Publishing Company, 1942.

——. "Egypt and the Early History of the Negeb." JPOS, 1924, pp. 131–61.

——. "The Administrative Divisions of Israel and Judah." JPOS, 1925, pp. 17–54.

——. "The Site of Tirzah and the Topography of Western Manasseh." JPOS, 1931, pp. 241–52.

——. "Contributions to the Historical Geography of Palestine." AASOR, Vols. II and III, 1922–23, pp. 1–46.

——. "Excavations and Results at Tell-el-Ful." AASOR, Vol. IV, 1922–23.

Amiran, D. H. K., and Gilead, M. "Early Excessive Rainfall and Soil Erosion in Israel." IEJ, Vol. IV, pp. 286–95.

Amiran, D. H. K. "Sites of Settlements in the Mountains of Lower Galilee." IEJ, 1956, pp. 69–77.

——. "The Pattern of Settlement in Palestine." IEJ, Vol. III, pp. 65–78, 192–209, 250–60.

Anati, E. "Subterranean Dwellings in the Central Negev." IEJ, Vol. V, pp. 259–61.

Antevs, E. "The Big Tree as a Climatic

Measure." *Quaternary Climates.* Carnegie Institute Washington publ. 352, 1925.

Arden-Close, C. F. "The Rainfall of Palestine." PEQ, 1941, pp. 122–28.

Aref el-Aref. *Bedouin Love, Law, and Legend.* Jerusalem, Cosmos, 1944.

Arundale, R. L. *Palestine, the Land and Its People.* London, Nelson, 1947.

Arvanitakis, G. L. "Essai sur le climat de Jérusalem." *Bulletin de l'institut égyptien,* Ser. 4, No. 4, pp. 128–89. Cairo, 1903.

Ashbel, D. *A Hundred Years of Rainfall Observations.* Jerusalem, Hebrew University Press, 1946.

———. *Bioclimatic Atlas of Israel.* Jerusalem, Meteorological Dept. of the Hebrew University, 1950.

———. "On the Importance of Dew in Palestine." JPOS, 1936, pp. 316–21.

Avi-yonah, M. "Map of Roman Palestine," in *Palestine Antiquities Department Quarterly,* Vol. V, pp. 139–93. Jerusalem, 1936.

Arnimelech, M. "The Geological History of the Yarkon Valley and Its Influence on Ancient Settlements." IEJ, 1950–51, pp. 77–83.

———. *Études géologiques dans la région de la Shéphélah en Palestine.* Grenoble, Allier, 1936.

Baedeker, Karl. *Palestine and Syria.* Leipzig, Baedeker, 1912.

Baikie, James. *Lands and Peoples of the Bible.* London, A. & C. Black, 1932.

Baldensperger, Louise, and Crowfoot, Grace. "Hyssop." PEQ, 1931, pp. 89–99.

Baly, T. J. C. "S'baita." PEQ, 1935, pp. 171–81.

Barnes, W. Emery (ed.). *A Companion to Biblical Studies.* Cambridge, Cambridge Univ. Press, 1916.

Barrois, Augustin Georges. *Manuel d'archéologie biblique.* Paris, A. et J. Picard et cie, 1939–53.

Ben-dor, M. *Beisan.* Jerusalem, Palestine Department of Antiquities.

Bell, Gertrude Lothian. *Syria, The Desert and the Sown.* London, Heinemann, 1908.

———. *The Letters of Gertrude Bell.* 2 vols., London, Benn, 1927.

Bentwich, Norman. *Israel and Her Neighbors.* London, Rider, 1955.

Bikermann, E. "La Coélé-Syrie, notes de géographie historique." RB, 1947, pp. 256–268.

Blake, G. S. *The Stratigraphy of Palestine and Its Building Stones.* Jerusalem, Printing and Stationery Office, 1935.

———. "Old Shore Lines of Palestine." *Geological Magazine,* Vol. LXXIV, pp. 68–78. London, 1937.

Blake, G. S., and Goldschmidt, M. J. *Geology and Water Sources of Palestine.* Jerusalem, Government Printers, 1947.

Blanchard, Raoul. *Asie occidentale.* Paris, Armand Colin, 1929.

Blanckenhorn, Max. *Naturwissenschaftliche Studien am Toten Meer und im Jordantal.* Berlin, R. Friedländer und Sohn, 1912.

Blyth, Estelle. "Palestine: Its Past, Present, and Future." JRCAS, 1918, pp. 25–41.

Bodenheimer, F. S. *Animal Life in Palestine.* Jerusalem, 1935.

Borland, Hal. "Animals of the Bible." *Frontiers,* Vol. VI, No. 2, December, 1941.

Braid, M. H. "Northern Palestine and the Lebanon Region." *Scottish Geographical Magazine,* Vol. 34, pp. 369–78. Edinburgh, 1918.

Brooks, C. E. P. *Climate Through the Ages.* London, Benn, 1949.

———. *Climate in Everyday Life.* London, Benn, 1950.

———. *The Evolution of Climate.* London, Benn, 1922.

———. "Changes of Climate in the Old World during Historic Times." *Royal Meteorological Society Journal,* Vol. 57, pp. 31–50. London, 1931.

———. "Geological and Historical Aspects of Climatic Change." *Compendium of Meteorology.* Boston, American Meteorological Society, 1951, pp. 1004–18.

Broome, E. C., Jr. "The Dolmens of Palestine and Transjordania." *Journal of Biblical Literature,* December, 1940, pp. 479–97.

Brunt, David. "Climate, Weather and Man." *Endeavour,* Vol. 3, 1944, pp. 87–97.

Burney, C. F. *Israel's Settlement in Canaan.* London, Oxford University Press, 1917.

Burrows, Millar. *What Mean These Stones?* New Haven, American Schools of Oriental Research, 1941.

——— "Biblical Background in Palestine." *Religion in Life,* Vol. 2, pp. 212–24. Cincinnati, 1933.

Caiger, S. T. *Bible and Spade.* London, Oxford University Press, 1936.

Chapin, Thomas. "Observations on the Climate of Jerusalem." PEQ, 1883, pp. 4–40.

Childe, Gordon. *New Light on the Most Ancient East.* London, Routledge, Kegan, and Paul, 1952.

Clerget, Marcel, *Matériaux pour une étude climatalogique de la méditerranée orientale. Types de temps.* Cairo, E. & R. Schindler, 1934.

Close, Sir Charles. "Agriculture and Forestry in Palestine." PEQ, 1934, pp. 149–50.

Cole, Grenville A. J. *The Geological Growth of Europe.* London, Thornton Butterworth, Home University Library, 1914.

Coleville, H. E. *The Accursed Land.* London, Sampson, Law, 1884.

Conder, C. R. *Tent Work in Palestine.* London, R. Bentley and Son, 1878.

——. *Palestine.* New York, Dodd, Mead & Co., 1890.

——. *Illustrated Bible Geography and Atlas.* London, Collins Clear-type Press, 1938.

——. *The Survey of Eastern Palestine.* London, Palestine Exploration Fund, 1889.

Conder, C. R., and Kitchener, H. H. *The Survey of Western Palestine.* London, Palestine Exploration Fund, 1889.

Cook, S. A. "The Foundations of Bible History." PEQ, 1932, pp. 88–97.

——. "The Confines of Israel and Judah." PEQ, 1934, pp. 60–75.

Cook's Guides. *Cook's Traveller's Handbook to Palestine, Syria, and Iraq.* London, Simpkin, Marshall, 1934.

Cooke, Arthur William. *Palestine in Geography and History.* London, Kelly, 1901.

Cotton, C. A. *Landscape.* Cambridge, Cambridge University Press, 1941.

Cressey, George B. *Asia's Lands and Peoples.* New York, McGraw-Hill, 1944.

Crowfoot, G. M., and Baldensperger, Louise. *From Cedar to Hyssop.* London, Sheldon Press, 1932.

Crowfoot, J. W. "An Expedition to Balu'ah." PEQ, 1934, pp. 76–84.

——. *Early Ivories from Samaria.* London, Palestine Exploration Fund, 1938.

——. "Megiddo—a Review." PEQ, 1940. pp. 132–47.

Curry, J. C. "Climate and Migrations." *Smithsonian Institute Annual Report*, pp. 423–35. Washington, 1929.

Dahl, G. *The Materials for the History of Dor.* New Haven, Yale University Press, 1915.

Dalman, Gustav. *Sacred Sites and Ways.* London, Macmillan, 1935.

Dana, L. P. *Arab Asia.* Beirut, American Press, 1923.

Day, Alfred Ely. *Geology of Lebanon and of Syria, Palestine, and Neighboring Countries.* Beirut, American Press, 1930.

Douglass, A. E. "Climatic Changes and Tree Growth." *Carnegie Institute Washington Publ.* 289, I, 1919; II, 1928; III, 1936.

Dowson, V. H. W. "The Date and the Arabs." JRCAS, 1949, pp. 34–41.

Driver, G. R. "Birds in the Old Testament." PEQ, 1955, pp. 5–20, 129–40.

Driver, S. R. *Modern Research as Illustrating the Bible.* London, Oxford University Press, 1922.

Dubertret et Weulersse. *Manuel de géographie. Syrie, Liban et Proche Orient. Première partie: La Peninsule Arabique.* Beirut, Imprimerie Catholique, 1940.

Duncan, J. Garrow. *Digging Up Biblical History.* New York, Macmillan, 1931.

——. *The Accuracy of the Old Testament.* London, Macmillan, 1930.

——. "The Sea of Tiberias and Its Environs." PEQ, 1926, pp. 15–22, 65–74.

——. "Es-Salt." PEQ, 1928, pp. 28–36, 98–100.

——. "Père Mallon's Excavation of Teleilat Ghassul." PEQ, 1932, pp. 71–78.

Dussaud, René. *Topographie historique de la Syrie antique et médiévale.* Paris, P. Guethner, 1927.

East, Gordon. *The Geography behind History.* London, Nelson, 1938.

Elliott-Binns, L. E. *Modern Discoveries and the Old Testament.* London, S.P.C.K., 1923.

Ellis, W. T. *Bible Lands Today.* New York, Appleton, 1927.

Epstein, E. "Bedouin of the Negeb." PEQ, 1939, pp. 59–73.

——. "Hauran: Rise and Decline." PEQ, 1940, pp. 13–21.

——. "The Bedouin of Transjordan." JRCAS, 1938, pp. 228–36.

Erskine, Mrs. Steuart. *Transjordan.* London, Benn, 1924.

——. *Vanished Cities of Arabia.* London, Hutchinson and Co., 1925.

Evenari, M., and Keller, D. "Ancient Masters of the Desert." *Scientific American*, Vol. 194, No. 4, April, 1956, pp. 39–45.

Febvre, Lucien. *A Geographical Introduction to History.* London, Kegan, Paul, 1932.

Finegan, J. *Light from the Ancient Past.* Princeton, Princeton University Press, 1946.

Fisher, W. B. *The Middle East.* London, Methuen, 1950.

Forbes, J. Rosita. "Palestine." *Fortnightly Review,* new series, Vol. 110, pp. 131–39. New York, 1921.

Forde, C. Daryll. *Habitat, Economy and Society.* London, Methuen, 1934.

Forder, Archibald. *Petra: Perea: Phoenicia.* London, Marshall, 1923.

Fosdick, H. E. *A Pilgrimage to Palestine.* New York, Macmillan, 1927.

Free, Joseph P. "Abraham's Camels." JNES, Vol. 3, pp. 187–93.

Garstang, John. *The Foundations of Bible History: Joshua, Judges.* New York, R. R. Smith, 1931.

———. *The Heritage of Solomon.* London, Williams & Norgate, 1934.

———. *The Story of Jericho.* London, Marshall, Morgan and Scott, 1948.

Gautier, Lucien. *Au dela du Jourdain.* Paris, 1896.

———. *Autour de la mer morte.* Geneva, 1901.

Gilead, M., and Rosenau, N. "Ten Years of Dew Observation in Israel." IEJ, Vol. 4, pp. 120–23.

Glubb, Sir J. B. "The Economic Situation of the Trans-jordan Tribes." JRCAS, 1938, pp. 448–59.

Glueck, Nelson. "Explorations in Eastern Palestine." AASOR, Vol. 14, pp. 1–113; Vol. 15, pp. 1–202; Vol. 18; Vol. 19. Philadelphia, 1934, 1935, 1937–39.

———. "Explorations in Western Palestine." BASOR, Oct., 1953, pp. 6–15.

———. *The Other Side of the Jordan.* New Haven, American Schools of Oriental Research, 1940.

———. "Further Explorations in the Negeb." BASOR, Feb., 1955, pp. 10–22.

———. "The Third Season of Explorations in the Negeb." BASOR, Apr., 1955, pp. 7–29.

———. *The River Jordan.* Philadelphia, Westminster Press, 1946.

———. "Surface Finds in Edom and Moab." PEQ, 1939, pp. 188–92.

———. "Kenites and Kenizzites." PEQ, 1940, pp. 22–24.

———. "Nabatean Syria and Nabatean Transjordan." JPOS, 1938, pp. 1–6.

———. "Three Israelite Towns in the Jordan Valley." BASOR, 1943.

———. "Some Ancient Towns in the Plains of Moab." BASOR, 1943.

———. "Wadi Sirhan in Northern Arabia." BASOR, 1944.

Golding, Louis. *Those Ancient Lands.* London, Benn, 1928.

———. *In the Steps of Moses.* Philadelphia, Jewish Publication Society of America, 1943.

Golub, J. S. *Geography of Palestine.* New York, 1939.

Grant, C. P., *The Syrian Desert.* London, A. & C. Black, 1937.

Grant, Elihu. *The Orient in Bible Times.* Philadelphia, J. B. Lippincott, 1920.

———. *The Economic Background of the Gospels.*

Gray, G. B. "Crocodiles in Palestine." PEQ, 1920, pp. 167–76.

Gregory, J. W. *The Structure of Asia.* London, Methuen, 1929.

———. "Is the Earth Drying Up?" *Geographical Journal,* No. 43, London, 1914.

———. "Geological Researches in the Judean Desert." PEQ, 1931, pp. 197–202.

Grollenberg, Luc H. *Atlas de la Bible.* Paris, Elsevier, 1955.

(Les) Guides Bleus. *Syrie.* London, Benn.

Gustavson, A. F. *Conservation of the Soil.* New York, McGraw-Hill, 1937.

Guy, P. L. O. "Archaeological Evidence of Soil Erosion and Sedimentation in the Wadi Musrara." IEJ, Vol. 4, pp. 77–87.

de Haas, J. *History of Palestine.* New York, Macmillan, 1934.

Hadlow, Leonard. *Climate, Vegetation and Man.* New York, Philosophical Library, 1953.

Halbwachs, Maurice. *La topographie légendaire des Evangiles en Terre Sainte.* Paris, Presses Universitaires, 1941.

Hall, H. R. "Early Relations between Egypt and Palestine." PEQ, 1923, pp. 124–36.

Hamilton, R. W. *A Guide to Bethlehem.* Jerusalem, Palestine Dept. of Antiquities, 1939.

———. *Guide to the Historical Site of Sebastieh.* Jerusalem, Palestine Dept. of Antiquities, 1936.

Hanauer, Canon J. *Walks about Jerusalem.* London, London Society for Promoting Christianity among the Jews, 1910.

Hart, H. C. *Some Account of the Fauna and Flora of Sinai, Petra and Wady Arabah.* London, Palestine Exploration Fund, 1891.

Headlam, A. C. "Archaeology and the Bible." PEQ, 1931, pp. 122–38.

Hillelson, S. "Notes on the Bedouin Tribes of the Beersheba District." PEQ, 1937, pp. 242–52; 1938, pp. 55–63, 117–26.

Hodge, R. M. *Historical Geography of Bible Lands.* New York, Charles Scribner's Sons, 1915.

Hogarth, D. G. *The Nearer East.* London, Frowde, 1902.

Hölscher, Gustav. *Drei Erdkarten: ein Beitrag zur Erdkenntnis des hebräischen Altertums.* Heidelberg, C. Winter, 1949.

Hornby, Emily. *Sinai and Petra.* London, 1901.

Horsfield, G. & A. "Sela-Petra, the Rock of Edom and Nabatene." *Palestine Dept. of Antiquities Quarterly,* Vol. VII, Jerusalem, 1937.

Hull, Edward. *Memoir on the Geology and Geography of Arabia, Petraea, Palestine and Adjoining Districts.* London, Palestine Exploration Fund, 1886.

——. *Mount Seir, Sinai and Western Palestine.* London, Palestine Exploration Fund, 1889.

Huntington, Ellsworth. *Palestine and Its Transformation.* Boston, Houghton Mifflin, 1911.

——. *The Pulse of Asia.* Boston, Houghton Mifflin, 1919.

——. *Civilisation and Climate.* New Haven, Yale University Press, 1933.

——. "The Climatic Factor as Illustrated in Arid America." *Carnegie Institute Washington Publ. 192,* 1914.

——. "The Climate of Ancient Palestine." *Report of American Geographical Society,* New York, 1908.

Ionides, M. G. *Report on the Water Resources of Transjordan and Their Development.* London, Crown Agents for Overseas Governments and Administrations, 1939.

——. "The Perspective of Water Development in Palestine and Transjordan." *JRCAS,* 1946, pp. 271–80.

Isserlin, B. S. J. "On Some Possible Early Occurrences of the Camel in Palestine." *PEQ,* 1949, pp. 50–53.

——. "Ancient Forests in Palestine: Some Archaeological Indications." *PEQ,* 1955, pp. 87–88.

Jack, J. W. *Samaria in Ahab's Time.* Edinburgh, T. & T. Clark, 1929.

——. *The Ras Shamra Tablets: Their Bearing on the Old Testament.* Edinburgh, T. & T. Clark, 1935.

Jacks, G. V., and Whyte, R. O. *The Rape of the Earth.* London, Faber, 1939.

Jarvis, C. S. *Yesterday and To-day in Sinai.* London, Blackwood, 1938.

——. "The Desert Yesterday and To-day." *PEQ,* 1937, pp. 116–25.

——. "The Forty Years' Wanderings of the Israelites." *PEQ,* 1938, pp. 25–40.

——. "Sinai: with Special Reference to the Forty Years' Wanderings of Israel." *JRCAS,* 1933, pp. 91–109.

——. "Three Deserts." *JRCAS,* 1935, pp. 535–55.

——. "The Goat Standard." *JRCAS,* 1937, pp. 318–26.

——. "Southern Palestine and Its Possibilities for Settlement." *JRCAS,* 1938, pp. 204–18.

Johns, C. N. *The Citadel of Jerusalem.* London, Palestine Dept. of Antiquities.

Kallner-Amiran, D. H. "Geomorphology of the Central Negev Highlands." *IEJ,* Vol. I, 1950–51, pp. 107–20.

——. "A Revised Earthquake Catalogue of Palestine." *IEJ,* Vol. I, 1950–51, pp. 223–46; Vol. II, 1952, pp. 48–65.

Kallner, D. H., and Rosenau, E. "The Geographical Regions of Palestine." *Geographical Review,* 1939, pp. 61–80.

Kammerer, A. *Petra et la Nabatène.* Paris, Geuthner, 1929.

Kaltan, Nicola. *The Geography of the Near East with Special Reference to Palestine.* Jerusalem, 1945.

Kelso, James L. "New Testament Jericho." *Biblical Archaeologist,* XIV, 1951, No. 2, pp. 34–43.

Kendrew, W. *The Climates of the Continents.* Oxford, The Clarendon Press, 1953.

Kennedy, Sir Alexander B. W. *Petra—Its History and Monuments.* London, Country Life, 1925.

Kent, C. F. *Biblical Geography and History.* New York, Charles Scribner's Sons, 1920.

Kenyon, Sir Frederick. *The Bible and Archaeology.* London, Harrap, 1940.

Kenyon, Kathleen M. "Some Notes on the History of Jericho in the Second Millennium B.C." *PEQ,* 1951, pp. 101–38.

——. "Excavations at Jericho." *PEQ,* 1953, pp. 81–95; 1954, pp. 64–68; 1955, pp. 108–17.

Kincer, J. B. "Is Our Climate Changing? A Study in Long-Time Temperature Trends." *U.S. Weather Bureau Monthly Review,* Vol. 61, pp. 251–59. Washington, 1933.

King, Eleanor H. *Bible Plants for American Gardens.* New York, Macmillan, 1941.

———. "Plants of the Holy Scriptures." *Journal of the New York Botanical Garden*, March, 1941.

Kinglake, A. W. *Eothen*. New York, E. P. Dutton, 1908.

Kirk, G. E. "Archaeological Exploration of the Southern Desert." PEQ, 1938, pp. 211–35.

———. "The Negev or Southern Desert of Palestine." PEQ, 1941, pp. 57–71.

Kirk, M. E. "An Outline of the Cultural History of Palestine Down to Roman Times." PEQ, 1941, pp. 9–49.

———. "An Outline of the Ancient Cultural History of Transjordan." PEQ, 1942, pp. 180–98.

Kirkbride, Sir A. S., and Harding, Lankester. "Hasma." PEQ, 1947, pp. 7–26.

Kjaer, Hans. "Shiloh." PEQ, 1931, pp. 71–88.

Koeppel, Robert. *Palästina, die Landschaft in Karten und Bildern*. Tübingen, J. C. B. Mohr, 1930.

Kraeling, Carl H. (ed.) *Gerasa—City of the Decapolis*. New Haven, American Schools of Oriental Research, 1938.

Lagrange, M-J. "Le site de Sodome d'après les textes." RB, 1932, pp. 489–515.

Larssen, T. "A Visit to the Mat-makers of Huleh." PEQ, 1936, pp. 225–29.

Lathrop, D. P., and French, H. D. *Animals of the Bible*. New York, Frederick A. Stokes, 1937.

Lawrence, T. E. *Seven Pillars of Wisdom*. London, Jonathan Cape, 1926.

Leary, L. G. *The Real Palestine of To-day*. New York, McBride, Nash, 1911.

Lewis, Naphtali. "New Light on the Negev in Ancient Times." PEQ, 1948, pp. 102–17.

Libbey, W., and Hoskyns, F. E. *The Jordan Valley and Petra*. New York, Putnam, 1905.

Lobeck, A. K. *Geomorphology*. New York, McGraw-Hill, 1939.

Lowdermilk, W. A. *Palestine, Land of Promise*. New York, Harper, 1944.

Luke, H. C. *The Traveller's Handbook for Palestine and Syria*. London, Simpkin, Marshall, 1924.

Luke, H. C., and Keith-roach, E. *The Handbook of Palestine and Transjordan*. London, Macmillan, 1930.

Luynes, H. T. P. J. d'A. de. *Voyage d'exploration à la mer morte*. Paris, Arthur Bertrand, 1874.

Lynch, W. F. *Official Report of the United States Expedition to the Dead Sea and the Jordan River*. Philadelphia, Lea and Blanchard, 1849.

Lysgaard, L. *Recent Climatic Fluctuations*. Copenhagen, Danish Meteorological Institute, 1949.

Maisler, B. "Canaan and the Canaanites." BASOR, April, 1946, pp. 7–12.

———. "The Excavation of Tell Qasile." *Biblical Archaeologist*, XIV, 1951, No. 2, pp. 43–49.

Mallon, A. "Notes sur le Ghor." JPOS, 1931, pp. 55–62.

———. "The Five Cities of the Plain." PEQ, 1932, pp. 52–56.

Malone, Thomas F. (ed.) *Compendium of Meteorology*. Boston, American Meteorological Society, 1951.

Margoliouth, D. S. *The Relations between Arabs and Israelites Prior to the Rise of Islam*. London, Oxford University Press, 1924.

Markham, S. F. *Climate and the Energy of Nations*. London, Oxford University Press, 1944.

Marr, John E. *The Scientific Study of Scenery*. London, Methuen, 1926.

Marston, Sir Charles. *Fresh Evidence about the Old Testament*. London, The Church Bookroom, 1936.

———. *New Bible Evidence from the 1925–1933 Excavations*. New York, Fleming H. Revell, 1934.

Masterman, E. W. G. *Studies in Galilee*. Chicago, University of Chicago Press, 1909.

———. "Crocodiles in Palestine." PEQ, 1921, pp. 19–22.

Mathews, Basil. *The World in which Jesus Lived*. New York, Abingdon Press, 1938.

Macalister, R. A. S. *The Excavation of Gezer*. London, J. Murray, 1912.

———. *A Century of Excavation in Palestine*. London, Religious Tract Society, 1925.

———. *The Philistines, Their History and Civilization*. London, Oxford University Press, 1911, 1914.

McCown, C. C. *Tell en-Nasbeh*. Berkeley, Calif., Palestine Institute of Pacific School of Religion, 1947.

———. *The Ladder of Progress in Palestine*. New York, Harper, 1943.

———. "The Wilderness of Judaea and the Nomadic Ideal." *Journal of Geography*, December, 1924.

———. "Climate and Religion in Palestine."

Journal of Religion, Vol. 7, pp. 520–39. Chicago, 1927.

MacGregor, J. *The Rob Roy on the Jordan*. New York, Harper, 1875.

MacInnes, R. *Notes for Travellers, by Road and Rail in Palestine and Syria*. London, 1925.

Makhouly, N. *Guide to Acre*. Jerusalem, Palestine Dept. of Antiquities, 1941.

McMaster, V. C. *A Guide-book for a Tour of Bible Scenes*. New York, Morehouse-Gorham, 1941.

Meistermann, P. B. *Guide de Terre Sainte*. Paris, Letouzey et Ané, 1935.

Merrill, Selah. *East of Jordan*. New York, Scribner's, 1881.

Meyer, Martin. *History of the City of Gaza*. New York, Columbia Univ. Press, 1907.

Miller, A. Austin. *Climatology*. London, Methuen, 1944.

Miller, Madeleine S. *Footprints in Palestine*. New York, Fleming H. Revell, 1936.

Miller, Madeleine S., and J. Lane. *Encyclopedia of Bible Life*. New York, Harper, 1944.

Mills, Clarence A. *Climate Makes the Man*. New York, Harper, 1942.

——. "Weather and Health." *American Meteorological Society Bulletin*, Vol. 19, 1938, pp. 141–51.

Mitchell, H. G. "The Walls of Jerusalem." *Annual of the American School of Oriental Research*, Vol. I, 1903, pp. 85–163.

Moldenke, H. N. and A. L. *Plants of the Bible*. Waltham, Mass., Chronica Botanica, 1952.

Montgomery, J. A. *Arabia and the Bible*. Philadelphia, University of Pennsylvania Press, 1950.

Morton, H. V. *In the Steps of the Master*. London, Rich & Cowan, 1934.

——. *In the Steps of St. Paul*. New York, Dodd, Mead, 1936.

——. *Through Lands of the Bible*. New York, Dodd, Mead, 1938.

Mowrey, Lucetta. "Settlements in the Jericho Valley during the Roman Period." *Biblical Archaeologist*, Vol. XV, 1952, pp. 26–42.

Muilenburg, James. "The Site of Ancient Gilgal." *BASOR*, Dec., 1955, pp. 11–27.

Murray, G. W., "Desiccation in Egypt." *Bulletin de la Société Royale de Géographie d'Egypte*, November, 1949.

Murray, Margaret. *Petra: The Rock City of Edom*. London, Blackie.

Myres, J. L. *The Dawn of History*. London,

Williams & Norgate, Home University Library, 1911.

——. "Gog and the Danger from the North in Ezekiel." PEQ, 1932, pp. 213–20.

Naish, J. P. "Tel en-Nasbeh." PEQ, 1932, pp. 204–10.

Neil, James. *Palestine Explored*. New York, Randolph, 1882.

——. *Everyday Life in the Holy Land*. London, Cassell, 1913.

Nelson, H. H. *The Battle of Megiddo*. Chicago, University of Chicago Press, 1913.

Newbigin, M. I. *Mediterranean Lands*. New York, Knopf, 1924.

Olcott, F. C. *The Bridge of Caravans*. Boston, W. A. Wilde, 1940.

Oliphant, L. *The Land of Gilead*. Edinburgh, Blackwood, 1880.

——. *Haifa*. New York, Harper, 1887.

Ovenden, G. J. H. "Mount Gilboa." PEQ, 1924, pp. 193–95.

Palestine Royal Commission Report. His Majesty's Stationery Office, 1937.

Perowne, Stewart. "Note on I Kings, Ch. X, 1–13." PEQ, 1939, pp. 199–203.

Pfeiffer, R. H. *An Introduction to the Old Testament*. New York, Harper, 1941.

Philby, H., and J. B. "The Dead Sea to 'Agaba." *Geographical Journal*, Vol. 66, pp. 134–60. London, 1925.

Phythian-Adams, W. J. "The Boundary of Ephraim and Manasseh." PEQ, 1929, 228–41.

——. "Israel in the Arabah." PEQ, 1932, pp. 137–46; 1934, pp. 181–88.

——. "A Meteorite in the Fourteenth Century B.C." PEQ, 1946, pp. 116–24.

——. "The Volcanic Phenomena of the Exodus." JPOS, 1932, pp. 86–103.

Picard, Leo. *Geological Researches in the Judaean Desert*. Jerusalem, Goldberg, 1931.

——. *Structure and Evolution of Palestine*. Jerusalem, The Geological Department, Hebrew University, 1943.

Picard, Leo, and Solomonica, P. "On the Geology of the Gaza-Beersheba District." JPOS, 1936, pp. 180–223.

Picard, Leo. *Geomorphogeny of Israel*. Jerusalem, 1951.

Picard, Leo, and Avnimelech, M. "On the Geology of the Central Coastal Plain." JPOS, 1937, pp. 255–99.

Porter, J. L. *The Giant Cities of Bashan*. London, Nelson, 1876.

Porter, G. S. *Birds of the Bible*. New York,

Methodist Publishing House, 1909.

Post, G. E., and Dinsmore, J. E. *Flora of Syria, Palestine and Sinai.* Beirut, Syrian Protestant College, 1932–33.

Pritchard, J. B. (ed.) *Ancient Near Eastern Texts Relating to the Old Testament.* Princeton, Princeton University Press, 1950.

Raczkowski, H. *The Dead Sea Chemical Industry.* Jerusalem, Palestine Potash Ltd.

Ramann, E. *The Evolution and Classification of Soils,* trans. by C. L. Whittles. Cambridge, Heffer, 1928.

Reifenberg, A. *The Soils of Palestine.* London, Thomas Murby, 1947.

——. "Soil Erosion in Palestine." *Palestine and the Middle East,* Vol. 13, pp. 168–70, 176.

——. *The Struggle between the Desert and the Sown.* Jerusalem, 1954.

Richmond, John. "Khirbet Fahil." PEQ, 1934, pp. 18–31.

Robinson, T. H. *Palestine in General History.* London, Oxford University Press, 1929.

Rosenstein, A. B. *The Climate of Jaffa-Tel Aviv-Sarona.* Tel Aviv, A. I. & S. Shoshany, 1922.

Rostovtzeff, M. *A History of the Ancient World.* London, Oxford University Press, 1928.

——. *Caravan Cities.* London, Oxford University Press, 1932.

Rothschild, J. J. "The Fortified Zone of the Plain of Esdraelon." PEQ, 1938, pp. 41–54.

Rouch, J. "Le climat de la mediterranée." *International Commission for the Scientific Exploration of the Mediterranean Sea. Rapports et procès-verbaux des réunions.* Paris, 1938, Nouvelle série, Vol. 11, pp. 219–79.

Rowley, H. H. *From Joseph to Joshua.* London, Oxford University Press, 1950.

Russell, R. J. "Climatic Change through the Ages." *Climate and Man. Yearbook of Agriculture.* Washington, U.S. Government Printing Office, 1941, pp. 67–98.

Saarisalo, A. *The Boundary between Issachar and Naphtali.* Helsinki, 1927.

——. "Topographical Researches in Galilee." JPOS, 1929, pp. 27–40.

Salmon, F. J. "The Modern Geography of Palestine." PEQ, 1937, pp. 33–42.

——. "The 'Land' of Palestine." JRCAS, 1938, pp. 542–53.

Salmon, F. J., and McCaw, G. T. "The Level and Cartography of the Dead Sea." PEQ, 1936, pp. 103–111.

Sanday, William, *Sacred Sites of the Gospels.* Oxford, Clarendon Press, 1903.

de Saulcy, L. F. J. C. *Voyage autour de la mer morte.* Paris, 1853.

——. *Voyage en Terre Sainte.* Paris, Didier et cie, 1865.

Savignac, M-R. "Sur les pistes de Transjordanie méridionale." RB, 1936, pp. 235–63.

Schmidt, H. D. "Palestine Trends of Power." JNES, Vol. X, pp. 1–12.

Schumacher, G. *Across the Jordan.* London, Richard Bentley and Son, 1886.

——. *Abila, Pella and Northern Ajlun.* London, Palestine Exploration Fund, 1889.

——. *The Jaulân.* London, R. Bentley and Son, 1888.

Semple, Ellen C. *The Geography of the Mediterranean Region.* New York, Holt, 1932.

Sergeant, G. *From Egypt to the Golden Horn.* New York, Revell, 1940.

Shalem, N. "La stabilité du climat en Palestine." RB, 1951, pp. 54–74.

Shapley, Harlow (ed.) *Climatic Change: Evidence, Causes and Effects.* Cambridge, Harvard University Press, 1953.

Sherlock, R. L. *Man's Influence on the Earth.* London, Thornton Butterworth, Home University Library, 1931.

Shipton, G. M. *Megiddo.* Chicago, University of Chicago Press, 1939.

Simons, J. "Two Connected Problems Relating to the Israelite Settlement in Transjordan." PEQ, 1947, pp. 27–39, 87–101.

Simons, Jan Jozef. *Jerusalem in the Old Testament.* Leiden, Brill, 1952.

Simpson, G. C. "Possible Causes of Climatic Change and Their Limitations." *Proceedings of the Linnaean Society,* 152, 1940.

——. *Past Climates.* London, Manchester Literary and Philosophical Society, 1929.

Smith, George Adam. *The Historical Geography of the Holy Land.* London, Hodder & Stoughton, 1894.

——. *Jerusalem: From the Earliest Times to A. D. 70.* London, Hodder & Stoughton, 1907–8.

——. *Atlas of the Historical Geography of the Holy Land.* London, Hodder & Stoughton, 1915.

——. *Syria and the Holy Land.* London, Hodder & Stoughton, 1918.

——. *The Book of Isaiah.* London, Hodder & Stoughton, 1927.

————. *The Book of the Twelve Prophets.* London, Hodder & Stoughton, 1899.

Speiser, E. A. *Ethnic Movements in the Near East in the Second Millennium, B.C.* Baltimore, Johns Hopkins, 1933.

Stamp, L. D. *Asia.* London, Methuen, 1930.

Stanley, A. P. *Sinai and Palestine.* London, J. Murray, 1905.

Stark, Freya. "The Sources of the Jordan." *Cornhill Magazine,* Vol. 149, pp. 438–50. London, 1934.

Starkey, J. L. "Tell Duweir." PEQ, 1933.

————. "Lachish as Illustrating Bible History." PEQ, 1937, pp. 171–78.

Steers, J. A. *The Unstable Earth.* London, Methuen, 1942.

Suess, E. *The Face of the Earth,* trans. by Hertha B. C. Sollas, Oxford, Clarendon Press, 1904–29.

Taylor, F. H. *Save Our Soil.* Soil Conservation Board, Govt. of Palestine.

Temple, A. A. *Flowers and Trees of Palestine.* London, S.P.C.K., 1929.

Theilhaber, F. A. *The Graphic Historical Atlas of Palestine, 2000–333 B.C.* Jerusalem, Dr. J. Szapiro, 1941.

Thomas, D. Winton. "The Meaning of the Name Hammoth-Dor." PEQ, 1934, pp. 147–48.

————. "Naphath-Dor: a Hill Sanctuary?" PEQ, 1935, pp. 89–90.

Thoumin, R. *Histoire de Syrie.* Paris, 1929.

————. *Géographie humaine de la Syrie centrale.* Tours, Arrault et cie, 1936.

Thomson, W. H. *The Land and the Book.* New York, Harper, 1886.

Tonneau, R. "Caravane biblique au pays de Samson." RB, 1929, pp. 431–32.

Toynbee, Arnold J. *A Study of History*—abridgment of Vols. I–VI by D. C. Somervell. London, Oxford University Press, 1947.

Tristram, H. B. *The Natural History of Palestine.* London, Palestine Exploration Fund, 1892.

————. *Bible Places.* London, S.P.C.K., 1897.

————. *The Land of Moab.* London, Murray, 1873.

————. *The Land of Israel.* London, S.P.C.K., 1866.

Ubach, P. B. "Excursion aux déserts d'Enggadi, Zif et Maon." RB, 1946, pp. 249–59.

de Vaumas, E. "La Palestine. Etude morphométrique." IEJ, Vol. 3, pp. 79–93, 178–91.

de Vaux, R. "Exploration de la région de Salt." RB, 1938, 398–426.

————. "Glanes archéologiques à Ma'in." RB, 1939, pp. 78–86.

————. "Notes d'histoire et de topographie transjordaniennes." RB, Vie et Penser, 1941, pp. 16–47.

————. "Les patriarches hébreux et les découvertes modernes." RB, 1946, pp. 321–48; 1948, pp. 321–47; 1949, pp. 5–36.

————. "La Palestine et la Transjordanie au IIe millenaire et les origines Israelites." *Zeitschrift für die Altetestamentliche Wissenschaft.* Berlin, 1939.

de Vaux, R., and Savignac, M-R. "Nouvelles recherches dans la région de Cades." RB, 1938, pp. 89–100.

Vincent, L-H. *Jérusalem: recherches en topographie, d'archéologie et d'histoire.* Paris, Victor Lecoffre, 1912–26.

————. "Les fouilles de Teleilat Ghassoul." RB, 1935, pp. 69–105; 220–44.

————. "La topographie des Evangiles, à propos d'un livre récent." RB, pp. 45–76.

Wainwright, G. A. "Caphtor, Keftin and Cappadocia." PEQ, 1931, pp. 203–16.

Warren, Sir Charles. "The Significance of the Geography of Palestine." *Victoria Institute Journal of Transactions.* Vol. 49, pp. 165–98. London, 1917.

Washburn, Roger. "The Percy Sladen Expedition to Lake Huleh, 1935." PEQ, 1936, pp. 204–10.

Wheeler, Sir Mortimer. *Rome beyond the Imperial Frontiers.* Harmondsworth, Middlesex, Penguin, 1955.

Willatts, E. C. "Some Geographical Factors in the Palestine Problem." *Geographical Journal,* 1946, pp. 146–79.

Willett, H. C. "Long Period Fluctuations of the General Circulation of the Atmosphere." *Journal of Meteorology* 6, 1949.

Willis, B. "Dead Sea Problem: Rift Valley or Ramp Valley." *Bulletin of the Geological Society of America.* Vol. 39, pp. 490–542.

Wooldridge, S. W., and Morgan, R. S. *The Physical Basis of Geography.* London, Longmans, 1937.

Woolley, C. Leonard, and Lawrence, T. E. *The Wilderness of Zin.* London, Palestine Exploration Fund, 1914–15.

Wright, G. E. "The Discoveries at Megiddo." *Biblical Archaeologist,* May, 1950.

————. (ed.) *The Westminster Historical Atlas to the Bible.* Philadelphia, Westminster Press, 1946.

Zeuner, F. E. "The Goats of Early Jericho." PEQ, 1955, pp. 70–86.

Zohary, D. "Notes on Ancient Agriculture in the Central Negev." IEJ, Vol. 4, pp. 17–25.

Zohary, M. "Ecological Studies in the Vegetation of the Near Eastern Deserts. I: Environment and Vegetation Classes." IEJ, Vol. 2, pp. 201–15.

MAPS

Palestine 1:100,000 (Government of Palestine, 16 sheets).

Transjordan 1:100,000 (issued by the War Office for the use of the British Army during World War II—unpublished).

Palestine 1:250,000 (Jerusalem, Government of Palestine, 3 sheets).

Israel 1:250,000 (Jerusalem, Government of Israel, 3 sheets).

Jordan 1:250,000 (Amman, Government of the Hashemite Kingdom of the Jordan, 3 sheets).

Jordan (archaeology) 1:250,000 (Amman, Government of the Hashemite Kingdom of the Jordan, 3 sheets).

Geological Map of Palestine, 1,250,000 (Jerusalem, Government of Palestine, 2 sheets).

Rainfall Map of Palestine (issued for the United Nations Special Committee on Palestine, 1947).

Villages and Settlements of Palestine (issued for the United Nations Special Committee on Palestine, 1947).

Old Testament Palestine 1:500,000 (Jerusalem, Department of Antiquities, Government of Palestine).

Roman Palestine 1:250,000 (Jerusalem, Department of Antiquities, Government of Palestine).

Bartholomew's Quarter-Inch Map of Palestine (Edinburgh Geographical Institute, John Bartholomew and Son).

Carte Internationale du Monde 1:1,000,000, *Asia*, Sheet *North H-37*, AL-JAUF.

Fish and Dubertret: *Rainfall Map of the Middle East.*

———. *Lithological Map of the Eastern Border of the Mediterranean.* (I greatly regret that, as a result of the loss of almost all my collection of maps during the fighting in Palestine, I cannot give any more accurate information about these two maps.)

Ashbel, D., *Rainfall Map of Palestine, Transjordan, S. Syria and S. Lebanon* (Jerusalem, Hebrew University).

COMMENTARIES, ETC.

Hastings, James and John A. Selbie. *A Dictionary of the Bible.* New York, Charles Scribner's Sons, 1898–1904.

The Expositor's Bible. London, Hodder and Stoughton, 1887–1896.

The International Critical Commentary. New York, Charles Scribner's Sons, 1899–1937.

The Interpreter's Bible. New York, Abingdon Press, 1951–

The Clarendon Bible. Oxford, The Clarendon Press.

Gore, Charles (ed.). *A New Commentary on Holy Scripture, including the Apocrypha.* London, S.P.C.K., 1928.

The Abingdon Commentary.

INDEX OF BIBLICAL REFERENCES

OLD TESTAMENT

INDEX OF NAMES AND SUBJECTS

NOTE: Place names beginning with the Arabic article "el-", or its equivalent, are listed under the first letter of the name, e.g., el-Azraq, es-Salt, esh-Shaghur, eth-Themed. Also names beginning with "Jebel" or "Wadi" are listed as follows: Jebel Tubeiq as Tubeiq, Jebel, and Wadi Sirhan as Sirhan, Wadi.

Set in Linotype Caledonia
Format by James T. Parker
Printed by The Murray Printing Co.
Bound by The Haddon Craftsmen, Inc.
Published by Harper & Brothers, New York

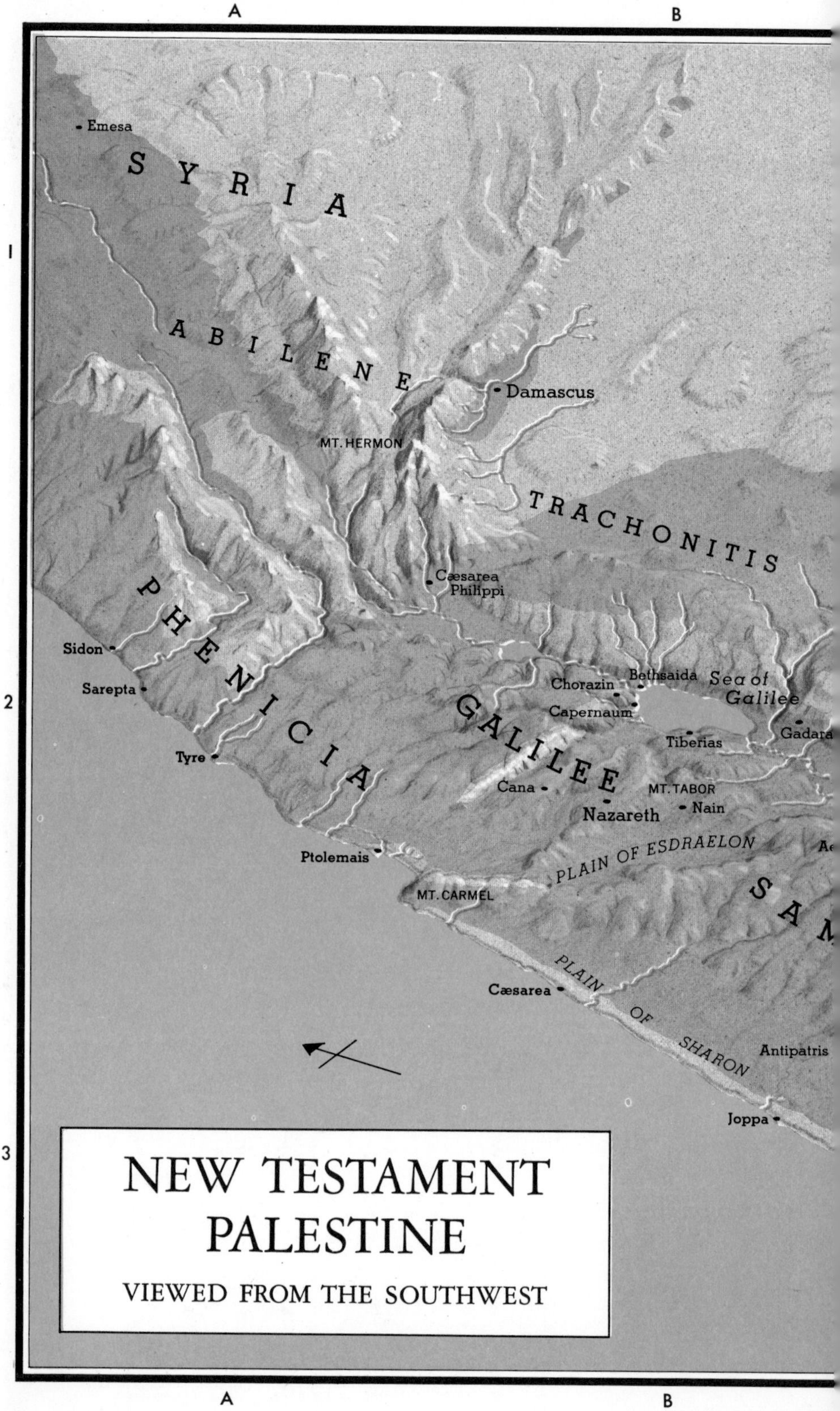

NEW TESTAMENT
PALESTINE
VIEWED FROM THE SOUTHWEST